RE-INTERPRETATIONS

Ernst Jünger: a writer of our time (Bowes & Bowes 1952)
C. G. Lichtenberg: a doctrine of scattered occasions
(Indiana University Press 1959, Thames & Hudson 1963)
(Editor) *Arthur Schnitzler:*
Liebelei, Leutnant Gustl, Die letzten Masken
(Cambridge University Press 1966)
Idylls and realities: studies in nineteenth-century
German literature (Methuen 1971)
On realism (Routledge & Kegan Paul 1973)
Hitler: the Führer and the people
(Collins/Fontana 1975)
A study of Nietzsche
(Cambridge University Press 1979)
(Editor) *The world of Franz Kafka*
(Weidenfeld & Nicolson 1980)
(With M. S. Silk) *Nietzsche on tragedy*
(Cambridge University Press 1981)

Re-interpretations

Seven Studies in Nineteenth-Century German Literature

J. P. STERN

*.. that we are not very reliably at home
in the interpreted world.*

R. M. RILKE

CAMBRIDGE UNIVERSITY PRESS

Cambridge

London   New York   New Rochelle

Melbourne   Sydney

Published by the Press Syndicate of the University of Cambridge
The Pitt Building, Trumpington Street, Cambridge CB2 IRP
32 East 57th Street, New York, NY 10022, USA
296 Beaconsfield Parade, Middle Park, Melbourne 3206, Australia

© J. P. Stern 1964

First published by Thames & Hudson 1964
Reissued by the Cambridge University Press 1981

First printed in Great Britain by The Camelot Press Ltd
London and Southampton
Reprinted in Great Britain at the
University Press, Cambridge

British Library Cataloguing in Publication Data
Stern, Joseph Peter
Re-interpretations.
1. German literature – 19th century – History
and criticism
I. Title
830′.9′007 PT341 80–49684
ISBN 0 521 23983 4 hard covers
ISBN 0 521 28366 3 paperback

To Sheila Stern

CONTENTS

ACKNOWLEDGEMENTS

My THANKS are due to the editors of *The Modern Language Review*, *The Cambridge Review*, *The Listener*, and to George G. Harrap and Company, Limited, publishers of *German Studies presented to W. H. Bruford*, London 1962, for permission to reprint in this book material which first appeared in the pages of their publications.

I am conscious of, and deeply grateful for, the encouragement and helpful criticism of many friends, colleagues and students. In Chapter I, 3 I have drawn extensively on an unpublished essay by D. H. Green, without which I would not have ventured into the hallowed precincts of medieval literature. Chapter V has benefited from the pertinent criticism of F. H. Hinsley. Several parts of the book, and especially Chapter III, were the subjects of conversations with Paul Roubiczek; to acknowledge something of what I owe to his generous friendship and wisdom is a very special pleasure. Similarly, the stimulus I have received from Erich Heller in the course of our old friendship has been a constant delight throughout the writing of this book. To my students past and present, willing and sometimes perhaps baffled partners in a common enterprise, I owe many an escape from obscure formulation. To Ellen Sutton I am grateful for many helpful comments and for her patient care in the preparation of the typescript; to Michael Wood and Terence Rogers for help with the proofs.

All my quotations are translated; the assistance I have received in that task, and in countless other ways, is acknowledged in my dedication.

St John's College, Cambridge

PREFACE TO THE
1981 REISSUE

While preparing this reprint of a book written some eighteen years ago I came across several passages which, partly as a consequence of re-reading the works discussed here, partly in the light of more recent criticism, I would have liked to alter. I also became aware of some additions I would have liked to make; in particular, discussions with Richard Humphrey convinced me that a consideration of the novels of Willibald Alexis would have enriched the range of the book as well as modified some of its conclusions. However, I had to content myself with correcting a number of plain errors, and I am deeply grateful to several friends—among them Alec Stillmark, and above all Nicholas Boyle—for helping me to do this. Whether the critical procedure outlined in the Introduction and followed in these pages amounts to a method it is for the reader to decide; in this respect, at all events, I have seen no reason for change.

J.P.S.

Christmas 1980

INTRODUCTION

THE AGE to which these studies are devoted begins with the death of Goethe in 1832 and ends in the heyday of the Wilhelminian Empire. At the end of that era, in January 1912, Rilke wrote the invocatory opening stanzas of the first of his *Duino Elegies*; when, in February 1922, he triumphantly completed the tenth and last, another age had begun. Possessed of an historical consciousness second to no other poet's, Rilke in the compass of a few lines defines the condition under which the life of men is enacted in the modern world:

> . . . *Ach, wen vermögen*
> *wir denn zu brauchen? Engel nicht, Menschen nicht,*
> *und die findigen Tiere merken es schon,*
> *dass wir nicht sehr verlässlich zu Haus sind*
> *in der gedeuteten Welt.*

> . . . *But who, alas, is there*
> *that we can use? Not angels, not men;*
> *and the knowing animals are aware*
> *that we are not very reliably at home*
> *in the interpreted world.*

His words ring true to us. The insecure condition they describe we recognise as ours; it is taken for granted and enlarged on in W. B. Yeats's, Valéry's and T. S. Eliot's poetry, it encompasses W. H. Auden's; the grand edifice of Rilke's *Elegies* rests upon it. Yet while these lines project prophetically into the European twentieth century, they also summarize the German nineteenth. The conclusion to which the most characteristic works of nineteenth-century German prose have led me is that they are distinguished above all by their special combination of the prophetic and the archaic, of the existential and the parochial, of the elements of worldly innocence and reflective profundity. They are almost always behind their times, and often peculiarly relevant to ours. And, as I see it, Rilke's lines, with all the 'contemporary' velleities they contain, amount to no less than a generalised setting-out of the theme of those works. If I have here concentrated on prose it is not because German poetry in the nineteenth century, from Hölderlin downwards, is irrelevant to my theme. It is merely because the poetic forms by their nature are less directly involved in the problems of realism which confronted the German writers of the age; and it is with this often unwilling involvement that I am here concerned.

I have called this book Re-interpretations for two reasons. First, because I see the prose-works which I have here considered as attempts at re-interpreting the world—at creating worlds—from points of view other than that of the common and commonly explored social certainties of their age; the world itself being presented in these writings not so much as a thing final and indisputably real but rather as in itself an 'interpretation'. And since the works discussed here do not readily adopt the mode of realism as that age (and largely also ours) conceived of it—sometimes the realism is directly challenged, sometimes it is silently by-passed, sometimes the writings are defeated by it—I have tried to suggest criteria, alternative to the common notion of realism, according to which the value of these writings, their especial charm and the weaknesses to which they are prone, may be more justly and fruitfully estimated.

In this second sense, too, what is offered here are re-interpretations. To present and evaluate these works, first, in accordance with one's understanding of the creative impulse to which they owe their existence and of the situation in which they are set— that is, in the light of what they are rather than in the light of what they are not—does not seem a very ambitious undertaking. Furthermore, to see them in the achieved round and as fully as possible (to see them also in the light of other literatures) seems a critical task no less obvious. Yet in attempting these two distinct and complementary tasks I have had less help from critics of the period than its voluminous bibliographies may suggest. Some of my fellow-critics, mainly German, are so deeply immersed in the ethos to which these works belong that they see in them not a

distinct tradition but simply a haven of spirituality, simply serene
emblems of high-mindedness; and they have tended to take the
question of specifically literary achievements for granted. At the
opposite end of the scale are the more or less casual foreign
readers or critics, so far away from it all that the bulk of nineteenth-century German literature (and its domestic criticism)
appears to them merely archaic and provincial, at best 'quaint'.
Then there are the Marxists: making their notion of 'socialist
realism' the only valid criterion of literary merit, they have indeed
gone roughshod over the ground. They have swept away many
an overblown reputation (Storm's), ignored another (Stifter's),
overestimated or distorted a third (Keller's). Yet it is they who
recall to us that which the study of German literature has been
prone to ignore—the social dimension of the literary work of
art. So that, although their ideological barrage is often aimed at
very modest targets, yet I have found them on occasion more
helpful than their exaggerations, patent in both method and conclusions, led me to expect. Whereas about the New Critics,
whose aims and procedures are diametrically opposed to the
Marxists', it can, I think, be said that nineteenth-century narrative
prose has brought out the worst in them. In extended prose
especially, the inability to see the wood for the 'image-clusters'
of the trees, the inability to hear the narrative voice for the 'sound-
patterns' and 'murmuring üüü-vowels', has led to singularly
absurd results.

I have no literary theory or critical method to offer. I have seen
no reason to eschew biography, anecdote or historical considerations; avoiding neither philosophical argument nor Wilhelm
Dilthey's notion of a 'Grunderlebnis' ('central experience'), nor
close attention to my author's words and imagery; choosing my
manner in each chapter as seemed appropriate. The very notion
of 'literature' could not be used at all rigidly where it was necessary
to proceed with as few prepossessions as possible. The distinction
between 'literature' and 'thought', by now a critical stereotype
and the source of much pedantry, becomes less than self-evident
where ideas are treated as living things. I have tried to keep the
distinction relative, as I have the notion of realism—relative, that
is, to the over-all creative achievement, which is, each time anew,

an exploration of human possibilities within a given historical setting.

The first draft of this book owes its origin to a course of lectures, some of them written in the usual weekly (and sometimes hectic) instalments. This procedure is not without its advantage, since it enables the writer to recall with some assurance that the similarity of the points made at each stage emerged gradually. As to the truth of the view presented here, therefore, I can at least claim that my central 'thesis' did not anticipate or determine the conclusions of each study. The late Ludwig Wittgenstein once compared the idea of a literary tradition to a hempen rope, where each short fibre overlapped a little, yet none reached from end to end; it is in this way that the studies of individual works are intended to contribute to and establish my central theme.

I have not attempted to write another history of nineteenth-century German literature, nor even of its prose. I have merely chosen a few representative examples of a literary tradition which I believe to be characteristically German, omitting many writings which seemed to me less interesting from my chosen point of view. Seeing in literature both a reflection and a source of social and national experience, I have suggested (where they seemed relevant) some of the reasons that make for the specific national character of the works interpreted in these pages. This has led me to consider several of the social and political facts which German literary historians have often either ignored or distorted. The claim that true literature, *Dichtung*, is a non-political thing few outside Germany have ever taken at its face-value. The common humanity and greatness of literary works, Goethe said more than once, can only lie in their specific character, of which their national origin is a part—sometimes an inconsiderable, at other times an important, part. And the claim that the true life of Germany is non-political—that too I have taken as part of the political atmosphere in which, both before and after 1848, much of German literature came to be written. The disastrous consequences of that 'non-political' attitude lie outside my present scope; yet their connection with the *Zeitgeist* I have tried to evoke in these pages is suggested more than once.

Hostility to arguments with some claim to coherence, and the suspicion that they are just so many rope-tricks, is in the very air we breathe. The consistent debunking of all general ideas has created a mental climate in which it is hard to tell the right from the wrong ideas. More especially, it is a situation in which criticism (as men like Matthew Arnold, Nietzsche or Péguy conceived and practised it) finds itself restricted by arbitrary limitations. 'Historians', we are sometimes told, have available to them 'concrete evidence' for the existence of a tradition; and this evidence consists in the 'beliefs and practices handed down the generations'; whereas 'critics', so the argument runs, merely make up a 'tradition' as they go along. The distinction, it seems to me, is based on what Whitehead called the 'notion of misplaced concreteness'. For where else is a society's recognition of its own beliefs and practices to be found at its most explicit, at its most interesting, but in its literature? And is it not there that 'the historian' *and* 'the critic' may look for it? The difference between them lies in the different means they use for illuminating the lived past. But the source of the illumination—a sense for the coherence of the past—is the same for both. And the point at which they come closest to each other is precisely in literature—it is there that the beliefs and practices of a society become most articulate and may thus be made available to posterity by means of a coherent argument.

All literary criticism is beset by the twin hazards of aestheticism and historicism. Works of literature don't live in total isolation, as timeless images or 'ikons', but then again their value is not to be measured in the light of our worries and preoccupations. In the case of German literature especially, it is not always easy to let the work speak to the reader in its own voice and yet to remember that the voice is, after all, part of a conversation that is social and historical as well as literary. Yet this is where, to the present-day reader at all events, lie the challenge and the appeal of that literature. The following scene, suggested by one of Stifter's stories, may perhaps indicate the kind of experience my reader is invited to consider in the following pages.

Imagine a wanderer, the cares of his ordinary city life still on his mind, arriving at a mountain hut to seek shelter for the night. The hut is clean and bare, a few pieces of ancient furniture stand in the room where he sits down. Tins and ingenious contraptions come out of his rucksack as he prepares his meal; all he requires from his solitary host is a little fresh water and a few slices of bread. While he bustles methodically with his precious accoutrements, offering this or that delicacy from his store, he notices his host's eyes, the poverty of the room. The exhilaration of his arrival dissolves as the embarrassment of possession, the shame of ownership before the tribunal of want, come over him and free him for an unaccustomed emotion. And he is stirred by the bareness and the truth of this scene in which he, a transitory guest burdened by many cares, will keep company with one who, for this night and thus in a sense for ever, is to be his bountiful host.

Perhaps my reader has found himself in such a situation; more likely he has not. Probably it will not strike him as revealing of the forces that agitate our contemporary world. But he cannot always see himself as part of that world. There are times when, however reluctantly, he is only himself, 'beyond the reach of common indication'. It is at such times that the truth of this scene may speak to him.

I ANTECEDENTS AND COMPARISONS

I

AMONG THE casual visitors in Goethe's house on the Frauenplan in Weimar was a young and ambitious *savant*, Arthur Schopenhauer, who had been introduced there in 1813 by his highly articulate mother and sister. On his last visit, Schopenhauer took away with him in his autograph album an inscription which is more indicative of the poet's attitude to life than it is of the future pessimistic philosopher's: 'If in thine own worth thou wilt rejoice', Goethe had written, 'thou must endow the world with worth'[1]—an exhortation which the young man is likely to have received with mixed feelings. By 1832, when Goethe died, Schopenhauer's *chef-d'œuvre*—in which those feelings were 'transfixed'[2]—had seen the light of a wholly incurious world for some fourteen years, and he had to wait another twenty before it would be accorded something of the importance he had never doubted was its due. What that book (and its systematic expansion in the second volume in 1844) contains is incomparably the most alluring, as it is the most comprehensive and detailed, re-interpretation of 'the world as an aesthetic phenomenon' the post-Goethean era (and European thought at any time) has to show. What, if anything, is Goethean about it? It certainly isn't Schopenhauer's intention in that work to 'endow the world with worth'. When we come to admire the high intelligence with which he describes

---

[1] '*Willst du dich deines Wertes freuen* / *So musst der Welt du Wert verleihen* . . / *im Gefolg und zum Andenken mancher vertraulichen Gespräche. Weimar, den 8. Mai 1814. Goethe.*' Quoted from Arthur Schopenhauer's *Sämtliche Werke*, (ed. E. Grisebach, *Reclam*) Vol. VI, Leipzig n.d., p. 186.

[2] See below, pp. 165–6.

the independence and the self-contained sublimity of the work of
art, when we observe how Nietzsche, in the 'seventies, at first
follows Schopenhauer's analysis and evaluation of the rôle of art
in experience, but then, with that sudden access of energy which
is characteristic of his thinking, begins to question the truthfulness
of the artistic process and turns upon the poet for being 'merely a
liar, merely a fool', for artfully deceiving himself and the world;
when, in brief, we find all the emphasis of later aesthetic thought
placed *not* on the humanity and abundance of the creative imagination but on the limitations and exclusiveness, and the otherworldliness, of the aesthetic experience, the connection with
Goethe looks thin. Yet I shall suggest that the truth of Goethe's
classicism was achieved, not indeed by any pessimistic disparagement, but at the price of a considerable curtailment, of the actual
world; and that the debt which he left behind grew larger as the
age of prose—by contrast a prosy age indeed—imposed its
conditions and demands.

Politics and social thinking are the chief victims of this process.
The old Goethe is merely 'not very interested', Schopenhauer
mordantly contemptuous. For Hegel, the 'real' world of contemporary politics comes to figure as an inopportune though alas
necessary obstacle in the Spirit's process of self-realisation. With
Nietzsche the Goethean reactions crystallise; the dichotomy
'Germany *versus* the West' hardens; he admires the French
political imagination, but regards it as something alien to the
German ethos. The nationalist writers of the Wilhelminian era[1]
endlessly reiterate the need for loyalty and for faith in the nation,
adding that political debate and social reform merely weaken
Germany and play into the hands of her enemies. Finally, with
Thomas Mann (in *Betrachtungen eines Unpolitischen*, 1919) 'German
politics' becomes an oxymoron, and the German ethos is pre-
cariously defined as almost anything but 'political'.

In that strange and moving 'war journal', written during the
Great War but published after the cause which Thomas Mann

---

[1] Men like H. Class (*Wenn ich der Kaiser wär*', 1913), P. de Lagarde (*Die
nächsten Pflichten der deutschen Politik*, 1874), J. Langbehn (*Rembrandt als Erzieher*,
1890).

had 'served with his pen' was lost, many profound things are said on the subject of the artist's isolation and of his ironical commitment to his age. Sartre's observations on the same subject[1] in a situation not wholly dissimilar thirty years later might well have profited from the generosity, the profound wit, the ironical openness of Mann's meditations. It is these qualities above all which give the work its permanent value, its unexpectedly contemporary ring, their absence which renders Sartre's insistence less memorable. But the finer Mann's insights, the more astonishing his omissions. 'Politics' to him is the ideology of the French Revolution, it is parliamentary representation, social amelioration, utilitarianism—'politics' *is* 'ideology'. The 'political writer' is the French egalitarian, the ideological propagandist. There is little suggestion here that the Reich too is a political organism; that the literary work, *Dichtung* itself, even when it is free from all overt propaganda, exhortation and precept, is (among other things) a political act; that Shakespeare's tragedies are not only explorations of the characters of individual men, of the soul's solitude, but also profound contributions to the political debate of the race; that Schiller's *Wallenstein* succeeds where Goethe's *Egmont* fails. The idea that social and political problems can be solved by an appeal to men's spirituality is only a half-truth. The point of view (e.g. Max Weber's) from which it is clearly seen as a half-truth is never considered seriously; nor ironically either. The 'non-political' attitude, Thomas Mann acknowledges, is conservative; yet the actual political implications of conservatism are never fully drawn. And the social and political dimensions of the novel—the dimensions so splendidly explored in Thomas Mann's own *Buddenbrooks*—are relegated to the inferior genre of the 'social novel' ('*Gesellschaftsroman*') which, in this polemical view, is French and English, and thus merely shallow '*comédie de mœurs*'. True, it is the Great War—the politics of the age—which accounts for the radical nature of Thomas Mann's political conclusions. But, as he himself knows and says, all his conclusions are implicit in the argument and in the literary art of the nineteenth century.

[1] *Qu'est-ce que la littérature?* Paris 1948.

Why have the German prose writers of that century not received much attention abroad? Why, on the other hand, have their most notable successors in the first half of the present century been acclaimed abroad as the spokesmen of modern European thought and feeling? The answer to both questions lies in the dissociation of German literature from the political and social realities of its encompassing world. The exploits and spiritual adventures on the margins of one age become the common itinerary of the next. When, in the 1920's, this dissociation ceased to be a peculiarly German phenomenon, it became, for the disaffected West too, the hallmark of authenticity and literary truth.

The situation of nineteenth-century German literature is one in which the literary imagination is but indifferently sustained by the worldly world. Quite often we shall notice, in that situation, a certain lack of feeling for the hard and ineluctable finality of experience—for the deed done that cannot be undone, the word said that cannot be unsaid. Indeed, a whole literary genre, the *Bildungsroman*, is at least partly conceived as an imaginative means for taking the sting of finality out of experience by making experience repeatable. The genre is fundamentally solipsistic. It leads the young hero from self-absorption into society, as though social life were a problematic task rather than a natural condition, the given thing; and his journey, inevitably, is more fascinating than his arrival. But the 'novel of spiritual education' is only one of the characteristic products of a culture which is reluctant to come to terms with its own material and social conditions. Whether experience is presented in the form of an 'educational' experiment or of unalterable fate, all that is of ultimate value in experience is here seen as removed from the socio-political world.

Where self and soul, art and eternity engage the imagination with a force, an abundance of interest, which contemporary society with its political and economic arrangements and the personal implications of its class-structure does not appear to yield; where all the lines and patterns traced by individual wills, historical circumstances and material objects on the social canvas are regarded as somehow sketchy, provisional, as not of the last importance; where solitude is depicted as the natural condition of man; and where the major religious tradition, or what is left of it, emphasises not a social cohesion, not a community of worship, but the single soul's striving for faith—there, certainly, the borderline between the literary and the philosophical imagination will not be easy to draw, and a mode of writing which *encompasses* experience and surveys it from a height will engage the creative imagination more powerfully than a mode which *retraces* experience in its particularities and living details. It is a situation which readily gratifies the taste for the unconditioned.

And as such it is not at all hostile to the claims of art. What here sustains art is not the world of our common interpretation, yet it is no abstruse chimera either. After all, nothing more particular can be imagined than a description of the solitary man, nor any thing more philosophical than the content of his far-roaming, unarrested thoughts.

2

'The situation of nineteenth-century German literature . . .' The difficulty about any argument based on a generalisation of this kind is that it so obviously fails to satisfy the 'principle of sufficient reason' by raising more causal questions than it ever answers. In all literary criticism that avoids the historical dimension there is a rough-and-ready convention as to the why's and wherefore's we may ask; once we bring in a phrase like 'the literary situation', causal questions are much more difficult to fob off. And no sooner do we start asking them than the hydra of teleology begins to rear its countless heads. For instance: if we argue that this literary situation in Germany was brought about by the lack of a unified political tradition, the objection is at hand that such a lack is as likely to be the effect of a cultural *impasse* as its cause. If we point to the absence of a homogeneous public and of cohesion on a national scale (of which Goethe and Schiller had complained), and turn to the Reformation and its consequence, the Thirty Years' War, for an explanation, we are left with the question why the political and social effects of Luther's teaching were so different from Wycliffe's or John Hus's, or even Calvin's; or again, why the Lutheran Church in the Scandinavian countries brought no such disruption in its wake. Conversely, we may

point to the uniquely intense spiritual energy freed by the Reformation, and see there the reason for the theological passion of
the German seventeenth and eighteenth centuries and for the
philosophical passion (the secularised theology) of the nineteenth.
This argument[1] offers as an ultimate reason the genius and energy
of Luther—yet his protest against the worldliness of Roman
Catholicism and his emphasis on inwardness (in the disjunction
between faith and good works) could not have affected the
national and literary history of Germany so profoundly had the
spiritual and social temper he expressed not been already present.
Or again, if we seek for an explanation in the arguments of
'geo-politics' (as Leibnitz, Kant and after them a host of less
reputable writers have done), we are in a worse plight still. For
we are then constrained to postulate (and account for) a national
cohesion which, though strong enough to overcome some of the
disruptive factors in Germany's geographical situation, was yet
not strong enough to overcome others;[2] and this is very much
like operating with those occult 'matters' of which little else is
known except the effects they are meant to explain. So, finally,
we turn to what looks like the most 'concrete' and down-to-
earth explanation of all, the Industrial Revolution. The fact that
it came to the German States from the West, and more than half
a century late,[3] looks like a convincing explanation of why there
is so much parochialism in the German literary tradition throughout the century, so much that is Wordsworthian, sylvan and
agronomic. The history of eighteenth-century particularism and
the economic conditions of the Metternich era could, not im-
plausibly, be used to account for that weakness of the social link

[1] See Wilhelm Dilthey, *Das Erlebnis und die Dichtung*[4], Leipzig 1939, p. 23.

[2] In other words, the argument runs aground in the statement *that* in Germany
this cohesion was stronger than among the Slavs and weaker than among the
French; which leaves the *why*-question open.

[3] The effects of this delay were by no means only negative, for it enabled
German industrial capitalism to avoid the worst mistakes and inhumanities of
English industrialisation. Hence we find, at all events in the Western industrial
regions of Germany, no such slums nor destitution nor inhuman labour conditions as are described in the English factory reports on which Marx drew.

and the relative paucity of a serious literary preoccupation with the body politic, which appear to us as the obverse of the philosophical passion and of the search for personal truth. (It would, for instance, be possible to find a place in the German literary tradition for Coleridge the poet and metaphysician—his speculations, we know, were much influenced by Kant and the *Naturphilosophie* of Schelling—but not for Coleridge the author of *The Constitution of Church and State*; while literary men with a highly developed and unsentimental social conscience—men like Hazlitt or William Cobbett—have no equivalent in Germany until the time of the Great War.) But then, to argue from the facts of the Industrial Revolution is only to beg the question why, given the ancient economic privileges and localised political rights of the *Bürgertum*, given traditions of responsible self-government which go back to the free cities of the late Middle Ages, industrialisation itself came so late and so precipitously, and why, when it finally came, it actually increased the political conformism and apathy of the middle classes.

The fact is that the argument from economic and industrial conditions—e.g. from bourgeois capitalism to realism—is based upon an aprioristic concept of causality whose actual working is shrouded in mystery. Even Marx, when he turned to this question in his unfinished *German Ideology* of 1845, did no more than assert *that* all consciousness, and thus literature and philosophy, are a product of material conditions, without showing *how* such a causal process ever took place, just as he merely asserted *that* 'the Germans . . . are lacking in "sensuous assurance"' and therefore don't understand their own history,[1] without showing *how* this lack had arisen.

---

[1] 'It is . . . clear that in Germany one cannot write that sort of history [of mankind in its relation to the history of exchange and industry], because the Germans lack not only the material and the understanding necessary for such a task, but also "sensuous assurance" [cf. Hegel's *Phenomenologie*], for beyond the Rhine you cannot have any experience of such things, since there history has stopped happening.' (Marx/Engels, *Deutsche Ideologie*, in *Gesamtausgabe*, I/v, Berlin 1932, p. 19; I have adapted W. Lough's translation from *The German Ideology*, ed. R. Pascal, London 1938, p. 18.)

At this point a comparison with Russia can hardly be prevented from showing up the dubious nature of the entire causal argument. We find in Russia at the beginning of the nineteenth century nothing like a firmly established bourgeois or '*bürgerlich*' tradition; industrialisation came even later; the influx of 'Western' democratic ideas was a good deal less steady; and the ideas themselves (in the writings, for instance, of Radishchev) were a good deal more alien to the prevailing ethos. In brief, compared with Germany, Russia at the turn of the nineteenth century was even more 'backward', even less ready to receive the impact of 'Western' economic, political and technological changes.

But what of the literature that now, from Pushkin onwards, comes to life? Its difference lies precisely where, according to the argument from economic and industrial conditions, we would least expect it: in the realism of its major achievements, in its serious commitment to the social scene. Here is the source of the great popularity of Russian literature in the West from Vogüét's time onwards, and the explanation, incidentally, of 'the apologetics indulged in by the West towards Russian realities'.[1] The contrast with the German literary tradition is striking on both sides of the argument. Social realism (by which I mean a thing different from the socialist realism of latter-day Marxists[2]) is adumbrated in Pushkin's and Lermontov's prose in their notion of 'odd people'; it is the condition of Turgenev's exquisite irresoluteness; care for the social realities of 'the Russian man' shifts from form to content in Gogol; in Goncharov the generalisation 'this is what we are like' is everywhere implied; social realism is the condition of life in Tolstoy, and the condition of the soul's salvation in Dostoyevsky; and the buttressing of the social dimension in literature by a critic like Belinsky or a propa-

---

[1] See E. Heller in the article 'Imaginative Literature' in *The New Cambridge Modern History*, Vol. X (1830–70), Cambridge 1960, p. 167.

[2] Although, as H. Gifford has shown, there is a remarkable 'Continuity in Russian Criticism' (*Essays in Criticism*, Oxford 1955, pp. 258–9) which, over the last hundred and fifty years, is insistently social.

gandist like Chernyshevsky points in the same direction. At the same time the 'Western' (here: the German) philosophical passion fades into fantasy, obscurity or those extravagant mis-understandings affectionately parodied by Chekhov and sharply satirised by Gorky. Yet even the naïve Platonism of a Solovev has social ends in view, even the strange messianic fantasies of the incendiaries and nihilists are informed, however pervertedly, by a social concern. What matters in a comparison with the German literary situation is *not* the writer's overt attitude to contemporary Russian society; the question is not whether the realists are hostile to or romantic about the life of their nation. What matters is that in its major productions Russian literature in the nineteenth century shows man as substantially involved in the *données* of the world around him.

Transcendentalism, obsession with inwardness, the manichean rejection of worldly power, extravagant spiritualism, Oblomov-ism[1] itself—the Russian realists know them all as parts of their own intimate experience, they creatively contend with them as with their own temptations. They are not 'thinkers', what sustains them is not their individual soul and passionate solitary thought. No Reformation divides them from their own past and nation, the secularism of the Enlightenment is largely alien to them, at no point do they identify Christianity with individual-ism. The protracted conflict between 'Western' thought and the 'populist' tradition is a conflict reflected in the social substratum,

---

[1] It would seem that Goncharov's novel, with its theme of 'boredom eating its way into Oblomov's eyes like some disease' (Part 4, Chapter 5) is an excep-tion to this argument. But my point about the Russian realists is not that social relations are their theme, but that they are the necessary condition of their view of man. Oblomov's *angst* and accidie are not explored in the void; they are manifest in his relations with the outside world no less than in the state of his soul. Thus he not only fails as a lover (of Olga), but he also shirks his duties as a master (towards Zahar) and as a landlord (the ruin of the estate); and Stolz, the 'efficient German', technologist and 'new man', succeeds wherever Ob-lomov has failed. In other words, the 'universal theme' is particularised not only in an emotional state but also in a social *locale*. On the other hand, Peter Schlemihl's accidie or the Romantic hero's *Weltschmerz* or Lenz's *Angst* (see below, Chapter III), are dissociated from their surrounding worlds.

often in the social substance, of their work. Their realism is
different in origin from that of their English and French contemporaries, and it has been convincingly argued that it begins at the
very point where the realism of the French novel—of Flaubert in
particular—is apt to be stifled by its self-imposed limitations.
Certainly their realism is neither secular and 'immanent' in range
nor 'aesthetic' in intention. Ironically enough, *fin-de-siècle*
European aestheticism enters Russian literature, with the
Symbolists, at the moment (1905) when, the main force of
realistic prose spent, the social concerns of Russian literature
and criticism are about to be translated into political reality.

The Russian realists are involved in a huge, sprawling yet
organic whole whose social claims they creatively acknowledge.
Why? Because, corrupt, absurd, reactionary, haphazardly illi-
beral as their society is, it and the claims it makes upon them are
not (as in the West) exclusively secular; because their outlook is
anything but 'immanent'; because in the actual circumstances of
their society, as well as in the conception of nationhood fundamental to their writings, enough of the traditional link between
Church and State survives to give substance and a rudimentary
unity to their social and spiritual preoccupations. The idea of such
a unity is to be found in the poetico-political speculations of the
German Romantics, in whose writings Pushkin and Lermontov,
but also Gogol and Dostoevsky, were steeped. But again it is the
contrast between the German and Russian situations which is
striking. The German Romantics from Novalis to Fichte are
inspired by an utopian and ideal vision of the unity of national,
social and religious feelings, but the very substance from which
they shape their vision is largely of their own creation. Whereas
for the Russian realists this kind of unity, tainted by corruption,
open to abuses, prosy and altogether remote from the ideal, is the
actual condition in which their work takes its shape: their vision
may be utopian but its substance is real.[1] There is little unity in
their understanding of the present and even less in their visions

---

[1] Marx and Engels, in their writings on 'The Russian Village Community',
were not likely to accept the religious element in the origin and continued
existence of the Obshtchina as anything but an 'ideological superstructure'. Yet

of the future of their society. Often enough their social, religious and literary concerns are all at war with one another; in all European literature there is not a more moving symbol of this strife than the Lear-like figure of the old Tolstoy. But these are battles whose outcome is anything but a foregone conclusion. However backward or 'unpoetic' the actual condition of the society which surrounds them or which they guiltily recapture from their hotel rooms in Paris or Baden-Baden, their writings form a continuity with it; that actual condition is never so base or unspiritual as to be unworthy of their consideration, as to appear unyielding to their creative interest and intentions. They transform it, as all creative writers do, but they do so according to criteria, conscious or not, which are *en rapport* with it: the questions that stir them to creative activity are not those concerned with the reality or otherwise of our experience, the validity or otherwise of our interpretations of the world. The questions that stir them are, 'Who can be happy and free in Russia?' and 'What is to be done?'

The 'German literary situation', then, cannot be 'explained' by any single set of historical facts; and it is hardly surprising that any one of the causal arguments I have mentioned is certain to take us on an erratic chase through the whole of German history. And comparisons too leave open as many questions as they were meant to answer. Yet such arguments, unenlightening as causes, do provide us with insights (to which we shall return when we come to describe the irony and exasperation with which Heine

---

they are acutely conscious of the historical continuity of the rural commune. Both (Marx in 1877, Engels again in 1894) stress that in by-passing the Western development of 'transforming its peasants into proletarians' and of thus having to undergo 'all the sudden turns of fortune of the capitalist system', Russian socialism can achieve its revolution not by destroying but by transforming the village communities. Even they, therefore, acknowledge a continuity of social organisms and of social criticism (in their quotations from Chernyshevsky, Danilevsky and others) unparalleled in Germany. (See *Karl Marx and Friedrich Engels: The Russian Menace to Europe*, ed. P. W. Blackstock and B. F. Hoselitz, London 1953, pp. 203–40.)

surveys the history of his country from his vantage point in
Paris). Inadequate answers to *why*-questions often turn out to be
illuminating as answers to *what*-questions; causes, after all, are
also in themselves states, and reasons descriptions. The re-
interpretations which this book describes have many antecedents
in the history of German literature. The moment on which I
shall now briefly dwell is intended not to *explain why* but to
show that the dissociation from the social world is a recurrent
phenomenon in that history.

3

The tale of Charlemagne's war with the Saracens and Roland's
death in the battle of Roncevaux has engaged the imagination of
perhaps all European nations and entered their literatures in
variously modified forms. The *chanson de geste* from which it has
been handed down through the centuries survives in a version
written probably some time in the first two decades of the
twelfth century,[1] and this was done into German, with significant adaptations, by a Bavarian monk, Konrad, at some later
date, most probably 1170. The narrative remains broadly the
same in both versions. At a Frankish council of war, Guenelun,
Count Roland's stepfather and enemy, is chosen by Charlemagne
to parley with the Saracens for the possession of Spain. Suspicious
of Roland's motives in suggesting him for the dangerous mission,
Guenelun conspires in Saragossa with Marsiliun the Saracen King,
and on his return to the French camp contrives to have Roland,
together with Oliver his comrade-in-arms and Archbishop
Turpin, put in charge of the rearguard that is to cover the withdrawal of Charles's forces from Spain.[2] The lengthy battle

[1] I have used R. Hague's reprint of the Oxford MS. of the *Chanson* (London
1937), Karl Bartsch's text of the *Rolandslied* (Leipzig 1874); my translations owe
a good deal to Hague's, to Dorothy Sayers's Penguin version, to Bartsch's
notes, and to Ottmann's lively '*Nachdichtung*' mentioned below.
[2] It is this scene of Roland's nomination as leader of the rearguard that is
the subject of Erich Auerbach's splendid analysis in Chapter V of his *Mimesis*[2],
Bern 1959.

between the French rearguard and the mighty Saracen Army contains some of the tale's finest moments. Too late Roland blows his horn to summon help. He and his warriors are slain by overwhelming odds, and only when Charles turns his main force back into Spain are the heathens, reinforced by the African armies of Baligant, defeated, Saragossa occupied and all the infidel leaders killed. Now at last Charles may bury Roland and his companions and return to his beloved Aix. Guenelun has knowingly exposed Roland and his men to mortal danger and has also caused the Emperor to ignore Roland's first call for help. He is tried for treason, and found guilty; after an ordeal by duel fought by two knights on his and the dead Roland's behalf, Guenelun is condemned to a cruel and dishonourable death. Oliver's sister Alde, Roland's betrothed, dies of a broken heart on hearing of Roland's death, Marsiliun's widow Bramimunde, a prisoner at Aix, is converted by Charlemagne. The French version ends with the Archangel Gabriel calling the bereaved, battle-weary Charles forth to another crusade ('*Deus*', *dist li rei*, '*si penuse est ma vie*'), while the Bavarian friar ends with a dedication to his ducal patron and a pious prayer 'that God of His Kingdom as heirs should secure us / *tu autem domine miserere nobis*'.

The contrast between the two versions is at its most obvious in the opening sections. The author of the *Chanson* plunges *in medias res*—'Charles the King, our great emperor, has been all full seven years in Spain . . .'—relying on his listener's familiarity with the previous events of Charles's campaign. He thus does almost nothing to motivate the enmity between Roland and Guenelun, the only reference to an earlier quarrel ('Roland wronged me in gold and in possessions', l. 3758) at the very end of the poem is suspect because it is a part of Guenelun's defence when he stands arraigned before the Emperor; also, we feel, it is too brief to explain their mutual hatred. On the other hand, this abrupt and dramatic opening is entirely characteristic of the terseness, vigour and energy of the whole *Chanson* as well as of that rigidity of action and ethos, that lack of any '*Problematik*',[1] which distinguish

---

[1] See Auerbach, *op. cit.*, p. 108.

it throughout. The German monk invents an earlier action. In
one respect this is an improvement on the French text: in a few
moving lines (1383–1404) Guenelun's hatred is shown to spring
from his fear that, in the event of his death, his real son Baldewin
will be dispossessed by Roland his stepson.[1] For the rest, the first
thousand lines of the *Lied* are taken up with a lengthy theological
placing of the action, Charles receives news of the Saracens' un-
clean and godless life, and an Angel is introduced in biblical
fashion (ll. 55 ff.) exhorting him to go and convert them. (Those
who will not be converted, the Angel adds, ll. 64–5, are of the
Devil and damned to eternity.) The religious aspect of the epic
is thus stressed from the beginning; explicit biblical parallels
abound; the story of Gideon and Joshua especially is invoked[2] as
a prefiguration of the religious significance and aim of the war;
and countless liturgical phrases and spiritual exhortations reinforce
the didactic intention of the author. In spite of the many words of
praise that Konrad lavishes on the Bavarians[3] and Naimes their
leader, he is not interested in the national aspect of the war at all.
What he has done is to turn a French national heroic epic into a
German spiritual one.

The absence of liturgical allusions and of an explicit religious
motivation does not mean that the French lay is lacking in
religious content. Far from it. In the story which the French epic
narrator puts before us the worldly actions of the battlefield are
so unproblematically set in a mode of pious heroism that they
don't need a theological placing. The religious, Christianising
aspect of Charles's war is a given spiritual circumstance—it is a
mode of the narrative—which is too self-evident, too firmly
established, to require much elaboration or even mentioning.
There is no significant hiatus between the secular and the religious.
Feudal loyalty, love of *la dulce France*, knightly valour and regard

---

[1] In the *Chanson*, ll. 312 ff., he merely commends Baldewin to Charles's care.
[2] See R. E. Ottmann's Introduction to his modern adaptation, *Das Rolandslied des Pfaffen Konrad*, Leipzig [*Reclam*] n.d., p. 11.
[3] Konrad found very little of this praise in the *Chanson*. Perhaps his reason for
inserting it was that, as a native of Rhenish Franconia, he was trying to in-
gratiate himself with the Bavarians at the court of Ratisbon.

for posthumous renown, love of companions-in-arms and hatred of the Saracen enemy—each of these secular motives has a religious value associated with it: unambiguous and inconspicuous, the association requires emphasis only in moments of extremity— moments in which it is quite natural to speak of the eternal rewards that do not make but complete the meaning of the secular deeds. As in Anglo-Saxon poetry, God is mentioned only when 'a man's time is no more'. There is no doubt that Roland's valour is Christian, Oliver's loyalty pleasing in the sight of the Emperor and of God, that Guenelun's treachery is condemned by both; that Turpin is both Archbishop (a 'gentle man', l. 2177, he absolves and blesses the warriors, 1137 f., allays their dispute, 1739 f.) and also among the bravest of knights, distinguished *par granz batailles e par mult bels sermons* (2243); that Charles is Emperor, God's viceroy on earth, and valiant defender of the Faith. All this is part of the French chivalrous tradition and, there being no need to dwell either on the piety of the French or on the wickedness of the infidels, the author's narrative energy is devoted to presenting the human side of the conflict, the characters of the agents, their motives and personalities. The characterisations, to be sure, are rudimentary, conventional, unprobing: the good are beautiful, the heathen almost always ugly, black, fantastic, Guenelun 'would have had the look of a baron had he been true' (3764), the war is above all a conflict over territories and worldly possessions.[1] The characters are statuesque and 'archetypal', yet they are sufficiently individuated to give rise to a remarkable play of affinities and differences.

The two great battle-scenes, for instance, have often been criticised for their length and goriness (though they are a good deal shorter than in Konrad); certainly, they are enacted in a formalised, almost dance-like, pre-ordained fashion. And yet the action is also shown to be determined by the individual

---

[1] Auerbach has shown in fine detail that the paratactic and firmly end-stopped verse produces a rigid and often disconnected narrative manner, which in its turn reflects the majestic narrowness and lack of concern with causal connections and close explanations of events characteristic of the French author's mind and, presumably, of the mind of his audience.

qualities (rather than by the theologically significant rôles) of the combatants. The affinities between the various warriors arise where the conflict of the two armies is depicted primarily as a war over the possession of Spain and for the glory of France, and only implicitly as a religious conflict: where the narrator lets his story be guided by its own dramatic impetus, there he must depict the heathens as capable of the same knightly virtues of valour and loyalty, and of the same warlike circumspection, as the Christians. But he also delights in working out full contrasts, as between Roland, Oliver and Turpin, or even between Marsiliun and the *amiral* Baligant, and above all between the wavering Guenelun and the impetuous Roland. And these contrasts are neither automatically determined by which side a man is on nor are they confined to the degrees of valour apportioned to each. In all this, and in many purposeful evocations of landscape, as in these lines from the opening of the last battle,

> *Between them is neither hill nor vale nor mound*
> *Nor wood. Hiding [asconse] there is none.*
> *They see each other clearly across the plain land*
> (3291 ff.)

we recognise the poetic imagination retracing the worldly contours of the war rather than its religious meaning. In fine, it is a deep human interest, indeed a rudimentary realism, which informs the *Chanson* and is allowed to shape its action.

The German monk writes for a different audience, in another age and land. His pious interpolations expand his poem to twice the length of the original,[1] the chivalrous convention of the *Chanson* is to him suspect and unacceptable. The praise he gives to the Christian warriors is put in words which belong to the religious traditions of the *miles gloriosus* and *gladius Christi* of an earlier era. The warriors' goal is now not worldly renown and

---

[1] Konrad writes (9082 ff.) that he 'first forced [the French book] into the Latin tongue / and thence turned it into the German /', and that he 'neither added nor left out' any part of the original. Actually his poem has rather more than twice as many lines as the French, although Konrad's irregular four-stress line is much shorter than the *Chanson*'s ten-syllable line with its strong caesura.

booty *and* salvation, but martyrdom and salvation in Christ alone.[1] Earlier in the twelfth century, in the Cluniac tradition within which Konrad was still writing, these had been monastic ideals, and it is Konrad's didactic intention to recommend these ideals to his patron[2] and to the knights at his patron's court.

There is nothing half-hearted about Konrad's didacticism. All virtues—now worldly virtues—are attributed to the heathens; feudal loyalty is changed to the Christian steadfastness of martyrs, *la dulce France* now becomes *rîche*, the Empire, which is above all *himilrîche*, the Kingdom of Heaven. Only one Christian fully displays, and praises in others, the worldly virtues—Guenelun, who is on the side of the heathens. And Guenelun's figure has little of the pathos of the *Chanson*. In Saragossa he is not so much the cunning plotter as rather Marsiliun's catspaw; his conflict is not so much with Roland his stepson as with the Emperor; and his relation to Charles is not so much that of a treacherous vassal to his feudal lord as that of Judas, the vassal of Satan, to Christ Himself. Where the religious conflict is stressed so much that even the Emperor's final victory over the Saracens is seen as a vengeance not for the death of Roland but for the dishonour done by the Saracens to God; where Guenelun is tried for treachery but Roland's death is no longer mentioned; where Charles himself comes to occupy the centre of the tale and yet remains a somewhat shadowy figure; and where, above all, the crusading idea and it alone carries the burden of motivation, there, obversely, we cannot expect anything like a sustained contrast in characters nor the same attention to the details of the worldly action.

The *Lied* has been called a 'supremely conservative anachronism'[3] because its author, far from being *au fait* with the contemporary courtly ideals beyond the Rhine, is still concerned with superimposing Christian virtues upon the passionate and turbulent

---

[1] See *Rolandslied*, ll. 4179 ff.: 'Targis [a heathen] fought for honour / Anseïs [a Christian] for his soul, / Targis for the worldly kingdom [ertrîche], / Anseïs for the heavenly kingdom.'

[2] Probably Henry the Lion, Duke of Saxony and Bavaria (1129–95).

[3] By D. H. Green in the essay mentioned above, now cf. his *Millstäter Exodus: a Crusading Epic* (Cambridge 1966), pp. 230–1 etc.

ethos of the Germanic warriors. (We shall see how, 700 years
later, in 1852 to be exact, Heine will diagnose the mind of contemporary Germany as still in the grip of the same conflict.)

If this is a correct statement of Konrad's intention, then it may
not be going too far to suggest that he himself felt something of
the passion which he hoped to assuage in his audience, and that
consequently there are two forces at work in his poem. The
length and number of his battle-scenes suggest that the monk
Konrad is as fascinated by valour and combat as is Turoldus,
the author of the *Chanson* (though he is much less terse and hence
less successful in his descriptions of them); but time and again he
draws back from these descriptions and allows the scene to dis-
solve into pious reflections or prayer.

The kind of tension of creative forces—between passion and
piety—that may have been present in Konrad's mind can on
occasion yield the finest and most memorable literary effects;
more than that, I shall suggest[1] that the narrative mode, whether
in the epic or in prose, not unlike the drama, derives some of its
greatest achievements from the tension, made explicit in narrative
contrasts, between just such forces as appear to be present in the
Rolandslied. Why, then, is it not really a masterpiece—why is the
Lied inferior to the *Chanson* in all except piety? Not because we
sense in it a tension between a religious ideal and worldly values
and passions, but on the contrary because the tension is inadequately worked out, because the contrast is blurred.

Obviously, the only way literature can present the harshness
of death is by contrast with the sweetness of life; and again, the
only way it can intimate the kingdom to come is by attributing
to it a perfection in *some* way related to all that is perfectible in
this world. Hence the more precise and powerful the portrayal
of men and things in the world, of all that we shall soon be
leaving, the more moving the evocation of the darkness of
death.

Turpin has been slain. In the *Chanson*, Roland weeps over his
dead body, lays him to rest,

---

[1] See below, pp. 206–7.

> *Upon his breast, where the keybone divides*
> *He has crossed his hands white and beautiful*

and then commends him, archbishop and knight, to God:

> *Never will there be a man more willing to serve Him.*
>
> (l. 2254)

Attending to the details of this scene—the description of the archbishop's hands, Roland's prayer that speaks of the *human* meaning of Turpin's qualities—we understand something of the way in which the *Chanson* succeeds in fusing valour with spirituality, of the way in which its majestic beauty is achieved. Not that Konrad is unaware of the particular problem of Turpin's personality: it cannot, for instance, have been easy for him to follow the *Chanson* and have Turpin say, on an earlier occasion,

> *He should truly ever be a monk*
> *Who does not here strike his sword:*
> *Such had never a man's worth.*[1]

But in the crucial scene of Turpin's death he fails us. It opens with the same gruesome detail of Turpin's wounds as does the *Chanson*, but this is immediately followed by a descent of the angels who take Turpin, now a martyr, into heaven where he is received by God. And it is not Roland's act of homage to the dead warrior and priest nor the voice of Roland, its prayer rising from this world *upwards*, that conclude the scene, but God's voice that *descends* from on high with the words, '*procede et regna*' (l. 6770).

Finally, we see the same difference of narrative attention in those scenes for which, above all others, the lay of Roland is still remembered, the scenes with the Olifant. The contrast between the valorous but prudent Oliver, who obeys Roland in spite of his misgivings, and the valorous and imprudent Roland who, in refusing to blow the Olifant when the lethal danger is first upon them, seals their common doom; their brief dispute and Oliver's bitter but eminently sensible expostulation on the difference between valour and recklessness—these come together in the

---

[1] Ll. 6296 ff. I wonder whether the *Chanson*, l. 1881, '[such a man] should be in *one of these* monasteries' ['*un de cez mutiers*'] is intended ironically.

Chanson, to form an emblem of loyalty, of the love unto death of
the fatherland and of one man for another, as heroic and moving
as any in European literature. All this Konrad must change.
Where, in the *Chanson*, Oliver calls Roland impetuous, there, in
the *Lied*, the Emperor calls them both brave; where Oliver blames
Roland for sacrificing the flower of France to his pride ('*Votre
olifan suner, vos nel deignates*', l. 1101), but later joins him in a
common regard for their kindred ('the shame of [our calling for
help] would last all their lives', l. 1707), there, in the *Lied*, Oliver's
first request is unmotivated; Roland's refusal is based entirely on
his trust in God and his desire for martyrdom (ll. 3870 ff.); he
eventually blows his horn at the Archbishop's request; there is no
real dispute[1] between the two friends and hence no reconciliation;
the fatherland ('Karlingen') which they call to mind is little
more than a name—it is quite unlike that '*dulce France*' where the
conduct of the heroes of the *Chanson* will be judged; and their
deaths are the less poignant for being entirely overshadowed by
their expectation of eternal bliss. Konrad fails, not because (as the
current cliché has it) 'the Christian faith makes tragedy impossible', but because his evocation of the world is too sketchy
and too partial to impress upon us at all deeply the value of that
which men must leave when they die.

Given the formalised, convention-tied nature of the *Chanson*, of
its descriptions, characterisations, of the pre-ordained action
itself and its determination, at least once or twice, by divine
interference—is it really meaningful to speak of its rudimentary
realism, to describe it as *the more realistic* of the two works?
There is here little concern with institutional or political matters,
and no resorting to low life, bourgeois intrigue or peasant guile,
or to a psychological devaluing of heroism. The meanings I shall

---

[1] In *Lied*, l. 6010, Oliver says, referring to his earlier request (3865), 'Had you
done it in time!' but, the worldly motive of glory being absent, had Roland
acceded to Oliver's request he would presumably have shown a lack of trust in
God.

content myself with throughout this book are *ad hoc* and relative meanings, emerging (for instance) from the contrast with Konrad's *Lied*, and denoting not a content but a condition of literary works. What I wish to designate and single out is the French author's greater readiness to shape the lineaments of his *Chanson* at least partly, at least on major occasions, by the *ductus*, the lineaments of living experience—possibly rare, exalted experience —in a world that a man shares with other men, and to go beyond that experience only on the margins of life itself. What I wish to designate is an author's readiness to shape his tale not by what shall be or should be; not by the single man's unshared experience of God and His commands; not by the author's spiritual fears, hopes and passionate injunctions; not by the content of his faith —*except* as these are realised, modified and alas worsted, in the living contact with contemporary reality, with other men. The world being what it is, the negative connotations of the term cannot be avoided: to write realistically is to retrace the shapes of the obstacles that men put into the ways of God, and these obstacles vary from age to age; or again, it is at once to enrich and refine, *and* to fulfil, the expectations with which the reader comes to the literary work of art.

Many philosophers, historians and literary scholars since Nietzsche have been amassing evidence in support of the view that there is nothing perennial or even stable about that conception of 'contemporary reality' which is central to any ordinary notion of realism. Though reluctant to see our own scene in that light, we are ready enough to agree that the common view of what is and what matters in the world changes from age to age no less than the props of civilised life itself, that the 'common view' is a time-bound interpretation. For the literary historian, whose task it is to make as relevant as possible the expectations with which to approach every literary work of art, this recognition is a truism, merely a further injunction to avoid anachronisms. Yet the perennial nature of realism remains unimpaired by historical considerations. It still designates a creative attention to the shapes and relations in the interpreted world where, for the space of the created work at least, for the brief respite of creation, that world is taken not as an interpretation at all but as that which alone is.

The shapes of things in the world and their relations change; the character, or rather perhaps the closeness, of the attending, of the exploration, changes. And yet there is a general direction, a bearing of the exploration itself, which remains sufficiently constant, sufficiently distinct as a creative activity, to offer a significant contrast to other modes of composition. There is no reason for thinking that 'mimesis' is the goal of every writer. Differences of creative attention are distinct from, and no less real than, differences in creative talent. What the *Chanson* presents is (as Wölfflin said of the Italian churches) 'an existence heightened beyond earthly measure, yet . . . conceived within the meaningful compass of human life', whereas what the *Rolandslied* attempts to give us is 'not the feeling in all its grandeur of life itself, but something that is beyond life.'[1] The former attends to the ways of men and of the God to Whom they turn in their hour of need, the latter to the ways of God and of men as they do or ignore His will.

A different age with its different beliefs and temptations, its different set of values, will yield a contrast between different contents of reality, yet it will be a similar contrast. And it would not be difficult to show how the contrast returns in different forms throughout the history of German literature. We sense it for instance in a comparison between Milton's *Paradise Lost* and Klopstock's *Messias* (begun in 1746). Milton's anthropomorphism, his immense feeling for the personal qualities and their conflicts, involve him (as Mr Empson has recently shown) in theological quandaries and moral dilemmas; but they also give his poem a dramatic quality wholly lacking in Klopstock's. What Klopstock's 'grand manner' yields is a devotional pæan, an attempt at a 'direct' evocation of the divinity and passion of Christ. Evil is named and execrated, but it is not shown in any-

---

[1] Heinrich Wölfflin, at the end of his essay on 'Das deutsche Formgefühl' [1922], in *Gedanken zur Kunstgeschichte*, Basel 1940.

ANTECEDENTS AND COMPARISONS   29

thing like a real conflict with divine goodness; and the biblical
stories to which the poem relates are mere illustrations, they are
not shaped into a recognisable narrative continuity. Thus the
poem is not a spiritual drama at all, but an immense elaboration
of a narrow range of sublime emotions attached to angelic agents,
to beings which remain (and, incidentally, are intended to
remain) ineffable. We discern the same contrast again in the German eighteenth-century imitations of *Robinson Crusoe* where (as
in the most famous of them[1]) the desert island is no sooner made
habitable than a pietist conventicle is founded there and it becomes the battleground of theological disputes. Again Gundolf,
writing of Shakespeare and the spirit of German drama,
makes the same point as Wölfflin: 'All that in Shakespeare is
essentially self-contained and at peace with itself is for Schiller
related to something outside, namely the moral order of the
universe. All the characters who in Shakespeare are symbols,
expressions of their own essential being, are for Schiller
allegorical examples of the moral order that obtains in the
universe.'[2]

In the nineteenth century the worldly exploration will no
longer discern the heroic, and the attention that is turned to
'something beyond life' will no longer see God in His heavens.
Dispossessed 'negative' heroes will take the place of Roland and
Oliver, many an *-ism* will take the place of Konrad's God. Yet
something of the politico-theological contrast between nation ('*la
dulce France*') and *Sacrum Imperium* ('*suoze Karlinge*' or more
simply, '*daz ríche*') is still recognisable in the contrast between
Stendhal's sure touch when he places his heroes in post-Napoleonic
France and the contemporary German writers' lack of social and
national assurances. Even the greatest of them fashions his works
outside the given realities of his age.

---

[1] See J. G. Schnabel's *Die Insel Felsenburg*, 1st ed. Nordhausen 1732, revised
by L. Tieck in 1828 and again by M. Greiner, Stuttgart [*Reclam*] 1959.
[2] Friedrich Gundolf, *Shakespeare und der deutsche Geist*, Godesberg 1947, p.
260. The same point is made by E. M. Butler (*The Direct Method in German
Poetry*, Cambridge 1946) when she contrasts the 'direct method' of Hölderlin
and the Romantics with the 'indirect method' of English poetry.

4

And so he [Napoleon] *came to speak dis-*
approvingly of our tragedies of fate. They
belonged to a darker age. After all, he said,
what have we to do with fate nowadays?
For us, politics is fate. . . .
From Goethe's conversation
with Napoleon, 2.10.1808.

My second sketch of antecedents takes us to the era immediately
preceding that of the *littérature embourgeoisée*, the era into which
Schopenhauer, the Romantics, but also Marx and Wagner were
born. It is dominated by Goethe, whose literary passion for what
is rather than what *should be* is a measure of his genius as a poet.
His deeply intelligent love of the created world, man-made and
natural alike, finds its beautiful reflection in every kind of European and exotic literary form (as well as in several of his own
making); the variety of genres which he fills out with his experience is in itself a measure of his creative generosity.

Of the three spheres of human experience which perennially
engage the literary imagination, he explores the first, *the personal*,
with an intensity of feeling that has rarely been equalled, never
perhaps surpassed. The self in and out of love, anguished, joyful,
serene, renouncing, failing and falling a prey to despair and then
again drinking the brave water of courage—of this self no poet
has ever spoken with greater passion and poetic felicity. And not
only of love and solitude, but also of the self in those social
groupings which are held together by intimate personal feelings—
the family, man tied by bonds of friendship, heredity, or un-
questioned fealty.

What is true of the first sphere of experience is also true of the
third, *the metaphysical and religious*. Both within the Christian faith
and outside it, in cosmic speculations which bear the hallmark not
of abstraction but of an intimate and wholly personal concern, in
reflective modes which are sometimes traditional, sometimes of
his own mythopoeic imagination, Goethe has depicted the greatness of the race more finely and the sweetness of life more

movingly than many another poet whose strength lay in that sphere alone. The poignancy of the moment as well as the consecration of habit and duration, the intersection of time and the timeless not in mystical ecstasy but in firm contact with the created world —these are among his finest themes.

But what does he say of the second, the realm of the Leviathan, the area of experience in which men are bound together not by love but contract, not by worship but agreement: that which he himself called 'the middle height of life': the *political* sphere? The answer, after many necessary qualifications, is, disappointingly little.

Not that he—patrician son, privy-councillor, cabinet minister, etc., etc.—was lacking in first-hand knowledge and strong opinion in these matters. True, he seems hardly ever interested in political principles. But his conversations, letters and auto-biographical writings bear witness to an intimate understanding of men *in politicis*; his many caustic observations about the national character of his fellow-countrymen, for instance, are among the most perceptive we know. But (and this is no less characteristic) little if any of this kind of knowledge enters his major works.

It is certainly not the *size* of the political events of his age which is responsible for his disengagement, nor indeed the size of his poetic genius. A smaller man on a smaller stage—W. B. Yeats— offers a revealing comparison. They have, after all, a good deal in common. Both are blessedly prolific and generously unfussy in their poetic production; to both, poetry is a manner of living, Sundays and weekdays alike; and both have the marvellous capacity for making occasional poetry great and for making the occasion great by means of the poetry. They share a nobility of outlook, an instinctive reaching-out for the highest values, an instinctive felicity in making of their poetry a vessel in which to preserve human worth. But Yeats's poetry, a smaller gift to be sure, takes for its occasions all three spheres of experience, it sees human worth alive everywhere, not least in the sphere of politics; and it may well be that here, rather than in its mythopoeic vein, lies the permanent value of Yeats's work. The parish-pump politics of a little island off the western shores of Europe, with all their pettiness, sordid patricidal intrigue and endless betrayals,

are an integral part of his finest poetry. Formulating the constriction of his world,[1] he escapes it. None of the defections, changes
of front and stifling loyalties are too base for his poetry. And since
they enter it, fully bodied forth in the sensuous detail of contemporary fact and circumstance, they emerge as poetic symbols,
no less, of all the world of strife and revolutionary turmoil. It is
to the complex whole of such a world of strife that his poetry is
committed, not merely to one of the contending parts. And it is
the ironical glory of the poet, as well as the despair of party men
and patriots, that his commitment to both sides is every bit as
passionate, every bit as serious, as the party men's allegiance to one.

Goethe's classicism is a literary style devised almost entirely apart
from the political reality, and it is least successful where, because of
the expectations raised by the subject-matter, that reality cannot
be excluded; and it is with such legitimate expectations that
I am here concerned. For different but equally irrelevant reasons
both Marxists and nationalists have criticised him because he
refused to enter the political arena and instead declared himself
to be 'a poet who, by his very nature, must remain impartial'.
The attitude, certainly, is unexceptionable, the censures crude.
The point of criticism is not where he 'stands' politically, but
what he sees and fashions, to what effect he 'immerses himself in
the circumstances of both contending parties';[2] for what we
expect is not advocacy but insight.

In *Götz*, *Egmont* and *Faust II* there arise situations, central to
the action, whose resolution hinges on political and social issues.
(I mean such issues as, to choose the most obvious comparisons

---

[1] See the last stanza of *Remorse for Intemperate Speech:*
> Out of Ireland have we come,
> Great hatred, little room
> Maimed us at the start.
> I carry from my mother's womb
> A fánatic heart.

[2] J.A. [*Jubiläumsausgabe*], Vol. XXVIII, p. 212.

of all, Shakespeare faces at the point where Caesar is murdered, where Prince Hal becomes king; or Racine, where Titus abandons Bérénice; or Sophocles, where he conducts the deadly dialectic between Antigone and the *raison d'état*.) And each time, in such situations, the political answer is avoided, or 'cooked' by being turned into an exclusively personal one. Götz's loyalty to the Emperor is not tested by exposing him to the real man and his weaknesses. The idea of heroic leadership which Götz and Egmont embody can only survive in a situation in which the political issues at stake are ignored; where the conflict between personal glory and social responsibility is avoided; and where all political prudence is identified with cowardice. We ask why Faust, at the opening of the Second Part, should find himself at the court of a medieval emperor; or rather, what is the connection with his previous life, as well as the purpose, of the strange antics he performs there; we wish, in brief, to rid ourselves of a persistent feeling of the unconvincingness and arbitrariness of it all. But there is no answer to these questions, except that Faust is 'meant' to go through these 'political' experiences because he is 'meant' to 'go through everything'—which is a bad, 'literary' answer because it depends on intentions rather than on immediate conviction through purposeful dramatic unity. We 'know' that Goethe intended anything but a political play. Its conception was to be utopian and idealising. It is on some such grounds as these that the peremptoriness of the action, its being 'left in the air', should be explained, we are told. But a comparison with another work written in the years of sublime maturity, *The Tempest*, shows that neither utopia nor idealisation is incompatible with that purposeful unity which *Faust II* lacks. Nor does Shakespeare leave unheeded those realistic considerations of time and place which (so the critics tell us) are irrelevant to Faust's grand journey through life. The 'philosophy', the heartbreaking wisdom of *The Tempest*, is achieved at the same time as the claims of men and their relationships are met: above all by Shakespeare's readiness to provide a full and sustaining and wholly relevant political background for his characters' sojourn on their distant and fabulous island.

Goethe's minor political pieces, such as *Der Gross-Coptha* and

Der Bürgergeneral, need not concern us in any detail;[1] there, certainly, the political issues are trivialised and allowed to fritter away into fancy and unreality. But the remarkable thing is that these plays, and several other productions, are fully intended as political comments, as the poet's responses to the major political events of his day. Of *Die natürliche Tochter* (1801–3), the most important of these works, Goethe himself wrote, 'I devised its outline to serve as a vessel in which I hoped to deposit with due seriousness all that over many years I had written and thought about the French Revolution and its consequences'[2]—an information likely to strike a reader who is ignorant of the biographical background of the play as very surprising. Mme de Staël called the play *'un noble ennui'*, a verdict which may be justly applied to everything in it except what obviously mattered to the author. Its main inspiration and poetic centre—the strange fate of the heroine with its mysterious betrayals and rescues—is presented with the deepest elegiac feelings. But of course the motivation of her fate lies in the actions of the other characters; and they, intended as dramatic comments on the revolutionary situation, are obscure and inadequate rather than mysterious. 'Time is out of joint', Goethe is saying; justice is perverted, ambition rife, loyalties are broken; bureaucracy has replaced mercy; even the King, for once, appears to be doing wrong. How—why—to what ends? Is there really no more to these sinister and obscure events than mean and complicated ambition and rank chaos? Are there no clearly conceived intentions for good or ill? Is it really true, or adequate, or even interesting, to say that in political situations in which 'expedient injustice' is done 'the powers that be act but rarely from free conviction',[3] and to say virtually no

---

[1] The more interesting war journal, *Campagne in Frankreich*, is discussed in a note on pp. 350–1.

[2] Quoted from E. Staiger, *Goethe*, ii, Zurich 1956, pp. 372 ff.

[3] In Act IV, Scene 1, the Councillor, spokesman of moderate, *bürgerlich* opinion, says to the heroine's chaperon:

Ich schelte nicht das Werkzeug, rechte kaum	Not for me to condemn the tool, to argue
Mit jenen Mächten, die sich solche Handlung	With those powers who permit themselves

more? Almost any other attitude would be more illuminating. Take Georg Büchner: his personal, 'subjective' dilemma remains (as we shall see) unresolved, he loses all faith in the meaningfulness of political action, yet his creative concern with the revolutionary ideas and practice is undiminished by his disillusionment. In Goethe's play, on the other hand, the ideas are never examined, the political situation (as opposed to the personal) is never properly articulated at all: all is covered as with a film of obscurity and undifferentiated suspicion. Verisimilitude, the interest and coherence of the action, the individuality of characters, all—except the tragic figure of a heroine blown by the winds of fortune past her destruction to a haven of domestic tranquillity—all crumbles in the hands of the reluctant dramatist.[1]

It is not my aim to survey or criticise Goethe's political attitude. Nor am I attempting an appraisal of the rôle of politics in the German literature of his age. In such an appraisal Schiller, Kleist and later Grillparzer would have to be given a more important place than he; certainly there is little in modern European drama to put by the side of *Wallenstein* when it comes to portraying the nature of leadership and the limits of power within the framework of a living political situation. But it is the 'fate-element' of these plays, not their political aspect, that engages the imagination of the later Romantics. As for Goethe, in the absence of a political and social interest he allows lyrical, elegiac, reflective or idyllic moments to obtrude on scenes which, for dramatic effect, require

Erlauben können. Leider sind auch sie	*Such action. They too, alas,*
Gebunden und gedrängt. Sie wirken selten	*Are bound, hard pressed. They act*
Aus freier Überzeugung. Sorge, Furcht	*But rarely from a free conviction. Care*
Vor grösserm Übel nöthiget Regenten	*And fear of greater evil compel princes*
Die nützlich ungerechten Thaten ab.	*To act unjustly from expedience.*
Vollbringe was du musst, entferne dich	*Do what you must do, and leave*
Aus meiner Enge reingezogenem Kreis.	*The narrow, carefully drawn circle of my life.*

[1] So uncongenial was the whole subject of the Revolution to Goethe that he never wrote the other two plays of the planned trilogy.

nothing so much as forthright action. But then, the ruthless
management of the turning-point is the business of the theatrical
'politician and schemer'[1] that lurks in every true dramatist, not
of the patrician Elder Statesman.

What so marks the literary and cultural tradition into which
the first generation of nineteenth-century prose writers was born
is the fact that its founder and admired exemplar should have remained relatively incurious about the major events of his day—at
least in the sense that the intricate, invigorating image of man as a
political animal, now despicable, now glorious and at all times the
inspiration of some of the greatest literary achievements, failed to
engage Goethe's creative imagination. This, after all, is the
generation which grew up to face the indignities of the Metternich régime, of the police-state, the upheavals of 1830 and 1848;
which, in the absence of any guidance, turned to a political
extremism as unsteady and unrealistic as it was short-lived.

One hesitates to speak of the breviary Goethe bequeathed to
that generation, *Hermann und Dorothea*, in political terms. In this
way one is apt to ignore its idyllic charm and its exquisitely subtle
interplay of ancient and modern; and it is these qualities, informed
by an immense creative affection and leavened by the finest
touches of irony, which are the sources of its greatness. Yet the
poem *has* a political significance. It depicts a world governed by
love, friendship and family relations, a way of life in which social
experience is seen entirely in terms of private virtues. It gives a
picture of a patriarchal society outside which reigns revolutionary
chaos. The image of life inside the idyll is complete and beautifully rounded, perfect in itself. However, the poetic image does
not live in isolation; and the more 'non-political' it is, the more
likely, in Germany especially, it is to become a precept. And it is
then that its political implications are drawn, that the poem turns
into an apologia for political quietism. The ethos of parochialism
which it extols is based on a nostalgic desire to reduce social and
political problems to family dimensions.[2] Not only did the poem

---

[1] See Emil Staiger, *op. cit.*, Vol. II, p. 180.
[2] Marx claims (in *Deutsche Ideologie*, 1844 ff., *ed. cit.*, p. 19) that this desire is
characteristic of the German middle classes.

meet that desire, but there was good reason why it should do so: its prescriptive character is, as it were, built into the poem. The old Goethe's view of himself and his work is based upon the deep conviction that poetry *should* form the basis of a national spirituality and culture, that Germany should look to her poets for guidance. For spiritual guidance certainly. But the emphasis itself, upon non-political *Dichtung*, connotes a political attitude—quietism and fear of meddling in politics become, not inadvertently, the consequences of Goethe's poetic undertaking.

This disengagement—from the political, but also from the full social, reality of his day—finally brings me to the question why Goethe's full-length novels do not, on the whole, achieve that comprehensiveness of worldly vision of which the genre is capable in the hands of Defoe, Fielding, and a little later Sir Walter Scott. The detailed realism of the first part of *Wilhelm Meister*, the psychologically revealing touches of *Die Wahlverwandtschaften*, come to be superseded, before the tales are told, by quite different modes and descriptive manners. The realism never lasts all the way. The central problem of each novel is not resolved within that mode, nor its full meaning attained. And what it is superseded by is a peculiar timelessness;[1] the social experience of the age is represented in a parade of shadowgraphs which yet has a very special charm of its own. The noble symbolism of the tragic tale of elective affinities is not without contact with contemporary reality. And it goes without saying that, in establishing this contact, Goethe is selective, as every writer must be. It is because that selection is a little recondite, and a little didactic too; because the principle of his selection is not so much 'life into art' as rather something like 'life-as-art into art', that the roots which sustain *Die Wahlverwandtschaften*, Goethe's most completely achieved novel, are aerial roots; that the ultimate impression it leaves is one of incompleteness.

---

[1] Thus the hermetically sealed social world of *Die Wahlverwandtschaften* takes us back to Schnabel's *Insel Felsenburg* of 1732, and to the communities described in early eighteenth-century Pietist biographies; at the same time this aristocratic mode of life is not very different from that described in the last part of Gottfried Keller's *Der grüne Heinrich* of 1855.

One's criticism here is not guided by a documentary interest. Completeness, in these matters, is not to be determined by the expectations of social historians, even less by premeditated stylistic rules or naturalistic dogma, but by the expectation which the work itself raises. *Werther*, in this and every other sense, is beautifully complete. Brief, even narrow and one-sided, passionate, it is a life in which nothing relevant is lacking, a portrayal which convinces and fulfils the expectation it itself raises, where conviction and fulfilment are but one thing. One style, and one reality, take the hero (and us) all the way.[1]

In all that I have said, the main dimension of Goethe's achievement—his true greatness—has gone unexamined. I have said nothing, for instance, of the supreme lyrical beauty of many a passage in *Faust II*, of his lines on Byron (perhaps the most moving homage ever paid by one poet to another), of the sensuously transcendent poetry of the last scenes ('... *wo es mit der geretteten Seele nach oben geht*'[2]). I have conveyed nothing of the conflict, portrayed in the pages of *Die Wahlverwandtschaften*, between the natural and the moral laws, with its grave and strangely violent conclusion.[3] Here indeed is *pesanteur* and charm in a unique combination. If I have concentrated upon a failing— a failing in realism—it is because that, rather than the lyrical or narrative charm, was handed down to the subsequent generation.

A failing in realism? Again, the meaning of the term is relative to the actual circumstances of the age; or rather to the ethos of

---

[1] In saying this I don't wish to imply that all great novels are necessarily written in *one* style; the Romantic '*Stimmungsbruch*' can on occasion be a highly successful device. The difficulty only arises where a 'mixed style' occurs inadvertently, where the reason for the change is lacking or unconvincing.

[2] To Eckermann, 6 June 1831.

[3] Which is reminiscent of the end of *The Cocktail Party*; but then, the atmosphere created and the wisdom conveyed in many of Goethe's later works, as well as their flaws, are all to be found again in Mr Eliot's latest plays, written in the years of his 'reconciliation' with Goethe.

that age as it is partly reflected in, and partly formed by, its literature.

This double relationship is as true of the 'Age of Goethe' as it is of any other. A case has been made for calling Goethe's lyrical poetry 'realistic', even though it is largely or wholly unconcerned with social circumstance: for is it not a loving, undeflected exploration of the whole of reality that comes into the purview of a poem? And is not our reading of it attended by the conviction that it *is* a whole? But the 'realism' of Goethe's poetry is not the realism of the subsequent age of prose. Yet it was this Goethean 'realism' which, in the hands of men whose experience was altogether less abundant than his own, became what he had never intended it to be: a restricting precept. Taken as a sanction for political and social disengagement, his poetry, and Weimar classicism generally, invited an attitude that was false both to the age and to the poetry.

And Goethe himself contributed to this development. It was, I think, Wilhelm Dilthey (in *Das Erlebnis und die Dichtung*, 1905) who first said that 'Goethe set out to make his life, his personality, into a work of art';[1] the view itself was common property of the intelligentsia throughout the century. Accepted uncritically and made into a recipe for living, the idea led to incongruous results. But what does it imply for Goethe himself? More than any other writer in the history of Western literature, Goethe was able to *create*, for the brief time of some four decades and in the narrow space of the Duchy of Weimar, the conditions in which his genius, his lyrical 'realism', had its flowering. The situation was unique. It was the result, above all, of his own creative energy. To an extent that seems hard to imagine today, he posited, *made* his values and those of his environment. But he could do this precisely because of the high-minded unpolitical susceptibility of Weimar society; because of the pliability, as it were, of the social clay from which he fashioned his existence as a poet, administrator, scientist, sage. The resistance he encountered, especially after the death of Schiller in 1805, was small indeed. The circumstances opposing his literary and cultural leadership, even the forces indifferent to it, were trivial when compared

[1] ed. Berlin 1921, p. 217.

with the resistance less fortunate men of genius have been compelled to face, and draw their strength from. Neither Shakespeare nor Racine ever set the tone of their societies in a comparable manner. Are not the trials and tribulations of the court of Syracuse among the sources of Plato's realism in *The Republic*? Had Goethe been less fortunate, might he not have been more so?

The balance is delicate, his attitude easily mis-stated. Reared on circumstances so largely of his making, Goethe's life was not an 'aesthetic interpretation of the world' (the phrase is Nietzsche's) if by 'aesthetic' we mean some sort of evasion or effete abridgement of living experience. He lived, we know, a uniquely full life. He conceived his art in a uniquely rich and generous way. And his life was more nearly co-extensive with his art than perhaps any other writer's. In *that* order: the man as great as the artist, the life co-extensive with and filling out the art: not the art straining to the life, not (as with Tolstoy) the artist as great as the man. In all the greatest works of the long and fruitful years of Goethe's maturity his art proceeds by selection not just from the life but from life-as-art.

His enthusiasm and his capacity for passionate feeling were great at all times, he was not always blessed with that 'natural sagacity of the heart'[1] of which he speaks in some of his later poems. It was his glory, but also his predicament, that his memory and creative imagination were one. He was for ever ready—perhaps at times too ready—to receive the consolations of poetry and to anticipate experience by the expectation of them. There is about him in that splendid house on the Frauenplan with its curving double staircase of fawn marble something of the guardian of his autobiographical documentation; all around him are the eminently exhibitable potsherds—some picturesque and rough, others highly polished—of former and present selves. His self-importance was frequently leavened by a sense of humour. The wryness and irony with which, in prose and verse, he liked to deflate the claims and importance of art (querying the value

---

[1] See *J.A.*, Vol. XXVIII, p. 174.

of poetry itself, querying the poetry of the German language, querying the value of 'Words, words, words') is one of the most engaging qualities of his greatness. Even on the subject of the immortality he cared for—that of artist and creator—he could be caustic and *désinvolte*. Yet he himself included the minutiae of his life among the things that his art was to preserve against the ruins of time.[1] But *that* part of his immortality, from which the recipe for living was formed, is not only the less valuable, for us it is liable to encumber and obscure the value of the poetry. His life was lived in circumstances which were unrepeatable, because all circumstances, and especially those of one's own creating, are unrepeatable. And it was when they had passed that his life came to be seen as an 'aesthetic interpretation' above all, as a 'work of art'; and only then were its incompletenesses magnified. Lesser men who had no imaginative right to his serenity and disengagement came to assert, and thus distort, what had once, free from all assertion, been *his* 'realism'. Like all expressions of the lyrical disposition, like all expressions of love, this 'realism' was uncontentious, indefensible. *They* offered to defend it against a realism whose challenge he had barely felt. Or else in his name they ignored the new realism, protesting against and deploring its limitations before ever they had probed its full European possibilities. Largely, of course, it was to be the old story of '*Les grands hommes, en apprenant aux faibles à réfléchir, les ont mis sur la route de l'erreur*'; largely, but not entirely.

Yet there were some who gave voice to the conflicting claims of soul and society. They succeeded in fashioning not a single alternative to European realism, but different solutions to what they came to feel as their personal and literary conflict of allegiances. Only in this indirect way could the Goethean heritage, to which they owed so much, be made fruitful.

---

[1] He satirises the contemporary cult of sensibility, he knows the attempt to hold up the passage of time with medallion, lock of hair and slab of stone for the vain thing it is, and he knowingly indulges in the cult. Thus, too, Charlotte, in *Die Wahlverwandtschaften*, at first ridicules this cult, but at the end of the novel it is she who collects the relics, plans the chapel decorations and the cemetery. . . .

II BEYOND THE COMMON INDICATION: GRILLPARZER

How oft, amid those overflowing streets,
Have I gone forward with the crowd, and said
Unto myself, 'The face of every one
That passes by me is a mystery!'
Thus have I looked, nor ceased to look, oppressed
By thoughts of what and whither, when and how,
Until the shapes before my eyes became
A second-sight procession, such as glides
Over still mountains, or appears in dreams;
And once, far travelled in such mood, beyond
The reach of common indication, lost
Amid the moving pageant, I was smitten
Abruptly, with the view (a sight not rare)
Of a blind Beggar, who, with upright face,
Stood, propped against a wall; upon his chest
Wearing a paper, to explain
His story, whence he came, and who he was.

Wordsworth, Residence in London

I

THE DIDACTIC IDEAL of German classicism, intimated in its finest creative achievements and propagated in its theoretical writings, is the aesthetic and hence the moral rebirth, or at least refinement, of mankind through the power of Art. The unity of the true and the beautiful which this classicism invokes is a unity imaged in its productions rather than observed in and reported from the world at large. Yet the claims of humdrum reality are not ignored. The vision of the poet as the legislator of mankind, for instance, is intended to illuminate the contact, turn to positive account the conflict, between the classical ideal and the actual world (or at least something like it). Thus the eponymous heroes of Goethe's *Torquato Tasso* and Franz Grillparzer's *Sappho* show the sometimes tragic, sometimes merely embarrassing limitations, imposed by an uncomprehending world, to which all attempts at translating the moral-aesthetic ideal into reality appear to be subject. But though the personal fate of the bearer of the message is likely to be catastrophic; though the artist is presented in a situation of very nearly absolute isolation (as though the sources of that isolation lay not merely in specific circumstances and personal temperament but in the very nature of Art)—yet the issue is not at all unmitigatedly tragic. The artist himself comes to grief; this much even the optimistic Schiller of the *Letters on the Aesthetic Education of Man* had envisaged. His is a life of renunciation and sacrifice, and as such meaningful. For there remains the work of art itself, imprint of the sensibility that fashioned it—it remains valid as the emblem of a life and spirit higher and finer than is to be found among ordinary men. True, the artist's contemporaries will probably fail to understand how vitally relevant the ideal is to their own situation, and hence fail to give the ideal its true, 'real' value. They may even show themselves unworthy of it. This is the deeply melancholy apprehension with which Goethe informed the lyrical songs of his unfinished dramatic poem *Pandora*, his most moving testament of beauty. But here again the apprehension and the doubt attach to the recipients of the gift, not to the gift itself. Perhaps the mind that has created it (as opposed to the artist's life in its raw, unformed actuality), and certainly the beautiful object of the mind's creation itself, are exempt from the doubt. The faith classicism has in the power of art is, after all, simple enough: the work will survive the incomprehension and faithlessless of those to whom it was given, and achieve its sublime task of educating, unifying, of pacifying the conflict. Not now, perhaps: but it is, after all, immortal.

By the time Grillparzer comes to reflect upon his own predicament as a man and writer, the tradition of German classicism has very nearly run its course. At any rate, his literary self-consciousness is that of an *epigonos*, a latecomer; his diaries abound with regrets at the passing of the Goethean era and with fears (even before the shock, as he felt it, of 1848) of a plebeian, egalitarian future. The present, to him, is all loss: he feels engulfed by an 'age of prose'.[1] Nor does he use the word only metaphorically. Indulging in a literal-mindedness which must at first strike us as odd, he restricts the noble appellation of *Dichter* to 'poet', and emphatically excludes from it the novelist or writer of *Novellen*. His polemical references to the topic are endless and not always illuminating;[2] his is not the sort of abundantly creative mind— as was Goethe's—which, having more urgent things to do than dwell on its own 'formal problems', solves them instinctively and without theoretical fuss. On the contrary, he is full of scruples, narrow discriminations and prescriptive rules on the one hand, and strenuously, self-destructively exalted visions of his calling on the other. Prose is to him a democratic, prosy form, essentially unsuitable for the high, the vatic task of the poet. Just so the contemporary social and political scene, whose language is to him so often the language of the mob, does not yield to his art a suitable subject-matter. The classical writers' trust in a *rapport* between the work of art and its audience, their faith that the didactic ideal is capable of realization—these, for the mature Grillparzer, have little contemporary significance.

This is not to say that Grillparzer repudiates the claims of the contemporary world upon his dramatic genius. In his last great play, *Ein Bruderzwist in Habsburg*, he gives us one of the two great political tragedies of German literature, its theme and message full of direct relevance to the politics of his day. But the message is nothing short of despair. Here no compromise is possible between a political reality, whose claims are presented as base, and the personal ideal, which is shown as unrealisable; the

---

[1] See, for instance, the diary entries for 1838-9, in A. Sauer's ed. *Franz Grillparzer: Sämtliche Werke*, II, Vol. X, Wien 1917, pp. 281-6; this ed. will be quoted as *S.W.*

[2] W. Kraft's 'Grillparzer und die Idee der Prosa', *Neue Zürcher Zeitung*, 7.i. 1956 (see also Kraft's 'Von Bassompierre zu Hofmannsthal: zur Geschichte eines Novellenmotivs', *Revue de littérature comparée*, Vol. XV (1935), pp. 724-5), and W. Naumann's *Grillparzer: Das dichterische Werk*, Wien n.d., pp. 1-21, contain collections of his remarks on the subject.

verse of the play, strangely unpoetic (as so often in Grillparzer) yet akin to the verse of the classical German theatre in its weightiness and dignity, bodies forth an unclassical pessimism. The Emperor Rudolf II's predicament—the conflict, which rends his mind, between the duties of kingship and the scruples of a warm humanity—is unsolved and indeed presented as insoluble. Didactic ideal there is none, not even—since Rudolf's refusal to act leads to chaos and war—in renunciation. It is not the political subject-matter—seen entirely as intrigue and machinations—but the dignity of the Emperor's insight into his own and his antagonists' motives which justifies the high poetic tone of the play. And this dignity and wisdom are presented as exclusively personal values, they are wrested from the play's political plot. (The Emperor's way out of the political dilemma is his way into inactivity, solitude and death.) The verse may be 'unpoetic' in the sense of riding roughshod over its own imagery, but its rhetoric is immensely dramatic, for it sustains the greatness, the portentous weight of the personal action, in the course of which the divinely appointed monarch moves from a culpable incapacity for his political office and its responsibilities to a repudiation of its claims upon his human person.

It is part of Grillparzer's rigidly conservative and hieratically Catholic view that each created being in the universe should occupy the station in life to which it has pleased God to appoint him. This feeling for propriety, for what belongs to each class of men and each occasion, leads him to the same conclusion as that which his contemporary Hazlitt (a man of very different political sympathies) had ruefully accepted, that 'the cause of the people is indeed but little calculated as a subject for poetry';[1] and it is this feeling which makes Grillparzer choose verse as the language of drama and dignity. His narrative prose, on the other hand, is reserved for occasions altogether more humble—such as those melancholy destinies which, involved as they are in the cares of the contemporary world, appear to lack both dignity and drama.

---

[1] In his essay on *Coriolanus*.

2

'Grillparzer is of the strange opinion that a literary work [*Dichtung*] written in prose cannot be called fully a work of art.' Grillparzer's frequent disparagements of prose amount to an exaggeration which is polemical but not pointless, and Hofmannsthal,[1] himself so often straining against the limits of conventional prose and labouring with similar problems of form, might have been expected to understand the older poet's point of view. The strands of Grillparzer's discontent—of which his remarks on the function and value of prose are but one expression—all lead back to his complex personality and to his manner of experiencing the world.

To begin with, the linguistic heritage upon which he enters is unstable, is less securely fixed than that of any other region of the German-speaking countries. A hundred years later the poet Josef Weinheber complains that he has to 'think in *two* languages, Viennese and High German',[2] that 'the Viennese language has no claim to a linguistic (nor, therefore, to an actual) harmony', and he describes the predicament which Grillparzer had encountered and failed to solve:

> Viennese had forfeited that claim as early as 1800, when the German classical writers from Lessing onwards sealed the victory of High German. The Emperor Francis's gesture of renouncing the Roman Imperial title was nothing but the visible albeit unconscious expression of the fact that the Imperial dialect was content to become the language of a region. We Austrians have had no classics: Grillparzer was not one, and Nestroy, who was one, came at least half a century too late. All he could do was to achieve his comic effects by contrasting Viennese with High German (which at that time sounded quite foreign and stilted).

The issue is of course not 'merely verbal'. The want of a distinct form of language of which Weinheber complains, the precariousness of the linguistic ('and therefore actual') habitation, faithfully reflect that unhappy 'Austrian problem' with which we are familiar from recent history; and so, from another angle, does

[1] *Buch der Freunde* [1929] Insel Verlag 1949, p. 78.
[2] Letter to Will Vesper, 31.xii.1938, in *Josef Weinheber: Sämtliche Werke*, ed. J. Nadler and H. Weinheber, Vol. V, Wien/Salzburg 1956, p. 199. See also Rilke's letter to August Sauer, 11.i.1914, in *Briefe* (ed. K. Altheim), Wiesbaden 1950, Vol. I, pp. 472–3.

Grillparzer's own unsettled consciousness of himself now as a German writer, now again as an Austrian patriot.

Grillparzer's 'strange opinion' and literal-minded insistence might seem to call for a definition of what is and what is not to be regarded as prose. Yet it is sufficient for our purpose to say that it is a form uniquely involved in the historical and social circumstances, the living customs and moral standards of its speakers and readers—that it is a singularly direct expression of that involvement. From which it follows that the less compatible these preoccupations and standards are with the artist's conscience, the more problematic will be his attitude towards the whole enterprise of conveying 'to his readers too', 'in *their* language', his vision of what the world is and what it ought to be. There is no end to the number of German writers who have experienced, and been unsettled by, this quandary, often long before it ever disturbed the consciousness of French or English writers. (And there is perhaps no end to the explanations of why this should be the case.) The very originality and creativeness of some of the greatest German prose writers from Nietzsche to Thomas Mann (and the idiosyncratic arbitrariness of many lesser ones) are a measure of how acutely the problem was and still is being felt. This is the situation in which arose that uneasy compromise between the artistic vision and the facts of life known in the history of nineteenth-century German literature as 'poetic realism', at a time when English and French novelists (not to mention the Russians) had as yet few qualms about the essential fittingness of their medium to their chosen task.

The novel especially, with its notorious tendency to looseness and shapelessness, has often been singled out as betraying all that Art should stand for, as a genre which offers insufficient resistance to the prosy outlook of its readers or to the indulgence in mere fancy. Recognising this, passionate novelists like Flaubert and Henry James preach and practise reform through imaginative discipline and high 'poetic' artifice. Other writers—Grillparzer among them—find it difficult to see how the genre can be salvaged at all. And the point of complete rejection is reached in the writings of the Viennese satirist Karl Kraus. In the wake of Nestroy, Kraus draws upon the contrast between Viennese linguistic and moral habits and his own vision of what the German language, and what life, should really be like. His own uncompromisingly intense and increasingly compact prose-style is utterly 'unpopular'; no bland Sunday reviewer could call it 'readable'; it is reared in conscious and deliberate defiance of the prevailing moral and linguistic preoccupations and standards. And when Kraus *'simply disclaims all interest'*[1] in the average novel's average plot, situation and message, when he proclaims that no sequence of words such as 'She looked at the sitting-room clock. It was half past two', or (more up to date) '"I told you Hugh said it was good of Felix to be so nice to Ann", said Mildred' can possibly belong to a work of art, he merely sharpens to a polemical point Grillparzer's contempt for 'the decline of poetry into prose'.[2] This scorn for all who don't even attempt that which alone is worthy of consideration and of the name of Art— namely, the masterpiece—Grillparzer had confided to his diaries more than half a century before Kraus. In view of the verbal inflations of our own day we need not, I think, discount these opinions as entirely absurd; nevertheless, like a great deal of the New Criticism they anticipate, the point of view is inadequate. It implies a radical rejection of quotidian language, experience

---

[1] *Die Fackel*, nos. 577–582 (1921), p. 47:

Da ich infolge einer angeborenen Insuffizienz Romane nicht zu Ende lesen kann, indem ich, der imstande ist, sechzehn Stunden ohne Unterbrechung und ohne Ermüdung zu arbeiten, schon beim geringsten Versuch, mir zu erzählen, dass Walter beim Betreten des Vorzimmers auf die Uhr sah, was mich so wenig angeht wie alles was weiter geschah, in tiefen traumlosen Schlaf verfalle ...	As a result of some congenital disability it is impossible for me to read a novel to the end, for although capable of working for sixteen hours without interruption and without fatigue, at the slightest attempt to interest myself in the fact that Walter entered the hall and glanced at the clock—which concerns me as little as all the subsequent events—I invariably fall into a deep and dreamless sleep ...

A similar impatience is expressed in Sartre's attack on *'la folle entreprise de conter'* (*op. cit.*, p. 256). Thomas Mann (in *Rede und Antwort*, Berlin 1922, pp. 19, 55) presents the story-teller's defence.

[2] *S.W.*, I, Vol. XIII, p. 288.

and standards, of the rendering of things and men in the world as it is, of the realism that must first encompass and then transmute the prosy world. Rejecting our annual harvest of prosiness and mediocrity, this attitude makes short work, too, of the verbal texture of the writings of a Dostoyevsky and Tolstoy.

Grillparzer stands at the unsophisticated beginning of this argument. He is not really concerned with technicalities. And even though he is tempted to equate 'prosiness' with prose, his scorn is, fundamentally, for 'talking', for all the lax, mediocre, uncommitted patter which, although not at all unsympathetic to the concerns of Art, is yet, in a peculiar way, its undoing. In one of his most moving compositions, the second of his memoirs of Beethoven, he makes the point with characteristic succinctness and asperity:

Ich habe Beethoven eigentlich geliebt. Wenn ich von seinen Aeusserungen nur wenig wieder zu erzählen weiss, so kommt es vorzüglich daher, weil mich an einem Künstler nicht das interessiert was er spricht, sondern was er macht. Wenn Sprechen einen Massstab für Künstlerwert abgäbe, so wäre Deutschland gegenwärtig ebenso voll von Künstlern als es in der Tat leer ist. Ja, der eigentlichen Schöpfungskraft kommt nur jenes, bereits im Talent gegebene Denkvermögen zugute, das sich instinktmässig äussert und die Quelle von Leben und individueller Wahrheit ist.[1]	*I truly loved Beethoven. If I cannot recount many of the things he said, it is mainly because what interests me in an artist is not what he says but what he does. If talking were the measure of an artist's worth, then Germany would at the present time be as full of artists as she is in fact empty of them. Indeed, the creative power proper can benefit only from that intellectual capacity which lies already in a man's talent and is as it were tied to it, which expresses itself instinctively, and is the source of life and individual truth.[1]*

Such was Beethoven's gift. Dare he claim it for himself too? Once, in 1823-4, the two men had tried to collaborate on an opera, but Grillparzer's libretto had proved barren ground for Beethoven's music and the plan came to nought. Three years

---

[1] S.W., I, Vol. XIII, p. 360. In connection with a reading of Tieck (II, Vol. X, p. 161) he writes, 'Eben so gut könnte jedes beliebige Thee-Gesalbader für eine [Novelle] gelten.'

later they met for the last time, in the small dining-room of the crowded, noisy inn where, at a separate table in a corner, the deaf composer came every day to take his meal. Their meeting is preserved for us in the heartbreaking record of Beethoven's contact with the world, his *Conversation Books*. Into one of these ghostly notebooks, in which the bewildering details of his daily life cluster round a silent centre, Beethoven's own unrecorded voice, Grillparzer scrawls his own *cri-de-cœur*:

If only I had a thousandth part of your power and fortitude![1]

Throughout the forty-six years which followed that conversation he was to remain a prey to such self-doubts as Beethoven, for all the tragedy of his life, had not known. But although Grillparzer was too diffident to claim for himself the gift of that 'creative power proper' (on the immediate and generous recognition of which his relation with Beethoven was based), yet he recognised and accepted the obligation which the gift confers on the possessor. To the end of his days he had a horror of prosy 'talking', the characteristic medium of his city.

Verse—even the kind of 'bungling'[2] verse Grillparzer is so often conscious of writing—implies a number of restrictions unknown to prose. But it also implies a certain freedom—the freedom, as it were, of being able to choose one's restriction; it leaves the artist something of a choice—and with Grillparzer the choice is conscious—as to which preoccupations and standards, which literary and moral tradition he will espouse. By taking over for his drama the language of Weimar classicism Grillparzer betrays not only his creative weakness (that is, his inability to create a classicism of his own: a task so immense that one fails to see how a single man could succeed in it); he also betrays his ambivalent

---

[1] *Grillparzers Gespräche und die Charakteristiken seiner Persönlichkeit durch die Zeitgenossen*, Vol. II, Wien 1905, pp. xxxiii–xxxvi; the transcription from Beethoven's *Konversationshefte* of their meeting in 'Zur Eiche', 10.iv.1826, is on pp. 284–7.

[2] In a conversation with Beethoven, Grillparzer had called himself '*einen Stümper in der Musik*', to which R. Backmann (*S.W.* I, Vol. XIII, p. 314) adds, '*Viel tiefer aufs Blut ging, dass er zeitweise in sich einen Stümper in der Poesie sah.*'

attitude towards his own public, the Vienna of his own day. The love–hate relationship, the *conubium infelix* that now binds him to his city and now again repels him; all those endless, unhappy oscillations between hot fear of involvement and grim, almost morose pride which mark most of his personal relations; the assurance and the deep, the devastating doubts with which he alternately views his own achievement—all these live for us in many of the characters of his dramatic *œuvre*, not least through its at times unpoetic verse. But, like his last great hero, the Emperor Rudolf II, he ultimately knows himself for what he is and where, in spite of all, he belongs. And when, after the catastrophic reception of his plays by the public of the city, he comes to reflect upon the emotions that rend his heart, he finds that he no longer has any choice of language. Like his hero he abdicates from grandeur—he now stands before us without formal and thematic support of the classical tradition. And he conveys his emotions to us, with wonderful poignancy and with all the humility that is, after all, proper to them, in the humble prose of his story *The Poor Minstrel*.

3

What is so striking about the writings of all the major Viennese authors of the last 150 years is *how* Viennese they are: how largely the atmosphere of their city, its concerns and moods, figure in their work: how deeply committed, for better and for worse, they are to its life. Its life and character may, like many another vital experience, be indefinable; to be a Viennese writer is indeed a complex fate. But there is little doubt that the thing is real enough, is 'there', that the city means so much more than mere 'background', that the insidiousness, the siren charm with which it intrudes its character into the literary works of its authors has no equivalent anywhere. It is not merely that the city possesses its literature. There is, after all, Dr Johnson's, Dickens's or George Gissing's London; there is Balzac's or Flaubert's Paris; Jan Neruda's Prague, Tolstoy's Moscow; there is Theodor Fontane's and Alfred Döblin's Berlin; and Joyce's Dublin. But it could not be said of any of these cities (except perhaps the last) that everything emerging from them has their character indelibly stamped upon it; it could not be said of the poets of the rue de Rome that they are Parisian to the extent that Hofmannsthal is Viennese. Dublin *is* comparable,[1] both as to the kind and also the extent of the influence it exerts upon its writers and intellectuals (though not as to the European importance of that influence). But when, after his famous declaration of '*Non serviam*', Joyce put Ireland and Dublin behind him, using it to the end of his life as the stage of his heroes' adventures but himself standing resolutely outside his city and seeing it from outside, he did something that no Viennese writer of comparable stature was ever able to do: he freed himself from its concerns, he repudiated its demands.

Any explicit invitation to consider what is characteristically Viennese[2] is likely to be regarded with a good deal of scepticism. Plain logic will object that to single out certain aspects in the writings of literary men who are known to have lived in the city, call these aspects 'Viennese', and claim that they give us a true and comprehensive picture of the city itself is to argue in a tautological circle; the sociologist will deprecate our 'sources of information' as 'hopelessly biased'; while the aesthetic sophist will 'feel acutely uneasy' at the suggestion that the testimony of Art should lay any claims to factual truth. All these objections, however, lose their point when we realise that the situation to be described is exceptional, and what the nature of the exception is. It is precisely because the atmosphere of Vienna was, for more than a century, uniquely artistic and abounding with artistic potentialities, that (to put the matter briefly and obscurely) the object described is uniquely involved in its descriptions. It is for this reason that the characteristic moods and concerns of her artists tally with and are an intimate part of the city's own moods: that the testimony of her poets and writers, of her lovers and

---

[1] And the comparisons which offer themselves between the two cities, not least in their relations with their large and largely uncomprehending neighbours, would yield a fascinating study.

[2] I have derived much pleasure, and profit, from G. Baumann's *Franz Grillparzer: Sein Werk und das österreichische Wesen*, Wien 1954, especially Chapter I, though concerning the Viennese *ethos* I confess to somewhat gloomier conclusions.

detractors, is reliable and to the point. Not only was the Viennese
public's attitude towards its musicians and authors, towards its
drama and opera, remarkably familiar and well informed, so that
here for once it is legitimate to speak of a—more or less genuine
—popular culture. Not only did the city attract and hold artists
and intellectuals from the whole of Central Europe and beyond.
What matters as much is *how* she held them; how, settling there
(for many were not born in Vienna), they found themselves both
warmed and chilled by an air of the utmost intimacy with Art:
by the sort of familiarity that inspires through its quick understanding and blights by breeding contempt. Now, the remarkable
thing is that this essentially middle-class dilettantism—a sort of
ornamental indoor ivy—pullulated much higher up, and especially much lower[1] down the social strata of the city than we are
likely to believe possible from our own experience of the cultural
life of big cities. In an age such as ours, when the arts depend for
their support upon a public whose real interests lie in technology,
material welfare and social manipulation—in such an age as this
the opposite dangers are difficult to envisage: I mean the dangers,
to the life and limb of Art, emanating from a public which is *au
fait* with every major and minor stirring of the Muses and unpredictably *blasé*; which is genuinely critical one moment and
merely choosy the next; whose very manner of life blurs the
proper distinction between creativeness and mere susceptibility,
and substitutes the play of art for the earnest of life. In one situation the artist is deprived of sustenance by being 'outside', in the
other he finds every Tom, Dick and Franzl 'in on' his most
private creative deliberations; as between exposure and suffoca-
tion, the choice is wide but hardly very auspicious. To the
Viennese writer the quasi-artistic, the histrionic and deeply un-
serious character of his fellow citizens is of course not without
its attractions: it is a thing equally hard to live with and to leave:
'Shall he go? Or shall he stay? / All resolve is taken away....'

[1] Grove writes (*Dictionary* ... ed. 1940, Vol. I, p. 264) that in 1794, when
Beethoven arrived in Vienna, 'Musical public ... there was none; musicians
were almost entirely dependent on the wealthy.' If this was true, things must
have changed greatly between that date and 1819, when Zelter visited the city.

The city's complex life testifies to the intimate connection in the human mind between light-heartedness and half-heartedness, between freedom from care and irresponsibility, between the historical and histrionics.

When Hofmannsthal, consciously taking issue with a remark of Grillparzer's, wrote

> *Dass wir sie überschätzen, dazu*   So that we exaggerate its value—
> *ward die Vergangenheit unserm*   that is the end for which the past was
> *Gedächtnis einverleibt*[1]   made a part of our memory

he coined an aphorism whose full meaning lies in this, that the state of mind he is summing up includes the consciousness of the exaggeration, and is histrionic by virtue of that consciousness. The traditionalism of the Viennese has often been remarked on. *Laudatores temporis acti*: Viennese writers and intellectuals—indeed even the ordinary people of Vienna—are notorious for their habit, developed far in excess of common humanity's need, of living in the memory of a golden age more or less recently past. To Grillparzer in his old age the world in which Beethoven had lived has a simplicity and purity of purpose for which he looks in vain among his contemporaries. Bauernfeld, his friend and biographer, harks back in the same vein to Grillparzer's own *Altwien* of the 'forties, and so, a little later, do Ferdinand Kürnberger and Ludwig Speidel, who might almost be said to have created a genre—the *feuilleton*—for the purpose of giving expression to their nostalgia; even the mordant tone of Karl Kraus mellows into lyricism when he speaks of the 'serene 'eighties'; so does Josef Weinheber's when he recalls Old Ottakring, his native district in the 1900's; and where Robert Musil, with his mixture of irony and nostalgia, sees a whole world coming to its tragicomical end, there his disciple Heimito von Doderer begins his saga of an

---

[1] Hofmannsthal, *op. cit.*, p. 49. Baumann (*op. cit.*, p. 119) quotes Grillparzer's repudiation of 'nationality, language idolatry and excessive estimate of history' in the wake of Hegel, but shows that in spite of his subtle awareness of the 'dangers of historicism' Grillparzer 'was not able to remain free of it'. Towards the end of the century the official Austrian ideology was in a similar quandary, hoping that it might replace separatist nationalisms by a monarchic, '*kaisertreu*' nationalism.

equally irretrievable but more recent golden age. A list of this kind could become endless, and the impression grows in the bemused reader that collective nostalgia is an invention of the Viennese. . . . Of one thing at any rate he may be certain: the consciousness of their own past is to the Viennese more acute, more real *in* its exaggeration, than the inhabitants of Paris or London, not to mention Berlin or New York, are likely to imagine. An integral part of a memory which is being re-enacted in the present, Vienna's collective past is an essential element in the potentially artistic and histrionic character of the city. Historians have often confessed themselves puzzled by the fact that the major cohesive force in nineteenth-century Austrian history was 'merely' the name and symbol of an obviously decadent dynasty. But the paradox is resolved once we understand the outlook of a population which takes the stage at least as seriously as it does politics, and for whom consequently an historical idea and a traditional symbol have all the force that elsewhere goes with a political idea and social precepts. In this as in many other respects the contrast between the Viennese and the North German ethos is as striking as the difference between metaphor-mindedness and literal-mindedness.

When the composer K. F. Zelter visited Vienna in 1819, he sent his friend Goethe a number of shrewd comments about its inhabitants.[1] They aren't much interested in politics, he writes, because 'politics comes from boredom and goes to boredom'. On the other hand, 'they know a thing or two about music . . . they really are deeply cultivated. True, they will put up with anything,'—as when they pretend to prefer Schuppanzigh[2] to Beethoven—'but all the same, only the best works remain alive

---

[1] *Briefwechsel zwischen Goethe und Zelter in den Jahren 1796 bis 1832*, ed. F. W. Riemer, Vol. III, Berlin 1834, letters of 20.vii. and 15.ix.1819, pp. 17, 22, 33, 38, 55.

[2] Who did, however, achieve his immortality, if not through his own compositions yet through Beethoven's choral variation 'Schuppanzigh ist ein Lump . . .', and Schubert's dedication of his Quartet in A.

here.' Yet what impresses Zelter above all—he is at the playhouse every night—is that 'the actors and the public *together* make the play'. (An admirer of Garrick's and Macklin's realism had made the opposite comment, praising the London stage for being 'a faithful imitation of all life, from the soup-kitchens of St Giles's to the salons of St James's'.[1]) The line between stage and world is blurred, all Vienna is like the Prater—an inextricable mixture of life, Art and artifice. But then, it will be said, a casual visitor like Zelter is apt to oversimplify the scene; North Germans are notoriously romantic about Vienna, and the Prater especially, as the English used to be about Dublin and the Horse Show. Another testimony is at hand, the more reliable since it is written without any intention of using the particular for a general insight. No artist, we know, had experienced the moodiness of the Viennese public more fully, nor reacted to it with more fiery scorn, than Beethoven. It was the beauty of the man (and the glory of the musician) that no adversity could ever make him uncertain of his genius; the clashes between his inward strength and the dilettante society around him left him enraged rather than embittered. Receiving at one time the highest honours and preferments (not to mention titles, which he took as a joke), he died, *not* indeed ignored and neglected, but recognised and appreciated *and* in degrading want; the little that could be done to lighten the burden of his last days on earth was done, not by the city in which he had lived for thirty-five years, but—by the London Philharmonic Society. Now lack of practical recognition, it may be said, is the common fate of genius anywhere. But since this is a Viennese story, it does not end here. Less than a week after Beethoven's death his companion and (*sit venia verbo*) friend Anton Schindler (who had found himself inconvenienced because Beethoven took such a long time dying) writes to London:

> The funeral was . . . that of a great man. Close on 30,000 people surged over the Glacis and filled the streets through which the procession was to go. In brief, the thing can't be described. Think of the Prater-feast at the Congress of 1814 [sic] and you will have an idea of what it was like. Eight conductors were the pallbearers . . . thirty-six torchbearers. . . . Seven bank shares and a few hundred guilders is all

---

[1] G. C. Lichtenberg, *Vermischte Schriften*, Göttingen 1844 ff., iii, p. 212.

the capital that was found. And now the Viennese papers clamour loudly and write publicly that Beethoven did not need any help from a foreign nation, etc. Everybody cries, 'How shameful for Austria!'[1]

The Prater as the one image which most readily comes to mind, even in connection with death, the histrionic even beyond the grave—word for word Schindler's lines could stand as the text for one of Karl Kraus's *'Glossen'*, those acid prose-poems in which, a hundred years later, the satirist called down the wrath of God and all just men upon his city. Accustomed to a different rate of turnover in events, attitudes and affectations, we find it difficult to believe that a century which opened with the Congress and ended with the defeat of 1918 should mean so little change.

From Zelter to C. F. Burckhardt (1941) and the late Reinhold Schneider (1957), visitors to Vienna have been fascinated (and the native moralists exasperated) by that constant to and fro—literal and metaphorical—between stage and stalls, by the exchange, lively *and* distracting, between stage and gallery, by the spectacle of life itself lived in the complex ambiguity of a spectacle. But then, this too is a part of the tradition-mindedness of the Viennese, for this mixed mode of life is connected, in no esoteric manner, with yet another tradition they are proud of, yet another golden age they love to summon up: the age (when many of their theatres were founded) of the Baroque theatre, with its central image of the world as a stage. The powerful image itself had outlived the religious sanction which once had given full meaning to it.

Like 'artistic sensibility'—like most terms that form our cultural vocabulary—'historical consciousness' is a morally neutral term. In one situation it brings with it a sense of obligation and moral standards, in another it serves as an excuse—for fatalism, irresponsibility, for defecting from the obligations not only of 'History' but of common decency even. And Vienna is a city of contrasts in this too, that she has bred both attitudes, in the highest Imperial places no less than in humbler stations of life. If it is true to say

---

[1] *Ludwig van Beethoven: Berichte der Zeitgenossen . . .*, ed. A. Leitzmann, Vol. I, Leipzig 1921, p. 370. Schindler's correspondent was the violinist Ignaz Moscheles, who became conductor of the London Philharmonic Society.

that every work of art springs from an over-estimate of a given
situation (and then proceeds to validate that 'over-estimate'), then
the exaggeration of the value and importance of the past, itself
determinable for good or evil, is potentially a work of art. But
only potentially, for not every exaggeration is a work of art.
Yet it is this artistic potentiality—the latent art—and the histrionic
at the root of every exaggeration which gave both sustainment
and offence to the Viennese artist. The city sustained him, because
he felt at home in an environment that was intelligently sympathetic to his thinking and doing; it offended and injured him,
because nothing is as corruptible and bad-tempered as the artistic
imagination living in mere potentialities. Improbably, the contrasts we have enumerated were lived—up to a point: the point,
that is, at which decisions could be avoided and life go on,
heedless of them, in its own bitter-sweet way. In a poem hopefully
entitled 'Farewell to Vienna' (1843) Grillparzer calls this mood
'semi-poetry', a state in which (his phrase, cloyed with a sequence
of qualifying particles, is untranslatably Viennese) 'one hardly
thinks at all / and feels the half-thought';[1] and we would add,

> [1] *Weithin Musik, wie wenn im Baum*
> *Der Vögel Chor erwachte,*
> *Man spricht nicht, denkt wohl etwa kaum*
> *Und fühlt das Halbgedachte.*
>
> *Man lebt in halber Poesie,*
> *Gefährlich für die ganze*
> *Und ist ein Dichter, ob man nie*
> *An Vers gedacht und Stanze.*

The force, or rather lack of force, of this Viennese *etwa* is difficult to convey
with words like 'perhaps', 'roughly speaking', beyond which it also connotes
the speaker's deferential or conditional attitude. Since what all this comes to is
indefiniteness and half-commitment, the word finds its appropriate place not
in Rilke (who would never use an indefinite or 'soft' word to convey his feeling
for the indefiniteness of situations) but in Hofmannsthal's plaintive lyricisms;
thus in the following passage from *Der Tor und der Tod*,

> *Es war doch schön . . . Denkst du nie mehr daran?*
> *Freilich, du hast mir weh getan, so weh . . .*
> *Allein, was hört denn nicht in Schmerzen auf?*
> *Ich hab' so wenig frohe Tag' gesehen,*
> *Und die, die waren schön als wie ein Traum!*

acts upon it, often with disastrous consequences. For it would be misleading to speak of Vienna only as an amalgam of charm and lassitude. Superficiality, after all, almost always signifies more than itself, and indecision too, even when raised to an institution, amounts to a decision. The potentialities for grossness, depravity and corruption which lurked behind the *trompe-l'œil* (to be depicted by Schnitzler half a century later) are sharply outlined to Grillparzer's prophetic eye, just as the capacities for silent devotion, for self-sacrifice and mute withdrawal move his wounded heart.

By the fickleness of his public's favours and the discrepancy between his inward exalted vision and their half-hearted (or light-hearted) unconcern, Grillparzer suffered ever new injury. So do many writers in many places. But he was typically Viennese in both clearly understanding his situation and theirs, and also in never emerging from it, from the malaise and the real suffering it entailed for him; he was Viennese in sharing it to the bitter end. 'He is said to be unbearably *maussade*',[1] Zelter reported of Beethoven; it could be said with much greater justice of Grillparzer, and indeed of a great many Viennese writers. A coincidence of individual temperament, perhaps. But there is also something specifically Viennese about it, whether the *maussaderie* is infinitely brittle and reserved,[2] as with Grillparzer; or in-

> *Die Blumen vor dem Fenster, meine Blumen,*
> *Das kleine wacklige Spinett, der Schrank,*
> *In den ich deine Briefe legte und*
> *Was du mir etwa schenktest . . . alles das*
> *—Lach mich nicht aus—das wurde alles schön*

(author's dots . . .), this *etwa*, if it does not actually remind us of a housemaid addressing the young gentleman (who is on the point of death), quite dissipates what little passion may have been contrived in the previous stanzas. Grillparzer's use of the word is ironical.

[1] *Op. cit.*, p. 47; Zelter describes Grillparzer as 'silent and ailing' (p. 56); words such as these are used by many of his friends.

[2] A. Klaar, in the introd. to his ed. (*Sämtliche Werke*, Wien 1909) speaks of Grillparzer's '*Sprödigkeit*'.

flammable and choleric, as with Nestroy; or bitter and harsh, as
with the proletarian Anzengruber; or gently ironical, as with the
prose-vignettist Peter Altenberg; or sweetly melancholy, as with
the aristocratic Hofmannsthal; or corrosive and polemical, as
with Karl Kraus; or plain alcoholic, as with Josef Weinheber.
The contradiction between these black humours and the gaiety
and charm so readily (and justly) ascribed to Vienna retraces once
again the real predicament. Where the outward force, now hostile,
now enticing, so saps the artist's inner strength, and where,
through the medium of his art and the direction of his artistic
conscience alike, he so remains committed to an encompassing
world which he must yet condemn, there *maussaderie* of one kind
or another becomes the habitual response of his *moral* nature. The
situation is essentially undramatic. Its representative hero is not
Timon but Tiresias, whose Viennese name (in Karl Kraus's
gigantic drama *Die letzten Tage der Menschheit*) is 'der Nörgler,'
'the Carping Critic.'

All that, of course, at a high level of sophistication. And
below it, in less exalted regions? While in the North there
grew up a metaphysic—indeed a religion—of work, Vienna
never knew the dour Protestant philistinism of the German
Sunday parlours. In the place of those unbending figures
which chill the air of many a play and novel from Hebbel
to Hauptmann we find characters of a wholly different
kind. Beyond the satirist's indignation, out of reach of that
notorious music-hall gaiety which stands for 'Old Vienna',
unexportable, they are yet no less 'typically Viennese', and
some of the city's greatest writers have paid their homage to
them. How to describe them?

Neither sentimental nor sentimentally portrayed, they are
symbols of a humanity that is silent in its deprivation: sustained
by a deep and unrequited love and a moral dignity: lonely yet
part of '*das Wiener Volk*', though without a trace of folkishness:
a subject not indeed for drama but for lyrical prose and poetry.
Altenberg, Hofmannsthal, Weinheber and a host of lesser writers
have portrayed them, they even find their way into Karl Kraus's
essays. A devoted servant, a lowly seamstress, a penurious pen-
sioner taking the air in the *Stadtpark*—all capable of a passion, a

pesanteur of feeling, endowed with an endless capacity for suffering, which show up strangely the spurious light-heartedness of their fellow-citizens. This kind of character too belongs to Grillparzer's experience of Vienna, it has a humble but not unimportant place in his work: and we know where in his heart to look for its origin.

Yet he does not disclose the origin and identity of these humble personages, for there is, after all, another part of him which knows that personal avowals, like the exaltations of feeling and faith, are oddly out of place in the context of his city; that to 'go on about things' is vaguely ill-bred or at least '*echauffierend*'; that passion is a bit of a bore. And irony—mode of the uncertain faith and the unexpressed truth—becomes the writer's habitation and far from impregnable stronghold. There are many dilemmas on which irony thrives: between character and destination, insight and action, between the good will and its profane realisation.

Again, the dilemma is familiar enough from other places. What is characteristically Viennese is the strange sympathy that springs up between intention and realisation, the overtures made by one to the other, and the radical negations of the real with which Viennese poets and prose-writers react to the lure around them. Satire and invective are built into the situation. And beyond them? Only once, in *Der arme Spielmann*, did Grillparzer allow himself to express the full negation and make it into art; only there is the ideal portrayed as unrealisable, the humble as all but silent. But the irony of that work, and its greatness, lie in the fact that the tale which achieves the negation becomes, by virtue of the narrative achievement, an affirmation: of faith, but also, implicitly, of art.

4

The almost contemporary setting as well as the prose form of *The Poor Minstrel* are something of an exception in Grillparzer's published work (and for this odd reason, and because of his disparagement of prose and 'stories' generally, the story has been less highly regarded than his dramatic work). Yet it is here that the innermost character of the man, and the true meaning of his

experience of life, are disclosed more fully and directly[1] than
in any of his dramas. Nor is this surprising, seeing that the self
that is explored here is not the vatic, Sapphic self, but the living
man as others see him. Unable to shake off the obligations that
imperil his art, unable also to oppose them by a positive didactic
ideal of his own creation, the living man here measures his
achievement with the standards of the world around him, and
finds it wanting. Speaking the language of the people amounts to
judging by their standards. And the scepticism that looms up for
him at this point is incomparably more radical than any the
classical writers ever knew, for it assails the work of art itself. Is
not, Grillparzer asks, even the work of art too deeply involved
in the world's substance—flesh of other men's flesh—to escape
the world's contamination? Words—tones—the pigments of
painters—marble itself: are they really exempt from the corruption of Vanity Fair? But then, where can a man find the materials
with which to give substance to the deep longing for perfection
that is within him, of what stuff can he fashion his pure vision?
Deprived of substance and working in a void, the artistic sensibility finds itself sustained by nothing but pure intention—the
intention to avoid the base, do the good and create the beautiful.
In brief, Art is reduced to the good will. Which to us who live
in the substantial world—and to the artist as a man among men—
also looks remarkably like a chimera, a mere nothing. How are
we to distinguish between the silence of incapacity and the
silence of abdication if not by the world of difference that lies
between them, which is our articulated world? This situation, in
which the good will is now everything, now again nothing at all,
is fraught with an unresolved tension of false expectations. The
narrative equivalent of that tension, once it is raised to the level
of consciousness, is irony; and to the extent that the tension is
presented in concrete events and living story only, uncommented
and bare, the irony becomes laconic.

---

[1] Which is why Grillparzer was deeply embarrassed by the story in later
years (*S.W.* I, Vol. XIII, p. 314); the caustic *Selbstbiographie* (*ibid.*, pp. 63 ff.),
written in 1853 at the invitation of the Austrian Academy, is much less
revealing.

5

Grillparzer's story *Der arme Spielmann*[1] was begun in 1831, completed some ten years later, and first published in 1847; between these two dates lies the disastrous première, on the stage of the *Burgtheater*, of his comedy *Weh' dem der lügt* (1838), and his decision (the public's catcalls still ringing in his ears) never to publish a play again. The episodic elements of the story Grillparzer took partly from newspaper reports of the flood of 1830, partly from an anecdote told by an acquaintance, while the setting is the Vienna of his day. It is the Vienna of the humble and poor artisans, victuallers and penpushers, now grasping, now charitable, now scornful and merciless towards failure, now again lost to the world in a song. The narrow streets, dark squares and dingy garrets of what were then the city's suburban quarters might be placed anywhere in Europe; but not so the fair, the *Volksfest* with which the story opens, or the story's inconspicuous hero and his modest yet very particular destiny. Following the convention established by the Romantics, Grillparzer gives his *Novelle* the framework of a first-person narrator, which reflects something of the actual relation in which the creative mind's eye first perceived its chance—the few casual encounters with a mendicant musician in the late 'twenties. It is here, in the narrator's point of view, that the laconic mode of the tale is established and sustained —with a sparseness, an economy of means rarely achieved elsewhere in German narrative prose.

To what extent the narrator belongs to the worldly world we are never told in so many words; but we know that, *vis-à-vis* the story's hero at any rate, he represents that world. On St Bridget's Day in July he goes out to Brigittenau beyond the Prater, to watch the rough-and-tumble of the fair. He doesn't take part in the merrymaking he has come to observe; his 'interest' (we are

[1] The text, with abundant biographical, historical and bibliographical details as well as explanatory notes, will be found in *S.W.* (ed. by R. Backmann), I, Vol. XIII (Wien 1930), pp. 35–81 and 307–51. Grillparzer himself disclaimed the designation '*Novelle*' for this story, calling it '*eine einfache Erzählung*' (*ibid.*, p. 288); I can see no other reason why he should have done so except his associating the word with Romantic literature, which he disliked.

told once or twice) is 'merely *psychologisch*'; the connotation of
the word is ironical rather than scientific. He is aloof, at times
caustic, he wishes merely to register. He emerges from his own
narrative as neither very friendly nor very *sympathique*; and his
few judgements on the hero (whom he meets for the first time
when the story opens) are sober, severe and just—just in the eyes
of a world that tolerates no nonsense, informed by the sort of
justice that is without warmth or affection. Beyond this we know
nothing about him. The *Novelle* thus shows an uncommon lack
of distraction from its line of narrative, an admirable fastidiousness
and precision in its presentation of the emerging theme; the
narrator's taciturnity about himself is one of its minor triumphs.
We know, as a matter of biographical fact, that his personality,
described by what is not said, is a fairly close (though, as far as
that goes, incomplete) portrayal of Grillparzer himself. In his
posthumously published diaries, for instance in the Prague and
London journals, there are revealed those moods of loneliness and
deliberate withdrawal, of determined disparagement of human
virtues and foibles, the *maussaderie* verging on plain bad temper,
which I have singled out as one half of the 'typically Viennese'
experience, and which makes plausible an identification of
author and narrator. Yet such an identification, were we to pursue
it further, would distort the story's truth by revealing less than
half of it, because the narrator's part is meaningful only as one
among several literary devices for revealing the whole truth: and
this truth is neither quite alien to nor quite at home in the world
to which he appears to belong. So that at this stage it is enough
to say that the narrator stands before us, with his curiously un-
friendly, or at least unbending, personality, the firmly sketched
presentation of an incomplete nature, and requires no reference
to Grillparzer himself, his antecedents and history. The description of the hero (at their first meeting) is detailed and yet succinct,
and serves to introduce both:

*Endlich—und er zog meine ganze
Aufmerksamkeit auf sich—ein alter,
leicht siebzigjähriger Mann in einem
fadenscheinigen aber nicht unrein-
lichen Moltonüberrock mit lächelnder,*

Last of all—he attracted my entire
attention—an old man, quite seventy
years old, in a broadcloth coat which
was threadbare but carefully brushed,
with a smiling, somewhat complacent

sich selbst Beifall gebender Miene. Barhäuptig und kahlköpfig stand er da, nach Art dieser Leute, den Hut als Sammelbüchse vor sich auf dem Boden, und so bearbeitete er eine alte vielzersprungene Violine, wobei er den Takt nicht nur durch Aufheben und Niedersetzen des Fusses, sondern zugleich durch übereinstimmende Bewegung des ganzen gebückten Körpers markierte. Aber all diese Bemühung Einheit in seine Leistung zu bringen, war fruchtlos, denn was er spielte, schien eine unzusammenhängende Folge von Tönen ohne Zeitmass und Melodie. Dabei war er ganz in sein Werk vertieft: die Lippen zuckten, die Augen waren starr auf das vor ihm befindliche Notenblatt gerichtet—ja wahrhaftig Notenblatt! Denn indes alle andern, ungleich mehr zu Dank spielenden Musiker sich auf ihr Gedächtnis verliessen, hatte der alte Mann mitten in dem Gewühle ein kleines, leicht tragbares Pult vor sich hingestellt mit schmutzigen, zergriffenen Noten, die das in schönster Ordnung enthalten mochten, was er so ausser allem Zusammenhange zu hören gab.

expression. He stood there as these people do, with his bald head bare, and his hat on the ground in front of him serving as a collecting-box. He was belabouring an ancient and much cracked violin, marking the beat not only by the tapping of his foot but also by a corresponding movement of his entire bent body. But all this effort to infuse unity into his performance was futile, for what he played seemed a series of disconnected notes with neither rhythm nor melody. Yet he was deeply absorbed in what he was doing; his lips moved, his eyes were fixed on the music that lay in front of him—yes, he actually had music! For where all other musicians would play from memory (and incomparably better at that), the old man had set up, in the midst of all the turmoil, a light portable stand with dirty, dog-eared sheet-music on it, which doubtless contained in the most perfect order what he was offering to the listener in such a chaotic form.

The man, ignored by the pleasure-seeking crowd, goes on playing. The narrator records its laughter and good humour but remains detached, observing the somewhat unusual mendicant from a distance:

Endlich hielt er ein, blickte, wie aus einer langen Abwesenheit zu sich gekommen, nach dem Firmament, das schon die Spuren des nahenden Abends zu zeigen anfing; darauf abwärts

At last he stopped. Like one whose thoughts have been far away and now return to him he looked at the sky, which showed signs of the approaching night; then down

—the laconic brevity of the zeugma aptly suggests the situation in which a just world rewards justly; but the suggestion is ironical and subtle, not ridiculous and gross—

darauf abwärts in seinen Hut, fand ihn leer, setzte ihn mit ungetrübter Heiterkeit auf, steckte den Geigenbogen zwischen die Saiten; 'Sunt certi denique fines', sagte er,	*then down into his hat, found that it was empty, put it on with undisturbed serenity, pushed his bow under the strings; and 'sunt certi denique fines', said he,*

—and here again the brief halt followed immediately by the quotation, instead of a full-stop and a new opening, deliberately draw back from a sentimental aside and hurry the reader through the description: on, to the Latin tag with its light suggestion (just enough to increase the observer's interest) of the strangeness of the encounter, to the encounter, to the sustained crescendo of the passage, simple in its realism and rich in its symbolical meaning—

; 'Sunt certi denique fines', sagte er, ergriff sein Notenpult und arbeitete sich mühsam durch die dem Feste zuströmende Menge in entgegengesetzter Richtung,	*; and, 'sunt certi denique fines', said he, took up his stand and with some difficulty began working his way through the mass of people thronging to the fair, in the opposite direction,*

—and thence to the final intimation, even at this unpropitious hour, of a final reward of quietus; here, finally, in the brief span of four words, all is laconic evocativeness and sustained pathos:

in entgegengesetzter Richtung, als Einer, der heimkehrt.	*, in the opposite direction, as one returning home.*

The account of the hero's life, much of it told in his own words, takes up the rest of the *Novelle*.[1] It is a life of failure at every step. Jacob—the hero—has failed to fulfil the promise which his father, a somewhat intimidating high official, had seen in him; he fails at school, in the inferior post which his father's influence had secured for him. Cheated of a considerable legacy, through honesty and stupidity he fails to save even a mean pittance from the bankruptcy which overtakes the man to whom he had entrusted his money. He falls in love with Barbara, a simple, warm-hearted

[1] A good deal of this story is taken over by Stifter into *Kalkstein*, including the hero–narrator relationship, but since Stifter is incapable of an ironic point of view, his story moves from pity to admiration.

girl of humble origin, yet his shyness and lack of confidence are so disabling that he falters in his effort to win her for himself. It is an absurd relationship, for although Barbara understands his simple-minded purity and devotion, she is repelled by his weakness. Here as everywhere else his contact with the real world is tainted with absurdity—when at last Jacob takes courage and tries to kiss her, it is through the glass pane of a closed door. Believing himself unworthy of her love, he accepts her impatience and reproaches as just, and sees her married to another man. And even his death is the death of a fool. Having helped to save her family and possessions in a flood, he wades back to the house to salvage the husband's account-book and a few unimportant valuables, and dies from exposure. He is humble—maddeningly yet also disarmingly humble. He is lacking in common sense and circumspection, in any kind of prudence that makes for life in society. And the narrator's judgements on him, his impatience and exasperation, merge with the rough-and-ready dicta of a world in which a man must either make his mark or go under.

The story is told in a wholly unromantic manner, partly in the slightly stilted and slightly pedantic phraseology ('threadbare but carefully brushed') of the old man himself. As for the narrator, he merely reports but never identifies himself with the unheroic hero's point of view. He never says (as Brentano or Tieck would have said), 'Poor Jacob, he was too good for this world. . . .' Instead, much more truthfully, much more beautifully, Grillparzer gives his hero a deep and sustaining pride which remains unacknowledged by the narrator. For the one positive value which informs Jacob's life, and the source of his unconscious and all but mute pride, is his integrity—his whole life and vocation are infused with a perfect morality. And his vocation is music.

Again, there is no romantic sacrifice involved. To sacrifice means to choose, yet Jacob has no real choice at any point. What draws him to his art is a vocation and a fate first and last, and his good will lies not in the exercise of any freedom but in acceptance. His life is stripped of all success, friendship and possessions, of the meanest comforts even, until in the end it is utterly bare, a mere instrument of his art, like that cracked violin he so treasured, which, in the story's last scene, the narrator sees hanging on a wall, 'balanced, with a kind of symmetry, by a Crucifix'. Yet there is order and propriety in his life.

Jacob's devotion to his art (if we are to call it 'art' . . .) emerges as the sole positive value intimated in the *Novelle*. But once again it is not a romantic, amoral passion that rules his life. On the contrary, his art is the source and repository of his moral integrity, of his untainted '*Redlichkeit*'.[1] The moral meaning of his art is manifest in the story through the 'impossibly' high, the exalted opinion he has of his calling. At the very opening of the story, for instance, we watch him returning home, 'in the opposite direction', at the hour when the crowd of revellers thickens and he might hope to collect a few alms at last, because he thinks it immoral to play to them; later on he recalls, not without some mild indignation, how he had refused to demean his art by playing 'popular valses, vulgar street-songs, let alone tunes to improper ditties'. In his own eyes he is not a beggar at all, but an itinerant professional musician;[2] his place in the world is fixed and clearly defined, at least to himself; his life is ordered with the utmost propriety:

'. . . *Die ersten drei Stunden des Tages der Übung, die Mitte dem Broderwerb, und der Abend mir und*

'. . . *The first three hours of my day are devoted to practising, the middle part to earning my bread, the evening*

---

[1] I have borrowed the term not from Grillparzer, who cannot use it since there is in his story no character for whom it would be proper to make the judgement expressed in the word, but from Nietzsche, who singles out '*Redlichkeit*' as the sole existent value worth salvaging from the contemporary social scene into his projected new world of revaluations (see his notes in Vol. 82 of the *Kröner* ed., p. 251). However, Nietzsche would also have recognized, and probably detested, Jacob's Christian meekness, and would have 'unmasked' him as an example of the 'slave morality' of the '*Schlechtweggekommene*' who are fobbed off by a promise of Heaven for their absurd failure on earth.

[2] On another occasion, when some children mock the old man, ' "Let me at least make good their ingratitude", I [the narrator] said, bringing out a silver coin from my pocket and offering it to him. "Oh, please! Please!" the old man called out, motioning me away anxiously with both hands "in the hat! the hat!" I put the coin in the hat in front of him, immediately the old man took it out and quite contentedly put in his pocket, saying with a chuckle, "I call this returning home with rich profit!" '

dem lieben Gott, das heisst nicht unehrlich geteilt,' sagte er, und dabei glänzten seine Augen, wie feucht; er lächelte aber.	*belongs to me and to our Dear Lord,' he said, 'I call this dividing one's time equitably,' and his eyes shone, as with tears; but he smiled.*

The life he leads—the very opposite of romantic dissoluteness, of the 'Satanic' or 'Sturm-und-Drang' genius—is the inconspicuous good life. Is his art not the vessel of those ideals of purity, nobility and goodness for which he is ready, if need be, to give his life? It is 'dæmonic' since it leaves him no choice, but the direction in which his dæmon drives him is towards morality. Are we then to understand that here at last, in this plain and unadorned piece of narrative prose, lies the answer to the old riddle, the consummation of Art in a unity of the true, the good and the beautiful?

The tale does indeed give an answer to the old riddle. But, for all the laconic temper and quiet tone of the narrative, the answer is little short of annihilating, for it is determined by the *quality* of Jacob's art.[1] Judged by any objective standard (the only standard the world knows) his 'art' is plain rubbish. Whether, after a morning's strenuous exercise, he 'pays his homage to the Great Masters' by playing from music carefully written out in his own hand, or whether he devotes himself to what he calls 'my proper Art, my fantasies', it is all one. He can scarcely hold a

---

[1] Our story has received the attention of many creative writers (including Stifter, Paul Heyse, Keller and Hofmannsthal) and critics (including Nadler, Gundolf, C. J. Burckhardt, and more recently W. Naumann and G. Baumann). Roughly speaking, their views follow and elaborate Keller's, who sees in it 'The absolutely pure soul's power over the world, that is the profound meaning which underlies this apparently slight work.' (Quoted from *S.W.*, I, Vol. XIII, p. 333.) This view, I think, is as far from being true as is Jacob's music from being beautiful, and it is only by disregarding what Grillparzer says about the music that the view becomes in the least plausible. Even Baumann (*op. cit.*, p. 174), quoting the passage where Jacob's 'improvising' is described, stops short of the narrator's revealing judgement. B. von Wiese (*Die deutsche Novelle von Goethe bis Kafka*, Düsseldorf 1956, pp. 134–53; see also his bibl. p. 346) comments illuminatingly, above all on Jacob's relation with his surrounding world, but then feels obliged to make of Jacob's otherworldliness something grotesque, 'skurril' and pathological.

note; he has no idea of rhythm; his fingers are clumsy and stiff from an absurd effort, utterly lacking in skill; and all that his 'improvising' amounts to (the narrator listens to it one night, standing outside Jacob's wretched garret, until the 'music' is cut short by the call—'indignant but not harsh or insulting'—of a neighbour) is a series of languid simple chords, a third, a fourth, then a fifth imperfectly sustained in a plaintive kind of sensuousness, then the same thing repeated, now quickly now slowly, over and over again.

Clearly, the emerging theme is less obvious and more profound than the themes we are likely to find in the average '*Künstlernovelle*' (which Grillparzer himself so despised). It is more profound, for instance, than Richard Wagner's ill-tempered piece of self-indulgence entitled *Ein Ende in Paris*, where the artist fails even more badly, in worldly terms, than does Jacob, but finally achieves spiritual triumph in his material misery by defying a wicked world composed mainly of evil (possibly Jewish) impresarios and rich English lords. Grillparzer's theme is more considerable than any of Gerhart Hauptmann's efforts in this vein, since the notion of a social 'creativeness' which is central to them has a very restricted, esoteric appeal. And it seems to me that the insight into the human condition which Grillparzer's *Novelle* vouchsafes is, after all, more important than that which we derive from Thomas Mann's early '*Künstlernovellen*' or from the last section of the *Buddenbrooks*,[1] though coming from Mann's work we are sure to be struck by the bareness and simplicity, the comparative naïvety even, of Grillparzer's narrative means. But then, his theme too is simpler and in a sense more fundamental. For while the driving force behind the art to which the 'heroes' of Mann's early stories are devoted is either pathological or aesthetico-satanic, the impulse behind Jacob's art is simply moral; hence the implications of Grillparzer's *Novelle* are not indeed less melancholy but more directly related to our own experience of

---

[1] As for the similarity between Jacob's and Hanno Buddenbrook's improvisations: the latter are more melodious if only because they are done not on a cracked violin but on a senatorial grand. But they are both objectively—that is, musically—of little value.

the world.[1] Grillparzer of course possessed none of Thomas Mann's up-to-date psychological skill and interest, being concerned with effects rather than causes. Thus few more 'modern' writers, or readers, would resist the temptation to make a great deal of the compensatory function of Jacob's 'art' (that is, of the consolation he derives from it for his manifold failures). Grillparzer is aware of it—he expresses it in his narrator's comments on Jacob's nocturnal improvisations—but leaves it unexplored, drawing our attention more firmly to the absurd discrepancy between intention and achievement than to the personal causes[2] that have led to the discrepancy. And this too I would count as one of the story's virtues, seeing how complete a picture of an incomplete personality he succeeds in giving, and how universal is the validity of the insight he secures for us. The absurdity of Jacob's unrequited musical passion (as of his love-affair) borders on the ridiculous; not until we realise that the *Novelle* never crosses that border, nor ever flounders in pathos, do we appreciate how important, and successful, has been the narrator's consistently laconic manner. The story is, after all, told in 'our' manner, the manner of almost any bemused, detached, worldly and slightly impatient observer, whose '*psychologisch*' interest is a disguise of his brittle and reserved humanity. And it is by virtue of the contrast between that manner and the fate it recounts that the story's theme, itself never more than darkly implied, is established and insinuates itself into our experience. But, for all that I have said about morality, psychological reticence and narrative detachment, what can there be that is 'central to our experience' in the absurd situation of a deluded fiddler?

Grillparzer's *Novelle* takes us back to the Quixotic origin of modern fiction. Its emerging theme is a complete rift in the living

---

[1] The point is made in T. S. Eliot's Introduction to the *Pensées:* '[Pascal's] despair is in itself more terrible than Swift's, because our heart tells us that it corresponds exactly to the facts and cannot be dismissed as a mental disease. . . .' (*Selected Prose* [Penguin] 1953, p. 159.)

[2] '. . . in the novel events often [appear] in mediated form, in the *Novelle* positively, so that in the former it is causes, in the latter effects which predominate.' (Written in 1839, *S.W.*, II, Vol. X, p. 286.)

unity of being and doing. And this, despite the contrary assertion of all kinds of pragmatisms, is an experience towards which any man's life is exposed; it is central in the sense in which the threat of absurd failure is attendant upon our thoughts, plans, hopes and fears, and upon all intentions. This disjunction is one experience at any rate which a man cannot share with the world, since the value buried beneath the débris of his failures is inaccessible to other men, to men as they share the world's manner of measuring and interpreting failure and success. What is he to them? Not an exemplar but a witness—*je suis mon propre témoin*—yet not consciously a witness either, since consciousness means separation, while his being, betrayed by every form of his doing, is one.

What emerges as the sole positive value is not, after all, the visible vessel of Jacob's morality—not the art which he has so faithfully 'practised' for a lifetime; nor his life, a clumsy failure from beginning to end; nor is it his way of keeping friendships alive, since he is as far from understanding other people's motives and actions as he is from understanding himself and his absurd obsession; nor is it his useless death. What emerges at the end, ironically hidden behind all these events (as irony always hides the insubstantial behind the substantial) is the intention and the pure heart alone, the disembodied good will as the absolute and only value.

Indeed, if a writer had intended to exemplify the circumstances in which the Kantian Good Will 'lives' in the world, he might well have written something like this story. When we try to account for one of its strangest effects—that of livingly presenting a life that is not quite a life—we are reminded of that thing-in-itself, that reality which lives its stern and lofty life, disembodied, without assured effect or palpable reward, behind the deceptive appearances.

Jacob's is a good will that conquers no world, and the only field in which it is undefeated is in Elysium. To convey this 'to them too, in *their* own language', yet uncontentiously, we can see, may be a humble but not a prosy task.

A little piece of world the pure heart does perhaps conquer after all. In the last scene, to which I alluded earlier, having learned of Jacob's sublime yet quite useless death, and attended, albeit from afar, his piteous funeral, the narrator goes out once more, to visit Barbara, the girl Jacob had unsuccessfully wooed, who is now respectably married to a butcher (it was in a garret in her house that Jacob had lodged in the last years of his life):

Ein paar Tage darauf—es war ein Sonntag—ging ich, von meiner psychologischen Neugierde getrieben, in die Wohnung des Fleischers und nahm zum Vorwande, dass ich die Geige des Alten als Andenken zu besitzen wünschte. Ich fand die Familie beisammen ohne Spur eines zurückgebliebenen besondern Eindrucks. Doch hing die Geige mit einer Art Symmetrie geordnet neben dem Spiegel und einem Kruzifix gegenüber an der Wand. Als ich mein Anliegen erklärte und einen verhältnismässig hohen Preis anbot, schien der Mann nicht abgeneigt, ein vorteilhaftes Geschäft zu machen. Die Frau aber fuhr vom Stuhle empor und sagte: 'Warum nicht gar! Die Geige gehört unserem Jakob, und auf ein paar Gulden mehr oder weniger kommt es uns nicht an!' Dabei nahm sie das Instrument von der Wand, besah es von allen Seiten, blies den Staub herab und legte es in die Schublade, die sie, wie einen Raub befürchtend, heftig zustiess und abschloss. Ihr Gesicht war dabei von mir abgewandt, so dass ich nicht sehen konnte, was etwa darauf vorging.

A few days later—on a Sunday—I was driven by my psychological curiosity to go to the butcher's house, using as a pretext a wish to acquire the old man's violin as a remembrance. I found the family assembled; no lingering impression appeared to trouble them. Yet the violin was hanging on the opposite wall by the mirror, balanced with a sort of symmetry by a Crucifix. When I explained what I had come about and offered a comparatively high price, the husband seemed rather inclined to look favourably on such a stroke of business. His wife however jumped from her chair and said, 'Whatever next! The violin belongs to our Jacob and we have no need to worry about a few guilders more or less!' So saying she took the instrument from the wall, inspected it all over, blew the dust from it and laid it in the drawer, which she then banged shut and locked, as though afraid of being robbed. Her face was turned away while she did this so that I could not see what might be passing in it.

The simple truth of the scene, of the couple's natural reactions (as greed and suspicion and fear of sentiment are 'natural'), stands in no need of comment. And at the point where it is enriched by a religious meaning, in the image of the mirrored world flanked by the symbols of the two passions, there too the realistic narrative mode, recreating a segment of our very own world, remains wonderfully intact. On an earlier occasion we learned that the woman too had been one of Jacob's pitiful delusions, for although

he had spoken of her in exalted terms, 'it seemed almost', the
narrator drily remarks after seeing her at Jacob's funeral, 'it seemed
almost as if she never could have been beautiful.' But now, as she
turns towards the departing caller, comes her moment of beauty:

<table>
<tr>
<td>

Da nun zu gleicher Zeit die Magd
mit der Suppe eintrat and der
Fleischer, ohne sich durch den Besuch
stören zu lassen, mit lauter Stimme
sein Tischgebet anhob, in das die
Kinder gellend einstimmten, wünschte
ich gesegnete Mahlzeit und ging zur
Türe hinaus. Mein letzter Blick traf
die Frau. Sie hatte sich umgewendet
und die Tränen liefen ihr stromweise
über die Backen.

</td>
<td>

However, as the maid now came in
with the soup and the butcher, ignor-
ing the presence of a visitor, began in
a loud voice to recite the grace in
which the children shrilly joined, I
wished them good appetite and went
out. My last look back was at the
woman. She had turned round, and
the tears were streaming down her
face.

</td>
</tr>
</table>

Here at any rate, in this piece of world that had never ceased to
be world, that had never given up the hard and practical point of
view, Jacob has conquered.

The annihilating conclusion towards which this quiet, unadorned
story takes us is no less than the intimation of a deep and consistent
distrust of the substantial world, which appears as a place radically
incapable of yielding form and substance to the good will. The
pure heart, in this vision, remains disembodied. The value of
every thing in the world, of art even—its 'objective' value—is as
nothing to the purity and goodness and devotion that reside in
the heart, mutely, unexpressed, perhaps inexpressible. The rift
between being and doing, the severing of intention from realisation, of spirit from matter—even the all but intangible 'matter'
of music—is complete. How deep is this distrust of all manifestations of the good will in the world we may fathom by returning
to our comparison with the classical point of view. In themselves,
Tasso's *faux-pas*, misunderstandings and embarrassing failures may
not, after all, appear so very different from Jacob's. What does
make them different is the fact that Tasso's artistic achievement is
never questioned by the 'objective' world; but that, on the contrary, it is presented by Goethe (and partly understood by Tasso's

friends) as a validation, *realised* and accessible to all men, as a sort of immanent 'redemption' of those failures. To Goethe the idea that the highest value is 'beyond the reach of common indication', that the highest virtue is mute, would not perhaps have been strange, but it would certainly have been unacceptable. Grillparzer's experience and insight are more melancholy; unsparingly, he reveals every fibre of his being. Many critics have commented on the transcendent beauty of the one and only song Jacob knows by heart—Barbara's song, which he endlessly repeats. Yet nothing could be further from the story's laconic truth, since to the 'objective' narrator the song sounds like any ordinary, disagreeably plaintive ditty, the weight of meaning and feeling which it is supposed to carry is absurdly out of proportion to its objective musical quality. The pæan to the Great Masters—full of treacherous double stops, threatening black with demiquavers and perilous runs—has only to leave the mind and the sheet of music, it has only to enter the concrete world of communicated experience through Jacob's cramped fingers, to turn into a caterwauling abomination. The implied devaluation of the world as we—as the narrator and his kin—commonly interpret it could hardly go further, does not in fact go further in that scene in Kafka's *Castle* where the finest and most aromatic of spirits has only to be exposed to contact with K., and the wintry world he inhabits becomes filled with a nauseous stench. Yet at a vital point the comparison with Kafka becomes false, for the simple reason that Grillparzer's is the story of a redemption (and as such it lies quite outside the range of Kafka's prose).[1] His narrative irony is so

---

[1] H. Politzer ('Die Verwandlungen des armen Spielmanns: ein Grillparzer-Motiv bei Franz Kafka', *Forum*, Vol. V, 1958, pp. 372–5) quotes Kafka's increasingly hostile comments on Grillparzer's story, of which the last, from a letter to Milena, is the most revealing: the story, Kafka writes, 'begins falsely, it contains a great many things which are wrong, ridiculous, dilettante and frightfully affected [*zum Sterben Geziertes*] . . . ; and especially Jacob's way of practising music is surely a miserably ludicrous invention; it's calculated to incite the girl [Barbara? Kafka is writing to Milena . . .] to throw everything at the story, in a rage which the whole world, myself included, will share, so that the story (which deserves no better) will perish of its own faults [*an ihren eigenen Elementen zugrundegeht*]'; and, Kafka adds, 'there is no better fate for a

familiar to us—is such an apt means for bringing home to us his
vision of the truth—since it conveys to us what we know so well
—namely, *how hard we find it* to speak of such a redemption. What
lies behind the irony is a truth of faith, wherein the loss of one
world intimates the gaining of another.

That intimation is as sparse as the rest: a crucifix, a plain,
middle-aged woman who remembers. Yet that is not quite all.
There is also the narrator's embarrassment, which finally gives
way to a humble recognition that his opinion of Jacob is not
the full truth, that his—and thus the world's verdict is not the
last word. 'I am ashamed of [Grillparzer's] story, as if I had written
it myself,' says Kafka. This is the feeling they share. Both
are ashamed of their writings because in them they reveal
their innermost feelings to the world. But while Grillparzer is
'ashamed' of his story because it reveals, in the last resort, a true
redemption, Kafka is 'ashamed' of *his* stories because, in the last
resort, they do not. Thus Grillparzer can free himself from his
'shame', through his narrator, by reversing the verdict of the
world; while Kafka, acknowledging the verdict of the hostile
world as absolute, can enter no such freedom and write no such
story as *Der arme Spielmann*.

The distinct and unique way in which Grillparzer's *Novelle*
contributes to the particular tradition which this book is to make
patent lies in its Christian character. We shall see how different
are the ways in which different authors convey to us their experi-

---

story than to disappear, and especially in *this* manner'—i.e. to perish at the
hands of an enraged world; and to this world, Kafka is guiltily aware, especially
vis-à-vis Milena, he does not belong. Kafka of course writes here not as a disinterested 'critic' but as a man who has been touched on the raw by another
man's intimate self-disclosure (the kind of disclosure he himself makes in his
story about *Josephine the singing mouse*); the embittered tone of his 'wrong'
identification of Jacob with Grillparzer indicates this. But, more important,
behind this 'wrong' identification lies Kafka's perfect understanding of the
story's pervasive disparagement of world and substantiation, which he shares
to the point of identifying himself with the author.

ence of the worldly world as 'merely' an interpreted and fundamentally unsteady world, with what different other worlds they
contrast it, and how often a poignant evocation of its unsteadiness
is an author's last word. Here alone the contrast is formed by the
age-old piety.

For what if a man could not help taking seriously that phrase
which he repeats on many a Sunday, *Domine non sum dignus*? If
all things were to fall away from him in his indignity, and the
pure will to receive the Lord were to inform his bared and deprived life? This would indeed be an absurdity, a 'scandal',
impracticable within the world as we interpret it, unrecognised
by the world and its narrator. But would not the dry and realistic
account of such an absurdity look something like the poor
minstrel's story? Grillparzer, we can now see, *is* neither just the
narrator (who corresponds to the caustic Self of the *Autobiography*)
nor just the narrator's chance acquaintance. He is both these and
a little more. He knows—with a creative artist's knowledge—in
what absurd manner the good will may find embodiment in the
substantial world and how little remains of it in the end. May it
not also be the case that by virtue of that encompassing knowledge, of that wisdom, the artist is freed from the good will's
absurd predicament? That Kierkegaard's 'either/or', his disjunction between 'the Aesthetic' and 'the Religious', is less than
absolute? The story itself, like the little piece of world that Jacob
had conquered, reaches into and is part of our own world; it is
a break in the gnostic vision, a *present* intimation. Yet perhaps
such knowledge is an unsteady possession after all. Of the
ultimate value of his work, the artist may well be as ignorant as
the narrator was ignorant of the true virtue of his interesting
acquaintance.

III A WORLD OF SUFFERING: GEORG BÜCHNER

I

THE PASSIONATE, febrile intensity, the concentration of intellectual effort, action and suffering which inform the twenty-three years of Georg Büchner's life endow it with a symbolical quality. He belongs to the revolutionary generation of the 1830's, which in Germany was silenced by a combination of violent measures and long-drawn-out oppression remarkably efficient for their time. Yet his literary genius, and the pace with which he rushes through and leaves behind the ideological attitudes of his contemporaries, distinguish him from all of them except Heine. Reading his biography we are reminded of certain phases in the lives of Byron, Leopardi, Baudelaire and Poe, yet unlike them he dwells upon no fortifying experience; the unhurried expanse of time—the condition, even in genius, of maturity and fruitful elaboration—is lopped off by his early death: 'Life is an epigram ... who on earth has time and breath enough for an epic!'[1] He never knew those moments of undivided love of life and nature which were the source of sweetness in Shelley's lyricism, nor the assurance of undivided friendship from which Keats drew heroic courage and strength. Not lyricism but a dramatic and infinitely vivid evocativeness is his medium; and betrayal in friendship one of the deepest injuries he suffered. Almost every line he wrote speaks to us of life experienced as a thing fragmentary, unsustained—but also undimmed—by the consolations of continuity. Abrupt openings, exclamatory assertions and sudden endings predominate in

---

[1] *Dantons Tod*, Act II; where the text is available, I shall quote from both Insel eds., *G.B.s sämtliche Werke und Briefe*, Leipzig 1922 (*S.W.B.*, p. 35), and *G.B.s Werke und Briefe*, Leipzig 1949 (*W.B.*, p. 34).

his life, in his dramas, as well as in *Lenz*, his only prose narrative.

Georg Büchner was born in a village near Darmstadt on 17 October 1813, the eldest of six children.[1] His father, Dr Ernst Büchner, began his professional career (as his forebears had done) as a field-surgeon, serving first in the Dutch Army and then in Napoleon's Old Guard, graduated as a medical doctor at Giessen, and took up a highly successful general practice at Darmstadt when Georg was three years old. The energy and the severities of the father's character are those of a self-made man who has subordinated all his interests (including early sympathies with the Revolutionary cause) to the attainment of professional success. Georg's mother, born into an upper middle-class family of Palatine civil servants, appears to be in every way Dr Büchner's opposite; and it is in the nature of this contrast of characters that, although she could not effectively resist her husband's domineering personality, her love and practical help offered some support to her son in his unhappy conflict with the father. After graduating in the Darmstädter Gymnasium (with a school-leaving speech in defence of Cato's suicide), Georg Büchner matriculated as a medical student at Strasbourg University in November 1831. Two years later he became engaged there to Minna, the daughter of his landlord, Pastor J. J. Jaeglé, but at his own insistence the engagement was kept a secret. Since his permit (from the Duchy of Hesse-Darmstadt) to study abroad was restricted to two years, he continued from October at Giessen University, whence he returned to Darmstadt, after an attack of meningitis, in August 1834. His revolutionary activities began at Giessen with the founding of a *Society for Human Rights*, and culminated in the clandestine publication of a subversive pamphlet, *Der Hessische Landbote*, in the summer and autumn of that year; addressed to the completely unresponsive[2] peasantry of his native Duchy, Büchner's original text was greatly toned down, and glossed with biblical quotations, by his friend Pastor F. L. Weidig. Living now at home, he

---

[1] The biographical data are taken from E. Johann's *G.B. in Selbstzeugnissen und Bilddokumenten (Rowohlts Monographien)*, and from K. Viëtor's and A. H. J. Knight's studies, mentioned below.

[2] See *S.W.B.*, p. 606; *W.B.*, p. 270.

continued his studies under the strict supervision of his father, who
suspected his son of revolutionary sympathies but knew nothing
definite about his activities. His fellow-conspirators were de-
nounced—he suspected a close friend, August Clemm,[1] of the
betrayal—and arrested; he himself lived in something like a state
of panic. (A present-day reader may be inclined to regard police-
measures in the 1830's as relatively harmless, or Büchner's fears as
exaggerated. It is therefore relevant to mention that Pastor
Weidig, the group's spiritual leader, was tortured, and committed suicide in jail two years after his arrest; August Clemm
served two brief sentences, but found himself ruined for life;
another friend, Karl Minnigerode, was released after three years
in a state of raving lunacy; yet another, August Becker, served
four years in jail. When, five years after the arrests, the verdict
was pronounced, twenty-six of the conspirators had fled abroad.)
Büchner narrowly avoided an interview with the examining
judge—a patient of his father's—in January 1835 by sending to
the court his brother Wilhelm, who was instantly released; it
may be (Wilhelm Büchner tells us) that the judge deliberately
wished to give him a chance to escape.[2] Meanwhile, in five hectic
weeks in January and February 1835, in constant terror of arrest,
Georg Büchner wrote *Dantons Tod*, keeping his manuscript
hidden from his father under his medical books, and hoping to
secure from the proceeds of it money for his imminent flight.[3]
The completion of the drama marks the end of his concern—his
practical, but also to some extent his literary concern—with
politics. On 9 March 1835 he fled to Strasbourg—without the
knowledge of his father,[4] who thereafter maintained a hostile

[1] See *S.W.B.*, p. 549; *W.B.*, p. 230. Karl Viëtor (*G.B.: Politik, Dichtung,
Wissenschaft*, Bern 1949, pp. 80 ff.) shows that the real traitor was K. Kuhn,
who was not known to Büchner.

[2] See *S.W.B.*, pp. 543, 639–40; *W.B.*, pp. 22, 287–8.

[3] *Dantons Tod*, the only one of Büchner's literary works to be published in
his lifetime, appeared in Frankfurt on the recommendation of the influential
critic and dramatist, Karl Gutzkow, but the royalties did not reach him until
well after his flight from Darmstadt (see *S.W.B.*, pp. 614, 636; *W.B.*, pp. 316,
284–5).

[4] *S.W.B.*, p. 638; *W.B.*, pp. 286–7.

silence, but with financial help from his mother and brother Wilhelm. (A warrant for his arrest was issued in June 1835, but no extradition from France seems to have been requested.) On his arrival in Strasbourg—this time as a refugee and without a passport—he began reading comparative anatomy and philosophy, resolved to make university teaching his career, but as yet uncertain of his subject. In concentrating on the theoretical foundations of the medical sciences he was once more turning against the authority of the father, whose wish it had been that he should qualify as soon as possible as a general practitioner, but who nevertheless appears eventually to have supported him with regular remittances.[1] Avoiding (so he reassures his parents[2]) all contact with other political refugees in Strasbourg, Büchner spent the summer and autumn translating Victor Hugo's *Lucretia Borgia* and *Maria Stuart*,[3] and writing the prose story *Lenz*. In the winter semester 1835–6 he seems again to have turned to dissecting and experimenting. He presented the results of his work on the nervous system of the barbel in three papers, written in French, to a Strasbourg learned society in April and May 1836. His only extant comedy, *Leonce und Lena*, was written for a competition (for which it was entered too late) of the Weimar publishers Cotta in the early summer of 1836. In October, after a visit from his mother and sister, he left Strasbourg for Zürich, where he received the Doctorate of Philosophy; he lodged there as a tenant in the flat of a liberal deserter from the Hessian Army, Lt F. W. Schulz. Early in November 1836 he was appointed *Privatdozent* at Zürich University and inaugurated his course on the comparative anatomy of fishes and amphibia with a lecture on their cranial nerves.[4] Later that year he wrote *Woyzeck*; and at Christ-

---

[1] *S.W.B.*, p. 626; *W.B.*, p. 341. Georg's brother Wilhelm, on the other hand, writes (admittedly, forty years after the event: see *S.W.B.*, p. 626, 8 and *W.B.*, 284, 6) that their father 'positively refused all financial support' to Büchner in Strasbourg.

[2] *S.W.B.*, p. 561; *W.B.*, p. 242.

[3] These translations were commissioned by the publisher of *Dantons Tod* in Frankfurt/M.

[4] Reprinted in *S.W.B.*, pp. 355–367; *W.B.*, pp. 187–198. A description of Büchner as a lecturer in *S.W.B.*, pp. 642–3; *W.B.*, pp. 290–1.

mas received a stern but friendly letter from his father, the first
since his flight.[1] He died of typhus, after an illness lasting seventeen
days, on 19 February 1837, aged twenty-three years and four
months. In addition to the writings I have mentioned we know
of at least one other possibly completed work, the drama *Pietro
Aretino*; it was destroyed, perhaps for reasons of prudishness, by
his fiancée (who was summoned to Zürich when he was dying)
or by some other person.[2] Apart from all this, Büchner has left
rather more than fifty letters, most of them of consuming interest,
a number of minor poems and addresses, and extensive critical
notes on the philosophies of Descartes and Spinoza. To those of
his critics who deplore that he wrote no comprehensive treatise
concerning his literary and aesthetic opinions we may quote the
tag he used in a letter to his parents, *Omnibus satisfacere non posset.*

The atmosphere of intellectual exertion and political enlightenment through philosophical books and radical pamphlets;
arrogance and aloofness paired with a capacity for intense friendship; the conspiratorial activities, utopian plans, naïvety in
practical matters and annihilating disillusionment; suicidal moods;
youthful cynicism alternating with a nihilistic rejection of
accepted values; the somewhat unreal love-affair, unsustaining at
the crucial moment; the ever-renewed attempts to repair the
shattered fabric of experience by a return to the natural sciences;
and finally the sudden yet not unexpected intervention of disease
and death—all these cohere in our minds into a strangely familiar
picture: it is as a character from one of Dostoyevsky's novels that
the young man stands before us. And seeing that only the waste
of his life, not the brief triumphs of his art, were discernible to
his elders and betters, we may easily imagine the sort of comment
one of the worthy civil servants or government officials of

[1] This masterpiece in the mode of 'More in sorrow than in anger' will be
found in *S.W.B.*, pp. 626–8; *W.B.*, 341–3.
[2] See *S.W.B.*, pp. 664–5; *W.B.*, 359; Minna Jaeglé, on the other hand (*W.B.*,
pp. 308, 363–4, not in *S.W.B.*), denied the existence of a completed MS.

Darmstadt society—an eloquent General Yepanchin from *The Idiot*—would make upon the erratic young man, or the sort of understanding he is likely to have received from his righteous and domineering father.

Is 'the Suffering through the Father' then the key that unlocks for us the mystery of Büchner's strange and untimely writings? Under that title there recently appeared a detailed and carefully documented psychoanalytical study[1] which, complementing facts with judicious conjecture, throws more light on Georg Büchner's emotional life than any previous fuller biographies have done. The father-son conflict, to which all the arguments of that revealing study are related, is seen as an unequal contest from beginning to end. Büchner's political activities are interpreted as the son's revolt against a paternal authority which is identified with the State. And the violent imagery of *Der Hessische Landbote*, together with its insubstantial proposals for political reform, suggest that hatred of those in power—'War on the Palaces!'—rather than love and pity for the exploited—'Peace to the cottages!'[2]—is the young pamphleteer's inspiration. *Dantons Tod* is seen (in this Freudian interpretation) as a 'drama ... of willingly accepted punishment for an act of rebellion against the established authority'.[3] The atheistic proclamations, and the sinister fascination which suffering and death have for most of Büchner's characters, intimate the young man's rejection of 'the world of the father' and the lure and fatal enticement by 'the world of the mother' respectively. The account of Büchner's emotional life as presented by the analyst is fairly complete. Everything in it seems to point

---

[1] J. S. White, 'G.B. or the Suffering through the Father', *The American Imago*, Vol. IX, Boston 1952, pp. 365–427. To those acquainted with the prejudices of German literary criticism it will not be surprising that this study is not so much as mentioned by any of the critics.

[2] *'Friede den Hütten! Krieg den Palästen!'* (*S.W.B.*, p. 165; *W.B.*, p. 171), the motto of *Der Hessische Landbote*, was used by Friedrich Engels as the motto for *The Condition of the Working Classes in England* of 1845. A detailed examination of Weidig's emendations and additions to Büchner's text in *S.W.B.*, pp. 165–77, and 733–38; a full account of the content in A. H. J. Knight, *G.B.*, Oxford 1951, pp. 35–9.

[3] J. S. White, *op. cit.*, p. 393.

in one direction. There is the apparently unnecessary secretiveness of his engagement to Minna Jaeglé, and his state of near collapse (preceded or followed—we don't know which—by an attack of meningitis) at the moment when all outward obstacles to an early marriage appear to be removed. There are the literal anticipations, in his letters to her, of the most cataclysmic phrases and images of *Dantons Tod* and *Woyzeck*. And there is his mention of an 'unspeakable fear' and of 'the certain prospect of a stormy life, perhaps soon on foreign soil' in the very letter in which he gives her leave to tell her father of their engagement (Giessen, March 1834[1]). All these, facts and conjectures, compose a portrait in which deprivations, velleities and emotional blocks predominate; and these in turn may plausibly be explained by the all-absorbing conflict with the father. (Kierkegaard's and Kafka's engagements, we know, were concluded and broken in very similar emotional circumstances, in the shadow of the same kind of conflict.) Even the identification (in the psychoanalytical study I mentioned) of Germany as the 'Fatherland' and France as the 'Motherland' is convincing, seeing that Büchner's return to Darmstadt was accompanied by severe migraines; while his flight to Strasbourg (it is hardly surprising) brought a 'relief from tension' and a freeing, no more than temporary, from the haunting, apparently inescapable conflict.[2] The analytical study ends with a conjecture which, given the convincingness of the detailed arguments that lead to it, given also Büchner's own recurrent premonitions, strikes me as plausible and illuminating:

> The rebellion against his father, the feeling of guilt, the urge for atonement, this trinity of contrasts that Büchner was never able to bridge over, constitutes the self-destructive drive in him to which he finally fell victim. For the morbid obsession to reactivate the original situation to which he was exposed as a child, and to which he kept an everlasting pathological loyalty, is the deepest reason for his premature death. The typhoid fever was only a casual agent, any other disease would have struck with equally lethal effect—would have struck his body, weakened in its resistance by the turmoil in his soul.[3]

[1] *S.W.B.*, p. 535; *W.B.*, p. 216.
[2] J. S. White, *op. cit.*, pp. 381, 399–400.   [3] *Ibid.*, pp. 424–5.

Beyond this conclusion, the psychoanalytical enquiry I have summarised attempts no evaluation of Büchner's literary work. I mean that it confines itself to what it identifies as the psycho-pathological causes of that work, using all available sources, including frequent quotations from the work, for the purpose of illuminating the personal circumstances and emotional climate of Büchner's life. But I also mean that as to *the truth* of the insights Büchner's work contains; as to their importance for us, their possibly more than personal validity: in brief, as to their quality as art, the psychoanalyst allows himself no explicit judgement. Now it may well seem rather naïve to see the study so, to fail to observe that in the analyst's insistence on their neurotic and morbid origins there is intended an implicit *de*-valuation of the human insights which Büchner's work yields. In which case this may be the appropriate point to insist on the hiatus—in the sphere of art and literature at all events—between causality and evaluation. The literary question at issue is not how or why Büchner comes to see what he sees, but whether what he sees matters, and is true. The world literary men inhabit would no doubt be a happier place were it less often necessary to insist on this disjunction. But however deplorable, or 'neurotic', or 'obsessional', or 'morbid' Büchner's preoccupations may appear to us; whether or not the God whom his heroes fear and deny, or the State which they would overthrow, are yet further father-images—as long as pain and suffering, death and the fear of death, and sin in the face of absolute commandments, in the face of the living experience of perfection, are *facts*, facts of our common humanity, so long will psychological 'explanations' remain incomplete, and, by virtue of their claim to completeness, misleading. Büchner's literary attempts to draw a meaning for life from the harsh reality of pain must be judged on their own merits, by their own success, and not by reference to the causes that led him to a preoccupation with that reality. And what is true for 'literature' is true for 'thought' also. Commenting on Büchner's propensity to 'see the world divided into two conflicting realities', the analyst invites us to consider *dualism* as 'due to a strong traumatic experience';[1]

---

[1] *Op. cit.*, p. 378.

while in respect of another author, with contrary propensities, another study treats us to the disclosure that there is '. . . an irresistible analogy' between *monism* and 'the desire to establish "whole objects" which is of such crucial importance in infantile development.'[1] In the light of such 'explanations', is not the whole world of ideas reduced to the dimensions of a Viennese *Kindergarten*? Are we not left wondering what strange subjective delusions all the writers of the last twenty-five centuries—out there, beyond the bars of the Freudian playpen—have been so earnestly concerned about?

Büchner's story *Lenz* presents the image—something, incidentally, like a clinical study—of a diseased mind. It is clearly impossible for an author to write out so powerful, so circumstantial an account of alienation without having experienced some emotions of the kind described, in some form or intensity. What this kind of argument leads to is banal tautology: to describe at any level of narrative intensity *is* to experience. The value for us of the image and encompassing story is as unrelated to its biographical origin as it is to the therapeutic effect it may have had on its author. Nor is its value connected with the value of the story as a clinical study. (In this respect, we shall see, there is some justice in regarding it as defective.) The interpretation of world and experience offered to us here is not one which any man in his senses would take as a literal precept. To propose that he should so take it, as the Expressionists did, is to propose an irresponsible sophistication. But Büchner's image of life *is* valid as a momentous exaggeration: as a mosaic of emotions and acts and reactions *each of which* represents a part—at once possible and actual—of our true self, flesh of our flesh, even though the imaged whole is a stranger to our sanity. So is the murderer Raskolnikov. Yet as we enter into his life and follow him upon his ever-narrowing daily round, from playful half-thoughts to the moment where for the first time he stares fully at the thought of the act, to the plan, the cold preparation, the wavering, the brutal resolve and finally the crazed—but is it so?—and bloody deed . . .: where, in that desolate journey, do we cry, 'Halt'? Everywhere and nowhere.

[1] R. Wollheim, *F. H. Bradley*, [Pelican books] London 1959, p. 283.

The journey and the deed—the completed image—are the price of our knowledge. And with such images—such imaginative explorations of our very own possibilities—before us and then for ever part of us, we may conjecture that the truth they yield is to be attained at no lesser price than that of the momentous exaggeration.

2

Between Grillparzer's tale of *The Poor Minstrel* and Georg Büchner's almost contemporary story *Lenz*, the contrasts of atmosphere, action and style could hardly be more striking. Where Grillparzer's narrative is ironical, laconic and reserved, Büchner's is fervent, passionately evocative and haunting. Where Grillparzer depends for his effects upon the distance between a ruminative and at times casual narrator and the inconspicuous subject of his tale, Büchner bursts upon us with an undeflected and stark description of setting and central character. From the story's first sentence he immerses the reader in an unsparingly tragic situation, leaving him no leisure for dissociation; dispensing with all ironical distance, the narrator remains throughout in the utmost proximity of his subject. Where Grillparzer's hero is modest to the point of self-effacement, Büchner's Lenz is violent, crazed into monstrous fears, egocentric to the point of complete solipsism. Where Grillparzer's style is circumspect and carefully modulated to place and illuminate the hero's absurd destiny by means of Austrian idioms and a close description of person and locale, within a very specific social ambience, Büchner's style is nervous, clipped and tense, unconcerned with expanding any thought beyond its first, briefest formulation, placing his hero on the icy margins of the social world. With Grillparzer ellipsis is used to express the narrator's laconic detachment, with Büchner it is carried to the point of disconnectedness. The coherence of his story is constantly threatened—not by some accident or literary failure but on the contrary by the very nature of the story's encompassing theme. He paints a portrait in stark, *fauviste* colours rather than in subtle hues; the absence of the worldly-wise *arrière pensée* and reflective judgement (where judgement implies distance) leaves hardly any space between events and

narration of events, story-teller and hero, leaves hardly any room
for conscious 'art'. With his refusal—or rather, since it is no
conscious act, his inability—to make any concessions to a discursive, leisurely understanding, Büchner writes as a man
possessed by a tragic vision. He is as it were *in* his story (while
Grillparzer's presence is sensed *behind* his). And while Jacob
seems as it were to depend on the narrator to give substance and
meaning to his life, Lenz is the sort of hero whose existence out-
grows, almost threatens his author. The impetus of events, but
also the intersection of events and natural setting, give Büchner's
Novelle a dramatic force unique in nineteenth-century narrative
prose; what it brings to mind are not literary parallels at all, but
the usurping art of Van Gogh. Even a comparison with E. A.
Poe is misleading, because here the violent conflict is in the mind
alone, presented without threatening contraptions or the show of
hostile forces, in short without patent outside causes. Yet although
the emerging vision stands before us almost entirely without
distinct outside causes, its origin being simply a rift in the mind,
there is ultimately no transgression of narrative convention—no
final incoherence—because Büchner's creative effort, his intense
presentation, is fastened to the mind's 'objective correlatives', the
objects of a recognisable and poignantly evoked natural world,
which give body and form to the conflict of the mind. But again,
although they belong to and are called up from our common
experience, these objects are not presented neutrally. They are
sucked into the vortex of a world other than our own, they are
usurped by a mind which does indeed distinguish and sever
things from things, but not in our way; a mind, in particular,
whose capacity for distinguishing between the inner and the
outer world is radically different. Büchner passes no judgement,
expresses no opinion, on the working of that mind. Instead, like
Grillparzer, he *shows*. And this showing forth of life is the one
means above all others a writer has (in literature everywhere) for
conveying what outside literature we take as opinion, or the
proving of a point, or abstract knowledge. Here it is the sheer
intensity of Büchner's portrayal which carries us away from our
habitual certainties to the vertiginous question, central to the
work, of what is real in experience: is it our own ordinary world,

so pale by comparison, or is it the coherent, vivid, lurid nightmare of Lenz's imagination?

And at this point of doubt, too, we recognise an intimate kinship with Grillparzer's tale. In each *Novelle* the narrative stress lies
on a radical *re*-interpretation of our common world, each in its
different way amounts to an imaginative proposal (the one hesitant
and caustic, the other intensely dramatic) to re-interpret the
world in a manner alien to, and indeed in conflict with, the
stable and commonly accepted assurances of society. To assert
this kinship is in no way to forget how different are the detail and
atmosphere of each story, how utterly different, too, the visions
which emerge. Büchner's *Novelle* presents us with an experience
infinitely more brutal and primitive than Grillparzer's. The depths
of soul uncovered in *Lenz* give one a feeling that it belongs to a
period much more recent than the 'thirties of the last century, a
feeling borne out by the fact that the story—and indeed Büchner's
entire work—remained almost entirely unknown until just before
the First World War. The unmistakable cadences of Büchner's
prose found no ready ear beyond the narrow circle of his closest
friends, his entire achievement went unrecognised until, attracted
by his personality and feeling a kinship with his unhappy fate,
the Expressionists tried to recapture—and imitate—his voice in
their own stories and plays in the 1920's.

The differences between *The Poor Minstrel* and *Lenz* are too
palpable to be in danger of neglect. Yet the common theme
which emerges beyond the individual themes illuminates each
and draws both together in a common narrative tradition. The
experiences presented are different; so are the narrative manners.
Yet in both tales we hear different and distinct voices asking one
kind of question: 'May it not be that the truth about the world is
really quite different from what the world claims it is? By the
light of its own wisdom, and to all practical intents and purposes,
the world is of course quite right in thinking that our heroes, who
regard it so differently from the way the world regards itself, are
deluded, or mad, that they aren't quite "there". But when a man
searches for an absolute, bedrock certainty, is being "there" more
than a relative reassurance? What *is* the world, to press its claims
upon our imagination with such peremptoriness? How firm is

its hold upon reality? Is the world's loud voice, it too, any more
than an interpretation? And, as such, nearer the truth? If the world
should turn out to be wrong, what then? What will *it* fall back on
save that which is not to be found *in* the world—the solitary search
of each individual man? And again: if the world is, conceivably, in
the last instance, wrong about itself, how much more questionable
is the value of its wisdom for each man as he stands on his own,
sheltering his soul against a hostile fate, as he emerges into his ultimate, inescapable solitude? Experience is experiment and solitary
venture. All other reassurance is false. Here is my interpretation.'

Putative questions such as these have a 'contemporary',
'existential', twentieth-century ring about them. They seem
incompatible with the bourgeois certainties and the sense of values
we associate with nineteenth-century realism, which is founded
upon an acceptance of and a creative assent to, the inalienable
reality, the fixity even, of the world's social character and institutions. The 'existential' questions to which the writings I have
singled out here propose their different answers are familiar to us
from more recent literary and philosophical works. Yet to impute
such questions to nineteenth-century German writers is no
anachronism. In some of the masterpieces of nineteenth-century
German prose the acceptance and creative assent of the realists
are partly or wholly absent; instead, in respect of the social
character of man, they have an air of the provisional, conditional,
interpretative about them. *Their* bedrock certainties lie outside
the social sphere (if anywhere at all); hence the descriptions of the
human situation which we are given in these works have unexpected affinities with our own age, with mid-twentieth century
dubieties about the social lot of man. Unless we are to repeat the
conventional error of judging these productions by standards
which are ultimately not relevant to them—and of which consequently they are bound to fall short—the standards relevant to
these works will have to be different from those relevant to
European realistic prose. To the extent to which they leave out
the sphere of social values—'the worldly world'—these literary
works are more innocent, to the extent to which they by-pass
'the world' they are more reflectively sophisticated, than the
works of European realism. (And where it is a question of

innocence, their 'contemporary', twentieth-century affinities are indeed misleading.) Their greatness lies in their capacity to illuminate the life of the human spirit 'beyond the reach of common indication', to illuminate the possibilities of the solitary soul.

The acceptance and the creative assent on which nineteenth-century realism is based, and which its productions reflect, are of many different kinds; the variety of the realists' responses to the social data is enormous; and, certainly, this creative assent is the opposite of uncritical (just as the realistic novelists' personal attitudes towards their social world are far from unambiguous). The intense contempt which Flaubert feels for the provincial and Parisian society of his age has few parallels in German literature. His feelings of estrangement from contemporary humanity—'*ils sont dans le vrai*', he exclaims enviously, watching the bathers from behind the window of his study—are perhaps as acute as any that German writers have experienced; and the complex process by which he 'sublimates' these feelings in his art is not my present concern. What I mean by 'creative assent' is reflected in the fabric of his prose, which is utterly steeped in the *données* of his world, in that social world's very own details of fact, character and atmosphere. Through his prose he commits himself, however scornfully, and with however many ironical reservations implied in the 'point of view' technique, to the common scale of values. At the points at which the characters of his novels attempt to escape from their given world, there especially he shares in the ways of that world, for the manner of their escapes is determined by the manners of their prison. And Flaubert's presentation of that world—*not* as an interpretation at all but as the one and only bed-rock certainty there is, without possibility of appeal, redress or redemption, as one-way ineluctable experience; hateful, deserving of contempt, humiliatingly inferior, no doubt, to the vision of a contentless 'pure' work of art which he (like Grillparzer) dreams of as the artist's only worthy goal[1]—his presentation of *that* is

---

[1] See A. Thorlby, *Gustave Flaubert and the Art of Realism*, London 1956, *pass.*; for Grillparzer's 'old dream' see *S.W.*, i, Vol. XIII, p. 315.

committed to the encompassing worldly reality with a creative passion which not so much cancels out the personal contempt he feels for the world, the nausea even, but which gives even to these feelings a *social* substance and a *worldly* reality and relevance. And the caricatures, the Breughel (or Hieronymus Bosch) monsters and dear little women who people Dickens's novels? It isn't at all that they 'have a life of their own' (as the critic resignedly concludes[1]), but that they have a life *in common*, that the exquisite distortions which give them their strange forms are all drawn from one perspective, all tend towards one focal point, for they live and die, act and suffer inalienably within their common social situation, than which there is, for them and for Dickens, no other. The vital point is that the more distorted they are the more light their existences throw on the horrifying, or absurd, or funny, or wicked imperfections of that to which their author irrevocably commits them, and himself. As fantastic as the least 'realistic' extravaganzas of German romanticism, *Bleak House* has hardly a character whose manners and speech and actions have not been imaginatively transformed into oddity, hypertrophy, sentimentality or grotesque. Yet what else is the novel's theme than an all but hypostatised *social* reality—'*Equity*, bleared Argus with a fathomless pocket for every eye and an eye upon it'—which both encroaches upon and stands above all the lives depicted? All England is enmeshed in its nets. It is dreadful in its power, abuse and pitilessness; it is inveighed against by all good men, ridiculed by the living and cursed by the dying, honoured by none but the mad; it is pompous, unjust and unjustified, oblivious of its true purpose—and *there*, inescapably part of the only world there is.[2] Nor is the *donnée* fundamentally different for Dostoyevsky. What the characters of his novels have in common is once again the

---

[1] E.g. George Orwell in *Critical Essays*, London 1946, pp. 50–1.

[2] In almost every one of the novels the place of one or several aspects of social reality is central: *Nicholas Nickleby* (school); *Little Dorrit* (the Marshalsea); *Dombey and Son* (London business, the railway); *Hard Times* (the industrial North); *Our Mutual Friend* (the Thames and the people who make their living from it); *Oliver Twist* (the Poor Law); even in mystery stories like *Great Expectations* and *Edwin Drood* personal destinies are inextricably intertwined with institutions (the legal practice; the cathedral and its environs).

reality of the encompassing social life and its institutions—the
Law, the penitentiary, the University, the government office, the
brothel, the shop, the clandestine meeting-place of revolution-
aries; and through this reality they all—Myshkin no less than
Raskolnikov, and even Alyosha Karamazov—must go: against
it they must measure themselves. And even when Dostoyevsky
does envisage another reality, even then the social here-and-now,
the worldly world remains as the necessary and (paradoxically)
absolute condition of his hero's ultimate emergence, the path (and
there is no other) which he too must tread. It is not in solitary
self-examination but in the law-court that Dmitri understands the
working of Grace. Like the virtue in one who has known temptation, the Christian spirituality towards which Dostoyevsky moves
is substantiated and enriched by what it ultimately renounces.

The diversity of European realistic literature, including some
German contributions, is in no danger of being obliterated by
my insistence on its common social foundation. It is, on the
contrary, this common foundation which is lost sight of by recent
critics who have stressed the moral (to the exclusion of the ethical)
and the existential (to the exclusion of the common and social)
aspects of that literature. The social commitment of the European
realists is a palpable literary fact, yet it is hardly too obvious to
require stressing when we contrast their work with the masterpieces of German prose. Through this contrast, too, we recognise
that the form in which the realistic novelists bring their personal
suffering and deliberate rejections into their work is determined
not by these feelings alone, not by the inward conflict only, but
by the imaginative world these feelings enter: which is the social
world as reflected in the rich humus of realistic themes and forms.
How complicated and unhappy were the realists' reactions to that
world we perhaps see more clearly today than ever before. That
they chose to have no other literary choice is the other, no less
important, half of their situation. For another choice was possible.

3

Büchner's few observations on his literary aims and method
amount to no more than hints where to look for his own

achievement. Isolated from the biographical or literary contexts in which he placed them, these observations have recently been made to serve a Marxist theory of literature[1] to which they do not belong. His own political activities culminate in the writing and distributing of *Der Hessische Landbote*, whose revolutionary import is reversed in *Dantons Tod*, and what follows is a turning away from all political loyalties and even interests. The political message of *Dantons Tod* is the futility of revolution—both because the means-to-end ethos of violence is shown to have corrupted those who wield power over others, and also because of the unworthiness of 'the People' whom the reign of terror was to have enfranchised. In view of this, it could hardly be expected that Büchner's subsequent writings would show any concern with the tenets of 'socialist realism' which Communist writers are ready to see in them. All the same, Büchner's own predicament in the autumn and winter of 1834 is complicated enough to require some elucidation.

His political views up to that point are pre-Marxist. In his early letters,[2] in *Der Hessische Landbote* itself, and also according to the legal deposition and testimony of his friends,[3] he advocates the overthrowing of the absolutist régime in the Duchy of Hesse-Darmstadt (and also probably in Germany as a whole) by revolutionary action.[4] Opposing the agitation of the Frankfurt Liberals and of the nationalist and middle-class reformers as ineffective, he singles out want and hunger as the only significant agents of historical change. He demands economic equality, attacks exploitation by the Princes, the bureaucracy and the army, rejects promises of constitutional reform as valueless. His view of the French Revolution, couched in the sort of simple narrative he

---

[1] See H. Mayer, 'G.B.s ästhetische Anschauungen', in *Zeitschrift für deutsche Philologie*, Vol. LXXIII, Berlin 1954, pp. 129–60. The conclusions here are all the more disappointing since they are at odds with the author's much finer argument, and much less 'orthodox' point of view, in his earlier book, *G.B. und seine Zeit*, Wiesbaden 1946.

[2] *S.W.B.*, p. 525; *W.B.*, p. 204.

[3] *S.W.B.*, pp. 605, 635–6; *W.B.*, pp. 269, 281–2.

[4] *S.W.B.*, p. 173; *W.B.*, p. 179.

was naïve enough to expect his peasant readers to follow, is positive and unproblematic. A nation has been freed by trust-worthy, honourable men from the arbitrary rule of a corrupt King and court (he writes), and this act of liberation is sub-sequently reversed by foreign intervention on behalf of the cor-rupt aristocracy. As for direct political guidance or precept, the broadsheet contains nothing beyond a prophetic peroration to the effect that in Germany too the day of reckoning is nigh. This is the 'programme', the 'ideology' for which he is prepared to risk his career and freedom. How sudden and how radical is the change of mind which makes him write *Dantons Tod*?

Two considerations arise at this point, and both flatly contradict the overt purpose of the broadsheet. First: during the very period in which Büchner is politically active he is visited by moments of annihilating doubt regarding the value and meaning of any personal act or historical change. One such moment is described in a letter to his fiancée (written from Giessen, probably in November 1833 and certainly not later than Spring 1834):

Ich studierte die Geschichte der Revolution. Ich fühlte mich wie zer-nichtet unter dem grässlichen Fatalis-mus der Geschichte. Ich finde in der Menschennatur eine entsetzliche Gleichheit, in den menschlichen Ver-hältnissen eine unabwendbare Ge-walt, allen und keinem verliehen. Der Einzelne nur Schaum auf der Welle, die Grösse ein blosser Zufall, die Herrschaft des Genies ein Puppenspiel, ein lächerliches Ringen gegen ein ehernes Gesetz, es zu er-kennen das Höchste, es zu be-herrschen unmöglich. Es fällt mir nicht ein, vor den Paradegäulen und Eckstehern der Geschichte mich zu bücken. Ich gewöhnte mein Auge ans Blut. Aber ich bin kein Guillotinen-messer. Das Muss ist eins von den Verdammungsworten, womit der Mensch getauft worden. Der Aus-spruch: es muss ja Ärgernis kommen,

I have been reading the history of the Revolution. I felt as though crushed by the hideous fatalism of history. I find in human nature a terrifying sameness, in human institu-tions an irresistible power, bestowed on all and on none. The individual mere foam on the wave, greatness a mere accident, the sovereignty of genius only a puppet-play, a ridiculous struggling against an iron law, to recognise it is our highest achievement, to control it impossible. Never again shall I feel inclined to bow down before the performing horses and the corner-boys of history. My eyes have grown accustomed to the bloodshed. But I am no guillotine-blade. 'Must' is one of the execra-tions pronounced at the baptism of mankind. The dictum 'it must needs be that scandal cometh to pass: but woe to him through whom scandal

aber wehe dem, durch den es kommt
—ist schauderhaft. Was ist das, was
in uns lügt, mordet, stiehlt? Ich mag
dem Gedanken nicht weiter nach-
gehen.[1]

cometh!' *is terrible. What is it in us*
that lies, murders, steals? I cannot
bear to pursue the thought.

The unrelieved determinism of this passage, with its antithesis of
knowledge against action, its spiritual and moral (that is, personal)
concern with the biblical paradox, its denial of any possible
ethical standards—all these read very strangely if we bear in mind
that they are written by a young man who is also composing a
revolutionary pamphlet which he will distribute, at great personal
peril, among the peasantry. Nor is this simply a passing mood of
doubts to which, it may be, any young revolutionary is prey.
For, secondly, such animadversions on the meaning of personal
action and human freedom lead him directly to the vision of
politics and history embodied in *Dantons Tod* (January–February
1835); they must therefore have occupied his mind more or less
continuously throughout the period in which he engaged in
subversive activities. His friend August Becker writes, many
years later:

> *His idea in writing the broadsheet was provisionally* only to explore *the mood of
> the people and of the German revolutionaries. Afterwards, when he heard that the
> peasants had given most of the broadsheets they found to the police, and that the
> patriots too had spoken out against the broadsheet, he gave up all his political hopes
> of a change in the situation.*[2]

This explanation is convincing as far as Büchner's subsequent disengagement from political action goes, but how does it illuminate
his state of mind at the time? As between the determinism of his
views and the activism of his deeds, what did he *really* believe in?
Is it true to say that 'the appeal [in the broadsheet] was only an
experiment'? That 'the determinist was trying for once to deceive
and deflect the "terrible fatalism of history",' but that he failed—
had to fail—because he was not prophetic enough to recognise

---

[1] *S.W.B.*, p. 530, dates the letter spring 1834; *W.B.*, p. 209, November 1833.
[2] *S.W.B.*, p. 636; *W.B.*, p. 281, my emphasis.

that 'the exploited class, once revolutionised, would be able to bring the solution'?[1] His last letters to Gutzkow, written *after* he completed *Danton*, seem to suggest as much: 'The relation of rich to poor is the only revolutionary element in the world; only Hunger can become the goddess of Freedom. . . . If you pamper the peasants and let them grow fat they will die of apoplexy.'[2] And again: 'Our age is wholly material[istic] . . .'—for the majority-class of the exploited 'there are only two effective levers: material want and religious fanaticism. Any party which knows how to work these levers will win.'[3] Yet here too (as in *Danton*) the horror of the *canaille* is infinitely stronger than the reformatory intention, and the desire *to understand* the situation has outlived the urge *to alter* it.

Büchner's fundamental preoccupation (as we shall see) is with suffering as the dominant mode of human experience. His plays and his *Novelle* are explorations of this theme, but so, partly, is *Der Hessische Landbote*. It is of course true to say that the direction of its arguments is 'not likely' to make it into 'an effective piece of propaganda'.[4] Nor, for that matter, is its style, its emphasis on corruption, lawlessness, violence and deprivation, which is utterly different from, say, the politically effective descriptions of a Karl Marx;[5] in a sense, Büchner's broadsheet is no more than a series of rhetorical and poetic variations on the image of 'the chains' with which *The Communist Manifesto* ends. Yet this style, so much more memorable than the sketchy revolutionary argument, un-mistakably anticipates *Dantons Tod* and *Woyzeck*. More than that. Together with these plays, as well as with certain passages in his letters, the style of the broadsheet reflects a unity of creative pur-pose more fundamental than the overt political purpose suggested in its argument. I think it is more fundamental, not from some preconceived belief that politics cannot be a writer's fundamental

[1] H. Mayer, *G.B. und seine Zeit*, Wiesbaden 1946, p. 169.
[2] Strasbourg 1835 [?], *S.W.B.*, p. 549; *W.B.*, p. 229.
[3] Strasbourg 1836, *S.W.B.*, pp. 562–3; *W.B.*, p. 243.
[4] A. H. J. Knight, *G.B.*, Oxford 1951, p. 39.
[5] See I. Berlin, *Karl Marx*, London 1949 (*Home University Library*), p. 182.

concern, but because I see Büchner's energy everywhere committed to an exploration of suffering rather than to its abolition;
because the reality of suffering is present in *Der Hessische Landbote*,
while even the possibility of meaningful political action is absent
everywhere else. His political act is indeed an 'experiment': not
because, writing and thinking in the pre-Marxist limbo, he hasn't
yet 'seen the light', but because a creative writer's fundamental
concern, even if it be with politics, has in the world of political
action always something experimental about it; its issue, after all,
is an illumination first and foremost, not a precept.

It is hardly necessary to add that the tragic imbroglio of his
political experiment increased the anguish of those last months
before Büchner's flight from home, that the fear of imminent
arrest by the police and the fear of detection by his father must
have been made almost intolerable by his far from momentary
doubts. What did he *really* believe in? We are, nowadays,
familiar with the 'irony' of this sort of situation, in which a young
revolutionary is very nearly arrested and condemned for incite-
ment to actions which his own play ('found among his possessions
at the time . . .') identifies as actions of meaningless delusion or
hypocrisy. It is the sort of 'irony' that perhaps only a Dostoyevsky
could fully recreate and transcend. The truth behind the 'irony' is
clear enough; of Büchner's fundamental belief in the all-encompassing reality of pain his every act, political and literary, is
a brutal confirmation.

This, then, is Büchner's predicament as a young revolutionary
and as a young writer at the beginning of his career. The political
'experiment' ends with his flight to Strasbourg. What remains is
a concern to which his political activities, to which even his
creative writings, are in a sense incidental. He did not, we know,
think of himself consistently as an author, seeing his vocation
first in medicine, then for a short time in philosophy, finally in
experimental physiology; yet it is not in this sense that I see his
writings as incidental. The studies he pursued, his politics, *and* his
literary work, are all means to an end—which is an existential
understanding; yet of all these, perhaps in his consciousness too,
literature is the most direct. Having yielded the figure of Danton,
his political engagement is abandoned. To see in Büchner the

theoretician and practitioner of a 'plebeian-democratic realism'[1] is to misstate the theme of *Woyzeck* by making of the play a political tract. Woyzeck belongs to 'the People', yet he has nothing in common with the *canaille* of *Danton* or with the peasants for whom Büchner had written his tract. His choice of a 'plebeian' hero for his last play is dictated by no 'ideology' save his own— the vision of human suffering—to which all political and even social considerations become increasingly irrelevant. This is equally true of the few scattered critical observations Büchner wrote, for they are as little determined by considerations of social justice or economic causality as is the essentially private vision which these remarks help to bring into focus.

4

Briefly, he insists that the writer's task is to reproduce reality as closely as possible; that he should give a faithful account of the historical circumstances of his chosen character, of the events as they actually happened. He is to refrain from all—Schillerian— moralising and didacticism (as always when the emphasis is on 'unadorned truth', the notion is at hand that the dirtier the truth the truer it is). In a letter to his parents, written at the time when he expected that news of the publication of *Dantons Tod* had just reached them,[2] he begins by arguing in anticipation of the usual philistine charges:

> As for the so-called immorality of my book, I would say this. The dramatic poet is, to my eyes, nothing but an historian, but he stands above the latter because he creates history for us a second time; instead of giving us a dry account, he transports us directly into the life of an epoch; instead of giving us characterisations he gives us characters and instead of descriptions, living figures [Gestalten]. His supreme task is to come as close as possible to history as it really happened. His book must be neither more moral, nor less, than history itself; but God did not create history as reading-matter for young ladies, and so I cannot be blamed if my drama is as unsuitable for

---

[1] See H. Mayer, 'G.B.s ästhetische Anschauungen', *loc. cit.*, p. 150. Mayer's argument and conclusions are clearly predetermined by the ideology for which he seeks support in Büchner, yet he stops short of misinterpretation; for this the enquiring reader must go to the Nestor of Marxist criticism himself, G. Lukács, in *Deutsche Realisten des neunzehnten Jahrhunderts*, Bern 1951, pp. 66–88.

[2] Strasbourg, 28.vii.1835, *S.W.B.*, pp. 551–2; *W.B.*, pp. 232–3.

that purpose. Surely I can't make virtuous heroes out of a Danton and the bandits of the Revolution. If I wished to depict their dissoluteness I had to let them be dissolute, if I wished to show their godlessness I had to let them speak as atheists. . . . Any man who objects [to my having chosen such a subject] could not study any history, because it contains many immoral things, he would have to go about in the streets blindfold because otherwise he might see indecent behaviour, and he would have to cry out bitterly against a God who has created a world in which so much depravity exists. And if it should be further argued that the poet ought to show the world not as it is, but as it should be, I would reply that I don't wish to do better than God has done —for surely he has made the world as it should be! As for the so-called 'idealising poets', I find that they have produced nothing but marionettes with sky-blue noses and affected pathos, not human beings of flesh and blood, whose suffering and joy make me feel with them and whose actions fill me with disgust or admiration. In fine, I think much of Goethe and Shakespeare, very little of Schiller . . .

—who, oddly enough, had used much the same argument in defence of *his* first drama, *Die Räuber*.[1]

In this and one or two similar observations Büchner shows his aims to be very much more 'realistic' than were those of his 'Jungdeutsch' contemporaries,[2] and seems to be anticipating the *ne-plus-ultra* imitation-theory of Naturalism. And this 'ultra-realistic' view of his writings appears to be supported by the fact that they abound with literal quotations from historical and bio-graphical sources. In *Dantons Tod* there are several speeches quoted verbatim from Thiers, Mignet, and from a German historical magazine to which his father subscribed.[3] In *Lenz* there are

---

[1] 'The economy of my play [*Die Räuber*] makes it necessary that there should appear many a character who offends against the finer feeling of virtue and revolts our tender morals. Every painter of men is necessarily put into this position, if what he wishes to offer is to be a copy of the real world and not idealising affectations and textbook-creatures.' (Quoted from H. Mayer, *op. cit.*, p. 144). Such anti-classical and anti-idealist views were common in the 1770's; passages from J. M. R. Lenz's *Anmerkungen übers Theater* (e.g. K. Viëtor's quot. in 'Lenz: Erzählung von G.B.', *Germanisch-Romanische Monats-schrift*, Vol. XXIV, 1937, p. 8) were undoubtedly in Büchner's mind when he wrote the 'aesthetic conversation' in *Lenz* (see below, p. 103).

[2] See H. Mayer, *op. cit.*, p. 135.

[3] See M. Jacobs' excellent edition of *Dantons Tod* and *Woyzeck*, Manchester 1954; quotations from the French sources in R. Thieberger's *La Mort de Danton*, Paris 1953.

extensive transcriptions and paraphrases from the diary of Pastor Oberlin, the man in whose house the poet Lenz had stayed during his wanderings in the Alsatian mountains in 1778.[1] In *Leonce und Lena* the borrowings, more directly literary, come from de Musset's *Fantasio* and the German Romantics;[2] in *Der Hessische Landbote* there are, surprisingly enough, echoes of Jean Paul.[3] And in *Woyzeck* the plot and some characterisation relate to an actual murder committed by a wig-maker of that name; the details of it Büchner knew well from a published account of the psychiatric expert who had acted as witness at the trial in 1823–4, and from the subsequent controversy (regarding Woyzeck's sanity) in a medical periodical in which Georg Büchner's father frequently published his own professional articles.[4] In short, what could be more 'realistic', we may well ask, than that a Danton, a St Just, a Lenz should be presented *ipsissimis verbis*? How much closer is it possible to come to historical or quotidian reality 'as it actually happened'?

It all depends on what kind of reality an author has in mind, or rather not 'in mind' only, but in the very fibres of his being, the very movement of his pen. The reality which informs Büchner's drama and prose is wholly different from that to which the realists' creative assent is extended (and *a fortiori* different from what nowadays stands for 'socialist realism'). The one characteristic and crucial point Büchner never mentions in his 'aesthetics' (I mean in those three or four isolated observations from which a Marxist 'aesthetic theory' has been constructed) is his experience and poetic vision of the fragmentariness and discontinuity of life. It is not the verbatim interpolations and literary borrowings that matter, but what he makes of them: how he draws them into his

---

[1] See E. Johann, *op. cit.*, pp. 138–40, A. Stöber, *Der Dichter Lenz und Friederike von Sesenheim*, Basel 1842, pp. 11–31, and *S.W.B.*, pp. 678–9.

[2] See A. Renker, 'B. und Musset', *Das Inselschiff*, Vol. III, 1922, pp. 284 f.

[3] E. Johann, *op. cit.*, p. 79.

[4] See F. Bergemann, 'Der Fall Woyzeck in Wahrheit und Dichtung', *Das Inselschiff*, Vol. I, 1920, pp. 242 ff., E. Johann, *op. cit.*, pp. 117–23; the actual trial seems to have been one of the first at which expert evidence in respect of diminished responsibility was admitted by a German court.

images of life seen as a broken vessel. Much importance has been
attached to the fact that several of the manuscripts he left behind
are incomplete. But really this bibliographical chaos—the joy and
despair of editors—leaves the dramatic argument unimpaired.
For even where (as in *Dantons Tod*) a more or less complete final
version exists, the reality apprehended and imaged is a thing
fragmentary and discontinuous; while even where, for one
contingent reason and another, our version is typographically
incomplete (as in *Woyzeck* and *Lenz*), the apprehension of reality's
fragmentariness is no less realised, the guiding poetic intention no
less achieved.

Another way of putting this is to consider the major dramatic
influence discernible in his plays, that of Shakespeare. Here he
follows, and indeed goes further than, the interpretation of
Shakespeare's stage technique as reflected in Goethe's *Götz*,
Schiller's *Die Räuber*, and in the other chaotically magnificent
productions of the *Sturm und Drang*, above all in Lenz's *Die
Soldaten*. Taking their norm from such plays as *Antony and
Cleopatra*, *Macbeth* or *Julius Caesar*, the generation of 1770 saw
the brevity of scenes and discontinuity of action not as a failure
to conform to classical standards, an inability to achieve a 'well-
made play', or an inconvenience caused by the practical limitations
of the Elizabethan stage, but as an essential part—the one most
readily accessible to them—of Shakespeare's vision of life. This
interpretation Büchner seems to take over from the poet J. M. R.
Lenz (our evidence here is indirect); more than that, he strains it
to its limit. It is as if he saw the essential Shakespeare all in that
final scene in *King Lear*, about eleven lines long, in which Edgar
leaves his blinded father in the shadow of a tree to wait the issue
of the battle and, after a sound of trumpets, returns to announce
that the day is lost. It is as if for Büchner the significant statement
were not 'ripeness is all'[1] but the heartbreaking incongruity of
'pray you, undo this button'. What he invokes (and the
Expressionist playwrights and film-directors follow him in this)

---

[1] P. Schmid's *G.B.: Versuch über die tragische Existenz*, Bern 1940, uses this
quotation as a motto to his book; it seems to me to describe a state of mind and
mode of writing Büchner did not reach, could perhaps not have reached.

is the discontinuity, almost, between cause and effect, assertion and reply, intention and realisation, stimulus and response; it is, very nearly, a severance of communication between men. And all this, a seeming chaos, belongs not to Shakespeare but to his vision alone.

The nearest he ever comes to describing this vital part of his 'realistic' intention is in the course of a literary discussion in *Lenz*:

> Ich verlange in allem—Leben, Möglichkeit des Daseins, und dann ist's gut; wir haben dann nicht zu fragen, ob es schön, ob es hässlich ist. Das Gefühl, dass was geschaffen sei, Leben habe, stehe über diesen beiden und sei das einzige Kriterium in Kunstsachen. Übrigens begegne es uns nur selten: in Shakespeare finden wir es, und in den Volksliedern tönt es einem ganz, in Goethe manchmal entgegen; alles übrige kann man in's Feuer werfen ... Man versuche es einmal und senke sich in das Leben des Geringsten und gebe es wieder in den Zuckungen, den Andeutungen, dem ganzen feinen, kaum bemerkten Mienenspiel ... Es sind die prosaischsten Menschen unter der Sonne; aber die Gefühlsader ist in fast allen Menschen gleich, nur ist die Hülle mehr oder weniger dicht, durch die sie brechen muss.[1]

'In all things [Lenz says to his friend Kaufmann] I demand life, possibility of existence, and that's all; once that is achieved, it's not our business to ask whether it is beautiful or ugly'—whether it is a meaningful whole or a fragment of the whole, Büchner might have added: for this, the tracing out of the *bare* 'possibility of Being', is his very own perilous enterprise. 'The feeling [Lenz continues] that there is life in the thing created is more important [than considerations of beauty and ugliness], it is the only criterion of art. Besides, he said, we meet it only rarely: we find it in Shakespeare, it calls out to us with a full voice in the songs of the people, sometimes in Goethe, everything else can go on the fire.'

What does Büchner[2] mean when he speaks of 'the possibility of Being'? Is that Being a thing *bare* and deprived, as I have

---

[1] *S.W.B.*, p. 93; *W.B.*, pp. 91-2; the similarities between this speech of 'Lenz's' and J. M. R. Lenz's 'Anmerkungen übers Theater', are not particularly close; the most striking are the passages on imitation (*Gesammelte Schiften*, Vol. I, München 1909, p. 227) and poetic (= dramatic) insight (p. 231).

[2] Of this identification of Büchner with his hero more will be said below, p. 155; in this passage it raises no problems.

interpolated, or is it 'the fullness of life'?[1] The reference to folksongs, and to Goethe, would appear to suggest the latter. Yet when
we look at the folksongs Büchner actually quotes—in *Lenz* itself, in
Leonce und Lena, and in *Woyzeck*—we find that they are all verses
of solitude and pain. And this, too, is the direction in which
Lenz's argument continues. After attacking the 'wooden dolls'
created by idealising authors, he asserts the true function of the
artist: 'Let him try for once to immerse himself in the life of the
humblest person and to reproduce it in its throbs and hints, in
the subtle, hardly perceptible play of his features.'[2] Here, literally,
is not only the language and substance of *Dantons Tod*, of Thomas
Paine's speech on the chasm in Creation—here is 'the programme'
of Büchner's entire work; and Lenz concludes in the same
vocabulary of pain: 'the artery of feeling is the same in almost
all men, only the shell'—the shell of unfeeling—'only the shell
through which the vein must burst is now thicker and now thinner.'

5

The experience fundamental to Büchner's vision of human
character and destiny, and the unifying theme of his literary work,
are the experience and the theme of the world under the aspect
of suffering. The rudimentary and often discontinuous dramatic
movement of his plays traces out a dialectic whose antitheses are
formed by boredom and insensateness on the one hand and its

[1] In his English version of *Lenz* (*Partisan Review*, Vol. XXII, 1955, p. 40)
M. Hamburger translates: 'Besides, it's only rarely that we find such fullness
of life', for which there is no authority. However, Mr Hamburger's version of
Lenz also contains several illuminating renderings (see below, p. 148).

[2] See also *Dantons Tod*, Act III, 'Das leiseste Zucken des Schmerzes...'
quoted below, p. 105, and, even more directly relevant to the present 'aesthetic'
context, Danton's reference (in Act II; *S.W.B.* and *W.B.*, p. 39) to the painter
Jacques-Louis David:

Und die Künstler gehn mit der Natur um wie David, der im September die Gemordeten, wie sie aus der Force auf die Gasse geworfen wurden, kalt-blütig zeichnete und sagte: ich erhasche die letzten Zuckungen des Lebens in diesen Bösewichten.	*And artists treat Nature as David did, when the bodies of the murdered men were thrown out of La Force on to the street in September, and he stood drawing them in cold blood and said, 'I am snatching the last throbs of life in these scoundrels.'*

conquest by feeling on the other. It is a movement from un-reality, adumbrated as the all but incommunicable region of solipsism, unfeeling and isolation, to reality, experienced above all as encroachment, violation and ravage of the self by another. The grim fact of pain is seen, initially, as 'the bedrock of atheism', the irrefutable proof that an omnipotent, just and loving God does not exist. Yet the recognition that 'the least twinge of pain, and if it stir only an atom, rends creation from top to bottom'[1] does not lead Büchner to the Hobbesian view that a man should put himself in a position where he can avoid pain, or to the Schopenhauerian view that he should regard it as illusory. On the contrary, in the visions which emerge from Büchner's work a man's capacity for suffering is his bedrock of reality, his one and only proof that he *is* and that the world *is*. Büchner's 'hero' is like a man waking from an anaesthetic or from a condition of total shock: the life and feeling that flow back into his limbs and flood his consciousness are the life and feeling of pain. The river of pain that flows through him yields the only proof he has of existing, but at the same time it is more than he can endure: the proof of his existence is also his undoing. Büchner's occasional use of the imagery of the dissecting table and of physiological experiments owes something to the laconic detachment and ribald humour of the medical student. But such images also indicate his view of men as specimens which are being 'prepared'—their every lethal spasm is watched—by a demiurge whose intentions remain hidden in sinister obscurity. The dialectic into which Büchner's characters are strung is not between good and evil, or fate and will, or hatred and love, but between feeling and unfeeling; and existence is manifest not yet in action but in endurance and suffering, not yet in pleasure but in pain. This far Büchner's work takes us, but no further; the 'not yet' belongs to our logic, not to his vision.

Leonce und Lena, Büchner's only comedy, is concerned mainly with the first half of the dialectic. The hero, Prince Leonce, is one of those 'who are unhappy, incurably, merely because they *are*';[2] and his escape from insensateness, which takes the form of an all

[1] *Dantons Tod*, Act III; *S.W.B.*, p. 51, *W.B.*, p. 50.
[2] Act II, Scene 3; *S.W.B.* and *W.B.*, p. 119.

but suicidal boredom, is effected by means of a fairy-tale device, convincing only in terms of a romantic convention of co-incidences. At the same time the device is barely compatible with the emotion of boredom which casts a deadly chill on the harlequinade, or rather not with the emotion itself but with the intensity this emotion is given by the playwright. Knowing each other as the world knows them, a Prince and Princess in Never-neverland frustrate the world's—the silly King's—matchmaking intentions; intended for him by Polonius, Ophelia becomes the object of Hamlet's vicious scorn. But ignorant of each other's identity when they don the masks of the marionettes they 'really' are, Prince and Princess fall in love and marry. The curtain comes down on a happy Lena and a caustic Leonce wryly reconciled to the ambiguity of their union. And the meaning of this happy ending? As a goal to his search for reality and reassurance Leonce recognises it as ludicrously arbitrary. The only meaning of the conclusion is as a proof—and again he ironically recognises it as such—that an inescapable determinism governs men's destinies, that freedom, and thus purposeful actions, are wholly illusory. Determinism—that is, the rationalisation of arbitrary actions—is the intellectual correlative of the emotion of boredom, and bore-dom is the soul's response to the void which encompasses it. Some of the most powerful lines of the play are devoted to character-isations of that emotion on the boundary of *Angst*. Just as boredom is interest without an object, a concern with nothing and over nothing, an encounter of the experiencing self with 'nothing in particular', so *Angst*, a negative boredom, is objectless fear, fear which fears 'nothing in particular' and thus everything; which fears existence itself as well as its end. Seeing in boredom not merely a trivial interlude between periods of meaningless action but a mode of life, a void which threatens all life, Büchner is writing out the experience of his post-Byronic, post-Napoleonic generation in Continental Europe everywhere. Lermontov and the Czech romantic poet K. H. Mácha, E. A. Poe, Leopardi,[1]

---

[1] K. Viëtor, *G.B.: Politik, Dichtung, Wissenschaft*, Bern 1949, p. 107, points to a parellel between Leopardi's poem 'Bruto Minore' of 1824 and Danton's image of the Moloch's arms in Act IV (*S.W.B.*, p. 76; *W.B.*, p. 75).

de Musset and, a little later, Baudelaire—they all speak of the atrophy of the heart and the dulling of the senses in a world where commerce and finance, the Civil Service and bourgeois orthodoxies have filled the place of heroism and adventure, and of faith. But taking this theme to its extreme point—the point of anguish of soul—Büchner upsets the precarious balance of comedy:

Komm, Leonce, halte mir einen Monolog, ich will zuhören. Mein Leben gähnt mich an wie ein grosser weisser Bogen Papier, den ich vollschreiben soll, aber ich bringe keinen Buchstaben heraus. Mein Kopf ist ein leerer Tanzsaal, einige verwelkte Rosen und zerknitterte Bänder auf dem Boden, geborstene Violinen in der Ecke, die letzten Tänzer haben die Masken abgenommen und sehen mit todmüden Augen einander an. Ich stülpe mich jeden Tag vierundzwanzigmal herum wie einen Handschuh. O, ich kenne mich, ich weiss, was ich in einer Viertelstunde, was ich in acht Tagen, was ich in einem Jahre denken und träumen werde. Gott, was habe ich denn verbrochen, dass du mich wie einen Schulbuben meine Lektion so oft hersagen lässt?—(Act I, Scene 3)

Come, Leonce, let's have a monologue, and I will listen. My life yawns up at me like a big white sheet of paper that I must fill with writing, but I can't produce a single letter. My head is an empty ballroom, a few withered roses and crumpled ribbons on the floor, broken violins in the corner, the last dancers have taken off their masks and are looking at each other with eyes weary unto death. I turn myself inside out like a glove twenty-four times a day. Oh, I know myself, I know what I shall be thinking and dreaming in a quarter of an hour, in a week's, in a year's time. God, what have I done that you should make me recite my lesson over and over again, like a schoolboy?—

In what follows the balance is not restored; the desolate anguish unleashed in the Prince, 'merely because he is', is stifled, not assuaged, by his subsequent happy fate.

In *Dantons Tod* the underlying emotion is substantially the same —the same region of soul is illuminated—but the emotion is rendered incomparably more intense because its proximate causes are intimated, its effects on the 'hero's' character more fully sustained, and because, above all, the dramatic situation is so much more commensurate with the emotion itself than it was in Büchner's romantic comedy. The drama opens on 24 March 1794; Danton is now on the point of complete disillusionment with the cause and development of the Revolution. He is haunted by nightmare visions of the September massacres in which he played a leading part. He now knows the sordid and trivial concerns, the greed and corruptness of 'the People' on whose behalf he conducted the massacres: he also knows the cowardice and cynicism and the hypocrisy (so strong as to be self-delusive) of his fellow-revolutionaries: and, having exhausted all physical pleasures, Danton has come to the end of experience, and knows himself to be alone. This is the end with which the play begins. He is like a man imprisoned in a maze, who knows the mechanism of every lock and of every guard's mind, yet who also knows that any door he may succeed in unlocking leads merely into another part of the maze. His knowledge is as complete as it is paralysing— the determinism, now projected on to a wide, historical plane, is reflected in boredom and *nausea vitae* which are almost suicidal. In this initial situation Danton is incapable of any meaningful human contact. Whatever happens outside him is unreal. 'They will not dare'—the phrase he repeats whenever his friends urge him to escape arrest by Robespierre's Revolutionary Tribunal— sums up his feelings, or rather unfeeling, about the world that surrounds him. Even to Julie, his wife, who tries to penetrate his insensate detachment with devotion and love, he can only speak of his isolation:

... *Wir wissen wenig von einander. Wir sind Dickhäuter, wir strecken die Hände nacheinander aus, aber es ist vergebliche Mühe, wir reiben nur das grobe Leder aneinander ab,—wir sind sehr einsam.*	*We know little of each other. We are thick-skinned creatures, we stretch out our hands to each other, but it is wasted effort, we are only rubbing our coarse hides together—we are very solitary.*
Julie. *Du kennst mich, Danton.*	Julie. *You know me, Danton.*
Danton. *Ja, was man so kennen heisst. Du hast dunkle Augen und lockiges Haar und einen feinen Teint und sagst immer zu mir: lieber Georg! Aber* (er deutet ihr auf Stirn und Augen) *da, da, was liegt*	Danton. *Yes, what passes for knowing. You have dark eyes and curly hair and a fine skin and you always call me 'dear George!' But* (pointing to her forehead and her eyes) *there, there, what lies behind there?*

| hinter dem? Geh, wir haben grobe Sinne. Einander kennen? Wir müssten uns die Schädeldecken aufbrechen und die Gedanken einander aus den Hirnfasern zerren.— | It's no good, we have crude senses. Know each other? We should have to break open each other's skulls and drag the thoughts out of each other's brain-coils.— |

Danton's and his friends' death under the guillotine is a fore-gone conclusion, the external action of the play leads towards it without being greatly modified by retarding events or by the stirring of a will to live. Danton's brilliant rhetorical victory before the Revolutionary Tribunal serves not to avert his fate, or even to delay it, but to demonstrate its arbitrariness: all rational argument, all personal and political action appear absurd. The dramatic movement that sustains the play is a movement of the ideas and emotions of men who are all caught up in the revolu-tionary situation.[1] They are distinguished not by virtue of the political or moral principles they proclaim, but by the degrees of self-knowledge of which they are capable, where knowledge is the enemy of the will to survive. Thus the one quality which, even at the beginning of the play, distinguishes Danton from his enemies, and from Robespierre in particular, is his candid insight into the motives of political action, and his lack of hypocrisy. But this is no virtue in him, since his understanding of the truth about himself and about the Tribunal that will soon condemn him to the death to which he has condemned so many others, is a detached, cynical understanding. Furthermore, Danton has no decision to make, no active part to play any longer, and is thus in

[1] The enthusiastic critical review of *Dantons Tod* which Karl Gutzkow wrote when it first appeared in July 1835 has been largely ignored by subsequent critics; yet it contains a great many remarkable insights, e.g. 'One may say that in Büchner's drama there is more life than action. . . . Instead of drama, of an action which develops, rises and falls, Büchner gives us the last quivering and rattle which precedes death. But the abundance of life which is massed before our eyes for a last time does much to supply the want of an idea resemb-ling a plot. We are enthralled by a content which consists of more events than deeds, and are astounded by the effect which a production would be bound to make on the stage—a production which is impossible because you cannot play Haydn's Creation on a barrel-organ. . . .' (Quoted from K. E. Franzos's ed., Frankfurt 1879, p. 449.)

possession of a negative freedom: he cannot escape the 'dreadful fatalism of history', but he can choose to become its conscious victim rather than its blind instrument—'I'd rather be guillotined than guillotine. I've had enough. . . .'[1] The sentient grasp of the truth of his guilt and his non-participation, his negative freedom, are the conditions from which a change proceeds: a change not of mind towards action but of soul towards suffering.

Imminent death appears to Danton not as punishment or retribution, but only as another kind of corruption, different from life merely by being less complicated.[2] He now recognises, with all the anguish of one who has had enough of life, that the annihilation which death will bring is not total. What then does it amount to, this apparently wholly negative insight at which Danton arrives, the insight that 'nothing can turn to nothing'? Less than a positive assent to creation, and scarcely more than a hiatus in his nihilism, it is merely the recognition of the unending reality of 'something', of an object, a being, a resistance of some kind, against which life, flowing back into insensate limbs, into the soul, strikes: and, striking, wakens body and soul to pain. Fear—now no longer objectless anguish and nausea but the definite fear of an unending death—is indeed a strange 'value' to emerge at the point where Danton's false fearlessness ('. . . they will not dare . . .') ends. Yet it *is* a rudimentary value when we compare it with the solipsistic insensateness with which the play opened. For Danton to fear death—to fear it for himself, but even more so for his friends—and to make his exit with the words (addressed to the executioner, who thrusts back Hérault as he tries to embrace Danton)—

Willst du grausamer sein als der	*Will you be more cruel than Death?*
Tod? Kannst du verhindern, dass	*Can you prevent our heads from*

---

[1] Act II, first scene; *S.W.B.*, p. 34; *W.B.*, p. 33. See also M. Jacobs' note (*ed. cit.*, p. 123): '. . . Büchner takes over from Mignet [*Histoire de la Révolution française*, Paris 1824] these words of Danton, but omits his outburst of anger against Billaud and Robespierre . . . instead of feeling personal animosity against Robespierre at this point, [Danton] sees both himself and his opponent involved in the wretched fate of mankind. . . .'

[2] Act III; *S.W.B.*, p. 65; *W.B.*, p. 64.

unsere Köpfe sich auf dem Boden des   kissing each other at the bottom of
Korbes küssen?[1]   the basket?[1]

—is to have undergone a change, a 'development' even: not
towards any traditional morality (which to the end he rejects as
a subtle kind of hedonism); nor towards heroism (which he
ironically deprecates as a mere theatrical gesture); but towards
the barest, the most rudimentary *apprehension* of reality through the
capacity to feel it and to fear its endlessness. Danton dies at
the point where, having freed himself from the negative infinity
of unfeeling, he is exposed to—but does not enter—the positive
infinity of creation. Yet it is a positive infinity: positive in relation
to the other side of the dialectic, the insensate Nothing from which
he awakens, and therefore also absolutely positive, in the sense
that life, however terrible, is a condition, a *sine qua non*, no more
than a bare foothold, of Grace. At this point the play—indeed
Büchner's literary work—stops. The proof of Danton's existence
is also his end as a living man.

The dialectic of pain is bodied forth, in *Dantons Tod* and everywhere in Büchner's work, not primarily by overt action and
events, but by strange mosaics of words grouped in a series of
individual scenes, their connections barely sustained yet never
quite abandoned. The measure of Büchner's 'realism' is, formally
speaking, his success in continuously conveying the discontinuity
of experience,[2] in making a rudimentary whole of his feeling for
life as a thing fragmentary and incomplete. The strange mosaics
of which the individual scenes of his plays consist are made up
of two kinds of contrasting images, one grey and one scarlet.
Insensateness and boredom are represented by an imagery, always
forceful and sometimes obscene, which is related to the physical—
the digestive and sexual—functions; the repetitiousness and
tedium of the daily ritual of dressing, eating, the 'symbols of

---

[1] Act IV; *S.W.B.*, p. 79; *W.B.*, p. 77.
[2] In all this his dramatic practice overtakes his capacity for, or interest in,
aesthetic theorising.

exhaustion' like discarded clothes, the smell of the grave, frozen ground and arid wastes, ashen skies and empty marshy landscapes, mechanical dolls, robots and marionettes—these are the images that give dramatic substance and poetic form to one side of the dialectic. In violent and dramatic contrast with these is the language of flesh and blood, of violence and of the Crucifixion.

No elaborate demonstration is needed to prove that this imagery owes much to Shakespeare; Macbeth's 'Life's but a walking shadow . . . a tale / Told by an idiot, full of sound and fury, / Signifying nothing'; Hamlet's 'Imperious Caesar, dead and turn'd to clay, / Might stop a hole to keep the wind away'; Lear's 'The wren goes to it, and the small gilded fly / Does lecher in my sight . . .', and countless other examples of this 'low' style[1] spring to mind. The fundamental difference lies in the framework of the total vision to which this double imagery of feeling and unfeeling belongs. Shakespeare too is intimately familiar with the experience of life's meaninglessness and pain. But he contrasts it with invocations, as realistic as they are powerful, of the greatness and dignity of man, dramatically portrayed in a man's capacity for loyalty, love and courage; a capacity often unavailing but always real, that is, an element in the fashioning of a man's character and actions. In Büchner the only contrast is between the scarlet and the grey, it lies within the double imagery itself; there is nothing outside or beyond it; the search for reality through the experience of pain and suffering makes up 'the whole', such as it is, of his work.

At this point, however, a vital question arises: what is it that makes the comparison with Shakespeare at all possible, that preserves Büchner's writings from the turgid pointlessness and horror-mongering of our 'Theatre of the Absurd'? What is it that preserves Büchner's ever-repeated variations on tedium from being tedious, on the pathos of the human situation from being merely 'pathetic', on the ghastly boredom of life from being ghastly and boring? In other words, what makes them into works of art? The answer lies in the paradox of all successful realism,

---

[1] 'Low' in contrast to the elevated style of classical tragedy, as E. Auerbach describes it in *Mimesis*, e.g. in the chapter on Shakespeare (pp. 298 ff.).

which the naturalists (among them Büchner's imitators) have failed to heed. His world is like a giant battlefield, a pattern of livid greys and blood. Yet form—the manner in which these two kinds of images are presented—is peculiarly at odds with the apparent content. For while in speech after speech and scene after scene death and decay are invoked, the immense creative, poetic *energy* which informs each invocation—the living force of each image: the violence, for instance, of Danton's tedium—belie its overt meaning. And this energy—Aristotle's *sine qua non* of all drama—is present not only in the individual parts but also in the achieved whole of each work. *Dantons Tod* and *Woyzeck* both end on the same note, and leave the same total impression in our minds: that life *is*, that it is not a delusion (as insensateness is) but reality, and that its meaning is in pain. This far his vision takes us, and thus he attains to a rudimentary meaning which escapes the horror-mongers; but it takes us no further. The next step in the dramatic argument—the meaning of pain as a means to some end other than itself, as expiation to forgiveness and Grace, he does not express.

Danton's discussion with his friends in the Conciergerie (Act III, Scene 7), immediately before the opening of the Tribunal, provides an example of Büchner's technique of advancing his dramatic argument by means of a mosaic of images. Meaning and action, pressed together into the smallest conceivable grouping of words, are made to depend not upon the abstract opinion expressed, but upon the colours of the imagery and the tone of the speaker's voice:

Philippeau. *Was willst du denn?*
Danton. *Ruhe.*
Philippeau. *Die ist in Gott.*
Danton. *Im Nichts. Versenke dich in etwas Ruhigeres als das Nichts, und wenn die höchste Ruhe Gott ist, ist nicht das Nichts Gott? Aber ich bin ein Atheist. Der verfluchte Satz: Etwas kann nicht zu nichts werden! Und ich bin etwas, das ist der Jammer!—Die Schöpfung hat sich breit gemacht, da ist nichts leer, alles voll Gewimmels. Das Nichts hat sich ermordet, die Schöpfung ist seine Wunde, wir sind seine Blutstropfen, die Welt ist das Grab, worin es fault.—*[1]

[1] S.W.B., pp. 64–5; W.B., pp. 63–4.

To Phillippeau's question what there is left to hope for Danton replies, 'Peace.' *Phillipeau:* 'Peace is in God.' *Danton:* 'In Nothing. Immerse yourself in something more peaceful than Nothing, and if the greatest peace is God—then isn't Nothing God?' This is the *credo*, the ontological argument of nihilism. And Danton demolishes it in the next breath: 'But I am an atheist.' Here is no statement of fact but a cry of despair: a piece of cold logical deduction *and* a violent assertion of existence; and as such the sentence is as far as it could be from its overt lexical meaning. There is no God, and therefore no 'peace'; no peace, and therefore no Nothing: 'Oh, that accursed proposition, "Something cannot become Nothing". And I am something, that is the horror of it!'[1] The something of creation is ubiquitous—'Creation has spread itself everywhere, nothing is empty, everything is crawling with it'—creation is the annihilation of peace: 'Nothingness has murdered itself, Creation is its wound, we are drops of its blood, the world is the grave where it lies rotting.'

All of which, as Danton adds, 'sounds mad'. And yet, in this assertion of the irreducible reality of existence, we have conveyed to us an experience less remote than Danton's enigmatic negation may suggest. For what he asserts is as it were negative existence (in the same sense in which boredom is 'negative' interest)—it is life as it appears to the man awakening from shock. The vision which emerges from the double negation is the very opposite of Heidegger's '*Nichts das selbst nichtet*'—an empty, meaningless void (such as Lenz experiences[2]), which sucks in and silences all emotion and thought. It is the opposite, too, of Schopenhauer's disembodied 'Nirvana', his atheistic parallel to (and parody on) the Christian's 'Peace that passeth all understanding'. What emerges is something more familiar than these: it is the world encompassed by suffering, it is Being filled out with pain, sensate

---

[1] One of the two English translations (*Danton's Death*, by Stephen Spender and Goronwy Rees, London 1939, p. 114), uninspiring at the best of times, here reaches complete incomprehensibility: '. . . and if the highest peace is God, isn't nothingness God? But I'm an atheist; that accursed phrase! Something cannot be nothing. . . .'

[2] See below, pp. 150 ff.

and throbbing with painful life. Peace—the Nothing—is desirable enough: it would indeed be an 'ideal' condition: *'das Nichts ist der zu gebärende Weltgott'*: 'Nothingness—*that* is the world's god that is yet to be born'[1] (= that should be born). But peace *is* not, has no place in creation. Consequently (and here again the astonishing combination of cold logic and hot passion) absolute solitude too does not exist, is breached and violated by another. But just as the existence asserted through pain was a rudimentary, 'negative' existence, so the contact of two beings which is based on the violation of their solitudes (of their 'brainboxes'[2]) is a rudimentary, 'negative' contact: Danton's love for Julie is love in the face of death, Woyzeck's love for Marie is sealed by murder; though the scene from which I have quoted began on a note of despair at the absence of Nothing, it ends with the fear of solitude:

...O Julie! Wenn ich allein ginge! Wenn sie mich einsam liesse!—Und wenn ich ganz zerfiele, mich ganz auflöste: ich wäre eine Handvoll gemarteten Staubes, jedes meiner Atome könnte nur Ruhe finden bei ihr.	*O Julie, if I were to go alone! If she were to leave me forlorn! And even if I could fall to pieces, utterly, dissolve entirely, I would be a handful of tormented dust, and every atom of me could only find peace with her.*

But since there can be no death, no peace, what remains to be done? Before, in his state of boredom and heedless unfeeling, Danton had considered that nothing—no political action, no attempt to escape or survive, not even the cry of pain and anguish —was worth the effort it involved. Now this one thing only remains: the cry which will assert the *ne-plus-infra* of bare existence:

Ich kann nicht sterben, nein, ich kann nicht sterben. Wir müssen schreien; sie müssen mir jeden Lebenstropfen aus den Gliedern reissen.	*I cannot die, no, I cannot die. We must cry out—they must tear every drop of my life's blood out of my limbs.*

---

[1] S.W.B., p. 76; W.B., p. 75. The other English translation (*The Plays of G.B.*, by G. Dunlop, London 1952) is not to be outdone in schoolboy howlers: 'The world is chaos—Nothing its too spawning god' (p. 203). For the rest, it makes up for incomprehension by an artificiality and archness of language likely to discourage the most enterprising of producers.

[2] See the opening of Act I, quoted above, p. 109.

To what end? Once again we come to the fragmentary, jagged
open edge of the vision. There is no God because there is pain,
which is the only, the terrible proof of existence: and if there is
no God—no peace—is there thus no cessation of pain, no end to
existence? Is existence pain into infinity? It is not so, D. H. Lawrence calls to us in his last poems, it cannot be so:

> *And if there were not an absolute, utter forgetting*
> *and a ceasing to know, a perfect ceasing to know*
> *and a silent, sheer cessation of all awareness*
> *how terrible life would be!*
> *how terrible it would be to think and know, to have consciousness!*
> *But dipped, once dipped in dark oblivion*
> *the Soul has peace, inward and lovely peace.*

But later still, on the very threshold of death, Lawrence adds that
question which had tormented Danton; which leaves the vision
open at the far end of life; and exposes all life—procreation and
the enduring of joys and sorrows—to infinity:

> *Oh lovely last, last lapse of death, into pure oblivion*
> *at the end of the longest journey*
> *peace, complete peace!*

> *But can it be that also it is procreation?*

> *Oh build your ship of death*
> *oh build it!*
> *Oh, nothing matters but the longest journey.*

Which is it: the bad infinity of pain or the good infinity of
Grace? It seems that in his hour of death Büchner was able to
answer the question, to complete for himself the vision of the
world under the aspect of pain. His last words, spoken to his
friend and fellow-exile, Wilhelm Schulz, sum up poignantly the
central experience of his short life and the theme of his literary
work:

Wir haben der Schmerzen nicht zu-   *We do not suffer too much pain but*
viel, wir haben ihrer zu wenig, . . .   *too little, . . .*

but to these words he adds the answer of faith which his writings
do not contain, and thus gives to suffering the meaning which his
creative imagination was not able to encompass:

, denn durch den Schmerz gehen wir zu Gott ein.[1]	, for through pain we go home to God.[1]

6

A singular progression is to be observed in the successive stages
of Büchner's preoccupation with the problem of pain; like Danton's growing apprehension, it is the opposite of what ordinarily
might be called a positive development. It is as if, from *Dantons
Tod* through *Lenz* to *Woyzeck*, Büchner were trying to come ever
closer to the experience and the problems it raises; as if, progress-
ively discarding all that, from *its* point of view, appears as contingent, he were intent upon grasping the dialectic in its barest
form. The complex and personal situation in which Danton is
involved is seen as the outcome of the blind, anonymous forces
of historical necessity. It is seen in this way by Büchner *and* by
his hero, who understands his situation well enough to be able
to expatiate on its absurdity. (And Danton's knowledge, as well
as his eloquence, is shared in various degrees by his friends and
fellow-prisoners.) Danton has no power—because he has no

[1] The quotation (*S.W.*, p. 650; *W.B.*, p. 298) is from the diary of Caroline
Schulz, in whose flat in Zürich (see above, p. 81) Büchner died. Although not
she but her husband was present at Büchner's death-bed, the absolute relevance
of these words—at any rate of the first sentence—to Büchner's writings leaves
no doubt in my mind that they are quite authentic. Here is the entire entry:
'16th [February 1837]. We had a restless night; the sick man repeatedly
tried to get up and leave the house because he was dreaming that he was going
to be taken or that he was already a prisoner and wanted to escape. In the after-
noon the pulse was only a flutter and the heart-beat was 160 to the minute; the
doctors said there was no hope. My piety forsook me and I bitterly asked
Providence "Why?" Wilhelm came into the room and when I expressed my
despairing thoughts to him he said, "Our friend himself gives you the answer;
just now, when a violent storm of fantasies had passed from him, he said calmly,
loudly and solemnly, 'We do not suffer too much pain but too little, for
through pain we come home to God! We are death, dust and ashes, how can
we complain?'" My misery dissolved in sorrow, but I was very sad and shall
be so for a long time to come.'

consistent desire: and no desire because no sustaining reason—to
avert his execution, but at least he faces death with a distinct and
highly articulated consciousness. Woyzeck has not even that. He
is victim pure and simple—victim of his own birth and circumstances, of society, of his own dark nature. Or rather, he is as
nearly a mere victim as it is possible—as we are made to accept
as convincing—for a living man to be; not the least of the young
dramatist's achievements is that he gives us an imaginative measure
of that state. And in creating Woyzeck as the embodiment of a
ne-plus-infra of the human condition, Büchner is wholly original.
For the figure of this down-trodden simple soldier, passive and
animal-like in his suffering, there is no literary precedent anywhere; in particular, not in Shakespeare, whose influence upon
many details of characterisation in *Dantons Tod* is powerful and
even, once or twice, overpowering. Here in *Woyzeck* it is as if,
taking up such minor figures as Poor Tom or Private Feeble—
'I'll ne'er bear a base mind: an 't be my destiny, so; an 't be not,
so'[1]—Büchner decided to enshrine a whole vision of life within
the boundaries of the helpless victim's soul. Nor is his originality
merely of historical interest. Creating situations in many ways
similar to Woyzeck's, neither the Naturalists of the late nineteenth
century nor the Expressionists of the early twentieth ever achieved
a dramatic portrayal comparable in intensity and uncontrived
pathos. Determinism, social indictment, the class-struggle—all
these are implicit in the play, but the vocabulary to which these
terms belong is altogether too intellectualised, it describes a
situation less primitive and fundamental than Woyzeck's. And
since solitude, here too, is a part of the 'hero's' deprivation, it is
still a single and distinct man, *an individual,* who occupies the
stage (and thus appeals to our sympathy in the traditional manner).
To think of a remedy for Woyzeck's situation—that is, to think
of it socially—is to think of a different play.

He is, during the early part of the play, passive, a slave in body
and mind. Words to him are strange, disconnected objects which
he uses as one who had never used them before—falteringly, then
again violently, hurling them at people:

---

[1] *Henry the Fourth*, Part II, Act III, Scene 2.

[Woyzeck] *Ich geh. Es ist viel möglich. Der Mensch! Es is viel möglich.—Wir haben schön Wetter, Herr Hauptmann. Sehen Sie, so ein schöner, fester, grauer Himmel; man könnte Lust bekommen, ein' Kloben hineinzuschlagen und sich daran zu hängen, nur wegen des Gedankenstrichels zwischen ja und wieder ja— und Nein. Herr Hauptmann, Ja und Nein? Ist das Nein am Ja oder das Ja am Nein schuld? Ich will drüber nachdenken.*

I must go. Many things are possible. Humanity. Many things are possible. Fine weather we're having, Captain, Sir. Look, such a beautiful sky, all grey and hard. It almost makes you want to knock a hook in it and hang yourself on it, only because of the little dash between Yes and Yes again—and No. Captain, Sir: Yes and No? Is the No to blame for the Yes or the Yes for the No? I'll have to think about that . . .

Earlier in the scene the Captain whom he serves as a batman had insinuated that Marie, Woyzeck's mistress, had been unfaithful to him. Thus Woyzeck's 'Yea and Nay' is tied to the action by expressing the torment of his uncertainty; but his words are also an appeal to the biblical injunction—'Let your words be . . .'; and they are finally a cry of despair in the face of the eternal bedrock of guilt—'Scandal there must be, but woe to him from whom scandal cometh.'[1] Her guilt? His own? He faces the question defenceless and alone.

Words, everywhere in Büchner's work, are such strange, isolated objects: now like gaudy beads of poison, now like knives quivering in the target, now like scalpels dissecting living limbs, now again like gory wounds. Büchner's style is 'dramatic' if by 'dramatic' we mean, not the coherence of sustained conflict recognisable to both parties and made meaningful by motivation, but annihilating tension and conflict compressed into momentary haphazard encounters. His tormented hero speaks without expectation of being understood or hope of being spared. He speaks, yet the world is silent to him—Woyzeck's tormenting doubt is silenced not by knowledge but by the irrational deed:

Weib!—Nein, es müsste was an dir sein! Jeder Mensch ist ein Abgrund; es schwindelt einem, wenn man hinabsieht.—Es wäre! Sie geht wie die Unschuld. Nun, Unschuld, du hast ein Zeichen an dir. Weiss ich's? weiss ich's? Wer weiss es?

[1] See Büchner's letter to Minna Jaeglé (*S.W.B.*, p. 530; *W.B.*, p. 209), from which I quoted above, p. 95, and *Dantons Tod*, Act II; *S.W.B.* and *W.B.*, p. 43; also, possibly, *King Lear*, Act IV, Scene 6, 'To say "ay" and "no" . . .'.

Is she guilty? 'Woman!... No, there would surely be some
visible sign on you!' But would it be visible to him? 'Each person
is an abyss. Giddiness takes you when you look down.' And yet:
'Could it be true? She walks like innocence itself.' But innocence
has no visible sign, goodness is silent, only evil and pain call
loudly from the void: 'Well, then, innocence, you have a sign on
you. Do I know? Do I know? Who does know?'

His sentences are discontinuous as his self is isolated. He uses
words the way Kaspar Hauser[1] had done—the youth who, fully
grown but with the mind of a savage or a child, had emerged
from the dark woods into the blinding daylight of the world of
men. Is not the first, the most 'obvious' thing we say of such an
'unaccommodated man' that he is defenceless? Do we not feel
that the harm and injury that we know will come to him are
somehow 'natural' and proper to his desolate situation? And yet,
is there not, even in that bare and primitive condition of a Kaspar
Hauser, of a Woyzeck, something that touches us with a recognition of ourselves? Is he not 'the thing itself', the very *a priori* of
man? Man in this vision is not the glorious survivor of a process
of natural selection but, on the contrary, a creature separate from
all other creatures by virtue of the utter openness, exposedness,
of the infinite vulnerability to which his organism and senses—
his 'useless' sensibility—have condemned him. And his capacity
for suffering, anguish and pain, is that not vastly in excess of,
irrelevant and even hostile to, the process of 'natural' selection?
Kaspar Hauser was a foundling; so, it seems incongruous to add,
was Tom Jones. The difference that lies between these two—
representatives of their respective national literatures—amounts to
almost the entire social dimension of man. The literary imagination of many German writers, from Feuerbach to Gutzkow to

---

[1] Born in 1812, Kaspar Hauser appeared mysteriously in Nuremberg in
1828, was said to have been brought up by an English nobleman, later by a
religious fanatic called G. F. Daumer. He was variously regarded as an impostor,
a German Prince, or l'Aiglon (Duke of Reichsstadt); the figure is in many ways
reminiscent of Boris Godunov (and thus contributes to Hofmannsthal's
Sigismund in *Der Turm*). He appears to have been murdered by exploiting
showmen, or to have taken his life, in Ansbach in 1833.

Wassermann, Trakl, Kafka, Hofmannsthal and Wolfgang Borchert, has been haunted by that figure—at once sinister and saintly: defenceless and accusing—on the shadowy margins of society, the man who entered the world only to leave it with a dagger in his back. And yet, when we have singled out the Kaspar Hauser theme as typical of a 'German' feeling for what the world is, we are recalled from the generalisation to another figure—no less 'typical' of *its* creator's feeling for the world— that of Poor Tom and his kin. The theme, after all, though Shakespeare never gives it so central a place, relates to no less than the condition of man. The *a priori* of which I spoke is no philosophical abstraction, but Lear's anguished cry to Poor Tom, 'Is man no more than this . . . thou art the thing itself; unaccommodated man is no more but such a poor, bare, forked animal. . . .'

Not all the speeches in *Woyzeck* are disconnected and incoherent. In contrast to Woyzeck's own violent and enigmatic utterances—as ashen grey stands in contrast to blood red—there is the fantastic coherence of rhetoric and rodomontade of the Doctor's physiological disquisitions, the Boothkeeper's exhibition of a calculating horse—

'. . . *Yes indeed, ladies and gentlemen, here's no stupid beast, here is a person, a human being, an animal human being—and yet* [the horse misbehaves] *an animal, a beast . . .*'[1]

—or the parody of a teleological sermon by a drunken journeyman—

'. . . *Why is man? Ah, why is man? Verily, verily I say unto you: what should the ploughman live on, the pargeter, the cobbler and the physician, if God had not created man?*'

None of these speeches[2] contains an ounce of truth or sympathy or

---

[1] There is an allusion to Woyzeck himself: when the Doctor experiments with his diet, he is reduced to a state of incontinence.

[2] There is a remarkable resemblance between these speeches and Lucky's monologue (in Beckett's *Waiting for Godot*, London 1956, pp. 42-4), 'Given the existence as uttered forth in the public / Works of Puncher and Wattmann. . . .'
The journeyman's sermon recalls Büchner's comment (in a letter to his parents, January 1833, *S.W.B.*, p. 524; *W.B.*, p. 203) on Lutheran sermons, and

insight, they are wordy lies against Woyzeck's inchoate truth. Their very rhetoric—the world's coherent discourse itself—is the harbinger of chaos, pain and death. To Woyzeck, crazed yet searching for reality, they are a meaningless rigmarole.

He is as solitary as any man can be in our world. The people around him rise up from the cracks in the earth's thin surface[1] as in a dream or a delirium. They stand in certain simple social relations to the 'hero', yet they involve him in nothing like a substantial plot, in no give-and-take of opposing wills. The Doctor (perhaps a sketch of Büchner's father) is a harsh satire on the 'scientific', that is, the mercilessly curious mind; the Captain, a sketch of hypocrisy and inadequate sympathy; the Drum-Major —'what a man! like a tree!'—a portrayal of physical violence and sexuality. Yet these three—outlined with astonishing dramatic energy and in the briefest possible way—are not Woyzeck's opponents and tormentors so much as the inescapable and—since he is defenceless—necessarily hostile facts of his situation. How bare can a man, 'the thing itself', be? Love is not of his essence, it is not part of his irreducible self. Marie, Woyzeck's mistress, a victim of degrading indigence but also of her instincts, is not the object of his love so much as the one hold Woyzeck has on existence, on life itself; the only thing, in the threatening void outside his tormented mind, that tells him that he *is*. Hardening her heart against him, she returns the Drum-Major's embraces, and Woyzeck, a good man and a good father to their child, murders her. The deed is done in a fit of jealousy, but the jealousy itself reaches to a still more primitive and more fundamental emotion. His is an act of self-assertion: the act of a man who must 'make a bruise or break an exit for his life': who must carve a notch upon the tree of experience before he is himself crucified on it: a man who must do *this* deed since no other, more positive, lies within his power.

his lampoon on Kant in *Leonce und Lena*, Act I, Scene 2; for the attack on teleology see below, p. 126.

[1] This is a recurrent image: see *Dantons Tod*, Act II (*S.W.B.* and *W.B.*, p. 38); *Woyzeck*, Act I first scene in *S.W.B.* (p. 145) and second in *W.B.* (p. 147), M. Jacobs (*ed. cit.*, p. 81) places the scene third; and repeatedly in *Lenz*.

Yet although he stands before us in this state of all but complete deprivation, Woyzeck is an individual nevertheless, sharply outlined against all others. Not so much by a distinct consciousness as by the capacity for feeling which his wandering consciousness reflects. Again—more briefly but also more powerfully than in *Dantons Tod*—the two contrasting imageries, of grey insensateness and of crimson pain—sustain and accompany the 'hero's' movement towards the reality of pain, the apprehension of which separates his hallucinative mind and injured heart from all around him. Andres, his fellow soldier, with his dull, mechanical reactions to everything—a mere human vegetable—provides a measure to Woyzeck's sentient soul. So does the Doctor with his laconic comments on the humiliating experiments he conducts on Woyzeck's body. But so too does Marie, whose last words before she succumbs to the Drum-Major are words of dead indifference. The Grandmother, a boothkeeper at the fair, a journeyman, a Jew who sells Woyzeck the knife he uses to murder his mistress, Marie's child which doesn't hear when told of its mother's death, a Policeman who sums up Woyzeck's passion, 'A good murder, a good honest murder, a lovely case. As nice a case as you could wish to see. We haven't had one like that in a long while . . .'—they all pass hurriedly before our eyes, figures in the icy void into which Woyzeck must reach, which he must somehow breach, and be it with a deed of violence:

[Waldsaum am Teich. Woyzeck, allein]: . . . *Das Messer? Wo is das Messer? Ich hab es da gelassen. Es verrät mich! Näher, noch näher! Was is das für ein Platz? Was hör ich? Es rührt sich was. Still.—Da in der Nähe. Marie? Ha, Marie! Still. Alles still! Was bist du so bleich, Marie? Was hast du eine rote Schnur um den Hals? Bei wem hast du das Halsband verdient mit deinen Sünden? Du warst schwarz davon, schwarz! Hab ich dich gebleicht? Was hängen deine Haare so wild? Hast du deine Zöpfe heut nicht geflochten? . . . Das Messer,*

[Woyzeck, alone, on the edge of the forest, near the pond]: *The knife? Where is the knife? This is where I left it. It will hang me! Closer, closer still! What place is this? What's that noise? Something moved. Sh! . . . close at hand. Marie? Ha, Marie. Hush. It's so quiet. Why are you so pale, Marie? Why have you got that red cord round your neck? Who paid you with that necklace for your sins? You were black with sins, black! Have I made you white now? Why does your hair hang down so wild? Didn't you plait your hair this morning? . . . The*

das Messer! Hab ich's? So! Leute— dort![1]	*knife, the knife! I've got it. Now. People! I hear them coming ... there!*

And the world, the empty void which engulfs Woyzeck? It is
described in the scene immediately preceding the murder: in a
fairy-tale the Grandmother tells the village children, the simplest
and surely also the saddest fairy-tale ever told:

Grossmutter. *Kommt, ihr kleinen Krabben!—Es war einmal ein arm Kind und hatt kein Vater und keine Mutter, war alles tot, und war niemand mehr auf der Welt. Alles tot, und es is hingangen und hat gesucht Tag und Nacht. Und weil auf der Erde niemand mehr war, wollt's in Himmel gehn, und der Mond guckt es so freundlich an; und wie es endlich zum Mond kam, war's ein Stück faul Holz. Und da is es zur Sonn gangen, und wie es zur Sonn kam, war's ein verwelkt Sonneblum. Und wie's zu den Sternen kam, waren's kleine goldne Mücken, die waren angesteckt, wie der Neuntöter sie auf die Schlehen steckt. Und wie's wieder auf die Erde wollt, war die Erde ein umgestürzter Hafen. Und es war ganz allein. Und da hat sich's hingesetzt und geweint, und da sitzt es noch und is ganz allein.*	Grandmother. *Come, you shrimps. Once upon a time there was a poor child that had no father and no mother, they were all dead, and there was no one left in the world. They were all dead, and so it set off and searched night and day. And as there was no one left on the earth it wanted to go up in the sky, and the moon seemed to have a friendly face. But when it came to the moon, it found it was a piece of rotten wood. So then it went to the sun, and when it came to the sun it was only a withered sunflower. And when it came to the stars they were little golden gnats, stuck on pins just as the shrike sticks them on the blackthorn. And when it wanted to go back to earth, the earth was just a pot that had been turned upside down. And it was all alone. So it sat down and cried, and it is still sitting there all alone.*
Woyzeck (erscheint). *Marie!*	Woyzeck (appears). *Marie!*
Marie (erschreckt). *Was is?*	Marie (frightened). *What is it?*
Woyzeck. *Marie, wir wollen gehn. 's is Zeit.*	Woyzeck. *Marie, let's go. It is time.*
Marie. *Wohin?*	Marie. *Where to?*
Woyzeck. *Weiss ich's?*	Woyzeck. *How do I know?*

---

[1] Whatever the sequence of the final scenes (I quote from M. Jacobs' text,
ed. cit., pp. 100–1 and 147), the appearance of a policeman suggests a trial and
perhaps (as in the case of the actual J. C. Woyzeck) execution. Alban Berg's
opera *Wozzeck* (see the English text by E. A. Blackall and V. Harford, London
1952) ends most poignantly with Marie's child being told of her death and riding
away on its hobbyhorse, uncomprehending.

7

Georg Büchner's sole work of narrative prose, the story, *Lenz*, was written in Strasbourg in the late autumn of 1835; as the periodical for which he intended it was banned before its first number reached the public, the *Novelle* was published two years after Büchner's death by Karl Gutzkow, his friend and literary mentor. Gutzkow received the manuscript, which has since been lost, from Minna Jaeglé, and the version that has come down to us is generally, but I think wrongly, regarded as an unfinished fragment. Critics have supported this view by referring to the story's abrupt opening, more often to an apparent break in the narrative, and to the absence—again only apparent—of a conclusion.[1] The view I wish to advance is that Büchner's creative capacity—his literary energy—is fully reflected in the *Novelle* as we have it; that he had nothing to add; and that the *Novelle*, though fragmentary in what one may call a typographical sense, is an achieved masterpiece.[2]

As for the abrupt *opening*, a few introductory hints will help the reader to place the events into which he is swiftly carried by the narrative; but before supplying these preliminaries I would suggest that their absence is not as adventitious as it may seem. The very opening raises the question of the continuity of experience: in our search for the truth about man, in our recital of a lifetime's stigmata, how far back can we go? How illuminating are our *whys* and *begats*? To these general questions the artist has only a specific answer, and each time a different one; thus here the story's dramatic first paragraph all but drowns out the question *why*, and transforms it into the assertion *that*.

[1] And of course the chaotic state of the MS. from which Gutzkow printed the story; as in *Woyzeck*, Büchner seems to have written out no fair copy (see *S.W.B.*, pp. 678 ff.). Thus the first version (as in K. E. Franzos, *S.W.*, Frankfurt 1879) prints the first 4½ pages, not inappropriately, without a paragraph.

[2] H. Pongs ('Ein Beitrag zum Dämonischen im Biedermeier', in *Dichtung und Volkstum*, Vol. XXXVI, 1935, p. 250), is the only critic to interpret the *Novelle* not as a fragment but as a finished work. His article is vitiated by a confusion typical of the age in which it was written—the confusion between pathological, 'dæmonic' and religious motivations.

In one of his scientific papers Büchner attacks the 'teleological method' in physiology ('If the eye is to function properly, the cornea must be kept moist, and this makes the lachrymal gland necessary. The latter exists in order to keep the eye moist, etc.'), and points to the *'progressus ad infinitum'* in which every *why*-question is involved. He proposes to replace it by a 'philosophical method', according to which 'the physical being of each individual' should be seen as a 'manifestation of a fundamental law, a law of beauty, which produces the highest forms in conformity with the simplest plans and outlines'.[1] In the context of Büchner's science this remains a mere suggestion. Yet is there anything to show that he was aware of its implications for his literary work? That he thought this 'law of beauty' relevant to it? In his literary work, certainly, a given state of mind is presented now without antecedents, now without consequences—at all events without the consolations of causality. Clearly, this literary practice springs from Büchner's experience of life as a thing inconsequential and incomplete, rather than from a conscious intention to shape his work according to a 'law of beauty'. But the idea of such a law is taken up in the *Novelle* itself: once in a conversation Lenz has with Oberlin, when he speaks of a feeling of harmony with the natural world, and a second time when Oberlin suggests to Kaufmann that certain 'statuesque groups' and 'images' in a mountainous landscape, which to Lenz represent true art, are themselves manifestations of 'infinite beauty'.[2] However, these emotions and this insight are not accessible to the hero of Büchner's story. Lenz sees beauty informing a world he cannot enter; the images which are formed in the world around him are perfect just because he knows himself to be excluded from their perfection. Büchner shares and exceeds Lenz's knowledge and experience: if the world were not the thing of pain his truthfulness shows it to be, it would indeed be governed by a law of beauty. But since Büchner's truthfulness is transfixed into image and poetry at a

---

[1] See his inaugural lecture at Zürich, 'On the cranial nerves' in *S.W.B.*, p. 355; *W.B.*, p. 187. This 'philosophical method' clearly owes a good deal to Goethe's morphological studies.

[2] *S.W.B.* and *W.B.*, pp. 90-3.

point far removed from elementary order, let alone from a law of harmony; since, further, his literary self-consciousness is casual and limited, there is nothing to suggest that he ever saw his own work as a 'manifestation' of such a 'law' (or that he derived any consolation from his achievement). On the other hand, *our* understanding is enriched by his notion to the extent that 'the law' of which he speaks helps us to silence the fretful questions of causality. Why does Danton understand his situation and his friends do not? What has made Woyzeck the man he is? Why is Lenz mad? The only answer we ever have is that, like Leonce, each man is what he is 'merely because he is'.[1] And the intensity of the description of what he is—of his bare being: of 'the thing itself'—renders all else irrelevant; 'the form', as Hofmannsthal once remarked, 'disposes of the question'. But 'the form', the narrative mode of *Lenz*, brings us back to 'the law': Oberlin's description of the 'statuesque groups' and static 'images' sums up the impression we have that the people in the story are transfixed, that Lenz himself is a man imprisoned in his world.

So much, then, for the story's abrupt opening. The *break* in its narrative presents no genuine problem. There is no reason to suppose that it would be noticeable to a reader who had no means of comparing the passage where the break occurs with the text Büchner was drawing on at this point; that a further recital of Lenz's actions could do more to clarify the story's theme.[2] And, lastly, the story's *conclusion* too, as we have it, strikes me as magnificently complete, and though critics seem to think otherwise, none has ever given any hint of what more could possibly be said when Büchner reaches the end of Lenz's passion. That the historical Lenz lived on for another fourteen years, recovering his sanity (though not his creative power) for long stretches of time, eventually to die in the streets of Moscow, does nothing to impair the realistic truth and conclusiveness of Büchner's conclusion.

---

[1] See above, p. 105.

[2] *S.W.B.*, pp. 681–5, and *W.B.*, pp. 257–61 quote the relevant passage from Pastor Oberlin's diary. It merely continues the list of Lenz's tribulations; the diary contains none of the emphatic comments or natural descriptions which make for the greatness of Büchner's *Novelle*.

Lenz is a biographical *Novelle* in the sense that it is concerned with
a certain period—which Büchner's narrative compels us to regard
as crucial—in the life of the *Sturm-und-Drang* poet and dramatist,
Jakob Michael Reinhold Lenz (1751–92). Büchner quotes from a
poem of Lenz's in a letter to Minna Jaeglé dated March 1834, and
he may well have read some of Lenz's dramas and his observations on Shakespeare much earlier, in Tieck's edition of 1828.
But it was in 1835, during his first year as an exile in Strasbourg,
that Büchner's interest in the poet's life was quickened. Pastor
Jaeglé, Minna's father, had been a friend of Pastor Oberlin's, and
had preached a sermon at his graveside in 1826. Oberlin it was
who had given shelter to Lenz during his wanderings in the
Vosges mountains in the winter of 1777–8. In 1831 Ehrenfried
Stöber had published a *Vie de Frédérick Oberlin*, and in 1835 his
son August,[1] one of Büchner's closest friends, gave him access to
the diaries on which the biographical memoir was based. For
Büchner the life which he pieced together from these diaries had
an immediate personal significance. More directly than any other
of his writings, *Lenz* is the issue of an act of self-identification.

J. M. R. Lenz's entire life—but in particular its early part—
is the life of a typical representative of the chaotic generation of
the 1770's; or rather, it is the life of a man who, perhaps more
sinned against than sinning, sought to live what others wrote and
thus avoided. His 'alternating moods of despair and enthusiasm,
irony and fantasy, satire and veneration'[2] all combine to obscure
not only the question of his sanity but even some of the facts of
his biography; Goethe begins an *aide-mémoire* on him by calling

[1] August Stöber himself edited extracts from these diaries in 1831 and again
in 1839, after Georg Büchner's death; in the latter, which relate to the Lenz
episode, are recounted some of the events which Büchner left out of his
narrative.
[2] R. Pascal, *German Sturm und Drang*, Manchester 1953, p. 32.

him 'a strange, almost indefinable individual'.[1] Having abandoned
his theological studies in Königsberg, Lenz arrived at Strasbourg
in 1771, aged twenty, as tutor to two Baltic barons, the brothers
von Kleist. A radical egalitarian in politics, he despised his job of
'Hofmeister', yet apart from achieving some literary success (but
no solvency) in 1774-5, he never found another livelihood. He
joined Goethe's Strasbourg circle and soon outdid all in their
worship of Shakespeare. He conceived a passionate admiration—
all *à la mode*—for Goethe, who very probably responded; and if
the tone of Lenz's addresses and letters strikes us as over-enthusi-
astic (as it did Goethe thirty-five years later), so, after all, does the
tone of Goethe's own or Herder's writings of that time. But from
its very beginning Lenz's passion appears to have been complex,
tainted with jealousy and feelings of inferiority. It is true that in
several of his works Lenz imitated Goethe; that in his travels,
affairs and friendships, he followed, as a man obsessed, in his
friend's tracks. Yet it is no less true that Lenz's own poetic talents
were not, to begin with, very far inferior to Goethe's; and that
Lenz's *Observations on the Theatre* are as original as Goethe's
Shakespeare essay. The emotional temper and creative aspirations of the two men who in 1771 met in close friendship, perhaps
in mutual love, were not, after all, very different. But while this
period was probably the most fruitful in Lenz's life, in Goethe's
it marked merely a beginning. What Lenz lacked—probably long
before he ever met Goethe—was the sort of purposeful strength
of personality that ultimately distinguished Goethe from all his

---

[1] *Jubiläumsausgabe*, Vol. XXV, p. 223; this hostile note was not intended for
publication. The portrait in Book XI of *Dichtung und Wahrheit* (Vol. XXIV,
pp. 57 ff.) is rather more friendly, while the later reference (Book XIII, in Vol.
XXIV, pp. 183–7) is once again lacking in charity and patience. It is, incidentally, a strange and chilling fact that Goethe's description of Lenz seems to fit
Büchner as we know him from engravings and from the data of the police
warrant: 'He was short but had a neat figure [Goethe writes of Lenz], a delight-
ful little head, charming in form, with slightly snub features, and blonde
hair....' At least one independent description of Büchner as a student (*S.W.B.*,
p. 633, *W.B.*, p. 279) also corresponds to Goethe's summary: 'The only word
I can think of to describe [Büchner's] cast of mind is the English word *whimsical*,
which, as the dictionary shows, subsumes under one notion many peculiarities.'

fellow-rebels. This strength lay in Goethe's intuitive understanding of the nature and direction of his own 'dæmon', his genius;
and to this was allied his capacity—not lacking in ruthlessness—
to act on his understanding. When he accuses Lenz of 'self-
tormenting introspection', the charge is borne out by what we
know of Lenz's life. It is not surprising that Goethe should make
it, for his own capacity for abandoning introspection, and indeed
any 'experience', beyond the point where it contributed to his
poetry, is a source of constant wonder to his admirers and of
occasional embarrassment to his apologists.

   The more biographers have written about Goethe's 'Sesenheim
Idyll'[1]—his love-affair, in the summer of 1771, with Friederike
Brion, the daughter of a village pastor in the vicinity of Strasbourg
—the less idyllic its conclusion appears to be. About Goethe's
enigmatic departure from Sesenheim we know little more than
that his own description of it comes under the heading of *Dichtung*
rather than *Wahrheit*, that it was sudden and to Friederike unexpected. Ten months later Lenz called at the Brions' house in
the company of one of the Kleists (with whom he shared garrison
quarters in a neighbouring fortress), and fell violently in love with
Friederike. Goethe's suggestion that in seeking out Friederike
Lenz was really engaged in some evil farce is based on an odd confusion of dates. Against it there is the evidence of Lenz's letters
to his friends and family as well as the poems he addressed to
Friederike (it speaks for their quality that the authorship of some
of them was for a long time ascribed to Goethe). All this suggests
that Lenz's love was in no way less sincere than Goethe's own had
been, and that Friederike herself may well have requited his

---

   [1] The whole issue is bedevilled by irate and partly scurrilous controversy;
there appear to be at least thirty-five books and articles, dealing wholly, or in
large part, with the 'idyll'. I have here followed the most recent and (as it
seems to me) most sober account, by S. Ley, *Goethe und Friederike*, Bonn 1947.
However, the legend of a 'happy ending' dies hard; although all the known
facts speak against it, the 1954 ed. of *D.N.B.* still repeats it. But the biographers'
curiosity, though irritating, is less than reprehensible if we bear in mind that
Goethe himself met it more than half-way, partly by making *Dichtung und
Wahrheit* the amalgam of truth, half-truth and fiction it is, partly by his habit
of collecting only *certain* documents relating to his life.

feelings. The end of Lenz's affair is obscure (and so, incidentally, is the end of Goethe's). With no clear idea of what to do, Lenz left Sesenheim in August 1772 for Strasbourg, where eventually he threw up his job as a tutor. And in April 1776, six months after Goethe, he arrived in Weimar. He had vast literary plans; he came to Weimar in hot pursuit of a lady-in-waiting, an acquaintance of Goethe's who appears hardly to have known Lenz and who anyhow turned out to have become engaged shortly before he reached the town; but what most drew Lenz to Weimar, now with the force of an obsession, was Goethe himself. For weeks on end he stayed on Charlotte von Stein's estate, teaching her family English, engaging in literary quarrels with Wieland, reading aloud to the young Duke, hoping for a court preferment. . . . In Weimar Lenz's every undertaking, blighted with the curse of imitation, ends in a minor catastrophe. His every action, drained of strength and independent purpose, turns ineffectual. His every creative impulse, its realisation anticipated by the young lion, wastes into silly, self-destructive intrigue. A few days after Lenz's arrival Goethe, who had just become one of the four members of the Duchy's governing council, notes in his diary that Lenz has been guilty of some 'asinine act' or other. Six months later Lenz was expelled from Weimar by ducal edict, possibly because of a lampoon on Goethe and Frau von Stein.[1] And from now on the sequence of disasters hardly breaks. Leaving Weimar on 1 December 1776, he went to stay with Goethe's sister Cornelia and her husband J. G. Schlosser in Emmendingen on the Rhine. He promptly conceived a passion for her, but appears to have had enough sense to leave before disclosing it to the Schlossers. In the spring of 1777 we find him staying with Lavater and other friends in Zürich and Basle, then again in the Swiss Alps. At the house of his friend Christoph Kaufmann of Winterthur he

---

[1] See J. Froitzheim, *Lenz, Goethe und Cleophe Fibich von Strassburg*, Strasbourg 1888, p. 15. Against this, Franz Blei (in his ed. of Lenz's *Gesammelte Schriften*, Vol. V, München 1910, p. 391) believes that what incensed Goethe was a passage from Lenz's fragment *Zum Weinen oder Weil ihr's so haben wollt*, in G.S., Vol. III, pp. 294–6; cf. also p. 471), where Goethe, in a conversation with Lenz, is made to boast of several particularly sordid actions.

received news of Cornelia Schlosser's death in childbirth (7.vii. 1777), to which reference is made in Büchner's *Novelle*. This news brought on an attack, probably the first, of insanity; it was so violent that Lenz had to be put in chains. When he had some- what recovered, Kaufmann sent him to a friend of his, Pastor Oberlin, who was in charge of a philadelphian community in Waldersbach (Büchner's 'Waldbach') in the Steintal, a little village in the foothills of the Vosges, thirty-five miles south-west of Strasbourg.[1] But instead of going directly to Waldersbach, Lenz proceeded from Winterthur to Strasbourg[2] and thence due north, to Sesenheim. What did he want of Friederike? Did he intend to take up again an affair that had ended five years earlier? Or—chaos turning into sordidness—did he come to extract from Friederike Goethe's letters to her, in order to blackmail his idol with them? Two years later, in September 1779, Goethe, who had so far not revisited Sesenheim, returned there for a last time. He called on Friederike who, he claims, told him of Lenz's false- hood and extortions; they appear, according to Goethe, to have talked of little else. Yet since she cannot have confused the two dates—1772 and 1777—of Lenz's visits, as Goethe does in his account of their meeting, the value of that account is doubtful. Goethe's own last visit to Sesenheim is no easier to explain than Lenz's; the one reason for it that we can find—and it may not be the true reason—is Goethe's fear that his letters to Friederike had come into the possession of a man whom by that time he thought capable of blackmail. (How much importance he attached to these letters even half a century later we know from other sources.[3]) If therefore Goethe's imputation can be neither sustained nor refuted, the true reason, sane or otherwise, for Lenz's arrival in

---

[1] In the course of a walking tour through the Vosges in July 1833 (*S.W.B.*, pp. 527-9; *W.B.*, pp. 206-8), which took him as far south as St Amarin, Büchner may have passed one or other of the villages mentioned in the *Novelle*, though we have no indications whether he knew of Lenz's journey through the mountains before reading Oberlin's diary in 1835.

[2] H. Düntzer, *Friederike von Sesenheim im Lichte der Wahrheit*, Stuttgart 1893, p. 121.

[3] See S. Ley, *op. cit.*, p. 65.

Sesenheim in December 1777 remains obscure, and so does the
nature of his feelings for Friederike. The account we have of his
behaviour there, on the other hand, sounds only too convincing.
At Christmas he delivered a sermon in the vicarage. At the end
of it, identifying himself with Lear and Friederike with Cordelia,
he pronounced judgement of damnation upon her, the world,
and himself.[1] The visit ended abruptly. In Friederike's presence
Lenz tried to take his own life (the attempt is described by Goethe
as 'ridiculous'), then wandered away, into the Vosges mountains,
reaching Oberlin's house at Waldersbach on 10 January 1778.[2]

Setting out on the present chapter, I hardly thought I would find
myself tussling with recalcitrant and obscure biographical facts.
But however incomplete my conclusions, they should adequately
determine the point at which Büchner breaks into the alien continuity of Lenz's experience; and they should also give substance
to the claim[3] that Büchner's *Novelle* is the issue of an act of
imaginative self-identification. What Büchner himself sees in the
figure of Lenz is a mind on the point of crossing the boundary-
line of sanity, a spirit before its annihilation. Only when Oberlin
asks after Lenz's father and family does Büchner hint—through
Lenz's terror—at the source of conflict in Lenz's mind. Goethe
himself is never mentioned in the story, indeed it is uncertain how
much Büchner knew of Lenz's attachment to him. I have dwelt
on that relationship because, so it seems to me, Büchner sub-
consciously identifies it with the conflict in his own soul. But to

---

[1] J. Froitzheim, *Friederike von Sesenheim: nach geschichtlichen Quellen*, Gotha
1893, p. 91, here supported by S. Ley, *op. cit.*, pp. 85 ff.

[2] After Lenz's brief stay at Waldersbach, he was brought under guard to
Strasbourg, then went to stay with the widowed Schlosser in Emmendingen
(O. F. Gruppe, *Reinhold Lenz, Leben und Werke*, Berlin 1861, pp. 114 ff.); later
still, at Duke Karl August's expense, he was put in the care of a cobbler. In
1779 his family at last sent for him and he returned to Riga, at first apparently
sane. In St Petersburg and Moscow he had to fall back on tutoring. He died in
the street in Moscow in 1792, aged forty-one years.

[3] See above, pp. 88 f.

speak of this identification is to mention merely the occasion which gave rise to the *Novelle*. The conclusions of biographical enquiry like those of psychological analysis lead us to the threshold of a work of art, considerations of the cathartic effects of composition begin beyond it. The work itself, occasioned by living experience and issuing into it, is as a thing transfixed between the exigencies of life. In this sense it is true that, whatever its biographical origins and implications, the vision that Büchner bodies forth through his image of Lenz's alienated mind obeys that 'law of beauty' of which he speaks in his scientific writings but which he probably did not see manifest in his own literary work.

8

I am not mad: I would to heaven I were!
For then 'tis like I should forget myself:
O! if I could, what grief should I forget.
(King John)

Den 20. Jänner ging Lenz durchs Gebirg. Die Gipfel und hohen Bergflächen im Schnee, die Täler hinunter graues Gestein, grüne Flächen, Felsen und Tannen. Es war nasskalt; das Wasser rieselte die Felsen hinunter und sprang über den Weg. Die Äste der Tannen hingen schwer herab in die feuchte Luft. Am Himmel zogen graue Wolken, aber alles so dicht—und dann dampfte der Nebel herauf und strich schwer und feucht durch das Gesträuch, so träg, so plump. Er ging gleichgültig weiter, es lag ihm nichts am Weg, bald auf-, bald abwärts. Müdigkeit spürte er keine, nur war es ihm manchmal unangenehm, dass er nicht auf dem Kopf gehn konnte. Anfangs drängte es ihm in der Brust, wenn das Gestein so wegsprang, der graue Wald sich unter ihm schüttelte und der Nebel die Formen bald verschlang, bald die gewaltigen Glieder

On 20 January Lenz went over the mountains. The peaks and high slopes covered with snow, grey scree all the way down the valleys, green plains, rocks and fir trees. It was cold and humid; water trickled down the rocks and gushed across the path. The branches of the firs were hanging heavily in the damp air. Grey clouds were moving across the sky, but all was so dense—and then the mist rose slow and clammy from the earth through the undergrowth, sluggishly and dully. He walked on, indifferent to everything, not minding which way he went, up or down. He felt no tiredness, only sometimes he found it a nuisance not to be able to walk on his head. At first there was a stifling pressure in him when the scree rolled underfoot, when the grey forest shook under him and the mist now swallowed up its outlines, now revealed its mighty limbs; there was

halb enthüllte; es drängte in ihm, er
suchte nach etwas, wie nach ver-
lornen Träumen, aber er fand nichts.
Es war ihm alles so klein, so nahe,
so nass; er hätte die Erde hinter den
Ofen setzen mögen. Er begriff nicht,
dass er so viel Zeit brauchte, um
einen Abhang hinunter zu klimmen,
einen fernen Punkt zu erreichen; er
meinte, er müsse alles mit ein paar
Schritten ausmessen können. Nur
manchmal, wenn der Sturm das
Gewölk in die Täler warf und es den
Wald herauf dampfte, und die
Stimmen an den Felsen wach
wurden, bald wie fern verhallende
Donner und dann gewaltig heran-
brausten, in Tönen, als wollten sie
in ihrem wilden Jubel die Erde
besingen, und die Wolken wie
wilde, wiehernde Rosse heran-
sprengten, und der Sonnenschein
dazwischen durchging und kam und
sein blitzendes Schwert an den
Schneeflächen zog, so dass ein helles,
blendendes Licht über die Gipfel in
die Täler schnitt; oder wenn der
Sturm das Gewölk abwärts trieb und
einen lichtblauen See hineinriss und
dann der Wind verhallte und tief
unten aus den Schluchten, aus den
Wipfeln der Tannen wie ein
Wiegenlied und Glockengeläute her-
aufsummte, und am tiefen Blau ein
leises Rot hinaufklomm und kleine
Wölkchen auf silbernen Flügeln
durchzogen, und alle Berggipfel,
scharf und fest, weit über das Land
hin glänzten und blitzten—riss es
ihm in der Brust, er stand, keuchend,
den Leib vorwärts gebogen, Augen
und Mund weit offen, er meinte, er
müsse den Sturm in sich ziehen,
alles in sich fassen, er dehnte sich aus

an urge in him, he sought for something, as though for lost dreams, but
found nothing. The whole world
seemed so small, so close at hand, so
wet: he would have liked to put the
earth to dry behind the stove. He
could not understand why he needed
so much time to get to the bottom of
a slope, to reach a distant point; he
thought that a few paces should be
enough to cover any distance. Only
occasionally, when the stormwind
hurled the clouds into the valleys and
vapour rose from the forest, and the
voices on the rocky cliffs awoke, like
thunder dying away in the distance
one moment and then again mightily
roaring in musical notes as though to
laud the earth in their wild exulta-
tion, and the clouds came galloping
up towards him like wild horses
whinnying, and through it all the
sunshine came and went and drew its
glittering sword over the snowy
slopes, so that a bright dazzling light
cut across the peaks into the valleys;
or when the stormwind drove the
clouds apart and tore open a blue lake
of light in them, and then the wind
died away and the sound of it floated
back from the depths of the ravines,
from the tops of the fir trees, like a
lullaby, like bells ringing, and in the
deep blue a shade of pink appeared
and cloudlets passed across it on
silver wings, and all the mountain-
tops, sharply defined, shone far out
over the countryside flashing in light
—then he felt a pain in his breast,
stood gasping, his body bent forward,
eyes and mouth wide open, it seemed
to him that he must draw the stormwind into himself, contain everything
in him, he stretched himself out and

und lag über der Erde, er wühlte sich in das All hinein, es war eine Lust, die ihm wehe tat; oder er stand still und legte das Haupt ins Moos und schloss die Augen halb, und dann zog es weit von ihm, die Erde wich unter ihm, sie wurde klein wie ein wandelnder Stern und tauchte sich in einen brausenden Strom, der seine klare Flut unter ihm zog.	*lay covering the earth, he wanted to confound himself with the Universe, it was an ecstasy that hurt him; or he would be still and lay his head on the moss and half shut his eyes, and then everything receded from him, the earth moved from under him, it became small as a wandering star and plunged into a raging torrent whose clear water was rushing past below him.*

This is how the *Novelle* opens. As for the 'story' which follows, it is simple and direct. Lenz arrives at Oberlin's house, stays with him and his family for several days, perhaps rather more than a week. He goes into the mountains several times; receives a visit from his friend Kaufmann; on hearing that a girl named Friederike has died in a neighbouring village, he goes to her house and tries to resurrect her; at Oberlin's invitation he delivers a sermon in the village chapel; tries to commit suicide; and is finally taken away, quiet, resigned, insane.

The value and effect of ellipsis, as of all literary devices, depends on the proximate context and on the ultimate whole to which it belongs. In Grillparzer's hand it served the purpose of laconic detachment and understatement. In Büchner's the effect is very nearly the opposite. The elliptical omission of verbs, striking enough in its effect of tension and immediacy, is not the most remarkable of Büchner's devices. More disturbing is the absence of preliminary qualifications, explanations and connections, of connecting particles, whereby the coherence of a brief and precise nature-study is disrupted. The natural description goes side by side with an evocation of the deranged mind's landscape, but the relationship between the two is as unsteady as the mind itself. Now the natural scene is described in its cold and independent reality, now again the meaning of that reality for the mind is emotively evoked—but there are no transitions. The effect of the ellipsis is to insinuate that what Lenz feels and sees in the grip of his state of alienation is the truth about the world.

The state itself is an acute form of schizophrenia, the mental disease involving a disjunction of standards of judgement and even perception, a sundering of thoughts, feelings and reactions from commonly recognisable goals; involving, above all, the juxtaposing of a shored-up inner world against the intrusion, experienced necessarily as hostile, of an outer world. Yet although the description of this state of mind is the most detailed and impressive we have in German, perhaps in any literature, the interest of Büchner's *Novelle* for psychopathology is incidental to his aim and achievement, if only because his concern with psychic causality is so limited. Nor do I wish to suggest that Büchner's identification with the hero of his story, whom he depicts as a schizophrenic, proves that he himself was, or inclined towards being, mad. The artist's power of empathy is greater than those deficient in that quality are likely to credit. Nor is empathy the mode in which the whole story is cast. For just as the natural landscape is presented now in its cold neutrality, now through the eyes of the deranged Lenz, so are Kaufmann, Oberlin and his family, and the people of the village; and so, above all, is Lenz himself. The detailed and intimate *in*sights into his mind are given to us at certain points in the story—more and more frequently as it draws to its end—as the delusions of a madman, while at other points the distance between narration and subject is suspended, and Lenz's vision itself is thrust at us with all the intensity and persuasiveness of a *true* vision of the world.

What Büchner does here seems to me altogether more telling than what we learn from a psychopathological study. It is reminiscent of Shakespeare's use of such figures as the truthsaying Fool, or Poor Tom, or the deranged Lear himself; it is what Shakespeare does, very briefly, with Ophelia's song; what Goethe with consummate mastery of gradation, achieves through the figure of Gretchen in the final scene of *Faust I*; what Dostoyevsky does on many occasions, especially in *The Possessed*. In all these instances the mad mind is used as a searching beam of light thrown on the world in which we all live, on the world which we take to be the very measure of our sanity. The idea of using the mind of the deranged in such a way is ancient lore, and in Greek drama especially, where the madness is shown to be divine in origin, its effect is not only to *tell* but also to put into jeopardy our plans, even to throw annihilating doubt on the substantiality of our experience. For the very question, But is Cassandra mad? amounts to no less. Her insanity, in the *Agamemnon*, is used primarily for a prophetic purpose rather than to make out the truth of the present situation, yet she *sees* more than all around her, and her 'madness' turns out to be merely their disbelief. In *Lear*, as in the Gretchen of *Faust I*, prophecy and present truth are combined. And in all these instances a transgression against the order— divine, moral or natural—of the world is more or less fully intimated as the cause of the strange gift. Yet with the Moderns the further implication is at hand that to see the truth—the truth either of what will be or of what is—to see the truth of the human situation, is disabling to the human spirit. Many examples from German literature could be cited to show that there the disablement, and the peculiar gift of insight which it denotes, are often taken not as exceptional states but as something like man's 'natural' condition. The issue there is an essential incommensurability between man's vital forces—his capacity for living—and his cognitive powers—his capacity for knowing. And this awareness is present, in various degrees of explicitness, in writers in other respects as different from each other as J. C. Günther and Kleist, in Nietzsche, Hölderlin and Trakl. Something of this awareness Büchner shares. The emergent conclusion of *Dantons Tod* and *Woyzeck*—that the proof of existence is its undoing— belongs to a catastrophic interpretation of life which these other writers elaborate from other points of view. In *Lenz* the situation is similar. Again pain and suffering are the means by which a man tries to grapple himself to the hard, icy rock of existence, to the common world and, failing, physically survives into spiritual annihilation. On this note, to which the comfort of 'where there is life, there is hope' is irrelevant, the tale closes. The world, or rather the earth herself, survives; but the hero has become a stranger to her.

In some ways the style of the opening section of *Lenz* resembles the style of Kleist's *Novellen*; and especially that strangely disconnected sentence[1] in which Lenz's madness is mentioned for

---

[1] See above, p. 134: '. . . only sometimes he found it a nuisance. . . .'

the first time reminds us of more than one opening paragraph in Kleist's prose. Yet there is a significant difference between the two writers; to single it out is to understand why, in spite of all, Kleist's work still to some extent belongs to the German classical tradition, whereas Büchner's does not. The idea of using the deranged mind for throwing a beam of truth on reality is one which we find in Kleist's work frequently enough; certainly he allows such characters a freer rein, he gives them a more nearly central position, than Goethe thought proper; and their effect on action and surrounding world is much more negative, destructive, than it ever is in Goethe. Yet in Kleist too—and here his tales differ radically from *Lenz*—there is action, plot and surrounding world—there is human *conflict*. And conflict, however devastating its issue, presupposes some common platform on which it is enacted, presupposes resistance, and thus a reality somehow shared by the antagonists: locked in mortal conflict, they yet feel each other. This reality of the outer world—which in most of Kleist's stories is a social reality—is not left unchallenged; it *is* highly problematic; and it does not amount to the realists' *donnée*. But it determines, or at least co-determines, the issue of the conflict, the story's plot. And in this sense Kleist's *Novellen* are radically different from *Lenz*, whose 'conflict' is enacted in solitude.

The absence of a plot here is not adventitious; to explain it by a lack of inventive power in the writer is only to beg a further question. More to the point is the recognition that 'you can only create if you can *care*'.[1] To invest creative energy in 'plot' and 'story' is to accept as meaningful, and care for, the *social* sphere in which alone a plot's convolutions and proliferations are enacted. It is to accept the world as at the very least susceptible of a common interpretation (and at the other, the Somerset Maugham, end of the scale the world is identified with an interpretation which is 'common' indeed). Where value is so much a matter of the soul and the solitary spirit, there the need for plot and invention is easily satisfied; and there the invocation of value or of doom is liable to be peculiarly direct, relatively unencumbered

---

[1] George Orwell, 'Charles Dickens', in *Critical Essays*, London 1946, p. 53.

(as it appears from that point of view) by the diversities of intrigue, deception and conflict of interests. There is of course a danger of exaggeration in my line of argument. No story is ever without a 'story'; no *Novelle* wholly without a plot; no solitude without an encompassing world; no situation wholly asocial. There *is* a social world from which Lenz has fled, which is present as a threat even in his solitary wanderings; there is, too, the cosy Biedermeier world of the parsonage, from which he knows himself to be excluded. But when we compare these with the embattled countryside and pillaged towns which defy Kleist's frenzied Michael Kohlhaas, we are aware of a radical difference. And our conclusion is again a *ne-plus-infra*: Lenz's isolation is as complete as a literary composition, in itself *also* a social act, appears capable of conveying.

What Büchner does, then, is to *use* his hero's insane mind, to ask what *it* is like, but also what the world, seen through it and in unstable contact with it, is like. And thus he suggests (I shall return to this 'suggestion') that, to the extent that the world is the thing of pain and suffering it is, such a mind is in a unique position to 'understand' it, to come close to it. Of causes (I have dwelt on this point) Büchner has little to say. Twice, very briefly, Lenz speaks of Friederike (*ipsissimis verbis*, if Oberlin's account is literal); once, when claiming that he himself has killed her, he seems to be confusing her with Goethe's sister Cornelia (with whose death, furthermore, Lenz was in no way connected). But so brief, so obscure are these hints that it would overstrain their meaning and import in the story were we to take them as explanations of the madness. Rather are we intended to see his stay in Sesenheim, which precedes his wanderings in the mountains, as the 'precipitating factor' of the disease, the last drop that overfills the cup of his tortured mind. Farther than that Büchner does not take us, Leonce's tautological circle is not broken; Lenz sees the world the way he does because he is mad, and he is mad because . . . But this means that we must look for the *Novelle*'s coherence not in its external causality, nor even in the sequence of its events, but (as in Büchner's other works) in the picture of what Lenz is and sees: in the 'statuesque image', into which his experience is transfixed; for thus, and not in terms of a causal *nacheinander*,

Lenz himself, in his discussion with Kaufmann,[1] describes a work of art:

> Sometimes one would like to be a Medusa's head, so as to be able to transform such a group [of girls he saw sitting on a rock] into stone. . . . They got up, the beauty of the group was destroyed. But the way they then descended [into the valley] between the rocks—again, it was another image.

The transfixed image of *Lenz*, this panorama of an alien world, is itself so convincingly done, is so powerful in its suggestion, its insinuation into the reader's mind, that from it alone the story's illumination proceeds, without a single line of comment or explicit injunction.

What is here proposed is indeed a revaluation of experience. Through Lenz's vision Büchner throws into doubt our common and stable cause-and-effect interpretation of the world. Furthermore he makes us recognise the worldly, sympathetic understanding of Lenz's friend and hosts as inadequate (like Grillparzer's narrator, they represent also 'our' understanding), and contrasts it with Lenz's 'understanding', which (like Jacob's) is both strange, alienated, and yet also closer than theirs to the predicament of man in his solitude. And so, finally, we accept Lenz's alien manner of apprehending reality as a contrast but also as a challenge, allowing it to influence our apprehension of the world and to to make it more sensitive. Yet all this is done without a word of comment. The recognitions to which we are led are derived from nothing but the immense energy and vigour of Büchner's art, from the narrator's abandonment to his hero's alien world. This he 'creates', for this he 'cares'.

Büchner does not say, or suggest, that Lenz is sane. What he does suggest, or rather show, is the dark side of the world. And though this dark side is revealed to us through the disease (whereas it would remain all but hidden to the normal and sane mind),

---

[1] *S.W.B.*, p. 88; *W.B.*, p. 93; see also above, p. 103. G. Anders (in his chapter, 'The Medusa's Head', in *Kafka: Pro and Contra*, London 1961) ascribes to Kafka's style the same qualities.

yet it is a part of our world. For every one of Lenz's moods and
actions, every one of his *symptoms*, is by itself—though not in the
totality of presentation which Büchner achieves—kin and cousin
to our apprehensions; mad, Cassandra is our sister. But these
piecemeal kinships with our individual moods are merely the
first footholds of our attention. What, then, of the total picture?
What pleasure is there in reading the story of a deranged mind?
Lenz is a work of art by virtue of making the dark realities of
experience into an imaginative whole. The totality (the 'exaggeration') that emerges from our reading of it yields no precept; and
as a thing to learn from, a clinical study may well be superior. It
is an image of life; it is entire in itself, but not the entirety of life;
a clarifying of an entire mode of experience which, but for that
image, will remain obscure and unattended. Coming to us as an
illumination, it also comes to us as knowledge (not of a disease
but of an extreme in man); and knowledge achieved and uncontentious is also a delight.

9

To judge by a recent study of the disease,[1] the clinical picture
Büchner presents is remarkably accurate and fairly complete.
The disintegration of a whole personality into a variety of actions
whose co-ordination is either entirely inward (and thus inaccessible) or absent is seen in Lenz's inability to concentrate on an
argument, respond intelligently and appropriately ('in conversation he frequently stuttered, an indescribable fear possessed him,
he had lost the end of his sentence'), to act with a set purpose
('he had to begin with the simplest things in order to come to his

---

[1] See M. Sakel, *Schizophrenia*, London 1959, especially Chapters V–VII. The
late Dr Sakel was a pioneer of insulin shock treatment for the disease. Believing that recent emphasis on psychological explanations and treatment have led
to a neglect of medical investigation, the author is predominantly concerned
with the physiological and chemical changes which occur in the course of the
disease. Thus his entire approach is one which Büchner himself would have
favoured. It is significant but not surprising that Sakel's book, which does not
mention Büchner or Lenz, should throw more light on the *Novelle* than do
J. S. White's remarks.

senses'). Apathy and indifference, accompanied by states of suicidal boredom ('Yes, vicar, you see: boredom, boredom! Oh, it's so boring! Really, I no longer know what to say. I've already drawn all sorts of figures on the wall!'), alternate with brief acts of violence and ruthless self-assertion. The disjunction between mood and thought[1] ('he felt as though he were double') is manifest in Lenz's fits of laughter and sudden fears,[2] which appear to be wholly unrelated to external circumstances. The diminution of mental energies appears in the form of Lenz's increasing forgetfulness and lethargy. Deep and obscurely motivated resentment, suspicion and paranoia, issuing from feelings (rather than clear recognitions) of inadequacy and inferiority, alternate unpredictably with hectic and equally unmotivated professions of love; overt hostility with sullenness. His senses are disturbed to the point of becoming the victims of auditory and visual hallucinations,[3] the disintegration of his reasoning powers leads to religious hallucinations[4] (as in Lenz's attempt to resurrect the dead girl), which are evoked by a chance recollection or association (the girl's name is Friederike); in these states all inhibiting criticism is suspended and reasoning recedes behind primordial fears and beliefs. Or again, the hallucinations themselves assume a destructive character—the very wording of Lenz's invocations of the 'dead' Friederike, and of the Cross, correspond to statements quoted from medical dossiers.[5] When the disintegration of personality reaches the stratum of the most rudimentary instincts, Lenz makes several attempts at suicide. These Büchner describes as 'not quite serious' and 'half-hearted'. Not because he believes (as Goethe did) that Lenz's state was wilful sham, but because what Lenz aims at with these violent acts is not death ('there is no peace in death') but physical pain. And pain is the means by which Lenz is 'to come to himself'; it is the last focus of his decaying psychic energies, the self-infliction is the one act that is still within the reach of this dying will. Hate, love and indifference merge haphazardly, *arbitrarily*, 'any decisive solution or adaptation of one or other of these feelings exclusively is impossible'[6]:

---

[1] Sakel, *op. cit.*, p. 141. [2] *Ibid.*, p. 151. [3] *Ibid.*, p. 87.
[4] *Ibid.*, pp. 128 ff. [5] *Ibid.*, p. 151. [6] *Ibid.*, p. 128.

The world he had wanted to put to some use had a monstrous rift; he felt no hatred, no love,—a terrible emptiness, and yet a torturing restless urge to fill this void.

And Büchner clearly understands that Lenz's final state of depression and apathy—his 'cold resignation'—is very far from an 'improvement' in his condition,[1] that it is simply the end of his agony and the irrevocable step into darkness.

Over all these symptoms of the 'impoverishment and devastation of the psychic life' there lies the shadow of isolation and loneliness. Lenz is alone and deprived of a stable contact with Nature. Secondly, he is alone among men, no warmth or sympathy can penetrate to him from his fellow creatures. Lastly, he is alone in his spirit, for his disintegrating thought tells him that he and the world are unreal, and his prayer echoes back at him from an empty firmament. Büchner presents these three forms of Lenz's isolation as closely interrelated—there is no hope for Lenz anywhere. Yet there is an order (the equivalent, almost, of a plot) in his presentation: the *Novelle* starts with an evocation of solitude in the natural sphere, proceeds to the human, thence to the religious and metaphysical, and ends with the return to the natural.[2] It may be useful here to separate these spheres and to show how each scene is constructed from essentially similar narrative elements: which, in its turn, is merely to show how comprehensive Büchner's vision is.

[1] Sakel, *op. cit.*, pp. 138, 148. Lenz's friends (see O. F. Gruppe, *loc. cit.*) took his depressive calm as proof of his recovery.

[2] Büchner himself, it seems, was not working to any premeditated plan; and seeing how interdependent these three states are, the importance of the 'order' must not be exaggerated. Also it should be added that Büchner does not adhere to the 'point of view' technique with any consistency—the alternations don't produce anything like an over-all regular 'structure'—a fact which, far from impairing the achievement, merely shows that here at any rate the criterion is irrelevant. H. Pongs (*op. cit.*) sees a 'turning-point' in Lenz's reaction when Kaufmann suggests he should return home; but to do this Pongs has to ignore the fact that Lenz's insanity precedes Kaufmann's arrival.

Thus a scene from Lenz's journey through the mountains begins with a neutral descriptive account,

Es war gegen Abend ruhiger geworden;	*Towards evening it had become less stormy;*

and then continues in a descending order, as one's eye might roam over the mountainous landscape, evoking the statuesque stillness of which Lenz speaks to Kaufmann and which reminds us of Woyzeck's disjointed words about 'the grey, firm sky'; yet here it is still part of the neutral description:

das Gewölk lag fest und unbeweglich am Himmel; soweit der Blick reichte, nichts als Gipfel, von denen sich breite Flächen hinabzogen, . . .	*the cloudbank hung solid and motionless against the sky; as far as the eye could reach nothing but peaks from which broad slopes spread downwards, . . .*

The transition into the personal idiom, into Lenz's reaction, is abrupt, the style is now *staccato*, hardly qualified by links and particles,

und alles so still, grau, dämmernd,	*and all so still, grey, dusky,*

and leads directly to the self, the human situation:

Es wurde ihm entsetzlich einsam; er war allein, ganz allein.	*He began to feel terribly lonely; he was alone, quite alone.*

All now has left him, clouds, sky, mountain offer no habitation, loneliness closes in upon him. And since there is nothing, no firmly integrated personality to oppose the annihilating pressure of nothingness, he responds by attempting to externalise his inward dread, to translate into physical reality his inner choking fear, yet there is no one to listen, to understand:

Er wollte mit sich sprechen,	*He wanted to talk to himself,*

but even this the self in the paralysing grip cannot do:

er konnte nicht, er wagte kaum zu atmen; . . .	*but he could not, he hardly dared to breathe; . . .*

(It is only a step from experiencing the pressure of this Nothing to hypostatising it, only one step from anguish to hallucination:

'Sehn Sie, Herr Pfarrer, wenn ich
das nur nicht hören müsste, mir wäre
geholfen.' — 'Was denn, mein
Lieber?'—'Hören Sie denn nichts?
hören Sie denn nicht die entsetzliche
Stimme, die um den ganzen Horizont
schreit und die man gewöhnlich die
Stille heisst? . . .'

'You see, parson, if only I didn't
keep hearing that, I should be well.'
'Hear what, my dear fellow?'
'Don't you hear anything? Don't
you hear the terrible voice, the
terrible cry round the whole horizon,
that people call Silence? . . .'

This hypostatising in Lenz's mind has its parallel in Büchner's
narrative manner, where intensity and depth are achieved through
ever-repeated alternations between mental states and their physical
correlatives). The description of the journey continues:

er wagte kaum zu atmen; das Biegen
seines Fusses tönte wie Donner unter
ihm, er musste sich niedersetzen . . .

he hardly dared to breathe; the
movement of his foot resounded like
thunder under him, he had to sit
down . . .

and concludes again with a short evocation of the mental state
and its physical parallel:

Es fasste ihn eine namenlose Angst in
diesem Nichts: er war im Leeren.
Er riss sich auf und flog den Abhang
hinunter.

A nameless anguish gripped him in
this Nothingness: he was in the void.
He leapt to his feet and rushed down
the slope.

Nature, which had been Werther's refuge, is for Lenz a threatening void. And Lenz's isolation among his fellow-men is essentially
similar, though here the dimension of time is brought into the
picture. A few people attempt to break his isolation: his friend
Kaufmann comes to visit him; a schoolmaster comes 'as if he
wanted to talk with Oberlin' (the narrator here slips strangely
into Lenz's wariness), accompanies Lenz on a visit to the dead
girl's grave, but turns out to be watching him; Oberlin speaks
kindly to him and prays with him; Oberlin's wife tries to occupy
him, engage him in conversation. Yet they all fail. They and their
good intentions are real enough to Lenz while he is with them,
in their immediate company, but as soon as he is left alone the

ring of his isolation closes round him, he begins to doubt their
very existence. The moment he is in his own room,

Es war kalt oben, eine weite Stube,	*It was cold up there, a big empty*
leer, ein hohes Bett im Hintergrund.	*room with a high bed in the back-*
Er stellte das Licht auf den Tisch und	*ground. He placed the light on the*
ging auf und ab . . .	*table and paced to and fro , . . .*

the picture of their company begins to fade from his mind. His
great effort is to recollect reality—

Er besann sich wieder auf den Tag,	*He returned to the thought of the day*
wie er hergekommen, wo er war.	*of his arrival, how he had come here,*
Das Zimmer im Pfarrhause mit	*where he was. The room in the*
seinen Lichtern und lieben Gesicht-	*parsonage, with its lights and kind*
ern,[1]	*faces,*

—and when he gets this far his sense of being utterly alone and
lost with his own thoughts, impressions and fears—the shadow
of that which alone is real to him—passes over and blots out the
reality of the scene recollected in his mind:

Das Zimmer im Pfarrhause mit	*The room in the parsonage, with its*
seinen Lichtern und lieben Gesichten,	*lights and kind faces, was like a*
es war ihm wie ein Schatten, ein	*shadow, like a dream to him, and he*
Traum, und es wurde ihm leer,	*felt the void again, as he had felt on*
wieder wie auf dem Berg; aber er	*the mountain; but he could no longer*
konnte es mit nichts mehr ausfüllen,	*fill it with anything, the light had*
das Licht war erloschen . . .	*gone out. . . .*

The darkness that fills his mind draws everything into itself. It
is a python-like 'Nothingness which annihilates', an increasing
apprehension of the worthlessness and insubstantiality of all
experience:

das Licht war erloschen, die Finster-	*the light had gone out, the darkness*
nis verschlang alles.	*swallowed everything up.*

Is not the perfectly sane mind too a prey to such moments?
There are few poets who have been free from that apprehension,
few who have not experienced it to the point where friends and

---

[1] H. Pongs (*op. cit.*, p. 250), suggests, plausibly, that the parsonage belongs to
a '*Biedermeier*' ideal of life.

the recollection of friends are drawn into the void, and where only love, the love of men and of God, the love that Büchner's Lenz has never known, survives and saves. But how is Lenz, who does not know that love, to be saved? What *is* there, that he could pray to it?

The last and most devastating form of his loneliness is the loss of his selfhood, of the feeling that he exists:

> *Eine unnennbare Angst erfasste ihn. Er sprang auf, er lief durchs Zimmer, die Treppe hinunter, vors Haus; aber umsonst, alles finster, nichts—er war sich selbst ein Traum.*

> *An unnamable fear took possession of him. He sprang to his feet, ran across the room, down the stairs, out of the house: but in vain, all was dark, all nothing—he was a phantom to himself.*

In this direct way Büchner calls up scenes in which the very foundations of Lenz's selfhood, of his existence as a creature in a created world, are undermined and broken. 'If only I could distinguish whether I dream or wake,' he says to Oberlin; and again: 'He felt as if he existed all alone, as if the world were entirely in his imagination, as if he were *the thing* eternally damned' ['das *ewig Verdammte*'], not a man at all but some shadowy presence, unredeemed into eternity. The most powerful description of this state is contained in those moments of dissolution where

> *er verwirrte sich ganz, und dabei hatte er einen unendlichen Trieb, mit allem um ihn im Geiste willkürlich umzugehen. . . .*

> *he became totally confused, and at the same time he felt an unending urge to do violence[1] in his mind to every thing and person. . . .*

[1] M. Hamburger's translation, *loc. cit.*, p. 139. Büchner's passage sounds like an echo of Goethe's second sketch of Lenz (*Dichtung und Wahrheit*, Book 14, J.A., Vol. XXIV, p. 184): '. . . *seine Liebe und Hass waren imaginär, mit seinen Vorstellungen und Gefühlen verfuhr er willkürlich . . .*'. Gutzkow's reference to Goethe's autobiography (*S.W.B.*, p. 622,; *W.B.* p. 327) implies that Büchner may have read it.

The emphasis here is on the *arbitrariness* of Lenz's actions. The sick mind, no longer able to contain and control the impressions that come to it from the objective world, swamps the world with a flow of its own, wholly arbitrary imaginings and would-be acts; like Lear, he can rave, 'I will do such things ... ! What they yet are I know not, but they shall be the terrors of the earth.' Ravaging the world with thoughts wholly fanciful and excogitated, he, the weakest of men, would be puppet-master,

Er amüsierte sich, die Häuser auf die Dächer zu stellen ...	He amused himself with turning the houses upside down on their roof-tops ...

he, the rejected lover, would bring his erotic vengeance upon mankind,

... die Menschen an und aus-zukleiden, die wahnwitzigsten Poss-en auszusinnen.	... dressing and undressing the people, making up the craziest tricks to play with them.

Here again Büchner shows an uncanny awareness and feeling for the underlying connection between arbitrariness and violence, between deprivation and the negative, destructive act; to read these passages is to know the meaning of absolute solipsism.

This solipsism, in which finally the self is reduced to an insubstantial *it*, reaches its climax in the disintegration of Lenz's religious beliefs. '*Das All war für ihn in Wunden*'—the universe itself, 'creation' as Danton said, 'is a wound': the wound which God, who for Lenz too dissolves into Nothing, has left upon the world. Lenz's attempt to resurrect the dead girl Friederike

... er sprach laut und fest: 'Stehe auf und wandle!' Aber die Wände hallten ihm nüchtern den Ton nach, dass es zu spotten schien, und die Leiche blieb kalt ...	... he said loudly and firmly, 'Arise and walk!' But soberly the walls re-echoed his voice, as though to mock him, and the corpse remained cold ...

is like a wager with God; and when he loses it—

Es war ihm, als könnte er eine un-geheuere Faust hinauf in den Himmel ballen und Gott herbeireissen und zwischen seinen Wolken schleifen;	He felt as though he could thrust an enormous fist up into the sky, and seize God with it and drag him through his clouds; as though he

als könnte er die Welt mit den Zähnen zermalmen and sie dem Schöpfer ins Gesicht speien; er schwur, er lästerte	*could crunch the world between his teeth and spit it into the face of its Creator; he swore, he blasphemed*

the earth, alien and absurd in its unreality, mocks at his frenzy:

. . . das ungewisse Licht dehnte sich hinunter, wo die weissen Stein-massen lagen, und der Himmel war ein dummes blaues Aug, und der Mond stand ganz lächerlich drin, einfältig.	*. . . the thin, uncertain light stretched down towards the white slabs of stone, and the sky was a stupid blue eye and the moon, quite ludicrous, stood in the middle of it, idiotic.*

Lenz's last sane words, after Oberlin's loving care has for a last time brought him back to reality, are the words of Büchner's life-long concern: 'But I, if I were almighty, you see, if I were that, I could not bear the suffering. I would save, save.'

I have already suggested in what sense, by virtue of what literary qualities, we are to understand Büchner's image of this unhinged spirit as true. What, then, if Lenz is right and all the rest is a lie, an elaborate conspiracy not to mention our true state? If the Nothing is real, and all our substantial being in the world ('*das Dasein alles Seienden*') is 'but a tale told by an idiot, full of sound and fury, signifying nothing'? Then, clearly, all our values too, all the things we hold dear and the hopes we cherish, collapse under the pressure of the annihilating Nothing. Or is there something that can save Lenz? Some aspect of his being that can withstand the void? Again, and more clearly than in his other works, Büchner sees pain and suffering as a mode of experience on the opposite side of that emptiness and unreality which constantly threatens Lenz and finally overwhelms him.

Lenz's repeated attempts at suicide Büchner describes as 'half-hearted' and 'not quite serious'. And he continues:

Es war weniger der Wunsch des Todes—für ihn war ja keine Ruhe und Hoffnung im Tode—es war mehr in Augenblicken der fürchter-	*It was not so much the desire for death—for him there could be no peace or hope in death—it was rather an attempt to bring himself back to*

lichen Angst oder der dumpfen, ans Nichtsein grenzenden Ruhe ein Versuch, sich zu sich selbst zu bringen durch den physischen Schmerz.	consciousness through physical pain in moments of appalling anguish or of stupefied tranquillity bordering on non–existence.

Again, and more directly than in his other works, Büchner contrasts the crimson language of pain, the images of resistant and thus pain-inflicting objects, with the leaden insensateness of Lenz's days; in pain if anywhere lies his salvation:

Er konnte sich nicht mehr finden; ein dunkler Instinkt trieb ihn, sich zu retten. Er stiess an die Steine, er riss sich mit den Nägeln; der Schmerz fing an, ihm das Bewusstsein wiederzugeben. Er stürzte sich in den Brunnenstein, aber das Wasser war nicht tief, er patschte darin . . .	He could no longer find himself, an obscure instinct drove him to save himself. He ran into stones, tore at himself with his nails. The pain began to bring him to himself. He hurled himself into the stone fountain, but the water was not deep, he splashed about. . . .

This invoking of pain as the spirit's last stronghold against the forces of unreality and madness, as the counterpoint to Lenz's isolation, is here carried to its ultimate conclusion. As long as Lenz is capable of 'being himself', of rallying himself in 'all in one single point', in his feeling, he is still in life, he still has a distinct and focused existence. He is not, even then, sane, but he takes part, however intermittently, in our world. At the end, at the point where he has no resistance to offer to the disintegration, no palpable object to cling to, he ceases to suffer. His state issues into absolute apathy and imperception. Ceasing to suffer, he has relinquished his hold upon our world.

The conclusion, then, is as convincing in psychopathological terms as it is in respect of the narrative itself: the exploration of the one makes for the perfection of the other. For when each broad slope of the alien landscape has been explored, each mode of isolation presented, the tale is brought to the point of absolute disintegration from which no mind returns. The prose itself, we have seen, is 'dramatic' in the extreme, yet in the course of the narrative the usual idea of drama is stood on its head. The story's

progress is not towards conflict, but away from it; the external
world is waxen, not embattled; all things give way; all reality
melts into gaping nothingness ... until, at last, mind and world
are severed. And at that final point the cold, impartial reality of
the world, or rather of the living Earth, now wholly separated
from the mind that would 'do violence to it', is set forth in two
images of remarkable lyrical beauty, strikingly reminiscent of the
elegiac evocations of Hölderlin and Trakl. Büchner's narrative
prose at first retains a factual descriptiveness of the kind we don't
find in their writings,

Er sass mit kalter Resignation im Wagen, wie sie das Tal hervor nach Westen fuhren. Es war ihm einerlei, wohin man ihn führte. Mehrmals, wo der Wagen bei dem schlechten Wege in Gefahr geriet, blieb er ganz ruhig sitzen; er war vollkommen gleich- gültig. In diesem Zustand legte er den Weg durchs Gebirge zurück. Gegen Abend waren sie im Rheintale ...	*He sat in the carriage in a state of cold resignation as they drove west- wards out of the valley. It was all one to him where he was being taken. Several times, when the carriage was in danger of being overturned on the bad roads, he sat there quite still, calm; he was completely indifferent. In this state he travelled the whole way through the mountains. To- wards evening they were in the Rhine valley ...*

but then the prose is intensified, reaching two brief lyrical moments unparalleled elsewhere in Büchner's work. It may be that
the first—

Sie entfernten sich allmählich vom Gebirg, das nun wie eine tiefblaue Kristallwelle sich in das Abendrot hob, und auf deren warmer Flut die roten Strahlen des Abends spielten; über die Ebene hin am Fusse des Ge- birgs lag ein schimmerndes, bläuliches Gespinst.	*Gradually they were getting further from the mountains, which now rose into the sunset sky like a deep blue crystal wave on whose warm tide the last red rays of the sun were playing; away over the plain at the foot of the mountains lay a shimmering bluish web.*

is still visible to Lenz himself. His eye, the eye of a poet, for a
last time roams the ether, focusing first on the mountainous
horizon and then losing itself, as it comes down into the valley,
in a ghostly blur. And there his vision ends. For now, after the
brief circumstantial report, which also intimates the mind's unfeeling state,

Es wurde finster, je mehr sie sich Strassburg näherten; hoher Voll-mond, alle fernen Gegenstände dunkel, nur der Berg neben bildete eine scharfe Linie; . . .	*It grew darker as they neared Strasbourg; the moon at the full, all distant objects dark, only the moun-tains closest to them formed a sharp outline; . . .*

comes the second and last image, the spirit holding firmly the earth's austere riches and splendour:

; die Erde war wie ein goldner Pokal, über den schäumend die Goldwellen des Mondes liefen.	*; the earth was like a golden chalice, over which ran foaming the golden waves of moonlight.*

But Lenz no longer sees anything. The image recalls for a last time what the earth is to us—that earth whose reality he no longer feels:

Lenz starrte ruhig hinaus, keine Ahnung, kein Drang . . .[1]	*Lenz was staring out calmly, not an idea stirred in him, not an im-pulse. . . .*

The urge to break open his prison, to communicate and be under-stood, to take part in and belong to the real world, is spent; all that is left is the sinister dread of unfeeling:

. . . kein Drang; nur wuchs eine dumpfe Angst in ihm, je mehr die Gegenstände sich in der Finsternis verloren.	*. . . no impulse; but a dull fear was growing in him, growing larger as the objects were lost in the darkness.*

Now at last the world gives way, the earth's hard, resisting objects[2] give way, insubstantial darkness swallows all. Life, of a sort, goes on,

Sie mussten einkehren. Da machte er	*They were obliged to stop for the*

---

[1] At the beginning of the *Novelle* (see above, p. 134) it was said, '*Anfangs drängte es in ihm . . .*'.

[2] Since it was only in the generation before Büchner's that the word *Gegen-stand* came into its present undifferentiated use (see Grimms' *W.B.*), it may not be too fanciful to suggest that the meaning-element of resistance offered by the concrete 'ob-ject' may have determined his choice of the word both here (*S.W.B.* and *W.B.*, p. 108) and in a similar context earlier: '*Er klammerte sich an alle Gegenstände*' (*S.W.B.* and *W.B.* p. 87).

wieder mehrere Versuche, Hand an	*night. There again he tried several*
sich zu legen,	*times to make away with himself,*

leading to new meaningless acts, new humiliations,

war aber zu scharf bewacht.	*but he was too well guarded.*

but the life of the spirit, the life which Büchner's *Novelle* encompassed, is at its appointed end.

10

If *Dantons Tod* and *Woyzeck* remained fragmentary because they left unanswered the question of the ultimate end towards which pain was the only valid means, *Lenz* is a whole by virtue of completing the dialectic. Since it is the spirit of a man whose struggle is enacted, Danton's death and Woyzeck's murder and subsequent execution (if that is what Büchner intended for him) do not conclude their struggles, whereas Lenz's last journey does. The defeat here is complete, and final; nothing can save him, not even pain. Pain is not denied, it is seen through to its end.

We conclude, it appears, with a paradox. The vital energy, in crimson and grey, and the poetic evocativeness of Büchner's language—the particular quality, at once dramatic and transfixed, of his images of life—endow his entire work with a unique distinction. These very qualities leave us, in *Dantons Tod* and *Woyzeck*, with a feeling of incompleteness, which we rationalise in the question, 'After the proof of existence through pain— what?' In *Lenz*, suffering is shown to be finally inadequate. Lenz goes one step further, to the point where pain too fails; and no other proof takes its place. In this simple sense, in the sense that 'the rest is silence', the *Novelle* is complete. Yet is not this conclusion, in what it tells us about life, even darker, even more tragic than the conclusions emerging from the plays? And if, then, I suggest that here in *Lenz* a perfection, a thing of beauty and value has been attained, am I not thus foisting upon my reader a wilfully catastrophic, sensational and 'morbid' view—in short the horror-mongering I was at pains to repudiate? There is, to this charge, no other reply but the appeal to the reader's experience; none, ultimately, but the assertion that such a gift as Büchner here shows forth cannot but make for 'a continuity and coherence much bigger than any disintegration';[1] that the creative gift, here too, cannot but make for order, meaning, and life.

The reality of being, of bare existence beyond the disintegration of lunacy, contrasts and thus sustains the central image of *Lenz* from beginning to end. And when the image finally breaks, we are left with more than the fragments. In its contact with the world the distorting mirror is shattered. But behind it, behind the incongruities it reflected, the earth itself is briefly revealed in its true shape. Is not the austere yet precious image of the earth's dark chalice of gold the more valid for having been secured from the ravaging grasp of unreality? Is not the assertion of value in *that* the more secure for having emerged from a fire of doubt? The day is lost, yet we are the richer for both battle and defeat. And Büchner? He, not Lenz, sees the chalice. His insight into the world of pain as a thing finite and bounded is, after all, the condition of his creative act. He too can say, as his hero could not,

> . . . *my grief's so great*
> *That no supporter but the huge, firm earth*
> *Can hold it up: here I and sorrows sit;*
> *Here is my throne, bid kings come bow to it.*

[1] The assertion comes from a writer who has often been falsely accused of ignoring the reality of pain, nowhere more fiercely than by his correspondent in *Henry James and H. G. Wells*, London 1958 (p. 162).

IV THE AESTHETIC
RE-INTERPRETATION:
SCHOPENHAUER

'Ce qui doit excuser le monde, c'est qu'il nous sert de modèle.'
(Anon., 1847)

I

THE ARTIST's disillusionment with contemporary reality is a mid-nineteenth-century phenomenon of European dimensions. And it is in Nietzsche's formulation, 'Only as an aesthetic attitude is the existence of the world justified', that it has been handed down to us. The thought and its many variations underlie his brilliant first work, the *Birth of Tragedy* (1872), it recurs in the retrospective Preface written for that book in 1886, eighteen months before Nietzsche's lapse into insanity: the thought spans the whole of Nietzsche's reflective life.

What is 'the aesthetic attitude': is it trivial, contemning, nihilistic, heroic? Beyond morality or immoral? What would an 'aesthetic revaluation of the world' mean in terms of man's vital, life-sustaining beliefs, in terms of his tragic existence? These questions no man has pondered more deeply and, in spite of his repeated exaltations of Homeric laughter and Mediterranean equanimity, less gaily or detachedly: that is, less 'aesthetically'; the fascination, for him, of 'the Apolline' is of a thing for ever alien. That Nietzsche comes to no conclusive answer to his questions concerning the rôle of the Aesthetic in existence is characteristic of his entire manner of philosophising, of his consistent distrust of all systematic consistency, his scorn for all neat conclusions and set precepts. Yet there is, apart from his habitual uneasiness, something peculiarly insubstantial about his attempts at an 'aesthetic theodicy'. He hypothesises, admires, questions; he conducts sorties against conventional morality on behalf of the aesthetic state: but to that state himself remains a stranger. The requisite quality of 'disinterestedness' is ultimately incompatible with his sense of personal truth. He is a little like Moses discoursing to his unworthy followers upon the beauties of the Promised Land; or perhaps like Wittgenstein, the least playful of men, proposing to consider experience on the analogy of 'language-games'. As so often, Nietzsche's guiding thought and perturbing insight are close to the central experience of his age, and prophetically projects into ours; yet it is not to him that we shall turn for the fullest and most consistent elaboration of the insight.

The idea of aesthetically validating the world (on the recognition that, left to itself, the world would be intolerable), together with conclusions of a highly systematic kind, was bequeathed to Nietzsche by Schopenhauer, his greatly admired 'teacher and exemplar'. The high praise (much of it misleading) which the young Nietzsche lavishes on Schopenhauer, as well as the fact that they both often appear on the same polemical front, have made some critics exaggerate their intellectual kinship. The contrast between Schopenhauer's comprehensively elaborated doctrine which culminates in the denial of the will, and Nietzsche's encomium of and aphoristic assents to the will, is striking rather than substantial; it is a contrast overshadowed by a very close similarity, amounting at times almost to identity, of the conception itself that is central to their thought. Thus it is not so much the will's denial in the philosophy of one and its far from unambiguous[1] assertion in the philosophising of the other that makes for the real difference in the vision each has of the human race. What arouses the young Nietzsche's admiration are not the didactic passages in Schopenhauer's work, where men are enjoined to renounce the will, as rather his precise and circumstantial descriptions of the will, where it is shown at work in nature and

[1] Thus, on the other side of the argument, Nietzsche's attack on Schopenhauer's 'fundamental misunderstandings of the will—as if cupidity, instinct, blind greed were its essence...' in *Wille zur Macht*, § 84, Kröner ed., no. 78, p. 63; and his rejection of the equation 'Will = Life'.

in men as Schopenhauer felt and saw it. It is the different functions
of the aesthetic in their work that provides a more significant and
fundamental contrast.

Ultimately, beyond the reach of shrill contradictions, for
Nietzsche the aesthetic mode is part of the heroic in man; while
for Schopenhauer heroism, it too, is aesthetic. A consistent
feeling for the tragedy of man's God-less existence engulfs almost
every one of Nietzsche's arguments, even those cast in a would-be
gay manner; while Schopenhauer, even at his most indignantly
serious, is not wholly free from the taint of sarcasm, irony, from
preoccupation with form. When he identified these qualities with
'the Aesthetic', his contemporary Kierkegaard may have had
Schopenhauer in mind.

As an aesthetic reinterpretation of a world in itself hostile to
the claims of the spirit, Schopenhauer's work has an obvious
relevance to the theme of this book. For one thing, the intermingling of philosophical and literary ideas—a commonplace of
German literary history—is nowhere more clearly ascertainable
than in his influence upon Grillparzer, Hebbel, Raabe, Otto
Ludwig, Fontane, Thomas Mann, and a host of lesser writers.
But equally relevant is the overwhelmingly *literary* nature of his
influence; is the fact that, of all major European philosophers, he
is undoubtedly the most literary. And finally, it is he who provides
us, even today, with one of the major descriptions of the aesthetic
mode. His line of argument, which stresses the distinction between
the empirical person of the artist and the timeless and impersonal
nature of the work of art, lies at the back of aesthetic and critical
theories from Mallarmé through Joyce to T. S. Eliot. It is through
his work—perhaps through it alone—that German literary ideas
have exercised a profound influence upon contemporary and
subsequent literary fashion in Europe everywhere.

The traffic between literature and philosophy is at this point at its
most complex and interesting. On the one hand there is the
'literariness' of Schopenhauer's philosophical system, manifest
(among other things) in the fact (as I hope to show it) that his

'philosophy' is co-extensive with, that it is scarcely more than, his aesthetics. On the other hand there is the nature of his undertaking itself, its amounting to yet another interpretation away from the world of 'common indication'. For the interest attaching to 'the world' when it is seen as the subject-matter, the 'basic text', of individual and varying interpretations and attitudes, is in itself *also* a philosophical interest. The whole variety of interpretative attitudes has *also* a philosophical aspect, while the question of interpretability, hardly ever far away, is a philosophical question *tout court*. It is the demands of this philosophical interest that Schopenhauer's system satisfies; and it does so in an elaborately literary manner.

By 'literary' I mean, to begin with, that he is not really 'deep'. The substance of his writings is co-extensive with his presentation of it. His presentation is clear, elegant, unambiguous, witty, ironical and sarcastic rather than poetic. The truth his irony hides is not a transcendent thing, nor does it remain hidden for long. What his presentation implies is not a vision 'behind' the written words and for some reason unfathomable by them: what he implies in one part of the argument is 'merely' another part of the argument, where it is made explicit. Thus the various images he uses to compare his system with—a house (not a pyramid or ladder, or a growing tree), a page, a book, a pattern, a painting— all point to its being mounted on a horizontal rather than a vertical axis. The great virtue of his system is that it is evolved in the dimension of width and comprehensiveness rather than of depth and symbolical evocation; in space rather than time; that it is written, emphatically, in prose rather than in any sort of poetry. The difference I have in mind was once described by Pasternak when he expressed amused surprise at the countless hidden meanings which Edmund Wilson had 'discovered' in *Dr Zhivago*: 'If you find a natural stone, you may learn a great deal about the earth's past. But what can you see in a brick?' Schopenhauer too is conscious of putting together an artifact, a fully determined, man-made thing, conscious of the strict limitations of the literary and philosophical mode. Thus it is significant that he should express scorn for those readers of Plato who wax enthusiastic about Plato's myths which he—Schopenhauer—

considers as little more than picturesque but regrettable departures from the philosopher's proper business. Significant, because the imagery he himself employs is always severely ancillary to the immediate point at issue rather than free-ranging and creative of a meaning unencompassed by the discursive prose.

Lacking—indeed deliberately eschewing—all 'poetic depth', Schopenhauer's prose achieves an intensely living picture of the human condition. His presentation is of course conceptual and in that sense 'abstract'; in more than one passage he describes the philosopher's task as strictly limited to giving a systematic account of concepts culled from experience in the world. Yet the connection between these concepts and actual experience is to be direct, self-evident. We are to see them as direct translations of our intuitive (and as such more or less hazy) feelings about the world into the stable and clear language of philosophy. The concepts must not take on a life of their own; for unless they are constantly checked against actual experience (through examples, anecdotes, psychological explanations), they are bound to lead to contradictions and abstruseness. Thus when he criticises the Stoic philosophy (which his own doctrine at some points resembles), Schopenhauer does not merely point to what he sees as its inherent contradiction—the unrealisable desire for a life without pain. For him the doctrine is refuted because its ideal image of man— the Stoic sage—strikes him as 'a being without life and without inner poetic truth, it remains a stiff, wooden puppet [*Gliederpuppe*] . . . which does not help us to arrive at a livingly embodied idea [*anschauliche Vorstellung*]'. It is not hard to guess that his conceptual refutation here merely rationalises his literary-critical insight, that inclination and taste come before the rationale.

Schopenhauer's own work, it is true, is not wholly free from the abstruseness which he dismisses as unconvincing. The heritage of eighteenth-century system-builders and enlightened worthies lies on several lengthy passages in which the argument is carried on by the heaving-about of concepts rather than by the life they are to retrace. But such passages are rare. Much more characteristic is the display of a literary intelligence such as we find it in Hobbes (whom he resembles in more ways than this), in Montaigne and Gracian, his favourite authors. He is very far from

THE AESTHETIC RE-INTERPRETATION 161

being 'open-minded', and has but a single point of view. Unlike the 'great knowers', Aristotle and St Thomas, he does not give us the impression of coming to experience ever anew with a wholly unprepossessed, purely enquiring mind; his frequent avowals that he is concerned with what is and not at all with what should be are in themselves a part of his tactics of persuasion. But the single point of view from which he presents the world is both wide and distinct enough to give his prose the authentic note of life itself:

Eine Gesellschaft Stachelschweine drängte sich, an einem kalten Wintertage, recht nahe zusammen, um, durch die gegenseitige Wärme, sich vor dem Erfrieren zu schützen. Jedoch bald empfanden sie die gegenseitigen Stacheln, welches sie dann wieder von einander entfernte. Wann nun das Bedürfniss der Erwärmung sie wieder näher zusammen brachte, wiederholte sich jenes zweite Uebel; so dass sie zwischen beiden Leiden hin- und hergeworfen wurden, bis sie eine mässige Entfernung von einander herausgefunden hatten, in der sie es am besten aushalten konnten. —So treibt das Bedürfniss der Gesellschaft, aus der Leere und Monotonie des eigenen Innern entsprungen, die Menschen zu einander; aber ihre vielen widerwärtigen Eigenschaften und unerträglichen Fehler stossen sie wieder von einander ab. Die mittlere Entfernung, die sie endlich herausfinden, und bei welcher ein Beisammensein bestehen kann, ist die Höflichkeit und feine Sitte. Dem, der sich nicht in dieser Entfernung hält, ruft man in England zu: keep your distance!—Vermöge derselben wird zwar das Bedürfniss gegenseitiger Erwärmung nur unvollkommen befriedigt, dafür aber der

On a cold winter's day a company of porcupines crowded close together in order to protect each other by their warmth against freezing to death. But soon they began to feel each other's quills, which made them move apart again. Now, when the need for warmth brought them together again, the latter evil recurred: so that they were tossed this way and that between the two painful situations, until they had found out an appropriate distance in which they could best endure each other.

Thus it is that the need for company, which arises from the emptiness and monotony of one's own mind, drives people towards each other; but their many repulsive qualities and intolerable faults drive them apart again, away from each other. The middle distance which they at last work out and which makes living together permanently possible is called politeness and good manners. 'Keep your distance!' is what they say in England to one who offends against this rule.

It is true that in this way the need to keep each other warm is but imperfectly satisfied, yet on the other hand there is no pricking of quills either. But whosoever has a great

Stich der Stacheln nicht empfunden.
—Wer jedoch viel eigene, innere
Wärme hat, bleibt lieber aus der
Gesellschaft weg, um keine Be-
schwerde zu geben, noch zu emp-
fangen.[1]

deal of inner warmth of his own had
better stay away altogether, in order
neither to give offence nor to receive it.

It seems a little heavy-handed to enquire whether porcupines do
in fact behave that way.

2

Schopenhauer's is a philosophical system like many another, in the
sense that it is a concerted attempt at describing in a unified way
the whole of human experience. Every such system, from Plato
onwards, has singled out one mode of experience, e.g. the moral,
or the religious, or the social, which it has set up as the crowning
pinnacle of the edifice, as a mode which is of greater value than
the rest. This is where Plato puts the contemplative life, the world
of the Ideas; where Spinoza puts the contemplation of the attri-
butes of the Supreme Being; where Hegel puts Hegelian philosophy. This is the place where Schopenhauer, in a manner to be
explained in due course, places ostensibly the Saint, whose
substantial qualities are adumbrated in the artist, his mundane
counterpart, and reflected in the work of art. And he does this in
such a way that, while it is the intention of his system to show in
the Saint's life the answer to the world's ineradicable faults and
incurable woes, yet it is with the artistic mode that he is most
seriously concerned; in other words, Schopenhauer's arguments
yield conviction not in what he has to say about sainthood but
in what he sees as a way towards it—namely, the aesthetic
mode.

The one thing that the various attempts at re-interpreting the
world which we have described so far had in common was that
they were conducted in the medium of art. To these re-interpretations Schopenhauer's work is complementary. What he does is
to provide a general philosophical outline of such attempts (that

---

[1] *Arthur Schopenhauer's sämtliche Werke,* ed. E. Grisebach, Leipzig (Reclam)
[n.d.] Vol. V, p. 689.

is, an aesthetic); and in so doing he offers an example of his own. His European influence is due to this double aspect of his work. For he not only provides a framework, he not only shows how the world may be aesthetically justified, but he also does the justifying; and is himself engaged in writing something like a work of art.

A single line of comparison between his philosophy and that of Hegel, whom he saw as his enemy, will give some idea of the kind of literary sensibility that is at work here. Significant from our point of view is the different place aesthetics has in each of the two systems. Hegel's system is a vast, 'natural' growth, forever changing and evolving. More than that, development, growth and change figure largely as elements in Hegel's description of the scheme of things, in the dialectical process as seen at work in the world; while the formal manner in which coherencies are established within the system, the dialectic, is in itself an example of the Hegelian vision of growth. The range of his images as well as his central preoccupation belong to historical growth; history as analogy, as a storehouse of examples, as a sanction for logic, epistemology and moral considerations alike— it is this that sets the characteristic Hegelian tone. The emphasis on fluidity in the states of mind, on relativity of values, on education, change, historical background—all these find their parallel in Hegel's strange and heavy style, for instance in his almost mechanical attempts at securing logical conviction for his argument by drawing on etymologies and historical semantics and by deliberately exploring the complex historical ambiguities of his own vocabulary. His near-mystical, 'poetic' style bears witness, certainly in the *Phenomenology of Spirit*, to his friendship with Hölderlin and to his membership of the Jena poetic circle. Aesthetics, in this system, plays a certain integral but subsidiary part. The Beautiful is one of the manifestations of the Spirit, its function and importance being determined not by anything intrinsic to it but along historical lines, according to the world-historical moment at which it manifests itself. Thus the Beautiful is only one among several epiphanies of the Spirit in time, in world-history. Hegel's conceptual summary of the whole is only partly determined by a consideration of the Beautiful, '*das*

Ganze' includes and exceeds the aesthetic and is preponderantly of a different kind.

Schopenhauer's system is not really the product of growth at all. Like Pallas Athene it sprang entire out of the philosophical Jupiter's head. His countless, often impatient, cross-references from one part of it to other parts bear out his conviction—or at least they are intended to sustain his claim—that his entire *œuvre* is based on one single, all-encompassing idea. In this idea the conception of natural, intellectual and experiential growth, with which Schopenhauer must have been familiar from Goethe, plays hardly any part at all. The man and the work give overwhelmingly the impression of being all of one piece.

3

As far as one can make out from the correspondence published by the philosopher's disciple, Eduard Grisebach (which was not available to Nietzsche when he wrote his panegyric), Schopenhauer was a bitter man, remarkable mainly for his vanity, and not much inclined to that emotion of pity and charity which he singles out as the better part of love and as the one positive moral value accessible to us. There may of course be many reasons why a man of genius may be bitter, self-assertive and vain, and the rejection of one's life-work by most of one's contemporaries is not in itself a trivial reason. It explains why, especially in the second half of his life, Schopenhauer seems to have had hardly any friends other than those who were prepared to propagate his doctrine by word of mouth—his 'disciples'—or by writing in his defence—his 'evangelists'. Nor did he suffer from any self-delusion, for his vanity is well sustained by several eloquent passages in which he dwells on the hypocrisy or idiocy (as the case might be) of the humble. But a further, not wholly unworthy, explanation of such vanity is, quite simply, that the man is co-extensive with his system. He 'goes into' the book, and nothing is left, as Hobbes goes into the *Leviathan*, as Joyce goes into *Ulysses*, as Rilke goes into his mature poetry. To argue and concede defeat on a point of one's conviction is not very hard if one isn't really in earnest about it (because one isn't really in earnest about anything); or if one rejoices in the possession of a wealth of ideas, experiences and feelings—a wealth of being—by virtue of which one can easily afford partial concessions. In either of these cases 'arguing' is beside the point. But if a man lives for, and has nothing else to fall back on than, the fruits of his thinking: if there is nothing whatever that he can regard with the same degree of seriousness, it is hard to see how such a man can genuinely give way on any fundamental point, how can he be anything but 'vain'.[1] The 'immanence' of the point of view is exemplified by the style, but also by the fact that it includes the man's entire being. What it omits or excludes is lacking in the man himself.

Schopenhauer first hit upon the central idea of his system in his early twenties, its introductory treatise was written in 1812 (when he was twenty-four), its first full exposition was published when he was twenty-nine. Forty years later (he died in 1860, aged seventy-two) he was still adding aphoristic snippets and elaborations—sometimes brilliant, sometimes boring—to the original insight, to the flash of understanding which he had experienced as a young man. There is perhaps no parallel among the major philosophers of the West to this concerted preoccupation with one central *aperçu*, to this utterly unchanging insistence on one comprehensive point of view, to the firmly outlined and achieved system he has created. On several occasions he speaks of the almost visionary experience in which his 'idea' came to him, stressing the immediate and personal quality of the inspiration. He insists on the meta-rational 'experience' as the source of his work—a source, usually, of art rather than philosophy. That this insight might be genuine, intimately personal and sensuously vivid, *and* wrong, never occurs to him:

Mein Kniff ist, das lebhafteste Anschaun, oder das tiefste Emp- finden, wann die gute Stunde es	*My trick is really this: to wait for a propitious hour and to freeze the most living sense-experience of the*

---

[1] The fact that such a measure of commitment to the work of one's mind is rare at the present time, and that our psychological cause-mongering offers to explain away the commitment and to supply all sorts of extraneous reasons for it, should not blind us to the meaning and value of the commitment when it does occur, nor make us identify it with truth.

herbeigeführt hat, plötzlich und im
selben Augenblick mit der kältesten
abstrakten Reflexion zu übergiessen
und es dadurch erstarrt aufzu-
bewahren.[1]

world or my deepest feeling for it,
which that hour has brought me,
suddenly and instantaneously with
cold abstract reflection and thus to
preserve it in a transfixed state.

To us, whose respect for authority based on personal conviction
has been somewhat shaken, the 'trick' commends itself as a
reaction against eighteenth-century rationalists, but for the rest
it sounds disconcertingly like the procedure of subsequent
ideologues and 'philosophical' charlatans. To base a philosophical
system (or, for that matter, a political one[2]) on an 'experience'
however vivid, however personal, however sincere, is not, as
Schopenhauer implies and Nietzsche proclaims, a guarantee of
its truth or value.

The philosophy, then, is a transfixed experience. And just as
there is no substantial development or change in Schopenhauer's
system-making; just as even the tone of the argument changes
only to the extent of becoming more self-assured and thus less
insistent and circumspect; just as it is true to say that the passage
of time itself seems to have little meaning in the life of the man
—so time itself has no fundamental reality in the system, it is
Being rather than Becoming which is explored, it is by exploration rather than intimation that he proceeds—it is the novel
rather than the poem that stands as an analogy.

Men like Hegel or Mallarmé or Rilke are engaged in a never-
ending series of battles—'raids on the inexpressible', Rilke calls
them—and undergo a spiritual growth which enables them to
reject this or that earlier 'opinion' as outmoded, as marking a
stage of their lives but no longer adequate to their subsequent
experience and understanding. Yet for the critic their rejection
may not always be a reliable guide. The fact that an opinion, or a
vision beheld in a poem, is *no longer* adequate to the philosopher
or poet who was once possessed of it, says little about its intrinsic
value. Of course, that earlier vision may have been immature

[1] Quoted from O. Jenson, *Die Ursache der Widersprüche im Schopenhauerschen
System*, Rostock 1906, p. 64.
[2] See below, p. 235.

and weak in comparison with what came after; that is the case with Rilke's early, pre-1906 poetry. Or it may have had a freshness and a force lost in the later work—as has been said of Hegel's work after the *Phenomenology*. But then again, the earlier may be merely different, equally beautiful and important—as is Goethe's early poetry. Hence, in our appraisal of the achieved thing we shall have to ignore one or several aspects of its genealogy and development. We shall have to take the poem out of the flow of chronology, and look at it as a thing out of time. Not that this is the only proper view of it. But certainly one vitally important aspect of it, one mode of understanding and evaluating it, is as a thing complete in itself, in a sense timeless and eternal. More than that, it is surely not implausible to argue that of all human achievements it is the artifact, the created work of art, which must be so regarded (though it may not be regarded in this manner exclusively). And the view of art that would so regard it is Schopenhauer's.

Die Welt als Wille und Vorstellung is a work composed of two volumes, of roughly equal length, where the first (1818) contains the reductive, abstract exposition of the system. This first part is divided into four books, in which the fundamental dualism inherent in the central insight is explored each time from a different angle. Schopenhauer's introductory treatise (1812) in which he showed that all propositions made about the real world are reducible to the principle of sufficient reason, is a sort of preliminary groundwork to the first and even more to the second book of the first volume, while all the subsequent collections of essays, aphorisms, reflections and meditations, including the second volume of the main work (1844), illustrate and apply the central idea of the first. There is, in all this symmetry, something elaborately pedantic; seeing that Schopenhauer himself has some wonderfully revealing remarks to make on the subject of pedantry, on the way that partial and unassured insights hide behind armour-plates of expatiation, on how pedantry is essentially an act of the assertive will, it is more than likely that he himself had some grim fun with following up the systematic elaborations. But it also soon becomes evident that the symmetry springs directly from the dualistic nature of the system itself: the substance and subject-matter of the work are reflected in, and determine, its expository manner.

There is here no identity of matter and manner, such as we are wont to claim for a poem. But there is undoubtedly an influence exercised by one on the other. Which is as much as to say that, unlike the work of any other modern philosopher, the scheme itself as well as its exposition has an aesthetic or literary appeal, that the thing is in a sense a work of art. In what sense? Again, the definition is supplied by the thing defined. It is a work of art according to that view which stresses texture, structure, architecture, the firmly determined artifact, 'brick' rather than 'natural stone'. The interrelation of sense-data and meanings of which Baudelaire speaks in *Correspondances*; the *leitmotif*-patterns in French Symbolist poetry, in Wagner's operas and in Thomas Mann's works; the severely structured whole of Joyce's *Ulysses*; the geometrical substructure in the work of Paul Klee or Henry Moore; the strictly elaborated architectonics of a Bach fugue[1]— these are some of the obvious examples of that modality of art to which the system is formally related. No doubt the element of structure is discoverable in all art, though whether it is as important as present fashions in aesthetic theory make out is another question. But it is to this element, in the first instance, that Schopenhauer's scheme owes its appeal.

The aesthetic, literary appeal of Schopenhauer's book is further founded in the clarity of its language. There is, given its initial premise, nothing in the least mystical or irrational in the book. Nor is the clarity due to a lack of content—it is not the kind that we see practised in some regions of contemporary philosophy where 'nothing is so conducive to peace of mind as not having any opinion at all'.[2] The lucidity is rather one of literary elegance and fine style, marked by a tendency towards *bons mots* and

---

[1] E.g. the '*Krebsfuge*' which 'works both ways' as the wide-eyed young Hanno Buddenbrook learns from his teacher in the organ loft.

[2] See G. C. *Lichtenbergs Aphorismen* (ed. A. Leitzmann, Berlin 1902–8), E 62.

aphorisms, succinct and laconic formulation, an almost wholly non-technical language of unforced, bright metaphors. The symbolists' technique of working within a structured whole is thus matched here with a diction quite different from theirs, a diction which owes more to *Le Neveu de Rameau* and Lichtenberg than it does to any poet or systematic philosopher. Again one is reminded of Hobbes, with whom Schopenhauer shares not only the relish of a whole-hearted contempt for most of the aims ordinary people set themselves, but also the typical literary manner of advancing the argument by a close look (in spite of the contempt) at the meaning of a word as these ordinary people use it, rather than by forcing new words and new meanings upon them.

The fact that his imagery remains ancillary and illustrative of an abstract meaning does not prevent it from displaying the abundance and intensity of a far-ranging literary imagination. To take but a few examples from the first volume[1] of his *chef-d'œuvre* will illustrate the riches of this literary imagination: the common man is seen as the 'stereotype factory product of Nature'; man in society as a 'beast of prey with a muzzle on': the *nunc stans* of the eternal present is the tangential point of a rainbow or of a rotating disc, or the refraction of the rainbow on a waterfall; man's existence is 'thrown into' time; existential *Angst* speaks to us in a disembodied voice out of the hollow of a crystal ball; life is a journey on a circular track of glowing coals with a few cooler places here and there; the singleness of tormentor and tormented is illustrated by 'the Will that sinks its teeth into its own flesh'; the genitals and the brain of man are the two foci (*Brennpunkte*) of the Will; and, finally, the 'silvery glance of resignation and knowledge [rests] smilingly and peacefully on the mirages of this world, which were once able to move and torment a man's mind, but now stand before him, indifferently, like chessmen after the game is over, or like masquerade costumes, cast off in the morning, whose shapes teased and disquieted him through the night of carnival'. If, furthermore, we mention

---

[1] In the account that follows I have not followed Schopenhauer's own order but have found it more convenient to begin with Book 2.

Schopenhauer's complex but highly controlled syntax, which (far ahead of its time) does all that it possibly can to lighten the notorious German 'ponderousness'[1] of final verbs; if, to conclude, we mention the vast range of his quotations—from the Vedas and Upanishads, through medieval mysticism and Platonic and neo-Platonic authorities, Patristic sources, to Spanish, French and English dramatists, poets and novelists, with the barest sprinkling of German quotations, and those mainly from the mystics, Meister Eckhardt in particular, and from Goethe: one might make a small anthology of the quotations from Shakespeare alone—we have perhaps done enough to substantiate Nietzsche's claim that Schopenhauer is the first German philosopher with a sense of European culture.[2]

Quite often the imagery is doubly literary, in the sense that my quotation will make clear. It comes from a passage[3] in which Schopenhauer is concerned to establish the world as a single and undivided reality, to establish in particular the continuity of dream and waking experience. In support of this view he has been quoting, as so often, the testimony of the poets, concluding with Calderon's 'Life is a Dream' and Shakespeare's 'We are such stuff / as dreams are made of, and our little life / is rounded with a sleep'. And then:

Nach diesen vielen Dichterstellen möge es nun auch mir vergönnt seyn, mich durch ein Gleichniss aus-zudrücken. Das Leben und die Träume sind Blätter eines und des nämlichen Buches. Das Lesen im Zusammenhang heisst wirkliches Leben. Wann aber die jedesmalige Lesestunde (der Tag) zu Ende und die Erholungszeit gekommen ist, so blättern wir oft noch müssig und

After these many quotations from the poets I too may be permitted to express myself by way of an image. Our life and dreams are leaves in one and the same book. When we read continuously, that is real life. But when our reading period (the day) is over and it is time to rest, we often go on, idly turning over the pages, here and there, without order or continuity. Sometimes we look at a page we have

---

[1] Schopenhauer himself describes it thus in his essay 'Über Schriftstellerei und Stil', *ed. cit*, Vol. V, pp. 530 ff.

[2] Kröner ed., no. 82 (*Nachlass*, Vol. I) p. 239.

[3] See *W.W.V.*, Vol. I, § 5 (*ed. cit.*, Vol. I, p. 51). Cf. Hobbes's famous passage on the continuity of thought in the *Leviathan*, Book I, Chap. 3.

*schlagen, ohne Ordnung und Zu-
sammenhang, bald hier, bald dort ein
Blatt auf: oft ist es ein schon
gelesenes, oft ein noch unbekanntes,
aber immer aus demselben Buch. So
ein einzeln gelesenes Blatt ist zwar
ausser Zusammenhang mit der folgerechten Durchlesung: doch steht es
hiedurch nicht so gar sehr hinter
dieser zurück, wenn man bedenkt,
dass auch das Ganze der folgerechten
Lektüre ebenso aus dem Stegreife an-
hebt und endigt und sonach nur als
ein grösseres einzelnes Blatt anzu-
sehen ist.*

*read already, then again it is one we
do not know yet, but they are all
from the same book. Such a haphazard reading of a single page is
not the same as our ordinary consecutive reading, but it is not all that
inferior to it if we consider that our
proper consecutive reading too, seen
as a whole, begins and ends haphazardly and must therefore be
regarded merely as the reading of a
larger single page.*

We come back once more to the 'literary' quality of the achievement, to Schopenhauer's insistence on his own, very particular way of formulating and organising the substance of his thought. Where Kant had said, 'Let others come and put the matter more clearly', he is inclined to claim convincingness from the very form of his argument—he may well (as Keyserling suggests) be the first intellectual to identify clarity and elegance of style with truth itself.

4

To be able to consider the whole of our life as a single book, as a completed and perfectly encompassed single thing, a man must place himself in the position of an observer at some distance from the details. He must put himself where he will find it possible to abstract from the untidy variety and apparently unwieldy diversity of single facts, phenomena, experiences. A moment's reflection—that is, a moment's abstraction from individual situations—will tell us that here lies the fundamental formal problem of every philosophy that is foolhardy enough to aim at making general statements about the real world. But this act of abstraction, the putting of a distance between the phenomena and the observing (account-giving) self, can also be the source of something like a distortion. It is likely to lead to the flattening out of some contours, the overstressing of others—the unified view, like all translations of experience from one 'mode' into another, will correspond to the phenomena in the world in a very particular way. If this is the formal problem every philosopher must face and solve (though he doesn't have to be explicit about his solution), it follows that to ask how he has solved it will always be relevant to a consideration of the philosophy he offers. In the present instance the question leads to the very core of the system.

For with Schopenhauer this 'formal' problem becomes the subject-matter of his philosophy, he makes a virtue of the philosophical necessity. His philosophy is a major reflective act in which this *distance* is turned into a source of *value*—ultimately, for him, the only source there is. He describes the various kinds of activity which achieve the distance, he shows to what degree they are capable of achieving it, and he elaborates all the implications arising from the undertaking.

Philosophers, poets and saints have said a great many un-complimentary things about man's life on earth. Some, stressing the haphazardness of a few moments' delight or lust, have shown these brief moments to be engulfed by otherwise unrelieved suffering or (at best) boredom. Others again have claimed that we are somehow not really at home in this grim world of ours, and some have compared our precarious worldliness very un-favourably with the assurances vouchsafed to us from other worlds. Schopenhauer will in effect say that these men are philo-sophers, poets and saints by virtue of having understood and enlarged[1] on this feeling we have, the feeling of our alienation. But he—and he alone among the major philosophers—is the one to say that this feeling of ours is an indication that we are not unredeemable: that if there is any goodness in us, its source is in that feeling.

If (to return to Schopenhauer's image of life as a book) the denial of a real difference between life and dream is something one might expect from a poet or dramatist, the other distinction implied in that passage, between 'life' and 'experience and its continuity', is a more directly philosophical one. It belongs to the kind of distinctions philosophers make when they speak of the

---

[1] The poets, however, enlarge in a special way; see below, pp. 195 ff.

objective world and its subjective interpretation, of noumena and phenomena, of 'das Ding an sich' and its 'Anschauungsformen', of appearance and reality. The dualism fundamental to Schopenhauer's philosophy, the dualism of 'Idea' and 'Will' (or 'World'), is of this kind. For him, as for Nietzsche, though the Garden of Eden is an illusion, the Fall of Man is not. His dualism is based on a feeling for the evanescence of all things human, which has traditionally led philosophers to postulate that meaning, significance, reality (or whatever other word they used to express their feelings for value) is not where *they* are, or where the world is.

It is our terminology rather than Schopenhauer's which makes for difficulties at this point. In reading him we must certainly give up our anxious habit of identifying 'real' with 'valuable'. For Schopenhauer the world and all in it is indubitably and unambiguously real. The fact that it is generated by the collective Will—and objectivised by each willing self—does not make the world into a chimera. Nor are we invited to another display of a gigantic solipsism. The fact that each thing in the world is posited, created by the individual will, makes no difference whatever to its status as a part of reality, to its 'being the case', to its being 'what the evidence compels us to believe', a thing firmly and indisputably *there*. The importance of the 'voluntarist' origin and nature of the world lies thus not in epistemology but in ethics, since this genealogy explains all human (and animal) conduct in terms of a conflict of willing selves. Never has the Hobbesian notion of universal war, of an endless, fruitless, meaningless bloody conflict, been taken up with greater gusto and elaborated by a more comprehensive imagination. For this conflict there is, *in* the world, hardly any abatement and little respite. True, Schopenhauer does speak of pity and charity. They are indeed the only values which, without fatally endangering the willing self—without permanently removing us from the strife—offer us brief moments of escape. Or rather not of escape since, pitying our fellow-slaves in the galley, we do not really leave the world, but only stand back from it for a while. For the rest, all is assertion and pitiless conquest, all is for the preservation and propagation of the self.

In the logic of the system, then, the world is the product of a

Universal Will (making its appearance by means of a large number of individuated wills, i.e. individuals), and the Idea, its antagonist, is not in the world. It is certainly not 'real' in the sense in which we count reality in the world, and yet, of course, the significance Schopenhauer attaches to the Idea is not just greater than that attaching to anything in the world: the Idea *is* significance, meaning, value. . . . And since it, the world viewed as Idea, has no bearing whatever upon the positive conduct of our lives, on our practical knowledge of the world, on our hopes and fears in it, the Idea is outside the 'vicious circle' of causes and effects. It is perfectly useless, purposeless, meaningless as the world, which is the world of the Will, recognises meaning and purpose. 'Perfectly useless?' It would appear, from the phrase, that we are capable of recognising perfection even where it does not serve an acceptable end. Oxymorons of this kind, and the feeling or experience they retrace, will provide Schopenhauer with a foothold on the rock of reality from which to preach his strange gospel of redemption.

5

The world is the product of a Universal Will, of which my subjective willing is a specific manifestation: this is one half of the argument. In trying to answer the question what sort of statement this is, what truth it expresses and what illumination it secures, I shall here leave out of account the logic and epistemology to which it belongs. More relevant at this point is the fact that Schopenhauer, like Stendhal, Heine, Hebbel and a host of other writers, belongs to an age that is dominated by the shadow of Napoleon. If this is the common situation[1] from which he and the majority of early nineteenth-century continental writers start, the reaction to it is a matter of individual experience and temperament. The personality of Napoleon does not explain the philosophy of Schopenhauer. It merely marks the point of its

---

[1] A critical account of the 'heroic ideology' of the age is to be found in P. A. Roubiczek's *The Misinterpretation of Man*. London 1949.

inception—the way it marks the inception of the later acts of *Faust II*, or of *War and Peace*. History—the European history of Schopenhauer's formative years—is determined by the great individual. The (at best) morally neutral nature of this conception of greatness preoccupies him as much as it does Stendhal, as much as it will Tolstoy. One need be no Hegelian to see that Schopenhauer's relations with the *Zeitgeist* are much more intimate than he likes to admit.

The principle which sustains and separates off the great individual from other men, and from the masses above all, is the principle of ambition: the lust for power, dominion, glory, sovereignty. In brief, it is the will. Its metaphysics is based on a generalised psychological and historical insight. The will, in its cosmic habitat a vast, undifferentiated drive, makes its appearance in the world as *the* principle of individuation; as that without which there would be no individuals, no particular phenomena, no distinct reactions; as that without which there would be nothing but undifferentiated chaos.

Nor is this postulation of the will merely a vast aprioristic generalisation innocent of concrete detail. The subtlety and variety of Schopenhauer's psychological observations and inferences is hardly inferior to Freud's, and hardly less original. But they all—observations, personal experiences, the evidence of poets, painters, prophets and saints—lead, in the interpretation of his powerful mind, to one central point. And, conversely, it is not too much to say that the philosopher's temperament is fully reflected in the doctrine, that it is a 'man of iron', a 'closed personality',[1] a philosophical Mr Dombey,[2] whose will is being

---

[1] The term itself, *'geschlossene Persönlichkeit'*, is central to Otto Ludwig's *Zwischen Himmel und Erde* of 1855.

[2] The comparison is not far-fetched. For instance: in perfect Dombeyan fashion, Schopenhauer broke off relations with his mother and (for a time) his sister because he suspected them of getting preferential treatment from his deceased father's creditors. He himself, in a lifetime of careful speculation, mainly in English gilt-edged (and, like the late lamented Mr Pipchin, not without some losses in the Mexican mines), doubled the modest fortune he had salvaged from the ruins of his father's bankrupt estate. It is also very much to the point that *Dombey and Son* (1846–8) is 'the first novel of Dickens to be

imposed upon the structure of the Universe. At one point Schopenhauer seems to recognise this himself. The central thought of his system ('a thought wholly without antecedents'), he proclaims, is entirely at one with the Universe itself; its manifold elaborations, on the other hand, 'cannot', he confesses, 'be wholly free from the vestiges of the personality in which [the thought] was produced for the first time'.[1] Thus 'truth' (the truth of his system) begins where this particular manifestation of the Will, called Arthur Schopenhauer, leaves off. As between the total disinterestedness of Kant's philosophising and the activism of a Marx or Nietzsche, Schopenhauer occupies a half-way position. He has not come to change the world, nor to 'philosophise with the hammer'. He is content to abdicate from all social activity—even from teaching—but not without first showing its utter worthlessness. Sour grapes here make a heady wine.

The unitary conception at the centre of Schopenhauer's statements about the world as the product of the Will is a speculative inference. It may be helpful to think of these unified insights as the radii of one circle—he himself speaks of the wheel of Ixion—which encompasses our world. They all run to its centre but are interrupted, short of their goal, by another, concentric circle, which draws the limits of our knowledge. Schopenhauer's generalisation of the will into *the* principle of individuation (and thus of all existence) amounts to an extension of the radii to the point where they presumably meet, and which is invisible to us. The one postulate required prior to the inference is that there is no God, no divine purpose, no redeeming meaning to the absurdity: more exactly, that the redeeming meaning cannot possibly come from a personal God, cannot possibly have assumed flesh and walked among us.

The major creative act of the philosophy, then, is the act of perceiving the will to be not merely that organ of the human psyche which shapes certain parts of the surrounding world according to its intentions (as common sense would see it), but

---

dominated by a leading idea, embodied in a single character' (K. Tillotson, *Novels of the Eighteen-Forties*, Oxford 1961, p. 163).

[1] *W.W.V.*, Vol. I, § 29, ed. cit., p. 226.

as that principle (and not merely organ) which actually makes, or creates, the world as that which we know it to be. And it is hard to see why, if there is to be no God, and if the philosopher's mind is vigorous enough not to be arrested by those half-baked 'purposes' which subsequent materialist thought was content to stop at, and if such a mind is not content with linguistic agnosticism— why the Will should not be thought adequate to provide an illuminating account (an account rather than an explanation) of the way the world has come to be what it is.

The Will, a huge undifferentiated force, makes the world what it is. It does so by a process of crystallisation into a large number of individual wills, all with different capacities for self-assertion, that is for life; all at war with each other; all irredeemably and endlessly positing themselves, and employing a variety of devices —not a very large variety at that—for the purpose of furthering their own ends. All this, it is hardly too much to say, is the philosophical, and scientifically unsubstantiated, anticipation of the Darwinian hypothesis of natural selection and survival. There is a place, in this scheme of things, for human intelligence and ingenuity. But these faculties are differentiated from blind instincts merely by their superior efficiency. A man has the capacity to take care not only of today, but also of the morrow and the day after. Practical intelligence, which finds its outlet in social activities, politics, lawmaking, the natural sciences and technology, is here not categorically distinguished from the cruder and blinder instinctive gropings of the animals; it merely embodies a more efficient way of dealing with much the same sort of concerns in much the same sort of environments.[1]

What this vision amounts to is a very specific disposition, a 'Weltgefühl' that Schopenhauer wishes to hand down to posterity.

[1] Another way of putting this is to say that Schopenhauer's conceptions of Verstand and Vernunft are different only in degree of abstraction and that the former corresponds roughly to Kant's conception of 'praktische Vernunft'; or again, as Schopenhauer himself says, that 'the intellect is merely derivative and secondary'.

The attitude which his complex and variegated reductions to a
first principle enable him to evolve is one of sublime indifference.
This is the moment of truth he conveys: the moment in which
the whole complex business of living in a highly developed
society, in the company of friends and against the pressure of
enemies; the whole business of enquiring, inventing, discovering,
interpreting, caring for things and one's self, having interests,
pursuing them and abandoning them for others, the whole
business, in fact, of belonging to 'this, our inalienable world', all
this, quite suddenly, appears as hopelessly, inescapably trivial and
unimportant. A generation earlier Schiller, fascinated by the
formality of the Kantian ethic, had praised '. . . the high value of
a philosophy of life which by its constant reference to universal
laws weakens the feeling we have for our individuality: teaches
us to lose our petty self in the comprehensive order of the great
Whole: and thus enables us to treat our own self as we would a
stranger'.ᴸSchopenhauer is more radical than that: the 'comprehensive order of the great Whole' for the sake of which he would
'weaken the feeling we harbour for our individuality' is nothingness, the void itself.

Like so many nineteenth-century arguments, this wholesale
relegation of the cares of the world *looks* Christian and is the
opposite. It is no accident that among the many quotations with
which Schopenhauer enlivens his work are the sayings of the
Christian mystics; though it is equally significant that these
quotations should always be irrelevant to the specifically *Christian*
nature of their mysticism. The difference between his teaching and
theirs lies in the moment of incarnation, which for the Christian
mystic is the necessary link between the null-and-void of this
world and eternal salvation. To the mystic the dual being of
Christ as man and as son of God is a guarantee that the flesh—the
world—though sinful, is yet in some way and in some measure
redeemable; that the Word—the spirit—was made flesh and in
its turn was redeemed by sacrifice into eternity. In order to be
able to claim that all great thoughts, including the Christian, are
united in his thought, Schopenhauer stoops to a fairly common

definitional sleight-of-hand: that which he pleases to call *real* Christianity he defines as a religion with no significant or positive contact with the here and now, whereas the doctrine of the Logos and of the exemplary sacrifice are to him either mere survivals of a barbaric Jewish tribal lust for blood or 'mere myths', anthropomorphic picture-books for children.[1] But this argument is conducted quite coolly—there is here no passionate feeling of deprivation, no despairing outburst of the natural believer. For Schopenhauer God is not dead: no *Zeitgeist* has killed him: he is, and always has been, a myth.

The other, and I think more relevant, comparison that springs to mind is with Heidegger's doctrine of *Sorge*,[2] according to which the world of our common interpretation is co-extensive with *care*. In this view all our activities in the world amount to the getting of things (*Zeug*), foraging, scrounging; all our discourse is but the patter (*Gerede*) that accompanies, and whiles away the time between, our trivial preoccupations;[3] and society is the sphere of '*man*', where our actions are governed, not by what '*I* say' or '*we* do', but by what '*one* says' because '*it* is done' ... Here again, in this resolution to see our ordinary world as determined by *cura rerum* and the clammy anxiety that goes with it, we have a view, not perhaps quite as comprehensive as Schopenhauer's, in which the range of everyday life, its values, intentions, hopes and fears, are disposed of with extraordinary nonchalance, in a stunningly cavalier manner. Both views are, in a sense, equally denigratory. But there is another sense—the

[1] Seeing that 'some of his best friends' and most devoted disciples were Jews, his anti-semitism is not consistent; but it is in his pages that we meet perhaps for the first time that division of Christian doctrine into 'Arian' and 'non-Arian' elements on which, towards the end of the century, H. S. Chamberlain founded his 'scientific' argument from race.

[2] See Martin Heidegger *Sein und Zeit* [1927],[5] Halle an der Saale 1941, Chap. 6, pp. 180–226.

[3] Schopenhauer's own observation on this is written in English: 'The *conversation* among ordinary people, when it does not relate to any special matter of fact, but takes on a more general character, mostly consists in *hackney'd common places*, which they alternately repeat to each other, with the utmost complacency.' (*Neue Paralipomena, ed. cit.*, Vol. IV of *Nachlass*, p. 307, his italics.)

one with which I am concerned in these pages—in which the contrast between them is as significant as the similarities: a sense we may call literary. By that I mean that one comes away from a reading of Schopenhauer with an impression which is lacking in Heidegger: the impression of his having been there.

To read what Schopenhauer has to say on the subject of 'the World as Will' is to experience the thrill of a great intellectual and imaginative enterprise. It is to understand that 'this "going right through to the end"' with an argument is by no means the prerogative of 'the full-length work' of art only—of the long novel—as a recent critic has suggested.[1] What follows from the initial hypothesis are consequences for all spheres of life. *All* positive action comes to be identified with suffering, since no action can fully achieve its end or, if it does apparently achieve it, can extend and make stable the enjoyment of the end. The tormentor and the tormented are one. *All* possession must figure as dispossession; *all* justice as the deterrence from crime; *all* government as the avoidance of anarchy. The State is not even the Hobbesian minimal condition which 'makes felicity not impossible', but merely the sum total of all egotisms; it is a safeguard against internecine war, but can never bring about permanent peace, if only because men would soon become too bored with each other and themselves to tolerate it. *All* 'positive' precepts of morality are the rationalisations of fear. *All* love (except *charitas*) is either propitiation or sex. (The one amounts to an imperfect safeguard against the necessarily hostile encroachment of one self upon another, the other has the propagation of the species and thus the endless repetition of meaningless tragicomedy for its end, and this end is temporarily rendered less intolerable by lust; thus sex is not even 'an expense of spirit in a waste of shame', for 'the spirit' is uninvolved.) And *all* 'empirical' knowledge and science, too, is but the knowledge of effects caused by the wills of individuals as they exploit each other and the natural sphere, which is but the sphere of inferior individua-

---

[1] See John Holloway, *The Charted Muse*, London 1960, pp. 225–6. However, this consequentiality is not true of the other side of the plot (see below, p. 202).

tions, that is, the sphere of less purposeful crystallisations of the Universal Will. The world, therefore, is wholly knowable: each individual will is wholly determined in every shape and form in which it makes its appearance in the world, and the world is but the sum total of the Will's appearances. Schopenhauer does not deny that we have, at any one point in our lives, a feeling of freedom of choice; he merely shows that this feeling is illusory since it is based on an imperfect knowledge of the relevant data, and is thus as transitory as all other feelings. Our lives are, after all, at best like a good novel, in which during our first reading, each new event had kept us in suspense by its unexpectedness, yet looking back on the whole we are at last struck by the necessity (the agreement between events and fully informed expectations) of each episode, by the unfreedom of each previously 'free' choice. Another freedom is possible; but its place is not in this world. As to the here-and-now, egotism, unhappiness and wrong-doing are in no way accidental and avoidable—they are of the very essence of life, it is their opposites which are the brief exceptions.

The world is not only wholly knowable but also wholly present. There is no past and no future; there are only the consequences of one and the expectations of the other, as they affect the present tangential point of particular and general, of individual and world. Similarly, guilt and apprehension alike are unreal except as indications which tell the willing self what it can do with impunity. There is 'eternal' justice, and its motto is 'Vengeance is mine'. That justice is the timeless, synchronous order of the world, a tableau of all events and phenomena as they balance each other in the total scheme, wherein all is as it must be, where the total world is its own court of law (*'die Welt selbst ist das Weltgericht'*), transgression its own punishment, and where whatever happens to a man happens to him justly and deservedly: 'for his is the will, and as the will is, so is the world': *'Tat twam asi—* thou art this.'

The regrettable fact that we are partly ignorant of the order of that timeless whole—that we are ignorant of what we are—is due to the blindness that is our lot as individuals. But for this individuation to which we owe our distinct existences—'the veil of Maya'—we would see the whole in its timeless, meaningless stability. But for this, we would see how the entire life and empirical self of a man is wholly and immutably determined in the moment and act of individuation—the moment we call birth —when the quiddity and quality of the will that is his humanity— that is *he*—is fixed, once and for all time. The liberating, 'redeeming' function of philosophy, art and 'sainthood', which lead to such a total knowledge, is the next step in the argument.

But what of the idea of freedom? Is it wholly illusory? In the eighteenth century the idea had been salvaged by the rationalists in their postulate of an infinite perfectibility (the 'monadic reordering') of the human mind. This postulate was taken up by the German Romantics in the form of the doctrine of 'infinite Becoming', and by Hegel in his dialectic of Progress. Seeing the mind (as well as the world) as a thing essentially static, Schopenhauer rejects this notion of 'Werden' and the entire *Weltanschauung* that goes with it. Like Dickens, Balzac or Melville, and quite unlike the authors of the post-Goethean 'novels of development', he sees the fundamental character of man as a thing immutable and fixed throughout his entire life. Mr Gradgrind can change no more than Captain Ahab or (when all is said and done) Mr Dombey. This unchanging self Schopenhauer calls a man's 'intelligible' character.[1] In itself uncaused, a part of the all-pervading Universal Will, this 'intelligible character' is the 'sufficient cause' (or sub-stratum) of our 'empirical character', which in its turn is wholly chained to causality in the shape of our *ad hoc* intentions and environment. Equating motives with causes (as is the novelist's practice), Schopenhauer has no difficulty —and a good deal of intellectual fun—in showing how each action of the 'empirical self' is part of that dreary causal nexus whose worthless ends are self-assertion, self-perpetuation and, *per impossibile*, the avoidance of pain. His task becomes rather more difficult when he attempts to show that the 'intelligible self' is free, if only because the freedom this self is to employ must lie

---

[1] Schopenhauer's practice of borrowing his terms from medieval ontology is as misleading as when, with caustic blasphemy, he calls the 'freedom' of the intelligible self, 'the efficacious working of grace'.

before the threshold of individuation, and thus of consciousness.[1]

The freedom of the 'intelligible self' (Schopenhauer argues) is a freedom which it derives from the Universal Will. Now, we can 'see' that Will, or think of it, only when it makes its appearance in the real world, yet all phenomena in this world are wholly determined by the chain of causality, and thus unfree. Therefore that freedom must, in this world, be a wholly negative thing. The 'intelligible self' *has* a choice, but its choice is, Heads you lose, tails the Will wins. Thus *either* the 'intelligible self' can (and most 'naturally' does) *choose to will* the world, and this is what the object of its choice looks like:

Denn, wie auf dem tobenden Meere, das, nach allen Seiten unbegränzt, heulend Wasserberge erhebt und senkt, auf einem Kahn ein Schiffer sitzt, dem schwachen Fahrzeug vertrauend; so sitzt, mitten in einer Welt von Quaalen, ruhig der einzelne Mensch, gestützt und vertrauend auf das principium individuationis, oder die Weise wie das Individuum die Dinge erkennt, als Erscheinung. Die unbegränzte Welt, voll Leiden überall, in unendlicher Vergangenheit, in unendlicher Zukunft, ist ihm fremd, ja ist ihm ein Mährchen: seine verschwindende Person, seine ausdehnungslose Gegenwart, sein augenblickliches Behagen, dies allein hat Wirklichkeit für ihn: um dies zu erhalten, thut er Alles, solange nicht eine bessere Erkenntniss ihm die Augen öffnet. Bis dahin lebt bloss in der innersten Tiefe seines Bewusstseyns die ganz dunkle Ahndung, dass ihm jenes Alles doch wohl eigentlich so fremd nicht ist,

Just as on the raging sea, endless in its expanse, that howling lifts up and dashes down mountains of water, a sailor sits in his boat and trusts in his frail vessel: even so in a world full of woes the individual man sits calmly, supported by and trusting in the principle of individuation, which is the way in which the individual perceives things as phenomena. The endless world, full of suffering in all places, in all its endless past and all its endless future, is alien to him, almost a fairy tale[2]: his own ephemeral personality, his immediate presence, his momentary well-being —these alone have reality for him: to keep and preserve all this he will do anything as long as a better knowledge does not open his eyes. Until then it is only in the innermost recesses of his consciousness that there exists a dark foreboding which tells him that yonder world of suffering is not, after all, really so alien to him, but that it has some connection with

---

[1] Of several criticisms of Schopenhauer's ethical theory, the most cogent is Nicolai Hartmann's in his *Ethik*[3], Berlin 1949, pp. 704 f.

[2] The same image is used in the same context by Stifter. See below, p. 271.

sondern einen Zusammenhang mit
ihm hat, vor welchem das principium
individuationis ihn nicht schützen
kann. Aus dieser Ahndung stammt
jenes so unvertilgbare und allen
Menschen (ja vielleicht selbst den
klügeren Thieren) gemeinsame
Grausen, das sie plötzlich ergreift,
wenn sie, durch irgend einen Zufall,
irre werden am principio individuationis, indem der Satz vom
Grunde, in irgend einer seiner
Gestaltungen, eine Ausnahme zu
erleiden scheint: z.B. wenn es
scheint, dass irgend eine Veränderung
ohne Ursache vor sich gienge, oder
ein Gestorbener wieder da wäre,
oder sonst irgendwie das Vergangene
oder das Zukünftige gegenwärtig,
oder das Ferne nah wäre. Das
ungeheure Entsetzen über so etwas
gründet sich darauf, dass sie plötzlich
irre werden an den Erkenntniss-
formen der Erscheinung, welche
allein ihr eigenes Individuum von der
übrigen Welt gesondert halten.[1]

him, against which the principle of
individuation cannot protect him.
This foreboding is the source of the
unconquerable horror common to all
men (and perhaps even to the more
intelligent animals) which suddenly
seizes them when, through some
chance event, the principle of
individuation seems to fail them by
reason of an apparent exception
occurring in one or the other manifestation of the law of causality; as
when it appears that some change has
come about without any cause, or
that a dead person has returned, or
that in some way a past or future
event has become present, or some
distant thing is suddenly near at hand.
The tremendous terror people feel
of this kind of thing arises from their
suddenly being confused about the
forms of knowledge under which the
phenomenon has appeared to them,
for it is these forms alone which keep
their own individual personality
separate from the rest of the world.

Or, acting on that 'dark foreboding', the 'intelligible self' can
decline to will its world and thus itself. Or rather, having once
willed the world, the 'intelligible self' can cultivate such a 'better',
that is, total knowledge of the world as will lead it to a renunciation of its willing, and hence to its own gradual, non-violent
extinction. Of that knowledge more will be said. But even here
it is evident that the hierarchy of philosopher, artist and saint
derives from the exercise of a freedom at each rung more negative,
from a knowledge at each step more disillusioning.

Schopenhauer's entire theory of character is eminently compatible with the Victorian notion of 'the great man': the man who
is subject only to the law of 'the great world'[2] which he alone

---

[1] Op. cit., p. 454.
[2] The last section of Dombey and Son begins (Chap. 51) with one of Dickens's
most powerful and, as it were, direct evocations of just this 'great world'. It

represents and holds his sway over. This is the predatory ethos of the early Industrial Revolution. At the point where Mr Dombey ceases to impose his will he not only fails as a man of business but also ceases to be the Mr Dombey we know. Thomas Mann is even more radical: ceasing to will, Thomas Buddenbrook has hardly time to wind up the family business before he dies, of a toothache. And Captain Ahab too, far from stock-exchange and counting-house, is not killed merely by a superior power or intervening circumstance. He too, 'in that all-pervading azure' of the day before the last chase, though still carried forward by the momentum of his mania, is overwhelmed by an insight and an understanding which maim his will: he too abdicates from his 'intelligible self'.[1] Each man, and each alone, is in his own frail boat. As soon as he ceases to ply his oars, the waves close in over him.

Schopenhauer's borrowings from medieval terminology are as misleading as his analogies with Christianity. Yet his conception of the 'intelligible self' does reflect his endeavour to establish a doctrine of Being which would not be wholly at the mercy of Doing. His attempt to oppose the Faustian ideology of 'striving' with a self-contained ontology founded in an immutable substratum in the personality seems to be valuable even if its negative implication is not. When he shows that non-being—the death-wish itself—is the only stable answer to the distractions of an endless doing, Schopenhauer argues towards a nihilism which one may be excused for thinking more honest than the notion of infinite perfectibility which, against all actual evidence to the contrary, lurks behind every activism. In a God-less world his is an altogether truer account of what we are and what are the limits of our individual possibilities.

I have called Schopenhauer's scheme a great intellectual and imaginative enterprise: the very tone, the circumstantiality and

is one of those passages which, cast in a poetic prose, moves (as Schopenhauer might say) 'beyond the confines of individuation'.

[1] See the conversation with Starbuck in the magnificent eighty-first chapter, 'The Symphony'.

detail with which he presents to us that world which he declares
to be an object, not indeed of his 'hatred', but of his scorn and
'contempt'[1]—the *way* he presents it to us conveys distinctly the
feeling that he has actually been there, that he himself has gone
through and imaginatively encompassed almost all of it, that he
has, in the fullest meaning, experienced it all himself; in much
the same way as a novelist conveys the impression of having been
involved, directly and immediately (whatever the mere facts of
his biography may indicate), in the human situation which his
book explores. Whereas (to return to a previous comparison)
Heidegger's presentation gives little if any of that kind of feeling,
for it proceeds in a wholesale, absolutist manner which intimates
little of the living experience, and relates but indifferently to our
imagination. The difference in philosophical doctrine is at least
partly determined by the literary quality and appeal of the argument.

To commend the tone, the literary quality, of Schopenhauer's
philosophy is neither to accept it as true nor to reject it as faulty.
The logical cogency of the whole remains to be examined, its
form—a mode of that whole—does not 'dispose of the problem'.
But to commend its form does mean that, even if the system itself
does not survive unimpaired, a good deal that is of value will be
salvaged. Even if we find that Schopenhauer's intricate rationalisation of his original experience cannot be defended, yet still
the experience calls to us in the tone of his voice. Of this too
Schopenhauer seems to have been aware. For when he comes to
speak of the superior conviction of evidence as against proof, of
the superiority of 'showing', '*erweisen*', over 'proving', '*be-
weisen*' and of '*Anschaulichkeit*' over mathematical deduction, he
is commending a mode of argument and conviction of which
he himself is the great practitioner.

---

[1] E.g. in a letter to one of his disciples, apropos of an enthusiastic essay on his
philosophy in the *Westminster Review* of 1853 (see K. Fischer, *Schopenhauers
Leben, Werke und Lehre*, Heidelberg 1934, p. 106). The distinction between
hatred and contempt may be a nice one, but it is precisely where Schopenhauer
proceeds by way of wholesale contempt—as in his arid scurrilities *On Women*
(*ed. cit.*, Vol. V, pp. 648–61)—that he becomes boring.

6

The world, apart from being the sum total of the objectivisations of the Will, is also a complex of ideas: or rather of '*Vorstellungen*', that is, the 'representational contents of my brain'.[1] Now the moment (and it is a moment in time, in our lives) these ideas quit the service of the individual will, they are raised to a higher order. Whereas the ideas ('*Vorstellungen*') vouchsafe to us a knowledge of what is the case in the world, and thus a knowledge with a definite mundane, practical end in view, the knowledge which the Ideas ('*Ideen*') yield is unrestricted by any such ends and thus less partial, giving specific answers to a total 'Why?'.

What is thus identified as the Ideas is not a certain part of the world but all of it, the world 'through and through'. The world is 'wholly Idea' at the same time as it is 'wholly the object of my willing'. The world is Idea 'from another point of view' (in Leibnitz's terminology), or 'under another mode' (in Spinoza's): that is, under the mode of disinterested knowledge. In trying to show how it can be both, Schopenhauer bases himself on an epistemological argument which is undoubtedly the weakest part of his scheme. What it amounts to is the formal assertion that all thinking about objects—that is, all knowledge—presupposes a subject, itself not an object and therefore not part of any knowledge; and this subject he hypostatises from its purely formal status into a metaphysical entity. Or again: all objects (all phenomena) and their relations presuppose, but are separate from, a knowing subject; they are distinct from an extensionless 'bearer of the world'; but what is that subject? It is identical with what we commonly call our self only to the extent to which that self is disembodied and thus outside the will-determined nexus of causality in space and time; whereas to the extent that the self is my body, it is an 'objectivisation of my will', and knowable to me only as such—that is, as an object (albeit the most proximate) among other objects. Now, Schopenhauer's reasons for hypostatising this formal assertion of a knowing subject are cogent enough. But the logic of it remains unconvincing, simply because it remains a statement about the relation between—the 'coincidence'

of—two things of which one is by his own definition
'always subject' and thus absolutely unknowable. And we have
already observed that Schopenhauer's whole style of writing is
the opposite of poetic in the sense of intimatory; that it is not
conducive, either here (§ 18 of Vol. I) or in the last implications
from the argument (Book IV), to conviction from myth or
analogy (from 'pretty pictures'), the way Plato's or the mystics'
writings are. Where he speaks of mystery we are apt to suspect
mystification.

If, psychologically speaking, it is the act of self-assertion—'the
world as will'[1]—that constitutes the intimate experience from
which Schopenhauer starts; if, historically speaking, it is in the
Kantian notion of aesthetic 'disinterestedness' that he finds the
only remedy against all worldly ills, then the need to postulate
the coincidence of willing and knowing subject in the self becomes obvious enough. The 'mystical coincidence' is his equivalent of redemption.

From the world-as-will all knowledge which is not purposeful,
'teleological' knowledge, is excluded. There is, in such a world,
no place for a philosopher capable of a comprehensive insight into
it all, no place for the artist who creates a beautiful and thus 'useless' image of any part of it, and no place for the saint who will
repudiate it all. Nor can they be in another world, for there is
none. In what sense, then, are they in this world at all? The answer
is again given in quasi-Christian terms: they—the philosopher,
artist and saint—are in this world, but not of it; in it as observers,
not of it as willing subjects. And since their knowledge of the
world and of its will-determined teleology is a knowledge of the
world's more or less blind self-perpetuation; since theirs is always
a knowledge of a *bad* world, their knowledge can have only one
'purpose': to illuminate the world, its object, in such a way that
the world will come to be seen more and more clearly in its
triviality and badness, until it (the object of their knowledge) and
they as empirical selves (as objects among other objects) will cease

---

[1] Schopenhauer's claim that the will is simply the Kantian '*Ding-an-sich*'
seems to me as unconvincing as the complementary claim that his Ideas are
identical with the Platonic (see below, p. 192).

to be. And their knowledge must do this unless it itself is to become 'bad'—that is, knowledge with a purpose such as the world accepts and is perpetuated by. The philosopher (and, *a fortiori*, the artist and the saint) is not merely 'not at home' in the world as men commonly interpret it; but, more than that, he must show up this 'being-at-home' as devoid of all value and all meaning, as unworthy of his most serious considerations *except* as a spectacle, a play, except as the subject-matter of his detached will-less contemplation. He is what he is by virtue of not participating: his being is not a doing. And he is truly free (as opposed to merely having an illusory and temporary feeling of freedom) in so far as he repudiates the doing of the world and distances himself from it.

Here indeed is the insoluble paradox of the argument: the truly knowing subject *is*, but only to the extent that it is not in the world, yet the world is the sum total of our knowledge. In order to get out of this quandary, Schopenhauer does not conduct an existentialist dialectic of Nothingness. The '*nihil*' he acknowledges is always the common-sense '*nihil privativum*', an absence of this or that thing or quality. He does not try to describe a 'positive nothingness', a *Nirvana*, or Rilke's '*Nirgends ohne Nicht*'; this (he says) is the 'task' of artists and saints, if indeed they have a task. His argument comes to rest on a *mystical* assertion. He postulates a Self, which is both an *individual*, in as much as it is the willing subject of the world and thus also one among the objects it wills; at the same time that Self is also *beyond individuation*, inasmuch as it is the purely knowing, uncaused and no longer causing subject of it all. The logic of the argument (one half empirical, one half mystical) is defective. Yet it wields a powerful attraction, because it expresses a certain intellectual disposition of his time and ours validly enough.

This 'mystery of coincidence' in the knowing subject is, after all, not wholly unknown to us. It marks, for us too, the moment of truth, falteringly put into words by poets and philosophers from Plato onwards, in which we feel ourselves in possession of a total knowledge. But in such moments a radical alternative faces us. Sustained by faith, they intimate to us the *positive* unity of all creation. Deprived of that, they intimate an apprehension of futility—Sartre's *nausée*, Heidegger's *Angst*—of the kind that

Schopenhauer knows well, and to which his doctrine of renunciation offers an absolute relief. That relief we are all too ready to accept. And what further makes him so much our contemporary is that the feeling which accompanies his deprivation is so lacking in passion. When he writes of God as 'the old Jew in Cloud-cuckooland' whose 'shares are falling', he writes as a man who more than once had to sell out in a slump. But he writes no better than that.

This, then, is his 'bedrock of atheism'. Rooted there is a vigorous, assertive and far from despairing philosophical mind which, having failed to find the world's meaning and value outside it, in a living God, and scorning utterly to identify any part of the real world as a worthy repository of them, attempts to recreate the ancient unknowable 'I am that I am' in something like its own 'mystic' image.

To Nietzsche this same situation is historically determined and tragic; in page after page of *Zarathustra* he evokes and comments on the monstrous event of the death of God in his time. And even where Nietzsche proclaims the event as a liberation, the violent rhetoric of rejoicing above the deep notes of despair is like the jarring sound of a seagull searching for land above the desolate waters of the sea.

For the anti-historical Schopenhauer there is neither loss nor compensation, the end of faith is neither the result of events in time nor tragic. (And indeed, seeing that the world is unchanging, and history the great '*nunc stans*', all 'tragedy' is but the unravelling of misapprehensions and 'absurd conclusions'.[1]) Coolly and caustically Schopenhauer unrolls his complex scheme. Irrelevant to any genuinely religious view, it accounts as well as may be expected for 'the coincidence', the 'moment of truth'; and for those creations of the human mind which, born in that moment, are in the world and yet not of it, those intimations of the timeless *Nirvana* which are flesh of our flesh and yet beyond the tyranny of purpose, space and time.

Schopenhauer's aesthetics (and thus his entire system) issues from his radically negative evaluation of the world, and this

---

[1] See Hobbes's *Leviathan*, Book I, § 5.

negation is deeply rooted in the spirit of his age (an historical consideration for which he would not have thanked us[1]). Yet both the negation and its resultant aesthetics belong no less to ours. Nietzsche's criticism is cogent enough:

Seit Kant ist alles Reden von Kunst, Schönheit, Erkenntnis, Weisheit vermanscht und beschmutzt durch den Begriff 'ohne Interesse'. Mir gilt als schön (historisch betrachtet): was an den verehrtesten Menschen einer Zeit sichtbar wird, als Ausdruck des Verehrungswürdigsten.[2]

Since Kant all talk of art, beauty, knowledge and wisdom is messy and sullied by the concept of 'disinterestedness'. I regard as beautiful (historically speaking) all that which, in the most revered men of an age, assumes visible shape as the expression of what is most worthy of reverence.

To the extent that this strikes us as an 'unrealistic' description of the art of his day and ours, we are still committed to Schopenhauer's idea of art as a process of indirection. But Nietzsche's repudiation is valid because it is based not on a mystical 'coincidence in the subject' but on a unity of world and art; that is, on a different, more generous conception of man. That Schopenhauer can cheerfully bear and expatiate on his knowledge of the bad whereas Nietzsche can do no more than polemically assert his knowledge of the good in men, is due as much to their individual temperaments as to the course of intellectual history itself.

7

If the world as Will is, according to Schopenhauer, the world as ordinarily experienced by men, the world as Idea is that of his

[1] Thus in 1855 he attacks Kuno Fischer: 'Hopelessly corrupted by Hegelianism [Hegelei], he artificially constructs the history of philosophy according to Hegel's a priori clichés, so that I as a pessimist become the necessary antithesis of Leibnitz the optimist. Which is deduced from the fact that Leibnitz lived in an age of hope, whereas ours is a despairing age. Ergo, had I lived in 1700, I would have been just such a smart and sly optimist.... Whereas ... [quite apart from other objections] my pessimism was worked out between 1814 and 1818 (at which date it was published in its complete form)—that is, after Germany's liberation, the time of her greatest hopes.' (Briefe, ed. cit., Leipzig n.d., p. 300.) Throughout his work, Schopenhauer's view of the Hegelian Zeitgeist is as crudely simplified as is the Marxists', though for a different reason.
[2] Kröner ed. no. 82, (Nachlass, Vol. I), p. 194.

re-interpretation. Is the knowing self wholly other than the willing self? It seems that he would have it both ways—the uncertainty of the answer reflects the obscurity of the '*unio mystica*' in the subject. Nor is the matter made clearer by Schopenhauer's invoking of the Platonic Ideas[1] to support his argument. For whereas in Plato the emphasis lies on the conceptual content of the Ideas (thus they subsume the virtues, etc.), Schopenhauer's Ideas have as their primary function the pure and disembodied re-presenting of the things in this world, and the relations among these things, all in a sphere that is not of this world. They are the most immediate and most adequate objectivisations of the Will ('*Objektität*'); that is, pure but partial renderings of that universal Will, unsullied and unarrested by 'base substance' (which owes its origin to its being an object to a willing subject). 'Objects' they too must be, but of our 'intelligible self'. As 'stable, indestructible forms' they lie between the self—'which is not the self as an individual but as a pure, will-less, knowing subject'[2]— and the real world. Art is the re-presentation of these Ideas in a sphere all but inaccessible to our individualised wills. Projected on to the consciousness of the self, these re-presentations are like the coloured images of the real world, like the panorama of waves and hostile vessels thrown by a periscope on to the sight-table below. Yet since they retrace the great Will itself as it is individualised in the world, and thus the true state of the world, they vouchsafe us a *true* knowledge the like of which is not to be had in the willed world at all. This whole scheme of the aesthetic Ideas is not without affinities with the old imitation-theory. If we were able to speak of a time sequence in this universe, we might well say that these pure objectivisations of the Will must follow upon the birth of the willed world; yet they are also patterns, archetypes of what has already become mundane reality. But here is no time or space (these belong to the world governed by the principle of sufficient reason). Here all is the

---

[1] Most of his account of Plato's theory of the Ideas appears to be derived from post-Platonic sources (see *ed. cit.*, § 25 of Vol. I, pp. 186–7 and § 41, pp. 281 ff.).

[2] *Ed. cit.*, § 38 of Vol. I, p. 264.

great *nunc stans*, a sublime and timeless configuration of the Ideas of all that is significant—or rather, is thus made significant —in the world. And if language, using such words as '*re*-presentations', is reluctant to yield descriptions of that timeless state, that is only to be expected, since language too, capable of rendering only that which is the case in the world, is obedient to the laws of causes and effects in space and time. This world of the Ideas is organised into a hierarchy whose apex is the point where its renderings are characterised by their greatest immediacy: knowledge in that world depends not on abstract proof but on sensuous conviction. Schopenhauer's is not the philosopher's but the artist's philosophy, for to him the most immediate and 'sensuous', as well as the most complete, re-presentation of the world as will in the medium of Ideas is art.

Art as a re-presentation of Ideas? Present-day criticism vaunts a cultivated disapprobation when statements of this kind are made; nothing comes more readily from the pens of intellectuals than the indictment of intellectualism. Rationalising their own deprivations, the New Critics especially have gone to remarkable lengths in trying to squeeze the products of the artistic imagination into the world of things. Time and again their analyses culminate in some such oracular statement as that a poem does not say or describe such-and-such a thing, but that it '*does it*'; as if reality resided only in what hurts upon impact, as if all ideas were parasites, at once malignant and abstruse, feeding on the healthy body of 'concrete Life'. To call such procedures egregious is not to deny that the work of art performs certain practical functions in the world of things. To recommend the superior intelligence and cogency of Schopenhauer's scheme is not to deny that he entirely fails to account for this function. That art cannot, for him, have a 'practical' function is, of course, the unavoidable consequence of his identifying the world with the Will and of his portraying this Will as a self-contained, windowless, complex whole which is for ever incapable of enlightenment from its full self-knowledge, that is, from the Ideas. So that in him the argument comes full circle: the 'intellectualism' he elaborates is so comprehensive that both 'abstract' and 'concrete', the pivotal yet vague concepts of modern criticism, are perfectly accommodated within it. And the differences between art and philosophy are the relative measures to immediacy and close-ness (in a non-spatial meaning) of the re-presentations to the world as it is.

The image in the mirror at the end of the room both is and is not in the room. The words on the page in the completed poem both are and are not the words of common discourse. The com-plex of pigments on the canvas both is and is not this landscape or that face. And Schopenhauer's aesthetics is that scheme which stresses the negative side of these contradictions. The work of art is for him a thing transfixed, as though experience, cleansed of everything adventitious, had escaped from the real world into the mirror, never to come back again.

Art, then, is a re-casting of the phenomenal world into eternal and incorruptible forms. The arts are the sublimates, or crystallisa-tions, of the phenomenal world in the world of Ideas, in their *immediate* and sensate form: not an abstraction away from that form but it itself. Containing significance, they must do more than merely imitate a world which has none. But how, being 're-presentations' or images of 'Ideas', can art achieve 'immediate-ness'? Schopenhauer goes beyond the intellectualist fallacy of equating ideas with concepts. His Ideas are the stable forms into which are cast all the *total* apprehensions of the world as Will of which we may be capable when we ignore the Will's peremptory demands to be given *particular* (individual) shape here and now. That total feeling we call 'foreboding'[1] is one such form, albeit an obscure and imperfect one. Even to these re-presentations a vestige of our individual will attaches: even they are not wholly image, being the creations of an individual. The perfect and ultimate objectivisation lies beyond art, in the silence of total renunciation. But *of* that silence little can be said, *in* that silence nothing; except that, unarrested by its individuality, the self there is a self no more, is at one with the Universal Will. 'Whereof we cannot speak, thereof we must be silent'? The entire scheme Schopenhauer unfolds before us issues in attempts at intimating what that silence, that *Nirvana*, might contain. But again, given

[1] See above, pp. 183–4.

the manner of his argument, the scheme is least convincing just where he places its apex.

Except in one important instance, Schopenhauer is not much concerned with a detailed examination of the various media in which the arts are cast, but rather with what we might call the foreign politics of art—that is, its relation to other and for him inferior modes of experience.[1] The place of art in his scheme of things, its peculiar relation to the world of the Will, determines its subject-matter; and its redemptive, anti-temporal function determines his criteria of what is to be counted as great art. There is no place here either for the fantasies of the Romantics or for the sordid and trivial imitations of Naturalism. His taste is severely classical, in the sense of preceptive and exemplary. Greek tragedy, Goethe's lyrical poetry, the perfect re-casting of the absurd in *Don Quixote*—these are high on his lists of recommended reading. Moralising of the kind he detects in Schiller receives short shrift, because he sees in it a mere translation of worldly—will-determined—considerations into a sphere which, to be true to itself, should be quite free from them. Shakespeare is for him an interesting borderline case. The tragedies—*King Lear, Timon of Athens* and *Macbeth* in particular—are great because, bare of all moralising, they teach us—or rather, they teach him—the only thing that art, in this scheme of things, is permitted to teach—namely, the vanity of all purposeful scheming and self-assertive action. Given the emphasis on the correspondence between the two realms of individual wills and the Ideas, Schopenhauer is bound to think little of all that Coleridge calls 'Shakespeare's fancy', because there cannot, in the nature of such a correspondence, exist an Idea whose content is unrelated to what we know to exist in the world of the Will. Thus very definite limits are set to the working of the artistic imagination, limits which exclude the purely fantastic or invented. Nor is Schopenhauer particularly interested in considerations of a detailed realism: it is a condition of great art, but no more than that. The pivot of the scheme is not verisimilitude but re-creation of what is weighty and

[1] The question of what 'interest' the work of art has for us is discussed below, pp. 243–4.

significant. The world, or at least all that is great and weighty in it, is *done again*. And only in the re-created thing lies a justification of our life down here.

Now, such a view of art would seem to be at odds with Schopenhauer's admiration for all those artists who have given their assent to the created world—his admiration, above all, for Goethe's lyrical poetry, surely the least qualified of all expressions of assent. How can he who says 'no' to the world admire him who says 'yes'? The solution to this apparent contradiction lies once more in the literary, aesthetic quality of Schopenhauer's imagination and hence of his philosophical scheme. The Stoic denial is worthless because the Stoic denies what he has experienced defectively[1] in the first place: the Ideas which re-present his will are necessarily dull and blurred: the game isn't worth the candle. Whereas the Goethean assent is exquisitely valuable as the necessary preliminary to an ultimate denial—the denial becomes significant when it is purchased at the highest price; the artist's task is *'reculer pour mieux sauter . . . dans le néant'*. The beauty and significance of lyrical poetry are seen as the result of 'a contrast between pure, will-less knowledge and the exigencies of an ever limited, ever deprived individual will,'[2] and the peaceful image of a Goethean landscape is the image of a conflict assuaged. The beautiful world which the poem creates is no longer of this world. When we read the lyrical poem as an invitation to enter the real world we read it falsely, since to enter the world is to shatter the peace which the poem intimates. The work of art is redemptive. Schopenhauer speaks of it as the Gnostic theologians speak of the kingdom of God. To us in the world-as-will it is nothing, yet as soon as we renounce the world it becomes everything. The prime postulate, here and everywhere, is a God-less world.

This entire conception of the otherness of art, though it had never before been taken to such radical conclusions, is not an invention of Schopenhauer's. At all times there have been voices

---

[1] *Op. cit.*, Vol. II, p. 498. Where all art vouchsafes total escape, 'escapist' literature would be rejected as defective for the same reason as Stoic philosophy.

[2] Vol. I, p. 330.

asserting the *differentiae* of art against other modes of experience: in Plato's condemnation it is a lie; in St Thomas's theory it is a *unique* synthesis of '*consonantia, claritas et integritas*'; in Dante's prosody it is described as a self-contained world of epic praise with its own modes of interpretation; in the Puritan rejection it is the source of iniquity; in Baroque theory it is extravagant artifice; in Kant it is the one 'disinterested activity'; in Goethe it is the great consoler, in Kierkegaard the great seducer, in Nietzsche the very justification of life. . . . Nor is the emphasis on its otherness as remote from our own understanding of art as a bare recital of the tenets of Schopenhauer's theory may suggest. To take an obvious example: the language of literary criticism is at once similar to and distinct from the language of everyday life, and it is this distinctness we invoke in order to do justice to the total effect of a work of art. Thus it is not, in criticism, a question of whether we 'like' Mr Knightley, but how Mr Knightley fits into the economy, the 'world', of *Emma*. Or again, when a dramatist portrays a character as deserving of punishment, he 'judges' him not only, or not even primarily, as we judge in ordinary life. He imposes his own scale of justice, which is likely to be subtler than, and different from, our common scale. He 'judges' according to the logic of the completed image of life he has set up before us, as a painter sights and thus 'judges' the distance between two objects on the canvas.

These are the kinds of distinction that Schopenhauer takes up and exaggerates into an absolute antithesis. That in his system the two kinds of 'judgement' I spoke of are forcibly sundered; that the knowledge which art vouchsafes is totally and thus falsely severed from the knowledge by which we live; and that he is concerned with increasing the distance between the two—all this I have already emphasised. What he does elaborate is that other aspect of art which, given our present infatuation with naturalism and with arguments on 'commitment' in full cry, it is the contemporary fashion to ignore.

8

Arguments concerning the function of literature are in no better state today than they were two centuries ago, when

Baumgarten[1] set out their conceptual framework. Our discussion
continues to oscillate between the extremes of 'commitment' and
'aestheticism', Left and Right, between history of ideas and syllable-
counting. Each extreme, whether its slogan is 'adult response to
society' or 'a poem is made up of words,' tends to falsify its opposite and so also itself. Eager to find in art the life-enhancing force
that will supply our wants, we 'look for a thing where we ought
not to look for it, and what is worse, we find it where we ought
not to find it: we wish to be edified in the theatre, aesthetically
impressed in church, we would be converted by novels, get
enjoyment out of books of devotion, we want philosophy in the
pulpit, and the preacher in the professorial chair'.[2] These con-
fusions, it seems to me, are not isolated. They reflect above all
our uncertainties about the function—the ethics—of knowledge
itself: the knowledge, for instance, that comes to us from a work
of art. For it is just this that we draw from it, and to say that art
is not among the sources of knowledge is to make these sources
more esoteric and abstruse, or more exclusively 'scientific', and
the rest of experience more irrational, than in our best moments
we know them to be. To learn the logic of the heart as the work
of art discloses it is perhaps the hardest, it is certainly the least
considered, lesson of all.

And on this point, at all events, Schopenhauer is refreshingly
clear-minded and positive. For him the work of art has an end,
and that end is knowledge; that is, knowledge not as the empirical
but as the 'intelligible' self understands it: a 'pure' knowledge
that is wholly free from mundane purpose and interest. (We are
of course bound to baulk at the absoluteness with which he posits
his distinctions. But put less absolutely the distinction is both valid
and helpful: 'aestheticists' and 'committed' critics alike need
reminding that the sort of knowledge we receive from a work of
art is both like, and also quite unlike, the sort of knowledge we
'learn by experience'.) It is a knowledge (Schopenhauer argues)
whose vehicle need not be words at all. In fact it is the more

---

[1] A. G. Baumgarten, *Reflections on Poetry* (1735), ed. Aschenbrenner and
Holther, Berkeley 1954, p. 62.

[2] Søren Kierkegaard, *Either/Or* (1843), Vol. I, Oxford 1946, p. 121.

complete and comprehensive the less it employs the media of a knowledge that is tied up with practical ends. And the structure of a work of art, as well as the genres and branches of art, are determined by this 'non-teleological' teleology. The law of causes and effects (whose servants, nay slaves, we are in the real world) is re-enacted in the image of the human ant-heap which the *camera obscura* throws on the table before us. The charm of the image, of the configuration, is in its life-likeness, certainly; but also in its dispassionate quality of 'as-if'. Art is not the only human activity to achieve this effect. When, 'chancing upon the forty-seventh theorem of Euclid, Thomas Hobbes exclaimed, "By G-d, this is impossible!" and thereupon fell in love with geo-metry', he experienced a delight[1] which was not fundamentally different from that experienced by an intelligent reader of Henry James. Only (Schopenhauer argues), art is more consistently the source of such disinterested delight than even the pure sciences, for it vouchsafes it from among the sensuous images of the 'Ideas' which are directly *en rapport* with the real world; ' "*schön*",' he writes in one of his etymological glosses, 'is undoubtedly con-nate with the English "to shew", "what shews well" . . . and thus it is the distinct expression of significant (Platonic) Ideas.'[2]

9

Among all the arts Schopenhauer singles out music as that which is at once most directly related to this world, most distinctly removed from it, and which re-creates a most complete account of it. The closeness of its relation is due to its being wholly free from conceptual ideas; its remoteness, to its 'purity' and lack of usefulness as moral doctrine or practical precept; while its com-pleteness springs from its capacity, wistfully remarked on by

---

[1] This is the cardinal term of a recent essay in Schopenhauerian aesthetics, M. Oakeshott's *The Voice of Poetry in the Conversation of Mankind*, London 1959. No doubt the stress on disinterested 'delight' as the end of poetry is salutary enough; but the only way I can see of distinguishing it from mere entertainment is by bringing out the connection of 'delight' with 'enlighten-ment' and thus knowledge.

[2] *Ed. cit.*, Vol. V, p. 449.

many literary men, to 'express all, even the inexpressible'. When
we look at Schopenhauer's account of music in strict accordance
with what he himself says about the function of all discursive
arguments, we must think it strictly irrelevant; a practising
musician is likely to find it as uncongenial as all other literary
'talk' about his art, from Plato to Thomas Mann. Granted that
irrelevance, for those who aren't musicians it is perhaps the most
illuminating and profound general account of music to be found
anywhere.

Music is, to Schopenhauer, both the consummation of the arts
and also fundamentally different from them. Unlike all the other
arts, it is not a re-presentation of the Ideas that lie between the
real world and the Universal Will. It is a re-presentation ('ein
Abbild') of the entire Will, an entire world in itself, like the world
of individual wills, like that of the Ideas. All three retrace the
total Will, they are related to each other not causally (as a thing
is not the cause of its representation in an image) but by way of
analogies in different media. Music cannot portray the individual
objects in the world, it does not retell the trivial little stories of
individual wills. Words or scenic presentation merely adulterate
it; they cannot make its meaning clearer or its effect more complete.[1] What it tells is the great cosmic story of the Will, what it
achieves is the fullest knowledge we can have of that Will.

The mundane world is all chaos and strife; the world of the
Ideas is passionless order; the world of music is harmony. The
fundamental tonalities of bass, tenor, alto and soprano correspond
to the order of creation in the real world. The lowest notes of the
double-bass correspond to the limits of individuation in the in-
animate kingdom, just as the highest, most 'spiritual', tonalities
of the violin or the human voice correspond to the highest, least
will-dominated degree of individuation in man. All that is

---

[1] Schopenhauer would have had little use for Wagner's notion of a 'Gesamtkunstwerk'. And when Wagner writes of the profound influence which his
reading of Schopenhauer had upon him (see his letter to Franz Liszt, Autumn
1854, in Hans Mayer's Richard Wagner, Hamburg 1959, pp. 79–80), what he
has in mind is not primarily Schopenhauer's theory of music but those parts of
the system (Book IV) which are concerned with a renunciation of the will,
realised by Wagner in the 'Liebestod' motif.

beyond these limits is inaudible, too indistinct and deep or too spiritual and high for our ears. There is a parallel between the intervals within each scale and between the scales themselves, and the 'intervals' obtaining between the rungs on the ladder of species and genera of mundane creation. Mutations away from the norm in the world of music as in the world of man (discords in one, freaks in the other) give us similar sensations of disrupted harmony. The slow rhythms of counterpointed bass, and the animation and swift runs in the upper registers, retrace the movement of life at its various levels of individuation. Flats and sharps reflect the fundamental moods of pessimism and hope, their alternation in a melody the complex continuity of our emotional life. And melody, guide and organising principle of the world of music, is the thread, the theme and guiding idea, the very meaning of the re-created life: 'Melody tells the story of the will, illuminated by contemplation, whose imprint upon reality is the series of its deeds. But it tells more—it tells its most secret story, it paints every passion, every inclination, every movement of the will, it tells of all that reason subsumes under the broad and negative concept of feeling and can no further accommodate to its abstractions: *"melodiarum motus, animi affectus imitans"*.'[1]

Instead of following Schopenhauer's well-nigh inexhaustible enthusiasm for such parallels we must now ask what they are based on. The answer we receive is at once candid and convincing. Of this grand analogy no proof is possible, for all proof is discursive and conceptual, whereas conviction of the truth must come from that very feeling to which music addresses itself, from those very apprehensions which it translates, completes and enlightens in its own way. And what is true of his account of music is ultimately true of the system as a whole. Its conviction springs not from its cogency (in which the philosopher's single-mindedness took such pride) but from the feeling, the very distinct and clear feeling, it gives us of a world without a Creator, whose

---

[1] Vol. I, p. 432. The final quotation is from Plato's *Laws*, vii. 'Feeling' here (as in Stifter, see below, p. 296³) is 'negative' in the sense of being unilluminated by reason.

total significance and ultimate justification are enshrined in its
aesthetic image.

Drawing on conviction rather than proof, the system before
us challenges the distinction between philosophy and art. Like
the great novels of its age it springs from the twin impulses of a
will to power over its own creation (the philosopher is as much
master of his world as the novelist is of his characters), and a
passion for knowledge (they both create as clearly and conse-
quentially as is in their power). Like every work of art, too, it
issues from a momentous exaggeration of a segment of experience
in the world. It satisfies similar imaginative, cognitive and
emotional needs of its readers. It is cast in a mixed mode, appealing now to the literal truth of facts in the world, now to the
literary truth of a concerted re-enacting of the facts, of a configuration of images. Where it is weak, it is so because the vision
has given out before appeasing the need of the system-maker—
just as a novelist's work may be weak where he finds himself
constrained to daub in a certain kind of character or scene which
the coherence of plot and theme required of him. And Mr Forster
is undoubtedly right when he observes[1] that this is most likely to
happen at the end of a novel; similarly, all that is said by Schopenhauer, in the last chapter of his story, about that state of bliss
which follows upon the renunciation of the will does indeed leave
us with an impression of deadness.

Schopenhauer is neither a poet nor a mystic. His inability to
do much to intimate that state of deliverance is not inadvertent,
for his re-interpretation is enclosed in the perfect circle of aestheticism. For him, only that is capable of being aesthetically re-
enacted which is significant in the world, and only that is
significant in the world which is aesthetically re-enacted; the rest
is either trivial or ineffable, it either falls short of or transcends
the philosopher's concern. What is re-enacted is a world grimmer
by far, and also poorer, than Goethe's world. At the same time
the function of art is exaggerated into an absolute, quasi-trans-
cendent function—what for Goethe had been a consolation here
becomes the only redemption (short of the ineffable *Nirvana*)

---

[1] See E. M. Forster's remark in *Aspects of the Novel*, Penguin ed., p. 102.

there is. And the Goethean practice of turning 'life-as-art into art' becomes 'life-as-art into the mixed mode of aesthetic philosophy'.

10

The fascination exerted by Schopenhauer's work upon the artists and literary men of his own country is as much a matter of its form and imaginative appeal as it is of its message. The mixed mode in which it is cast fulfils a complex need in a culture whose efforts to catch up with the ideological developments in France and England are first frustrated by the repressive measures of the 'thirties, then encouraged and disappointed by the débâcle of '48, then again strengthened by the beginnings of parliamentarianism in the 'fifties, to be rendered ineffectual in the anachronism of the Second Reich. The realism of the European novel, founded in an acute political and social consciousness and in its turn perpetuating and refining that consciousness through its productions, is here replaced by a form that lies between discursive argument and fiction, blurring the distinction between analytical and creative prose; a genre somewhere between philosophy, art and religion; a form which expresses with memorable precision the feelings of an unaccommodated intelligentsia. And the message this philosophy of the religion of art propagates—to re-enact the world of the will, not to participate in it—is most perfectly realised in Schopenhauer's panegyric of music, 'the purest of the arts'. To an age of waning faith he offers the 'religion' of music[1] as a doctrine of redemption, commending the musician as one in whom the most complete separation has taken place between 'the man who suffers and the mind which creates'.[2] Unsullied by

---

[1] Even earlier, e.g. in Herder, there had been a tendency to infer from the greatness of German sacred music the sacredness of all great German music.

[2] Mr Eliot's formulation (in *The Sacred Wood*, London 1922, p. 48) is anticipated by Schopenhauer's (*ed. cit.*, Vol. I, p. 343): 'The composer reveals the innermost being of the world and expresses the deepest wisdom in a language which his own reason does not understand: like a somnambulist, who tells of things of which he has no clear knowledge in his waking state. This is the reason why, in a composer more than in any other artist, man and artist are quite separate and distinct.'

base interests, invulnerable to material defeat, its very medium
perfectly useless to the service of the will, music vouchsafes a
salvation with which the real world cannot compete; here indeed
is that world's most perfect re-interpretation. In spite of his caustic
Voltairean wit, Schopenhauer is a profoundly German writer.

And (as Nietzsche said) a European phenomenon. We have
already had occasion to observe how, in so many 'typically
German' arguments, the parochial and the prophetic are strangely
united. Schopenhauer's influence on the aestheticist movements of
the *fin de siècle* in Italy, Spain, France, in England, in the Russia
of Gorky's student days, has been examined more than once.[1]
Is it due simply to his nihilism—to his having formulated, in a
Germany hardly touched by the Industrial Revolution, dis-
affections and discontents with the material world felt more than
half a century later throughout Europe? This wider influence too,
I think, derives not from the bare message but also from its form,
from its immediate and imaginative appeal—an appeal no less
alluring for being based on a fundamental paradox. For here is
a doctrine which condemns the entire real world as worthless,
but not before having recreated it, in much of its bright splendour
and intricate detail, not before having re-enacted it *realistically* for
its readers. The entire world is placed in a set of brackets, and
before them is a minus-sign. While it is the inside of these brackets
that really 'interests'—fascinates and attracts—the artists of the age,
yet they are not allowed to forget that the whole thing is negative;
an acute interest in what is inside the bracket seems to belie the
minus-sign, yet the lie is a part of the artifice. For Schopenhauer
shows them that they can be both inside the brackets, in among
the bright and sordid details of daily life, and yet contract out:
that they can remain disengaged by putting the distance of
aesthetic contemplation between the world and their image-
making selves. He *shows* them: to the abundance of this showing
the efficaciousness of the doctrine is due. There is, after all, more

---

[1] E.g. A. Baillot, *L'influence de la philosophie de S. en France*, 1870–1900, Paris
1927; O. Eichler, *S. y la literatura española*, Granada 1926; Belyi and Pasternak
came under the spell of his philosophy when they studied in Germany in the
1900's, Gorky describes it in *My Universities*.

living substance in Schopenhauer's sublime indifference than there is in the exaltations of the earth's sanctity and worth which fill the pages of many 'poetic realists', 'vitalists' and 'life-worshippers' of his and later times.

In more than one place Schopenhauer speaks of the actual living situation on which Goethe drew for his lyrical poems. These scenes, he tells us, were blighted by unattainable desires. But the poems themselves are bearers of peace; even the desires themselves, transfixed in art, no longer impel to action but intimate a rest. Thus the creative act as Schopenhauer sees it is based on a distinction between the 'bad' knowledge of the world (the knowledge which the individual needs for his meaningless perpetuation) and the 'beautiful' knowledge of the bad world (from which the artistic self fashions its 'redeeming' images). The distinction is precarious but it is no chimera; Baudelaire, for instance, knew it:

Tu m'as donné ta boue, et j'en ai fait de l'or.

The absoluteness with which Schopenhauer posits the distinction is ultimately destructive of both world and art, yet in a less radical form it has a validity not confined to its own age. The power of art to refashion the ugly and sinful world in its own terms has always been inseparable from art itself, even though earlier ages would have shown little understanding for an aesthetic which made of *this* re-fashioning the sole end of art, let alone the only redemption there is. For what strange thing is it that makes 'beautiful' the tale of lawlessness, carrion and carnage called *Antigone*? What is it that makes poignant Dante's condemnation of a pair of lovers whose very love he has put before us in its serenity and passionate beauty? Is not this the meaning of the word 'tragic', that it points to a conflict between two laws, one of life and the other of a judgement divinely ordained and more powerful than life? Does not the appeal—the beauty—of the tragic tale derive both from the splendour or sweetness or strength of life *and* from the inexorable severity of the ordinance?

From the conflict, stilled only in death, of the two? And does not the weakness of literature in our own age lie in this, that our writers are as defective in evoking the strength as they are hesitant in invoking the severity? Are not the 'heroes' of our tales for ever being crushed before they have ever lived? The art of Schopenhauer's age lies somewhere between the old strengths and the modern velleities. What the realists transformed were no longer the bloody deeds of kings, calling to heaven for vengeance, but the sordid realities of city-life, and passion and hunger in humbler places. Yet in their own ways they too follow the practice of the transformation through art. To this practice one thing above all is alien: the weakness betrayed in the image of a world that has never been really alive.

It is surely no anachronism to say that there was a conflict in Dante between his passionate humanity and the teaching of his faith, and that it is the translation of this conflict into poetry which makes the episode of Paolo and Francesca the poignant and beautiful thing it is. The horror of eternal damnation would be unmitigated and poetry itself find no foothold had he not also shown us what living worth lay in their love. Their passion is at once ugly and beautiful, yielding at once a 'bad' knowledge and a beautiful knowledge of the bad. And is not this conflict, re-enacted and resolved in Dante's presentation, similar to that which Schopenhauer presents and resolves by negating, in accordance with *his* doctrine, all that his literary imagination and sensibility had first enabled him to put before us?

The conflict he describes is similar in form and different in substance. As in Dante, it is a conflict between passions as the world knows them and a higher ordinance (a would-be divine one) which destroys those passions and their world. Yet the conflict is also substantially different—and here the parallel ends—since the condemnation of the ordinance which governs Schopenhauer's world is so much less compelling and hence the tale so much less poignant. What I have in mind is not merely the difference between a 'philosophy' and a poem. Dante's condemnation is founded in a doctrine that judges human conduct with the force of tragic necessity. If we do not accept the doctrine, the condemnation must strike us as arbitrary and absurd. And, conversely, the poignancy of the scene—its 'aesthetic effect'—is the measure both of our feeling for the loveliness of the life condemned and of our belief in the authority behind the condemnation. In Schopenhauer, on the other hand, the relationship is a good deal looser. For one thing, the doctrine is not cogent enough for any condemnation that follows from it to have the force of tragic necessity; it remains a fascinating 'system', one among several. And the logical flaw in the system has a parallel in its form, in the disparaging tone of his voice. The world that is here condemned is, after all, no more than the world of his experience, of his own 'willing': has he not himself insisted that no man can jump over his own shadow? And the world of his experience is bereft of many things, among them of a knowledge of the love that Paolo and Francesca bore each other, which was neither 'only sex' nor 'only pity'. It is a poorer thing than the great poets, Goethe among them, have shown the world to be; a weaker thing, for all the realistic details he lavishes on it, than we in our best moments know it to be. The thing condemned is not beautiful enough, so that the contrast between world and ordinance is a good deal less than tragic. In the end it comes to one that the condemnation is too easy, that after all the philosopher does not care enough.

V   HISTORY AND PROPHECY:
HEINE

I

THE PROSE WRITINGS with which I am here concerned (it should
by now be clear) convey a feeling for the world as a thing
hypothetical, interpreted, not unquestionably given. How did
this feeling arise? What would it lead to? There are good reasons
for thinking that such questions are never likely to be answered
conclusively. Nevertheless, it may be relevant to ask how the
writers of the age itself saw these questions, what answers they
themselves gave.

Perhaps the most interesting, possibly the most contentious,
and certainly the most amusing of these answers is given by the
grandfather of modern German journalism, Heinrich Heine, in
his book *Zur Geschichte der Philosophie und Religion in Deutschland*.[1]
Never has a more extraordinary book sailed into the world under
a more ordinary and discouraging title; yet for sheer literary
panache, for bizarre anecdotes, historical snap-judgements, and
sheer intellectual wit and vigour, the book has few equals. Heine
first wrote it in the early 1830's at a time when his poetry was
most fully inspired by his pantheistic views; and he republished it,
with some additions but no substantial changes, in 1852, after that
much-vaunted conversion to a Christian-Judaeic theism which he
traces out in *Letzte Gedichte*. The very circumstances of its publication surround the book with an ironical aura. As in some of
Nietzsche's and Thomas Mann's writings, the autobiographical
interest—the '*ecce homo*' undertone—is sustained by a confession

[1] 1st ed. Paris 1832, 2nd ed. Paris 1852; my text is taken from C. P. Magill's
excellent ed., London 1947.

to the irony of a changed point of view. But (we may ask) is it likely that the author's spiritual adventures will affect the arguments of a book that purports to deal with so austere a subject as that indicated by its prosy title? No question could be wider of the mark. Heine had neither the scholarly equipment nor the detachment to write anything that a respectable historian would wish to put his name to. Is the whole thing then a huge and heavy 'Germanic' joke, carried on over 180 pages of quite exacting reasoning? This is somewhat closer to the point, except that, far from being in the least heavy, the 'Germanic' joke is as subtle and light as an early Hock. But, if it is a joke, could it possibly repay the prolonged mental effort of understanding it? Another piece of irony: the joke of the joke is that so much of it is true, that so much of the book consists of brilliant, apparently casual and quite unexpected insights—that more truth and good sense is said here about certain important aspects of German history and culture, about the German mind, than in any other single book I know—said implicitly and by innuendoes, but also explicitly, also in a grand rhetorical style.

Yet even here the paradoxes are not over. Heine's *History* was first written in French, for the Paris public of his 'long night of exile', as a sort of intellectual Baedeker for contemporary France, and as an antidote, incidentally, to Mme de Staël's *De l'Allemagne*. Wherever, in his account of German religious and philosophical thought from the days of the Germanic gods to Hegel, Heine gets stuck, wherever he runs out of sources or knowledge, wherever he gets bored, there he makes a little curtsy to the French public, briefly remarks that such-and-such a phase in the aforesaid story is unlikely to be of much interest to them, and elegantly by-passes the point at issue. But wherever he feels within sight of his main theme, of that most personal and intimate concern which preys on his mind, there the French public goes hang and he sets to with a closeness and regard for detail, and an animus, that have no precedent in nineteenth-century German prose; and perhaps only Nietzsche's essays have a comparable vigour.

Heine's subject, it so happens, is a part of Bertrand Russell's as he describes it in the Preface to his *History of Western Philosophy*:

There are many histories of philosophy, but none of them, so far as I know, has
quite the purpose that I have set myself. Philosophers are both effects and causes:
effects of their social circumstances and of the politics and institutions of their time;
causes (if they are fortunate) of beliefs which mould the politics and institutions of
later ages. In most histories of philosophy, each philosopher appears as in a vacuum;
his opinions are set forth unrelated, except, at most, to those of earlier philosophers.
I have tried, on the contrary, to exhibit each philosopher, as far as truth permits,
as an outcome of his milieu, a man in whom were crystallised and concentrated
thoughts and feelings which, in a vague and diffused form, were common to the
community of which he was a part.

In the book itself Russell hardly ever comes back to the intention
avowed in the Preface, contenting himself with an occasional
aside on the nature of Athenian democracy or on the iniquities
of clerical censorship. The passage I have quoted is therefore only
occasionally relevant to the book itself; but it is revealing for the
lack of conviction in the second half of its argument. The idea
of 'philosophers as causes' is no sooner mentioned (and paren-
thetically queried) than it is dropped again; and by the time
Russell comes to reiterate the argument ('I have tried . . .'), he is
only concerned with 'effects'. To the Whig heir of the empirical
and nominalist tradition the idea that 'ideas' are the causes of
'history' has a certain formal plausibility ('if "effects", why not
"causes"?'), but it has no more than that.

Heine on the other hand does precisely what Bertrand Russell
says he is going to do. He calls his history '*sozial*', but his way of
proceeding has little to do with the 'scientific' enquiries of present-
day sociologists. His criterion of inclusion and omission is determined by his intuitive understanding of—his poetic feeling for—
the character of the country to which, in spite of all, he belongs.
He writes no encyclopaedic work. The obscure mystic Johannes
Tauler, Frederick the Great and Karl Philipp Moritz (who in the
1780's wrote the first German psychological autobiography),
Lessing, and the 'poor old Berlin bookseller Nicolai' have as
proper a place in this history as have Luther, Leibnitz, Kant and
Schelling. His account is '*sozial*': given the loose national and
geographical entity of Germany, given her even looser social
whole, given finally her linguistic cohesion and all that follows

from *that*, Heine sets out to describe what to him is the main intellectual and spiritual conflict that has shaped her ethos, her *Weltanschauung*, and thus her history. Germanic paganism and Roman Catholicism, Luther's protest, the eighteenth-century philosophic movement, and the *Naturphilosophie* of his own day represent the five phases of this account. Each of these he sees as a stage of one great conflict, of a millennial disputation that moulds the German national consciousness.

His account of German paganism starts with some pretty grim and scurrilous stories, the purport of which is to show that the job of christianising the lands east of the Rhine was rather different from anything the Church of Rome had ever tackled before. The Nordic mystique and orgy-porgy of the *Walpurgisnacht*, the barbaric cruelty and obsessive sensuality of the pagan cults, prove to him that proselytism in Germany had to take more drastic and more repressive measures than those required among the gentler Angli and the more sophisticated and better-mannered Gauls of France. And so to the Middle or rather Dark Ages. Again, it is the witch-burning and intense spiritualisation of transalpine Catholicism that engages his attention and mordant wit—the Middle Ages are to him a 'romantic' period, an era of intense longing for an otherworldly realisation of dogma and beliefs; and these beliefs (he tells us) were held the more fanatically for being in themselves fundamentally alien to the nation upon which they were imposed. It would be easy to indict Heine for oversimplification, excessive generalisation, and so forth; equally, it could be shown that his arguments are to some extent antici- pated in the writings of the Romantic School, that sometimes he is doing no more than drawing the last consequences from ideas and *aperçus* which go back to Novalis and Friedrich Schlegel. Such criticisms would be beside the point. We need only look at the terms he uses, the line of argument he puts before us, to see that both are still with us, that in the meaning and form *he* gives them they directly contribute to the image of Germany as we know it from the works of Nietzsche, Wagner, Thomas Mann,

and also of his great admirer Karl Marx. Furthermore, his book
not only describes a certain spiritual and cultural tradition; it also,
by virtue of its self-consciousness, offers itself as an integral part
of that tradition.

The spiritualisation which Rome forces upon Germany issues
in what he calls '*die Durchteufelung der Natur*':

> The Church transformed the pantheistic world view of the Germans into a
> pandemonic one.

This force and the spiritual process which Luther sets in motion
between them dispose of the Catholic belief in miracles; at the
same time they keep alive and strengthen the Germanic belief in
the Devil. Luther is a spiritualist—he believes in the supremacy of
the spirit over matter,

> *a way of thinking which would glorify the spirit by attempting to destroy the
> flesh,*

but, as a spiritualist, Luther wishes to give Germany a spirituality
of her own, and not a Roman one. His moral doctrine is fundamentally different from Roman morality, for the simple reason
that he is a Northerner. In the discussion that follows we are in
no danger of being overwhelmed by doctrinal or philosophical
argument. It is the poet Heine who takes over—the poet whose
chief privilege it is that he was there when it all happened. And
so he gives us, not an intellectual abstract or a learned dissertation,
but a living, 'first-hand' account with all the irrelevancies and
embroideries by which his omnipresent imagination appeals to
our senses:

> *Leo of Medici . . . must have smiled when he saw that poor, celibate, simple-
> minded monk who believed that the Gospels were the Charter of Christendom, and
> that this Charter was the truth! Perhaps he didn't really notice what Luther was
> after, seeing that he was at that time much too busy with building St Peter's, the cost
> of which was being met with indulgences; which means no less than that sin itself
> provided the money for the building of that church, the church itself becoming, as it
> were, a monument to sensual lust, like that pyramid which an Egyptian courtesan
> built from the money she had earned by prostitution . . . It was the triumph of
> spiritualism that it forced sensualism to build its finest temples—that the concessions
> made to the flesh should yield the means to glorify the spirit; and this, of course, was
> a triumph which they didn't understand in the Germanic North. For here indeed,*

rather than under the glowing sky of Italy, it was possible to practise a Christianity which made least concession to the sensual. We Northerners have colder blood, and we didn't need as many indulgences for sins of the flesh as Leo in his paternal care sent us. The climate facilitates the exercise of the Christian virtues, and on the 31st October 1515, when Luther nailed his Theses against indulgences on the door of the Church of St Augustin, the moat of Wittenberg was probably already frozen and you could skate on it, which is very cold fun and therefore no sin.

Yet while Heine sees the emancipation from the alien rule of Rome and the making of a new spirituality as the main sources of Luther's greatness, his interest is quite as much engaged by another of Luther's achievements—and here again the poet speaks to us through the 'social historian'—namely, his creative invigoration of New High German, of that language to which Heine's own poetic experience is totally committed. But for this gift of Luther's, the next phase in that history, the philosophical revolution of the eighteenth century, could not have taken place. To Heine, Luther's gift to his nation—that gift which not merely confirms but itself creates that nation's coherence—is little short of a miracle. And although (once again) our lexicographers and grammarians may demythologise the miracle and show it as part of an historical continuity, the tone of Heine's imaginative description of this act gives it the authority of incontrovertible poetic truth. The importance of that truth lies in Heine's understanding that the new language is more than a mere 'medium'; that it is both the repository and the source of the new vision. He understands that, for Germany especially, national life is intimately bound up with the life of her language, that for several centuries the linguistic is the only hallmark of the national. The spiritual need from which the language of Luther's Bible was born, as well as the need it came to supply later, have become a commonplace in German historical thinking. And his character-study of that choleric and fanatical miner's son from Eisleben, of the tough and hard-working monk, at once ascetic and gluttonous, at once aggressive and sin-conscious, at once coarse and deeply spiritual—Heine's image of the man has fully and permanently entered the German and European consciousness, merely to be confirmed by the labours of historical scholarship.

Act Four of this strange nation-drama is the philosophical

revolution of the eighteenth century. It is heralded by Spinoza, the patron-saint of all moralists and nature-philosophers alike, the one man of whom Heine, like the less witty Bertrand Russell, has no discreditable anecdote to tell. Not without ironical emotion does Heine recount the story of Spinoza's expulsion from the Synagogue, and of the ancient sacred horn which was sounded on that occasion:

> The sound of that horn accompanied the excommunication of Baruch Spinoza, he was solemnly expelled from the community of Israel and declared to be unworthy henceforth to bear the name of a Jew. His Christian enemies were magnanimous enough to leave him that name.

Like Goethe, Heine is content to take from Spinoza's teaching the catchword *Deus sive natura*, or, as he puts it, the identification of God with the world. Spiritualism is, for Heine, the denigration of the flesh and the exalting of the spirit; sensualism is for him the opposite movement, the extolling of the flesh and the world against the claims of the spirit; and Spinoza's pantheism is the omnipresence of the Divine Being in all things in the natural world at large.

Spinoza is the prophet of this new dispensation. What remains to be done after him is to clear away the vestiges of the old spiritualistic beliefs. (These Heine calls 'Deism', though eighteenth-century deists would hardly have recognised their beliefs in the form he gives them.) The destruction is accomplished, after some preliminary tidying-up by Christian Wolff, in the critical work of Kant; and again, Heine's treatment of Kantian criticism displays that ambiguity, that ironical illumination of the truth, which are his most successful stylistic devices. The account is both false and true. It is preceded by the briefest possible exposition of Kant's epistemology—of how we cannot have any reliable knowledge of things as they are in themselves and by themselves and undisturbed by the human onlooker, of how all we can know is dependent upon the forms in which things appear to our senses. The things-in-themselves are out there, in the inaccessible world, untouched by us, and God is one of them, and thus deism is disposed of:

Ihr meint, wir könnten jetzt nach	*And so you think we can now go*
Hause gehn? Beileibe! es wird noch	*home? No, by God! There is*

ein Stück aufgeführt. Nach der Tragödie kommt die Farce.	*another play coming, after the tragedy comes the farce.*

And now, in the grip of his fancy, of his intensely poetic and direct presentation of this drama of ideas, Heine the poet lets himself go. First comes Kant the slayer of the dragon of deism:

Immanuel Kant hat bis hier den unerbittlichen Philosophen traciert, er hat den Himmel gestürmt, er hat die ganze Besatzung über die Klinge springen lassen, der Oberherr der Welt schwimmt unbewiesen in seinem Blute, es gibt jetzt keine Allbarmherzigkeit mehr, keine Vatergüte, keine jenseitige Belohnung für diesseitige Enthaltsamkeit, die Unsterblichkeit der Seele liegt in den letzten Zügen—das röchelt, das stöhnt. . . .	*Up to this point Immanuel Kant acted the inexorable philosopher. He sallied forth against the heavens, he let the whole crew run his gauntlet. Deprived of the proof of his existence, the Lord of the world swims in his blood, now all Christian charity is turned to nought, there is no paternal love, no heavenly reward for earthly self-denial, it's all over with the immortality of the soul—oh the death-rattle! oh the gasps! . . .*

And when the gruesome fun is at its best, another actor enters, Kant's aged servant and amanuensis:

. . . und der alte Lampe steht dabei, mit seinem Regenschirm unterm Arm, als betrübter Zuschauer, und Angstschweiss und Tränen rinnen ihm vom Gesichte. Da erbarmt sich Immanuel Kant und zeigt, dass er nicht bloss ein grosser Philosoph, sondern auch ein guter Mensch ist, und er überlegt, und halb gutmütig und halb ironisch spricht er: 'Der alte Lampe muss einen Gott haben, sonst kann der arme Mensch nicht glücklich sein—der Mensch soll aber auf der Welt glücklich sein—das sagt die praktische Vernunft—meinetwegen— so mag auch die praktische Vernunft die Existenz Gottes verbürgen.'	*. . . and old Lampe stands by, an umbrella under his arm, sadly watching, the sweat of fear and tears run down his face. Immanuel Kant takes pity on him, shows that he is not only a great philosopher but also a good man, thinks a while, and in good-humoured irony speaks thus: 'Old Lampe must have a God, otherwise the poor fellow won't be happy—but man should be happy on earth—practical reason says as much—that's all right by me—so let practical reason stand as a warranty for the existence of God.'*

It would be boring to interpolate any comment. The prose—a unique compound of the eternal *raconteur's* fun and the precise intellectual wit of the ideal guest at an ideal High Table—can look after itself; every nuance of it, down to the disarmingly

Jewish interjection—'*meinetwegen*'—makes for superb liveliness.
And the caustic conclusion

Infolge dieses Arguments unter-scheidet Kant zwischen der theoret-ischen Vernunft und der praktischen Vernunft, und mit dieser, wie mit einem Zauberstäbchen, belebt er wieder den Leichnam des Deismus, den die theoretische Vernunft ge-tötet hat	Consequent upon this argument, Kant distinguishes between theo-retical and practical Reason, with which latter, as with a magic wand, he revivifies the corpse of deism which had been killed by theoretical Reason

completes the final effect by a show of succinctness which, in this
context, turns the whole thing into supreme intellectual irony.

This account is, as I have said, both false and true. It is false
because in Kant the rabbit comes out of the hat in a different
context—namely, in his deduction of the moral law which is
logically antecedent to the critique of 'practical Reason'. Hence it
is not for the sake of deism at all that Kant explores the possibility
of man's knowing at least one thing as it really is, at least one
'*Ding an sich*', which turns out to be the moral law. It is not Kant
the crypto-deist who performs this philosophical prestidigitation,
but Kant the moralist; while the moral law in its turn is postulated
by Kant in the context of his epistemology, it being his express
intention to contrast the phenomenal nature of the objects of our
cognition with the absolute, nouminal intuition we have of the
moral law within us. So that it is as a consequence of this moralist
concern (of which Heine says not a word), itself based upon his
epistemological analysis (which Heine treats in a cavalier manner)
that Kant puts forward the hypothesis, 'to satisfy the need of practical Reason', of an impersonal creator bound by the laws of his own
creation. And at this point, of course, we are back where we started:
Heine is once again right: the restoration of deism is achieved,
though it has not in fact come about the way he described it.

The prose in which this serious joke is told amounts to an enormous liberation. The lightness of touch, the effortless responsiveness
of the medium, the quickness of the insights and the melodramatic

sharp edges of Heine's expressiveness ('*das röchelt, das stöhnt*')—all these are quite unprecedented in the annals of German prose; the best in present-day German journalism as well as its least stilted productions during the last hundred years owe many of their nuances, their shades and points, their very turns of phrase and syntax, as well as their affectations, to this book of Heine's and to his other works of '*sozial*' popularisation. The aphoristic and epigrammatic quality has its antecedents in Friedrich Schlegel's writings, but the unaffected closeness to the voice and inflections of everyday language is Heine's own. The debt that Nietzsche owes to this act of liberation, though acknowledged by himself, has never been explored, for the simple reason that Heine's influence on Nietzsche has never been taken very seriously. With his wisecracks, his anecdotes, his ironical detachment Heine seems to be moving in a different world from Nietzsche's. Is that world really so different? Are his wit and irony really so detached?

2

What rouses Nietzsche's invective and his most telling criticism is the *parvenu* mentality of the 1870's. It is the State founded on a mixture of *Realpolitik* and a medieval idea of Empire—the German State as an industrialised and militarised anachronism: as the improbable compound of two incompatibles, Prussian bureaucracy and the Romantic idea of '*Volk*'. Heine did not live to see that State. What this *History* gives us are the antecedents that led to the foundation ceremony on the balustrade outside the *Salon de la Guerre* at Versailles. It is the story of the German mind, or rather perhaps the German soul; and it is seen in terms of a conflict, to the antagonists of which he attaches the names of sensualism and spirituality. Faust's theme of 'Two souls, alas, live within my breast' is projected on to a millennial scale. It begins with the Germanic dæmonology and ends with the apparent death of spiritualism and the consequent transformation of its old enemy. By 1852, when Heine published the complete version of his book, he himself had undergone a spiritual development which, though it didn't turn him into a believer, nevertheless brought him a faith in spirituality (a belief in religion, perhaps, rather than religion itself). His state of mind was certainly quite

different from that which had made him launch upon the attack
carried on in these pages. Why did he republish the book? Why
did he not modify its tone? 'Of course, I could resort to milder
expressions, I could obscure the issue by putting in a phrase here
and there,' he says in the Second Preface. Is it really, as he
goes on to claim, because of his honesty and dislike of circum-
locution? How are we to reconcile the statement from that Preface,

Der Deismus lebt, er ist nicht tot . . .	*Deism lives, it is not dead.* . . .
Und am allerwenigsten hat ihn die	*Least of all has it been killed by the*
neueste deutsche Philosophie ge-	*most recent German philosophy.*
tötet. Diese Berliner Dialektik kann	*These Berlin dialectics won't make a*
keinen Hund aus dem Ofenloch	*tired trout rise, they won't kill a*
locken, sie kann keine Katze töten,	*dead dog, let alone a God* . . .
wieviel weniger einen Gott . . .	

with the grand peroration at the end of the second book:

Unsere Brust ist voll von entsetz-	*Our heart is full of terrible pity.* . . .
lichem Mitleid . . . *Es ist der alte*	*It is the old Jehova Himself preparing*
Jehova selber, der sich zum Tode	*for death.* . . . *Can you hear the*
bereitet. . . . *Hört ihr das Glöckchen*	*ringing of the bell? Kneel down—*
klingeln? Kniet nieder—man bringt	*they are bringing the sacraments to a*
die Sakramente einem sterbenden	*dying God.*
Gotte.	

The truth on which Heine is intent is a complex poetical truth.
We saw how he modified his account of Kant's deism according
to a literary criterion, ordering his material (as any dramatist
might) so as to present it most effectively, most tellingly. When
he comes to his own era he again presents each side of the case,
he again—and more dramatically than before—identifies himself
with each side of the conflict. And what issues from the contra-
dictory evidence reveals both an historical situation and also the
conflict within Heine himself. It is much the same sort of conflict
as that fought out three decades later by Nietzsche, and three
decades after that by Thomas Mann in his *Meditations of a Non-
Political Man*. Each time the revealing confession and self-
examination sees the light of day well *after* the author has overtly
ceased to 'believe' in the truth of his earlier position; each time
the paradoxical double-belief reveals a *German* self-consciousness;

and each time the mind offers itself, naked yet sheathed in irony, for public inspection. In spite of Heine's cosmopolitan airs, his gallophile moods, his romantic Judaism, he remains fundamentally German in the sense which he himself gives to that word in his book. To be German is for him, as it is for Nietzsche and Thomas Mann, to feel this conflict, to assert the one principle at the point at which the other looks like carrying the day. It is to be in search of the reality of the worldly world, to reach after success—even of the most material kind—with one hand, and to repudiate and invalidate success and world as insubstantial with the other. And to feel the conflict is to be on the other side, on the side of the world-as-interpretation.

That 'death-wish' which Wagner dramatised and set to poly-phonous music in *Tristan*; which Nietzsche intimately under-stood *and* attacked in Wagner; which Freud named, and placed at the root of all devaluations of the substantial world; which Thomas Mann, and many lesser writers, dramatised in the personages of their novels—that death-wish Heine describes in terms of *isms* and tags of philosophical argument. He is ambi-valent in his attitude towards the problem of religion in Germany. But then, ambivalence is the form of his commitment to the 'German ideology', it is his creative acknowledgement of the conflict of which he himself, acute intellectual and subtle poet, is the battlefield.

Small wonder that there is so little of Goethe in the pages of this history of the German mind. For Heine, as for his whole generation, Goethe the Olympian figure overshadows the author of *Werther*, the *Urfaust*[1] and *Tasso*. And while the earlier Goethe gets a paragraph or two to himself, the author of *Faust II* is left out of Heine's account, because he seems to have resolved the conflict. We know that the truth about the old Goethe is more complex. The sublime irony of Faust's end and avatar bears witness to the fact that the theme remains alive for Goethe; and there is neither detachment nor equanimity, there is no standing above the conflict, in the two figures of Epimetheus and Pro-metheus of Goethe's unfinished *Pandora* (1811, published 1828).

---

[1] Which, incidentally, was not discovered until 1887.

But for Heine a true reading of these works was obscured by the elaborate façade of the patrician palace on the Weimar Frauenplan.

3

For Heine the author of this book (though not, as we have seen, of the Second Preface) the strife between the opposing principles ends in the victory—sometimes present, sometimes imminent— of *Naturphilosophie*; which in its turn is the up-to-date form of Spinozism as it emerges from the works of Fichte, Schelling, and the young Hegel. The formula of '*Welt-Gott-All*' by which he designates this new creed strikes me as neither particularly accurate (it fits Schelling's work better than the others') nor particularly interesting; whatever attraction it has for the poet, pantheism is not a doctrine that seems to gain much from being argued out in prose. But just at the point (three-quarters of the way through the book) where Pantheism rears its weary head and the argument is about to grow flat, Heine throws analysis to the winds, turns his horse about, and gallops off into the future. Or so it seems— when we look closer we find that the change is one of tone rather than of substance, for it is from the analysis of the past that he extrapolates the drama of the future.

The concrete prophetic conclusions which Heine now thrusts at his reader are truly astonishing. Can there ever have been a writer, we wonder, whose prophecies were so fully, so mercilessly vindicated? He now sees the German philosophical revolution not as abstruse verbiage ('which couldn't harm a stray cat'), not as a top-heavy intellectualist system with feet of clay, but as a living force, and a violently destructive force at that. He—so recently a mourner at the funeral of deism—now recognises the new ideology for the living 'religion' it is: he understands its revolutionary explosive nature, and he prophesies, on the last pages of his book, its catastrophic consequences for the rest of Europe:

A spectacle will be performed in Germany, in comparison with which the French Revolution will look like a harmless idyll.

The tidy-minded German intellectuals[1]—spiritualists and ascetics who deny reality to the 'phenomenal' world, fanatics and icono-clasts—these are the ones (Heine tells us) who will march the length and breadth of Europe and force their revolution on their hapless neighbours: the less piety they feel towards the 'phenom-enal' world, the more violent their outbreak into action:

The German revolution will not be any the gentler or milder for having been pre-ceded by Kant's Critique and Fichte's transcendental idealism, let alone by the Naturphilosophie of our age. By means of these doctrines revolutionary forces have evolved which are only waiting for the day when they can break out and fill the world with horror and amazement. Kantians will come forward who will treat the phenomenal world without piety, and will rage with sword and claymore through the very foundations of our European life, extirpating its last roots in the past. Fichteans will appear on the scene, armed in their self-willed fanaticism, knowing neither fear nor self-interest; for they live in the spirit and defy the material world, like the first Christians who were similarly not to be overcome either by physical torture or physical temptation. But more terrifying than any of these will be the 'Natur'-philosopher . . . for he will be in league with the primæval forces of Nature, conjuring up the dæmonic powers of the old Germanic pantheism, and because in him that lust for battle will reawaken which is known to us from the Germans of ancient times, which does not fight to destroy, nor to conquer, but simply for the sake of fighting. It is the finest merit of Christianity that it has somewhat tamed that brutal German lust for battle, though without destroying it completely. And on the day when that potent talisman, the Cross, will break, the savagery of the old warriors will flare up again, and the mindless Berserkers' fury of which the Nordic bards have sung. That talisman is rotten, and the day will come when it will fall to pieces al-together. Then the old gods of stone will rise up from the ancient ruins and will rub the dust of a thousand years from their eyes, and Thor with his giant hammer will leap up at last and shatter the Gothic cathedrals. . . .

Be warned, you people across the border, you Frenchmen, and don't interfere with what is going on at home in Germany. . . .

Don't laugh at these fantastical visionaries who are expecting that the realm of appearances will be shaken by the same revolution as that which shook the realm of the spirit. The idea comes before the deed, as lightning comes before thunder. Now, the German thunder, like the German himself, is not very subtle and a little slow in coming. But come it will. And when at last you hear such an explosion as you have never heard in all history, then you will know that the hour has struck. And when they hear this gigantic noise, the eagles will drop dead from the air, and the lions in the distant deserts of Africa will hide in their regal caves, their tails between their legs.

[1] 'It seems to me that a methodical nation like ours had to begin with the Reformation, could only then go on to philosophy, and proceed to the political revolution only after having completed the philosophical.'

And his prophecy of that unholy 'matrimony between bloodless
intellectuality and bloody barbarism'[1] issues in a grand tirade
which seems to anticipate the events of 1870–1 and of 1914 (not
to speak of later ones) with unparalleled precision.

How true is Heine's prophecy really? Is it really true to suggest
that Christianity, in the nineteenth century, lies like a thin crust
on the volcano of Germanic paganism? Are we justified in
concluding that the wars of 1870 and 1914 were the direct,
'dynamic' expressions of that complex ethos of which (as Heine
claims) the philosophers and ideologists were both effects and
causes? Heine's entire analysis of Germany's part from the earliest
Middle Ages to his day, we can now see, was undertaken with
these prophetic conclusions in view.

In order to understand the truth of his 'prophecy' we had perhaps better first ask (in Nietzsche's phrase[2]) why Heine too is 'so
clever'. His intelligence (and Nietzsche's too) is that of a *modern*
prophet. The biblical prophet receives the gift of foreknowledge
from God for a certain end, that of preaching moral improvement to his countrymen. It could hardly be said of Nietzsche,
and not at all of Heine, that this was what they were aiming at.
What Heine is after is insight. Philosophical and moral insight,
perhaps. But insight and self-examination alike he pursues above
all for an aesthetic end, for a high intellectual entertainment. His
remarkable gift for intimating the truth is a matter of individual
genius, certainly: but it is genius at work in a remarkably free and
unrestrained situation. Like Nietzsche's, his criticism is bound by
no loyalties, no institutions.[3] He sees what others see, yet sees more;
he soars above the rest, yet he belongs; and yet he is not firmly
rooted in the common soil.

[1] Erich Heller, *The Ironic German: a Study of Thomas Mann*, London 1958,
pp. 270–1.

[2] See the opening of *Ecce Homo*, Kröner ed., no. 82, pp. 299 ff.

[3] It seems that where a critic is not prepared to pay this price, there not
only does insight stop short of prophecy, but criticism itself is not easy to
distinguish from the things criticised.

4

It has been said of the Jews of Western Europe—and not necessarily by anti-Semites[1]—that their peculiar and unique position in the countries of their domicile has enabled them to see with an especial clarity the characters of their surrounding societies.[2] That position, a compound of familiarity and critical detachment, of acceptance and 'the freedom which distance gives', is not exclusively Jewish. It is from such a position, for instance, that Nietzsche criticises the German national ethos of his day. For the Jew it is never entirely a matter of choice; but then, it wasn't for Nietzsche either—hence his occasional self-identification with the Jews, which is at least as significant as his anti-Semitic remarks —indeed, the one is the context in which the other must be read.

It cannot here be my aim to explain the monstrous history of German anti-Semitism in the twentieth century; nevertheless, the argument of these pages is relevant to its antecedents, and through them to the 'Final Solution' of our own days.

Thomas Mann once wrote[3] that 'the German character *est essentiellement anti-sémitique*', adding (again it is the qualifying context that gives the full meaning) 'but then, as you know, *Deutsch* is a Jewish surname.' Two things make German anti-Semitism after the *débâcle* of 1848 radically different from that in the rest of Europe: first, its considered and intellectually elaborated quality, and secondly, the fact that it is instinct with fratricidal feelings. The testimony of their intellectual spokesmen makes it clear that the Germans among the nations of Europe felt as the Jews did among the Germans. And this similarity of feelings

[1] E.g. in Isaiah Berlin's essay *Jewish Slavery and Emancipation*, New York (Herzl Institute pamphlet no. 18) 1961, pp. 5 ff.; or René König's 'Judentum und Soziologie', *Der Monat*, Berlin, August 1961.

[2] When Stefan George's friend and disciple Friedrich Gundolf remarked 'Now I know what sociology is! Sociology is a Jewish sect,' he was underlining how much German sociology, from Marx through Georg Simmel to the end of the Weimar Republic, owed to Jewish intellectuals who, unless they let themselves be lulled into the false safety of complete assimilation, had a vital interest in observing the world around them accurately and without illusion.

[3] *Doktor Faustus*, Chapter XXXVII.

sprang from a similar experience of alienation, of being in-
securely and somehow provisionally accommodated in the social
and political world of the age. (It was for similar reasons that
France went through her phase of anti-Semitism after the defeat
of 1871.) The common-or-garden anti-Semitism that flourished
in the lower and upper classes, though more pronounced than
elsewhere,[1] was not peculiar to Germany. The considered, and
eventually would-be 'scientific', character of the phobia came
from the middle classes—the professional men, the writers and
musicians, above all from the teachers at all levels. For them, as for
the Jews, positive nationhood was not self-evidently given. For
them, as for 'their' Jews, it lay in their otherness, and in the mind:
hence the unbounded respect for the intellect common to both;
hence, too, the cultivation—the over-cultivation—of compensatory virtues, of Jewish astuteness and German technological know-
how and efficiency. There is in all this something like a common
feeling towards the world—indeed the idea of 'the world' is only
distinct and clearly delimited to those who feel themselves to be
outside it. But there was one big and simple difference. On the
German side there was thrust over this common feeling towards
the world the simple, brutal fact of power. For, however limited
their use of the franchise, however restricted their freedom for
independent political action, the middle classes of the Second
Reich were virtually free in the association of *opinion* against the
Jews (and also against other minorities). Improbable as it may
seem in the light of the recent past, on more than one occasion
before 1870 and after, it was the Prussian and other governments
that protected the Jews against the 'non-political' middle classes,
against their converting of opinion into open action.

    Jewish assimilation on one hand, German jingoism and anti-
Semitism on the other, are different responses to a similar experience. They are different compensations for a similar deprivation.
And they are divided by no more, and no less, than the factor of
power. Or rather of potential power—for here as well as in inter-
national politics the atmosphere of the Second Reich is one of

[1] E. Sterling, *Er ist wie du. Frühgeschichte des* [deutschen] *Antisemitismus*,
München 1956.

expectancy, of waiting for the day. . . .[1] Where the Jews had
never quite lost the inward sense of their 'chosenness', the Germans were to wage war upon their neighbours in order to prove
to themselves that 'they have a mission for all the nations of the
earth',[2] that *they* are now the Chosen Race.

But what of that sense of solidarity and nationhood—reputedly
so strong in the Jews, so lacking in the Germans? Doesn't that
mark a major difference? Here precisely lies the monstrous (and,
as histories of races and nations go, perhaps unparalleled) irony
of the 'Jewish question' in Germany. This ancient cohesion—this
of all things—the Jews were willing, eager to sacrifice on the
altar of assimilation. Religious in its origin and aims, their national
and social bond was weakened in the same way and by the same
process as the Christian faith was weakened and undermined
among the Gentiles—not least by the secularising spirit of the
Enlightenment. It was the enlightened ethos of tolerance that had
first enabled the Jews to enter German life; but the price of that
tolerance was the desuetude of their ancient faith. And again, the
experience, common to Germans and Jews, of the waning of
faith resulted in situations whose difference lay simply in the
possession of power. In the Germans it unleashed those forces
which Heine, with a good deal of poetic exaggeration, connects
with the Germanic past; the Jews it left spiritually and physically
defenceless. One doesn't have to subscribe to the propagandist
notion of the '*furor teutonicus*' of the First World War to perceive
that the character of German nationalism which Heine forecasts
was in fact different in intensity from similar emotions in Western
Europe; that (to mention the most telling instance of all) the
bellicose atmosphere in the Germany of August 1914—the
moment in which the emergencies of the immediate past were
consummated—constituted a break with anything Europe had
known for many centuries.

[1] See above, p. 221: 'Be warned, you people across the border . . . But come
it will. And when . . .'

[2] Paul Lagarde in 1886, quoted from H. Pross, *Die Zerstörung der deutschen
Politik: Dokumente 1870–1933*, Frankfurt 1959, p. 278; in the remainder of this
chapter I have drawn on the documents assembled in this book.

The Jews, on the other hand, were left defenceless. If not only the Christian 'God was dead' (as Nietzsche wrote) but 'the old Jehovah' also (as Heine had written two decades before)—for whose sake, then, were they to cling to the signs of their election, which were also the signs of their alienness? Where the religious sanctions waned, the social cohesion (which was based on them) could not survive for long: it was on the altar not merely of assimilation but of Germany herself that the Jews sacrificed their God. Did they know how questionable a deity they chose to serve? Many of them knew well enough.[1] But their knowledge sprang from that very detachment which they were sacrificing in the effort of assimilation, so that the more they 'belonged', the less well they knew. Increasingly sensitive to the charges of cosmopolitanism and a foreign outlook, they were more and more ready to abandon what was surely the one task for which they were uniquely fitted: to be Germany's reminder of all that bound her to the rest of Europe. Instead, they acted as though their own history had come to an end and now at last they could settle down and belong. Their German patriotism; their hostility to Eastern Jewry; their exaltation and defence of the German language, literature and culture; their notoriety (among the Slavs) as 'Germanisers'—these were some of the ways in which they avowed their loyalty, thus the seal was set upon their new Covenant. Heine himself stands in the middle of this journey towards assimilation.[2] What is so fruitful about his precarious position is that he never ceased to be Germany's European conscience; and in this too Nietzsche was his ally.

[1] See *Selbstzeugnisse des deutschen Judentums 1870–1945*, ed. Achim von Borries. Frankfurt 1962.

[2] Thus, in the best German nationalist tradition, he wrote vile anti-Polish jingles; while Nietzsche liked to think of himself as descended from the Polish aristocracy: each attitude corresponds to a different mood, or rather to a different stage, within the ambivalence of German national feelings.

5

It is in these regions of problematic nationhood[1] that we must look for the kinship between Nietzsche the German and Heine the German Jew. Here lie some of the reasons why they are both 'so clever'; in their concern for the country to which they belong— an impatient, ambiguous and embarrassingly self-revealing concern—the minds of the two 'prophets' come closest to each other.

Their position is at once individual and representative. The 'prophet' (I suggested) hovers above his society. But what happens to prophecy if that common soil is itself unstable, if society itself, at all events in those intellectual regions to which Heine and Nietzsche[2] addressed themselves, is unsure of its proprieties: what if significance, 'reality' itself, is felt to rest in intellectual and artistic experience, 'in the mind alone'? Then indeed prophecy has more than its usual chance of coming true.

This is why German literature from Heine to the end of the Weimar Republic abounds in such 'dynamic'—and accurate— visions of the future, of which Heine's peroration is the first. Put positively, they arise in a society which takes its intellectuals, artists and 'prophets' with that seriousness which Matthew Arnold had urged upon English society. Put negatively, these visions are offered to a society liable to be swept off its feet by all that goes on in the realm of the mind. There is, after all, something remarkably untrammelled about ideas—'elles se promènent dans l'espace', Leibnitz once said of them—and there is something alarmingly unresistant about the manner in which the reality of German

---

[1] Isaiah Berlin writes (op. cit., p. 9): 'Much of what Heine wrote was derived not from a first, but from a second order of experience—he saw himself as a German, as a Jew, as a poet, as an inhabitant of too many worlds, and wrote with a particular kind of self-consciousness alien to a normal member of a recognised community.' But then, the point of my argument is precisely this, that a large number of non-Jewish German intellectuals wrote from much the same vantage-point.

[2] When Nietzsche dedicated his *Zarathustra* (1883) 'To None and All', I suppose he meant that the people worthy of his book were only to be found outside contemporary society; this is the sort of 'public' the nationalists addressed.

politics after 1850 comes increasingly to be moulded by ideas and images whose sources are literary, poetic, religiose, mythopoeic, musical, philosophical . . . indeed anything but political. 'In this book,' writes Spengler in 1917, at the end of this era, 'the attempt is made for the first time to determine history in advance.'[1] The claim to originality is quite untrue, Spengler is merely explicit about what has always been the case—the fact that histories aren't written on desert islands. Whether literary or political in origin, the doom-filled prophecies from Heine onwards had also their political significance, often perhaps unsuspected by their authors. To a greater or lesser extent they too are not merely prophecies but expressions of intent.[2]

How different is the internal situation in Germany from the rest of Europe? How much is it really influenced by her intellectuals? The vigorous power-politics of Bismarck are, in the European concert of nations, exceptional only in being extremely successful. They are supported by right-wing ideologists who propagate a Romantic nationalism alien to Bismarck himself, and their views (which Heine polemically anticipates) gain the upper hand in the vacuum that follows Bismarck's dismissal. It is then that Heine's vision begins to come true; nor is this surprising, seeing that what he proclaims *is* the moulding of empirical reality by ideas:

> Don't laugh at these visionaries who are expecting the realm of appearances to be shaken by the same revolution that shook the realm of the spirit. . . .[3]

The conflict he sees is between the new naturalism, the *Natur-philosophie* which is a new intellectual paganism, and the Western

---

[1] '. . . *die Geschichte vorauszubestimmen.*' See the Introduction of *Der Untergang des Abendlands*, München 1920.

[2] Nietzsche at all events knew this well enough: 'The abbé Galiani once said: *La prévoyance est la cause des guerres actuelles de l'Europe. Si l'on voulait se donner la peine de ne rien prévoir, tout le monde serait tranquille, et je ne crois pas qu'on serait plus malheureux parce qu'on ne ferait pas la guerre.* Since I don't at all share the anti-war views of my friend the late Galiani, I am not afraid to predict and thus to conjure up the causes of wars.' (See F.N., *Werke*, ed. K. Schlechta, Vol. III, München 1956, p. 848).

[3] See above, p. 221.

(for him, French) political outlook, the common interpretation of Western society based on the ideas of the French Revolution. However (the point is worth making in view of subsequent nationalist disclaimers), this is a conflict of ideas against ideas, realities against realities. Ideas: the spiritual claims of individual interpretation of the world versus the social ideas and claims of political democracy and parliamentarianism. Realities: the German Reich versus the European states. Heine himself does not always make it sufficiently clear that this is, after all, a plain power-political struggle like many another. And the nationalists, and even some major historians, of later generations, with their insistence on the 'non-political' nature of the German ethos, will go out of their way to obscure the true nature of the struggle.

A writer like Bertrand Russell is not very good at showing the influence of ideas upon political and social reality, mainly because he has little direct experience of such a situation, and little sympathy with it. He 'theoretically' knows about it (it is certainly the commonplace of German histories of ideas), but in the culture to which he belongs the ideas are too complexly modified by inert and conserving forces, by the recalcitrance of society, to afford a clear view of their philosophical pedigree.

The thought that philosophy does not yield a categorical distinction for politics would hardly bother him; so much the worse for philosophy, he is likely to say. In Germany, on the other hand, the philosopher's failure to find an unambiguous place for politics in their systems determines their attitude towards it. For Schopenhauer (as we have seen) politics is merely the self-destructive wrestling of the impure, unenlightened Will with itself. In Hegel it is but an imperfect realisation of that vast, super-personal Spirit of History which accounts for, justifies, and subordinates to itself, all actions in the 'real' world.[1] But something like this is true also of Marx who, reducing politics to the outward symptoms of the struggle between those who own and those who are owned as means of production, disposes of it in economic terms. Yet politics exists, whatever the philosophies

[1] See Hegel's inaugural lecture in Berlin, 1818 (G. W. F. Hegel: *Auswahl aus seinem Werk*, [Kröner ed.] Stuttgart, 1942, pp. 224 ff.).

which fail to fit it in may say. Unaccommodated by any philosophical system, untouched by any 'categories', it is liable to
become untouchable, unworthy of the most serious thought.
And it is painfully obvious that, if politics is regarded as a relatively
unworthy occupation for long enough, it becomes the occupation
of those without philosophical scruples, backed by the starry-eyed
idealists who are inexperienced in distinguishing between what
does and what does not approximate to their dreams. Instead of
helping to decide between courses of political action, the intellectuals merely support and justify—that is, 'rationalise'—decisions
taken by those in power. No longer does Dr Pangloss merely endure
the world's evils: but he still must vindicate a pre-established harmony. And when the 'real world' comes to overwhelm the 'ideal
world', the latter becomes its unresisting victim. Let us think and
prophesy, cry the intellectuals of Heine's and the subsequent generations: leave us to write our poems, compose our music, pursue
our ideas; or again, leave us to get on with our trade and industries.

Surprise has sometimes been expressed—most recently by
C. P. Snow[1]—at the enormous technological advances achieved
by Germany in the course of the nineteenth century. Yet the
reason why 'in the Germany of the 1830's and 1840's ... there
were excellent courses in electrical engineering' is plain enough.
That higher technological expertise which Snow is pleased to call
a 'culture' was achieved at the cost of a political non-involvement
on the part of those who contributed to the industrial expansion
of the national economy. This is the concomitant he fails to
understand. Implying 'the strongest possible wish that we should
forget about politics',[2] Snow's argument leads, in our present
situation, to precisely the same attitude as that which I have
described, and which the German intelligentsia sought to justify:

> The truth is [one of them writes in 1919] that before the Revolution [of 1848] we
> could, on the whole, rely upon the honesty and the objective attitude of our govern-
> ment, and save ourselves the trouble of meddling in the affairs of our excellent
> bureaucratic state. These are among the circumstances in which is rooted the superiority

[1] In his pamphlet *The Two Cultures*, Cambridge 1959, p. 23.
[2] See Lionel Trilling, 'A Comment on the Leavis–Snow Controversy', in
Commentary 1962, pp. 470-1.

which Germany showed in the nineteenth century, generally and above all in her scientific and technological development.[1]

But the real world tolerates no vacuum, certainly not in the heart of Europe. It makes its demands on the *savants* too, and it creates its own emergencies in order to drive home these demands.

The author of the lines I have just quoted was one of the many intellectuals who, after the defeat of 1918, sought solace in Germany's past and found it in her *'geistig'* tradition. Now, this tradition includes a number of writers who did not denigrate responsible political debate as mere 'meddling'. Even Hegel's theory of the State, for all its notorious complexity, lays down the participation of 'individual wills' and the realisation of 'particular interests' as the necessary 'substantial correlative' to the idea of the modern state.[2] And Hegel's conception of the *'Rechts*staat',[3] not unlike any democratic theory, is based on the need to prevent the arbitrary exercise of power. But the idea of freedom behind that conception is a high metaphysical idea, and leaves no room whatever for independent political action. Not for nothing does Hegel speak of the *destiny* of individuals and nations; and these he sees as stages in the great *moral* process of the Spirit's self-realisation. But morality again, like freedom, is for him determined by the world-historical scheme. And that scheme issues in a metaphysical absolutism which was used to sanction every act of bureaucratic tyranny by an appeal to the *raison d'état* at such-and-such a stage in world history. It was this 'metaphysical superstructure' which became the politically effective ideology of the Prussian hegemony, and not its roots in the moral consciousness of the individual. This ideology it was which, fortified by success in the 'real' world, drowned out the

---

[1] G. Roethe, *Deutsche Dichter des 18. und 19. Jahrhunderts und ihre Politik*, Berlin 1919, p. 5: '... *dass wir uns das Mitreden ... in unserem vortrefflichen Beamtenstaat ... ersparen konnten.*'

[2] See Hegel's *Grundlinien der Philosophie des Rechts* (1821), paras. 257 ff. (*G. W. F. Hegel, Auswahl aus seinen Werken*, ed. cit., pp. 314 ff.).

[3] To which Schopenhauer opposes his own idea of the State as an institution properly concerned with no more than the protection of its citizens.

voices of the many political thinkers in the wake of the 1848
Parliament who warned against the consequences of the emerging
conformism. The German liberal tradition did not end with the
collapse of that Parliament. But as a minority-view it enjoyed
few safeguards and wielded no effective power. The work of men
like Max Weber is more important in the context of present-day
sociology than it was in the context of German politics at the
end of the Second Reich. The mental climate with which he and
his predecessors had to contend is summed up memorably in the
testament of the great Roman historian, Theodor Mommsen, one
of the last members of the generation of 1848:

> *I have never held a political position* [Mommsen writes in 1899], *and I have never
> had, nor aspired to, any political influence. But in my innermost being and with the
> best that is in me I have always been a political animal and have always desired to
> be a citizen* [Bürger]. *In our nation that is not possible, for with us the individual
> man, even the best among us, never rises above doing his duty in the ranks* [Dienst
> im Glied] *and above political fetishism. It was this inner estrangement from the
> people to which I belong that firmly decided me to shun the German public whenever
> it was possible for me to do so—a public for which I lack respect.*[1]

Hegel in his discussion of the State emphasises that 'patriotism'
should not be confined to 'extraordinary sacrifices and actions'
but should be 'the frame of mind which is accustomed to see in
the commonwealth its substantial basis and end.'[2] It is as though,
writing in 1821, Hegel had anticipated the crisis-atmosphere of
the Second Reich.

In one respect at any rate the Wilhelminian age in Germany is
wholly different from the Victorian: it is an age of ever-renewed,
ever newly created emergencies. And the apparatus of uniquely
progressive social legislation, brought in by the Conservatives;
the enormous technological advances of German industry; the
disastrous policy of repressive measures against *both* the Church
(*Kulturkampf*) *and* the working classes (*Sozialistengesetze*); the
notion of *Lebensraum* and the policy of African and Middle-
Eastern expansion pursued by Wilhelm II—they all belong to the

---

[1] See Alfred Heuss, *Theodor Mommsen und das neunzehnte Jahrhundert*, Kiel
1956, p. 282.
[2] *Op. cit.*, p. 322.

atmosphere of those ever-renewed emergencies which were
designed as focal points for a national effort otherwise centrifugal
and diffused.[1]

Why did the middle classes contribute so little to the political
life of the Reich? Why were the political prospects of an enterprising *bürgerlich* citizen about as limited as they had been in
France before 1789? The several pressures which the English and
French middle classes were able to accommodate over a period
of several centuries, one after another, the *Bürgertum* had to face
all at once. From the right, they had to contend with the hostility
of a rigidly exclusive aristocratic society (to which belonged the
higher ranks of the Civil Service), whose one concession to the
demands for reform was a debating chamber without real
political power. At the same time they had to cover their left
flank against a proletariat which grew in numbers with all the
momentum of the delayed industrial revolution. Behind them
lay the sad *débâcle* of 1848. Before them, industrial expansion and
rapid economic progress—power to be wielded concretely, in the
factory yard and in the counting-house, not through a sham
parliament. In this predicament the conception of nationhood
emerges as a rallying call, as the only point of positive contact
with the State. The sequence of French and English—but also of
Austrian and Russian—history is reversed: the Reich is founded
as a political derivative of 'the Nation', itself based upon a common language and literature, not upon a common political past;
which is why the Reich has constantly to be defined, why it
cannot be taken for granted.

What is *das Volk*, that conception on which the vast propagandist literature of the German nationalists of the Second Reich is
based? For the critic and historian the simple and unambiguous

---

[1] Thus Fontane writes to his son Theodor (19.x.1889) of the mood of dis-
affection: '... the only reason why anybody obeys is because he imagines
cannons closing in on us in a circle and shooting the whole thing to bits.' And
again (to von Heyden, 5.viii.1893), 'The collapse of the whole glorious edifice
that was built between 1864 and 1870 is being openly discussed. And while
ever new six-figure armies and millions are sanctioned, nobody has the least
faith that our position is secure.'

answer is that, in the 'German ideology', *das Volk* is the substitute
for social concerns and political thinking.

For the nationalists, on the other hand, it is all manner of things.
They see it as a God-given thing, natural, 'organic', chthonic,
pristine and innocent; now it is superbly powerful, now again
under-privileged and threatened by its neighbours; now the up-
shot of Herder's 'poetry' of historical ideas, now again the living
proof of a 'scientific', Darwinian sociology, or of a biologically
verifiable theory of race. . . . In the sphere of art, no doubt, it is
an image which bears witness to 'the genuine liveliness of the
archaic [or rather archaicising] imagination'. In the documents of
German nationalism, on the other hand, it stands for almost anything except what it really is: a political fact among other facts
of European politics. For the nationalists it is an entity to appeal
to in one self-created emergency after another; an entity of which
almost anything can be predicated, and which will not belie any
of its predicates as long as they remain on paper. It is an entity
posited at the expense of the politically effective and ethically
responsible conception of statehood—a nation *qua* nation can
neither do, nor be held responsible for, anything, a fact which
does not prevent those in power from appealing to it as an authority by which to justify their actions.[1] It is an exemplar, an embodiment of the Categorical Imperative, or again the nearest thing
in the sphere of politics to approximate to the literary ideas of
genuineness, unworldly purity and truth. The source of literature
is personal experience, '*Erlebnis*'; the source of political action is
the need to satisfy common social interests: *das Volk* is intended to
bridge the gulf between the two. But again, the manner in which
the attempt is made is literary rather than political in origin.
Literal-mindedness is the refuge of the underprivileged intellectual. And it is with an unrelenting, vindictive literal-mindedness[2]
that the nationalist writers create and explore a vast range of
antitheses:'*Volk*' vs '*Nation*', '*Staat*' vs '*Reich*', '*Gemeinschaft*' vs
'*Gesellschaft*', '*Kultur*' vs '*Zivilisation*', '*Geist*' vs '*Seele*', '*Literatur*'

---

[1] H. Pross, *op. cit.*, p. 264.
[2] As distinct from the metaphor-mindedness on which I remarked in the
Austrian context, see above, p. 55.

vs '*Dichtung*', and also Arian *vs* Jew, 'German' *vs* 'Western'.[1]
How 'real' are these distinctions? It often looks as though they
belonged to 'realism' in the medieval meaning of the word, as
though these were words which created their realities. Of course,
inside the unchallenged constructions of the 'non-political'
nationalists these antitheses are illuminating enough, mainly of the
state of mind that has created them. And if the real world outside
the solipsism seems not to contain such antitheses, then the real
world will have to be modified accordingly. If, for instance, there
is no political reality, past or present, which would bind the '*aus-
landsdeutsch*' minorities of Eastern Europe to the Reich, if *das
Volk* does not coincide with the frontiers of the State, then
organisations (such as the *Alldeutscher Verein*) can be created in
order to convert the idea into a reality, and the literary fact of a
common language can be turned into a power-political factor.
(But then again, this need not be applied to the 'minorities' in
the West.) If the consequences of the Enlightenment and the trend
towards social equality between German Jews and Germans look
like blurring any real distinctions between them (and the conservative politicians are unwilling to legislate in favour of discrimination), then a 'scientific' theory of race will do the trick. And each
time, for each antithesis, the sanction will be sought in personal
feeling, in an appeal to a creed or ideology based upon a 'genuine'
personal conviction, an '*Erlebnis*'[2] itself not subject either to
reasoning or the facts of the real world. The temper of the
nationalists of the Second Reich is the temper of expectation,
rising in impatience, against the day when their vision may
become reality: the day when the State shall collapse and *das
Volk* emerge from its ruins.

---

[1] The antitheses of '*Bewegung*' *vs* '*System*', and '*Weltanschauung*' *vs* '*Ideologie*'
were added in the 1920's.

[2] The 'idolatry of "sensation" and "personality"' is brilliantly analysed
in Max Weber's essay *Wissenschaft als Beruf*, 1919 (see his *Schriften zur
theoretischen Soziologie* [ed. Graf zu Solms], Frankfurt 1947, p. 5); and the
critique of '*gesinnungspolitische Parteien*' and the politics of '*Weltanschauungen*'.
and of the 'non-political' bureaucracy in his *Politik als Beruf*, 1921 (*op. cit.*, pp.
185 and 169).

Literary in their origins and apocalyptic in their conclusions, the ideas of German nationalism lie outside the range of the political realities of their age; they influence these realities mainly by rationalising middle-class conformism and making of it a national duty. And the ideas don't become fully effective until there is nothing to conform with: until the State *is* in ruins; and it is not irrelevant to add that the politically effective amalgam formulated in the party-programme of National Socialism in the 1920's contains not a single tenet, not a single 'idea',[1] that had not been formulated, expounded and advocated, as yet ineffectively, in the age that followed Heine's prophecies.

By saying that Heine's prophecies came abundantly true, I don't have in mind the coxcombical vanity of the Kaiser, even less the machinations of such semi-intellectuals as Hitler and his immediate entourage. *They* indeed were not the heirs of the *Naturphilosophie* which Heine saw triumphant. Yet the intellectual *élite* of their followers—admirers of nordic nationhood, racialists and theoreticians of the Greater Reich, superannuated ramblers and acolytes of Valhalla, hot-house open-air intellectuals to a man—these are the true heirs of that 'paganism' whose millennium Heine predicts. Heine himself would not have been among them (and not merely because he was a Jew), nor Nietzsche, any more than Thomas Mann was.

But by virtue of that imaginative intuition of which the poet Heine was master and slave, he felt as they did. He knew intuitively what conflict it was that rent them, what dilemma it was they attempted to silence by their violent outbreak into action; and, knowing these forces, succeeded in expressing them for the first time and with a validity as lasting as the 'German problem' itself.

[1] Except, perhaps, that the effectiveness of that ideology was greatly enhanced by Wilson's doctrine of self-determination.

6

Yet what of Heine the lyricist? Is it not eccentric to devote a
chapter to Heine's prose and say nothing of his poetry? The
course of German history since his death has made it difficult to
speak of his poetic achievement in an unembarrassed way. Karl
Kraus's famous assault upon his reputation[1] has made the writings
of all those critics who have blithely ignored it look like exercises
in irrelevance, while the few who have not ignored the 'demoli-
tion' are left with little to say,[2] the essence of which is that the
lyrical poet's reputation is discredited together with the ethos
which saw itself flatteringly reflected in his poetry. More than
any other major poet Heine the lyricist wrote with an eye on his
public, harping on its expected responses, extending but hardly
challenging its sensibilities. Hence the lyrical poetry and its
reputation are all but inseparable. His fame rests upon his
felicitous adaptations of Goethean and Romantic feelings to a
mid-nineteenth-century domesticity of philistines and their sentimental wives; and these adaptations ring false to our ears.

The real greatness of Heine's poetry, I would suggest, lies where
he is not at all a 'serious lyrical poet'. It lies in much the same
regions of ambivalent commitment as does his splendid prose.
The anecdotal extravaganzas and mocking rhetoric; the romanticism of 'deep' moods alternating with easy colloquialisms; the
double-take and the jokes (sometimes a little off, occasionally
downright obscene); the recurring references to the German
political and social scene; and the multilevelled sententiousness—
serious, ironical, and then again fundamentally serious behind the
veil of pastiche, irony, sarcasm—these are the devices of his
greatest poetry, here lies its perennial value. Where it is serious
and 'deep', his poetry no longer speaks to us in the authentic
voice of uncontentious lyricism. His unique achievement is that
of a political poet: it lies where the poetry reaches depth and truth,
and Germany, through the veils of irony, and where the pre-existent

---

[1] 'Heine und die Folgen', in *Die Fackel*, Vol. XIII (1911) nos. 329/330, pp.
1–33.
[2] T. W. Adorno, 'Die Wunde Heine', in *Noten zur Literatur*, Frankfurt
1958, pp. 144 ff.

forms bequeathed to him by Goethe and the Romantics are
no longer explored but exploded. As in this poem, in which
the poet in exile begins by calling up an idyllic picture of the
German countryside in the month of May, with linden-trees,
river, mill, and all the other pretty details of a landscape by
Caspar David Friedrich, and which ends:

Am alten grauen Turme
Ein Schilderhäuschen steht;
Ein rotgeröckter Bursche
Dort auf und nieder geht.

Er spielt mit seiner Flinte,
die funkelt im Sonnenrot,
Er präsentiert und schultert—
Ich wollt', er schösse mich tot.

Beside the old grey tower
There stands a sentry box;
A lad in a bright-red tunic
Is marching to and fro.

He's playing with his musket,
The sun makes it shine red,
Presenting arms and shouldering—
I wish he would shoot me dead.

VI PROPITIATIONS: ADALBERT STIFTER

I

THE SECOND VOLUME of Nietzsche's *Human, All too Human* (1886) contains several reflections on the tasks of literature in his day. Literature (he writes there) is to be a guide to the future, to the age, presumably, of the Superman. In *Zarathustra*[1] he had described that age as one of heroic dimensions. Its leaders would be different from all previous mankind by virtue of their absolute assent to life; they would love their fate not in spite of but because of their knowledge of its ultimate senselessness; they would be heroic by virtue of assenting to the supreme tedium of life's 'eternal recurrence'. What present intimations are there, he now asks, of the literature of such an age, what will it be like?

Dichtungen solcher Dichter würden dadurch sich auszeichnen, dass sie gegen die Luft und Glut der Leiden-schaften *abgeschlossen und ver-wahrt erschienen: der unverbesser-liche Fehlgriff, das Zertrümmern des ganzen menschlichen Saitenspiels, Hohnlachen und Zähneknirschen und alles Tragische und Komische im alten gewohnten Sinne würde in der Nähe dieser neuen Kunst als lästige archaisierende Vergröberung des Menschenbildes empfunden werden. Kraft, Güte, Milde, Reinheit und ungewolltes, eingeborenes Mass in den Personen und deren Handlungen:*	The works of such writers would be distinguished by being evidently cut off and secure from the heat and atmosphere of the passions. The irreparable error, the destruction of the whole range of the human instrument, mocking laughter and gnashing of teeth and everything we mean by 'tragic' and 'comic' in the old sense would be felt, in the presence of this new art, as a tedious archaic coarsening of the human like-ness. Strength, goodness, gentleness, purity and spontaneous, innate moderation in characters and their actions; a levelled surface, restful and

---

[1] The reference here is mainly to the third (1884) and fourth (1885) parts of the book.

ein geebneter Boden, welcher dem Fusse Ruhe und Lust gibt: ein leuchtender Himmel auf Gesichtern und Vorgängen sich abspiegelnd: das Wissen und die Kunst zu einer neuen Einheit zusammengeflossen: der Geist ohne Anmassung und Eifersucht mit seiner Schwester, der Seele, zusammenwohnend und aus dem Gegensätzlichen die Grazie des Ernstes, nicht die Ungeduld des Zwiespaltes herauslockend: dies alles wäre das Umschliessende, Allgemeine, Goldgrundhafte, auf dem jetzt erst die zarten Unterschiede der verkörperten Ideale das eigentliche Gemälde—das der immer wachsenden menschlichen Hoheit— machen würden.[1]

pleasant to the foot; a radiant sky, reflected in faces and events; knowledge and art merging in a new uni.., the mind living without contentiousness or jealousy beside its sister the soul, and drawing from the contrast between them the grace of seriousness instead of the harassment of rivalry: all this would only be the framework, the general climate, the gold-leaf background upon which the delicately nuanced colours of personified ideals would create the actual painting—a representation of the ever-increasing sublimity of man.

Built from things that are here and now, Nietzsche's utopia imposes upon these things an order which is different from the order we know. Here grace, charm and sublime humanity shall replace those contradictions, irremediable errors and unappeasable passions, and also the velleities, which he saw in the world around him.

This is the world of Adalbert Stifter's *Der Nachsommer*, and I know of no better brief description than these lines of the tone of that novel, of its purpose, and of the narrative dimensions within which it moves. In writing these words, Nietzsche may well have had Stifter's masterpiece in mind;[2] we know that he greatly admired it and placed it on his very short list of German prose masterpieces.[3]

However, Stifter's achievement has not always elicited such

[1] *Menschliches, Allzumenschliches*, II, Kröner ed., no. 72/ii, p. 51.

[2] Though the context of Nietzsche's reflection (quoted below, p. 299) makes me wonder whether the suggestion that he had Stifter in mind is as certain as several critics (including E. Bertram, W. Rehm and K. Privat) would have us believe.

[3] It includes, besides Stifter, the *Aphorisms* of G. C. Lichtenberg, Eckermann's *Conversations with Goethe* and Keller's *Seldwyla* stories, and Jung Stilling's autobiography.

praise. In his secret diary, written in the dark years of the Nationalist-Socialist régime, the Catholic and existentialist writer Theodor Haecker notes:

Nicht jede Traube ist der Edelfäule fähig. Eine 'Kultur' ist die Voraussetzung. So gibt es in der Literatur eine Edellangeweile. Eine Kultur ist die Voraussetzung. Ihr grosser Name ist Adalbert Stifter.[1]

Not every grape is capable of pourriture noble; this presupposes a 'culture'. So in literature there is such a thing as a noble ennui, and this too presupposes a culture. Its great name is Adalbert Stifter.

The serenity and harmoniousness which Nietzsche exalts are not denied in Haecker's reflection; but, Haecker adds, the product of such an anti-tragic 'culture' is also magnificently, exquisitely boring. And the point he makes is borne out, somewhat surprisingly, by Stifter himself when he notes in a letter to his Budapest publisher (16 February 1847) that he was 'really terribly bored' when going through the proofs of one of his books.

There is something irresistibly funny in the picture of an author who is 'really terribly bored' by his own proofs. And since he was presumably not bored while writing his stories, it follows that their appeal—even to him, let alone to others—is restricted. Clearly, we have here an author who, somewhat like Henry James, confines himself with more than usual circumspection to one range of human experience, actual or potential, and has little to say about life outside that range. And we shall see, too, that this is an author whose great strength and limitation lie in the implicit claim that the meaning of life is encompassed by his art, and that all that lies outside it is 'irreparable error, the destruction of the whole range of the human instrument', and as such 'a coarsening of the human likeness', a monstrous misunderstanding. So that to understand and appreciate Stifter's work we must immerse ourselves, more directly and unreservedly than with other authors, in the particular mode of experience he conveys. He is at the opposite pole from a writer like Tolstoy, of whom it

[1] Theodor Haecker, *Tag- und Nachtbücher*, München 1947, pp. 122-3.

is often said that he has something to say to every kind of reader, and to each reader in almost every one of his moods.

But what happens if we fail to immerse ourselves so unreservedly, if (for instance) we allow something to distract us from the narrative argument on the page before us? Of course, any author's work may become the victim of bad reading. The characteristic difficulty Stifter's work offers is that, once distracted, we don't quite know how to find our way back into the page; suddenly bewildered by the complexity and elaborateness of the sentences, by the long paragraphs in front of us, we don't, for the world, know how to slip back and repair the damage which a distraction has wrought in the narrative web. But then, most prose writers make a fuller use of the vehicle of plot or story than does Stifter, so that, when the moment of wandering attention is over, the tale itself reclaims and then holds our attention. In Stifter the plot is replaced by a meticulous exploration of the scene, usually of the natural setting: so much so that, in a very special sense, the 'setting' *is* the story.

For many years Stifter was undecided whether to make painting or literature his career, and he continued to produce watercolours and unpretentious landscapes in oil to the end of his life. The subjects of his paintings and their colour-schemes owe a good deal to the German Romantic school of landscape art, and the love of domestic detail evokes the contemporary *Biedermeier* convention. His draughtsmanship, on the other hand, is meticulous, often ambitiously planned and firmly executed—and these are the qualities which will go into the prose-works of his maturity. This is not to suggest that he writes in the sort of excessively epithetic style that Lessing had criticised in his famous argument in *Laokoon*; Stifter would, I imagine, agree with Lessing's dictum that the portrayal of 'a sequence of events one after another', rather than of 'the parts of an object next to each other', is the poet's proper task. And yet his writing has a particular static quality which challenges Lessing's distinction almost as radically as do the configurations of imagist poetry.

Stifter does indeed portray sequences of events; he does, too, certainly in his *Novellen*, tell stories. But as his style reaches the assurance of maturity, so the story-element is attenuated, until in

his greatest novel it all but disappears. What takes its place is a
kind of tracing-out of contours. There is a scene in *Der Nachsommer* where the young hero discovers a statue on the staircase
of the house in which he is a frequent and welcome visitor. The
point about the discovery is that, although the statue has always
been there, he was not sufficiently mature to see and appreciate it.
There is thus a certain 'before' and 'after' to this discovery, a
rudimentary sort of action; and again, when the youth goes round
the statue and retraces, in contemplating its beauty, each part of
it in his mind, it is this retracing that provides the narrative
thread, and there is at that point no other—the story has come to
a halt. The tenuousness of Stifter's plots is not due to a lack of
inventiveness. His early stories, written under the impact of Jean
Paul and Romanticism, are full of picturesque adventures and
often fantastic action in outlandish settings. As he reaches his
maturity, so the tales become simplified, external events are
reduced to a minimum, the palpable interest of the story wanes.
And when we compare some of the original versions of these
stories with their later, heavily revised forms, we see that the
elimination of striking images, dramatic action and involved plot
is a matter of deliberate artistic intention. It is as though he wished
to do the impossible, to give us 'pure beauty unadulterated by
anything beautiful'.[1]

But how is one to appreciate a story lacking in palpable
interest? It was this *impasse* which Schopenhauer had to face when
he came to consider the appeal of the 'will-less' or 'disinterested'
work of art. He could hardly deny that what is set in motion
by poetry or great art is our will—that 'interesting' means whatever appeals to our individual will, *quod nostra interest*.[2] And yet
the work of art is to be a '*Quietiv*' of that will, a peace-maker.
Schopenhauer gets out of the difficulty by distinguishing between
'the body' of the work and its 'soul'. Our interest in 'the body' of
a work of art, he argues, is merely the means leading to a 'will-
less' contemplation of its 'soul', its 'significant idea'. (The 'interest'

[1] The phrase is Wittgenstein's, in the *Blue Book*, Oxford 1958, pp. 17–18.
[2] See his essay 'Ueber das Interessante', 1821, in *Sämtliche Werke*, ed. P.
Deussen, vi, München 1923, p. 382.

of the work of art, we may paraphrase, has the purpose not of sugaring the pill but of spicing the fudge.) But the possibility of at least partly dispensing with 'the body' is already inherent in Schopenhauer's argument; and the impression of a sublime and so to speak beautiful boredom which we sometimes receive in reading Stifter's work springs from just such a dispensing with the palpable 'body' of art, with many of the things 'that interest us'. Not because Stifter follows Schopenhauer's view of art, let alone his metaphysic, but because he, like Schopenhauer, banishes much of the world of our common interpretation from the world of 'the significant idea', the world of his art. Plot is the concrete witness, in literature, of social involvement, and of the imperfections of knowledge and morality to which men in society are prone. Whereas what really 'interests' Stifter is the world of the individual soul, freed from all that does not belong to, or cannot be drawn into, its orbit. In setting out to transform that 'middle sphere of experience',[1] to which the spirit of his age was so reluctant to accommodate itself, Stifter proceeds altogether more radically and consciously than Goethe ever did, and thus less spontaneously. But then, *pace* Schopenhauer, the imperviousness behind his determination to present 'beauty unadulterated by anything beautiful' is itself an act of the will.

Stifter's exploration of the world of the single soul is entirely characteristic of the 're-interpretations' to which this book is devoted; more than that, here the tradition of nineteenth-century German prose reaches its peak: Stifter's work is the greatest and (for all its strange 'boredom') most fascinating achievement of that tradition.

2

Adalbert Stifter[2] was born on 23 October 1805 in the little town of Oberplan in the Bohemian Forest, not far from the mountains

---

[1] See above, p. 3.

[2] The biographical facts are taken from A. R. Hein, *A.S., Sein Leben und seine Werke*[2]. Wien 1952; Urban Roedl, *A.S.: Geschichte seines Lebens*, [1]Berlin 1936, [2]Bern 1958; and K. G. Fischer, *A.S.: Psychologische Beiträge zur Biographie*,

which for a thousand years have formed the frontier of the ancient kingdom of Bohemia, not far also from the sources of the Vltava, its main river. This is the landscape to which he returns in many stories throughout his life, and in which he places the beginning and end of his last great novel, *Witiko*. He was educated in the Benedictine monastery of Kremsmünster in Upper Austria, and became a student of Law at the University of Vienna in 1826. The death of his father during Stifter's childhood[1] brought the family to the verge of poverty, and as a student he had to make his way by tutoring in the prosperous houses of Viennese aristocrats and patricians.

The two great emotional experiences of his life occurred at this time. In Friedberg (not far from Oberplan) he fell in love with Fanni Greipl, the daughter of a well-to-do merchant family; in Vienna, a short time after, he met Amalia Mohaupt, a simple working-class girl who made a living as a milliner. Both encounters brought him a great deal of suffering, and in their different ways were decisive in the shaping of his emotional life. The affair with Fanni shows the full extent of his velleities; in his letters to her, fervent declarations of love alternated with devastating doubts as to his own worthiness, and the end was no less painful for being anticipated. The affair with Amalia, dominated by a powerful sexual attraction, led eventually to a marriage which it is difficult to see as anything but disastrous. Characteristically, the Friedberg engagement was kept secret—there is about his attitude to Fanni an air of defeat and resignation almost from the beginning. It is as if he never really believed that the social differences between them could be overcome, and his wooing of her appears throughout marred by the expectation of ultimate failure. The liaison with Amalia was broken off and resumed more than once—each time with many heart-searchings, to him mortifying and to her probably quite unintelligible. And when in 1837 he did at last marry her, his conscience was

---

Linz 1961. Stifter's letters are quoted from A. Sauer's ed., *A.S.: Sämtliche Werke*, Prague, &c. 1904 ff. For a discussion of the literature see note 3, pp. 358 ff.

[1] A fragment containing Stifter's account of his childhood impressions will be found below, pp. 352-8.

riddled with many feelings of guilt: towards Amalia with whom
he had consoled himself for the loss of Fanni, towards Fanni for
having betrayed her with Amalia, towards himself and his high
moral ideals. . . . He continued to think of Fanni, even after her
death in 1839, as his true bride, the more so since the erotic bond
with Amalia, which appears to have been deep and lasting,
brought him no peace of mind. But of all this, as of so many of
his own feelings, we know very little; on the whole his letters
are lacking, not so much in introspection as in insight, possibly
candour.

The mood of his student days in Vienna in the 1830's was
exuberant and lighthearted. Why it was soon to be superseded
by a state of mind deeply spiritual at its best, and often ponderous
and anguished; why indeed so much of his life lies submerged
under a heavy burden of psychosomatic disturbances, neither his
writings nor his letters nor even those of his biographers who
admit as much make entirely clear. The present sketch attempts
to do no more than enlarge a little on some of the facts which
contributed to that depressive disposition; many of the events of
his life must figure here not as causes only but also as effects and
symptoms of what they purport to explain.

In the early years of his married life Stifter made a number of
unsuccessful attempts to secure a teaching post at the State
Gymnasien, but again, as during his wooing of Fanni, he anticipated failure by paralysing self-doubt; and again eventually
drew from defeat the substance of poetic affirmation. He continued, meanwhile, to earn a living as a tutor (for a time to Metternich's son Richard), contributing stories and sketches to magazines
and very occasionally selling a painting.

One could compile quite a long list of German writers who
went through the dispiriting business of private coaching and
ended up by having their social pride and self-regard broken.
Stifter speaks for them all when he describes the arrogant way he
was treated by the parents of his charges, who regarded him as
little better than a mountebank or tamer of wild animals; the
pupil's attitude, as he watched the humble tutor's departure after
a lesson, is hardly more encouraging: 'Lingering by the window
and drumming with his fingers on the pane, he gazes at you as

you stand below, bespattered by the mud of the passing carriages.'
Yet Stifter harboured no feeling of revolt, and admired but was
uneasy with those who did; the feeling of social inferiority never
left him. At the same time he was a devoted and painstaking
teacher, acquiring the reputation of a serious pedagogue, even
though it brought him little practical reward.

Many professional failures and humiliations came his way, yet
they were not the only source of that heavy anguish which
increasingly oppressed his life. There is also something of the
déraciné peasant about him, of the townsman who has never
come to terms with his rustic past and whose occasional visits to
his childhood home leave in him feelings of betrayal and guilt.
These feelings find their appropriate expression in his images of
the big city as an emblem of superficiality, worldliness and ir-
religion, of all that is unauthentic and unnatural. But again,
Stifter's *déracinement* is characteristic of countless German authors
and their heroes throughout the nineteenth century; the mood
stands in complete contrast to the adventurousness with which
bright young Frenchmen from the provinces came to conquer Paris.

In the early 'forties Stifter's writings were gradually gaining
him a devoted reading public among the upper middle classes
and the families of his pupils. During that period he and his wife
lived increasingly on his literary earnings, though even then he
did not entirely abandon the idea of becoming a professional
painter. The tale of his perpetual financial worries is told in his
correspondence with Gustav Heckenast, his Budapest publisher;
from these letters, too, we get a very full impression of the
anxieties and misgivings which accompanied the publication of
many of his stories.

He is an indifferent critic of his own work, but the statements
of his literary intentions are revealing. By and large, he disclaims
any artistic ambition; or rather, identifying artistic achievement
with a high morality, he sees his art strictly as a means to a moral
end, and is anxious to erase from his work all that does not
obviously have an ennobling influence on the reader. Thus in
art, as in politics, in education, and also in human relations, his
overt judgements are absolute and flatly moral, and removed
from the reality of his own life. The simple and absolute ideal

which, in art as everywhere else, he professes to follow is described
in exalted and unworldly terms—neither the obstacles on the way
towards that ideal nor the fact that it might not be self-evidently
valid to others interest him.

No honest biographer can ignore the complex psychological
background of Stifter's art, nor its value, to him, as compensation
and make-believe; and it may well be that he himself had a fuller
understanding of all this than is apparent from his own statements.
But the signs of such an understanding are at best indirect.
Everywhere in his biography we are faced with the questions of
his truthfulness, but as often as not the answer eludes us. Did he
see the gulf between the reality of his life and his writings?
Between his grey days and the 'gold-leaf background' on which
he painted his figures? Between Amalia and the women that
appear in his stories? Between their marriages and his?

The thirty-one years of Stifter's married life with a barely
literate working-class girl are eased by none of that good-
humoured liberality and affectionate understanding which
marked Goethe's marriage with Christiane Vulpius. Irritations
and wounding quarrels, passionate reconciliations and unctuous
sermons were the order of their days. The marriage remained
childless,[1] and there are indications that Stifter, who showed
himself deeply affected by the deprivation, saw it as a punishment. (He also, on infrequent visits to his native Oberplan, found
the noise of children intolerable.) In the last decade or so of his
life, he set out on a strange literary transfiguration, as though,
through his poetic gift, he could make Amalia into something
she was not: he apostrophises her (in letters intended for publication) in a high-minded, unconvincing style, with expressions
which were probably incomprehensible to her. One strains hard
not to think of Dulcinea addressed by her elderly Don. Instead,
one tries to think of the Jamesian prescription—the loving refusal
to see the partner's blemishes until, through the agency of love,
the blemishes have disappeared. Yet the comparison is unconvincing, perhaps because Stifter hadn't enough emotional strength

---

[1] It may be that in November 1836 they had a child, which died a month
later; see K. G. Fischer, *op. cit.*, pp. 45, 52.

and patience to spare, more likely because in his homilies he wasn't addressing the real person at all. And if he deceived himself about Amalia, who grew bitter with the years, how true was his memory of Fanni? Was it perhaps the case that in their different ways both women were equally unsuited to the man: that neither had much understanding for his temperament, his anxieties, for the nature of his genius? It is a hard thing to say of a man that in many important moments of his life he drew strength from self-deception. Yet the conclusion seems to me unavoidable; and I mention it because it offers something like a key to Stifter's writings, for they, in many important parts, are precisely what his life was not. In many—not in all. The romantic view which would see the *artist* endowed with all the clarity which the *man* lacks is less than the whole truth. Thus, if it is true that Stifter never fully understood his own part in the affair with Fanni, the parallel situation in *Der Nachsommer* too is, as we shall see, marked by a strange unclarity.

Several of his biographers have suggested that it was the political events of 1848 which brought about for the first time those states of depression and anxiety from which he intermittently suffered for the rest of his life. What is certain is that his enthusiasm for the revolutionary cause, although it lasted only a few weeks, was duly noted by the Austrian Ministry of Education and later held against him—and this, we know, filled him with much apprehension. His attitude to the Revolution has often been likened to Grillparzer's. Both had suffered a good deal under the absurd censorship of the *Vormärz* era (Stifter was refused permission to give a series of public lectures on aesthetics), without ever voicing a radical disapproval of it, though Grillparzer was far from toadying to the régime as Stifter did. At first they were both among the enthusiastic supporters of the uprising—Stifter even gave a number of public addresses and helped to choose a deputy for the Frankfurt Parliament; and they both soon became disillusioned and increasingly hostile to the revolutionary cause, seeing their high hopes corrupted in the chaos which came to a head in the renewed fighting of October 1848. Their subsequent attitudes, however, are very different. Grillparzer is no less bitter than Stifter, no less full of anxious forebodings about the consequences of the mob-rule and of its collapse. But his feelings are informed by a profound understanding of the social forces at work in the chaos, and from this understanding springs the greatest of his dramas, *Ein Bruderzwist in Habsburg*. Compared with that work, the political essays which Stifter wrote in the next two years are without much significance. He speaks in them of ideals of justice, morality and humanity, in arguments which are as noble as they are unrealistic. The only practical means of achieving these ideals he ever discusses is the moral education of the individual; whereas the real source of positive political action—the scrupulous adjustment of means to ends, to which Grillparzer had devoted some of his finest dramatic argument—remains unconsidered. The great *'Staatswissenschaft'* which Stifter continued to invoke throughout the 'fifties is cast in absolute moral ideals, against which most of what actually happens on the political scene is weighed and found equally wanting. Thus he condemned Bismarck's conduct of the war of 1866 in such absolute terms that its speedy conclusion and the subsequent conciliation (which were the planned result of Bismarck's political genius) appears to have left him bewildered.

What is interesting in all this is not Stifter's anxious and dogmatic conservatism. It is his appeal to a *'science'* of politics—and indeed to a 'scientific' point of view in the study of nature, man and education, history, and hence also in the writing of literature. We can sense the beginnings of this attitude in his life as a penurious tutor in Vienna, where he came to think of 'culture', of the systematic cultivation of the mind, as the true stronghold of and compensation for a life deprived of all emotional and worldly assurances. Against the real world with its compromises and humiliations, and against fate too, with its sudden, annihilating visitations, he would erect a scheme of ideals—ideals of conduct, knowledge and feeling. It is to be a scheme of absolutes, regular and clearly determined, and thus 'scientific'. Like Goethe, he was deeply and actively interested in the natural sciences, and some of his finest nature-descriptions draw extensively on his own observations and on the work of his friend, the geologist Friedrich

Simony (whom, ironically enough, Stifter admired for possessing that freedom from social constraints which he himself never achieved). Like Goethe, Stifter is deeply concerned with a humanist ideal of *Bildung*, of which the natural sciences should form an integral part. From Herder and Goethe he takes over the ideal of a world-view which is to be unified by virtue of being equally concrete and anthropocentric in all its parts. But here, as in other contexts, he overstates the Goethean point of view. He lacks the inner freedom, and hence the stylistic adaptability, which enabled Goethe to treat each (or almost each) part of the natural world with the kind of precision he intuitively knew to be appropriate to it. The ideal of a 'scientific' precision which on occasion Stifter hopes to impart to his descriptive prose leads to a kind of encyclopaedic enumeration of data, which sometimes succeeds in imitating Nature's abundance but sometimes leaves the reader gasping for air. And here once more Stifter is typical of the intellectual climate of his and the subsequent age: with him too the '*wissenschaftlich*' attitude, intended to offset so many dispossessions, tends occasionally to degenerate into that pedantry which Nietzsche devastatingly attacks in his portrait of the '*Bildungsphilister*'.

In the early summer of 1848, full of deep misgivings about the political developments in Vienna, Stifter went on his annual vacation to Linz, and there, apart from several brief visits and journeys, he remained to the end of his life. In 1849 he was nominated inspector of primary and secondary schools in Linz and Upper Austria, a post which he at first held without any pay and to which for many years he gave much of his time and energy. The salary which the governor of the province eventually secured for him was at first a mere pittance, but the post did make it possible for him to devote a good deal of his time to writing. By the middle 'fifties, when his position had become more secure, discouraged by petty chicaneries and frustrations, he had already lost some of the enthusiasm with which he had entered on his career of educator and reformer.

In one of the most self-revealing of his stories, *Der Waldgänger* (1847), there is a prophetic and faithful description of his feelings. Here, first, is the whole passage:

> *Jedes Ungeheure und Ausserordentliche, welches sich in der Zukunft des Wanderers vorgespiegelt hatte, war nicht eingetreten, jedes Gewöhnliche, was er von seiner Seele und seinem Leben ferne halten wollte, war gekommen, was er sonst anstrebte, erreichte er nicht, oder erreichte es anders, als er gewollt hatte, oder er wollte es nicht mehr erreichen; denn die Dinge kehrten sich um, und was sich als gross gezeigt hatte stand als Kleines am Wege, und das Unbeachtete schwoll an und entdeckte sich als Schwerpunkt der Dinge, um den sie sich bewegen.*

It begins, unremarkably enough, with generalities, but towards the end of the first phrase we notice a strange life and plasticity entering into the abstraction:

> *All that was tremendous and extraordinary in the Wanderer's expectations of the future had failed to come to pass, whereas all the common-place things that he had intended to keep away from his inner and outer life had been his lot, . . .*

And now the situation is explored more insistently; its logic moves in two, three different directions, each abstract 'thing', each phrase becomes more plastic, each cog in the wheel of the argument is given a life, a slow mechanical movement, until the whole thing turns before us, almost like one of Kafka's menacing sentence-contraptions:

> *. . . all his other aspirations had either remained out of his reach, or had been attained in other ways than he had wished, or he had ceased to find them desirable; for things had reversed themselves, so that what had seemed great had become small and stood by the wayside, and what had been inconsiderable had swelled up and revealed itself as the focal point round which all other things revolved.*

Resistance to this fatal machine there is none.

The idealism with which, consciously reacting against the events of '48, he had set out to reform the education of his country, was not spent. It found its reflection in the most famous of his works, *Bunte Steine*, which appeared in two volumes in 1853. The book is intended as a collection of stories for children, and in the Preface, written partly as a reply to attacks which Hebbel had made on his work,[1] he speaks of the tales as 'playthings for young hearts'. Yet only three of the six stories can be read as simple children's tales. The others show that preoccupation with solitude and tragic fate which, as we shall see, is characteristic of some of his greatest work.

His daily life in the large apartment in the centre of Linz, the capital of Upper Austria, was monotonous and sombre. Although Amalia could share with him none of his literary ideas, she satisfied his obsessive need for order and tidiness (yet his own study was chaotic), and proudly looked after all the elaborate furnishings with which he filled the house. From precious ornaments and bric-à-brac he, the descendant of a long line of poor smallholders and village tradesmen, hoped to draw the assurance of possession —the massive beauty of his Baroque secretaire with its pedestal of dolphins is fully described in *Der Nachsommer*. He began collecting and restoring antique furniture and pictures—the restoration of the 'Kerberger' altar in the novel derives from his visits to the late Gothic church at Kefermarkt. He continued to wrestle with his paintings; grew heavy and listless with large meals,[2] heavy wines and lack of exercise; he chain-smoked cigars and made of the habit an elaborate ritual; and, as though intent on not omitting a single item of a typical *Biedermeier* existence, he kept a dog—whose death was followed by days of melancholia—and took to cultivating cacti—the centennial flowering of a *cereus peruvianus* is one of the great solemn events in the novel. It is hardly surprising that with the mounting expenses of the household his financial worries never diminished. *Der Nachsommer*, published in 1857, brought him back some of that recognition which his early stories had won while he lived in Vienna. The adverse criticism it also received, especially from

---

[1] In a dreary epigram published in the periodical *Europa* in 1849. (See Hebbel's *S.W.*, ed. R. M. Werner, Berlin 1904, I, Vol. VI, p. 349; Vol. XII, pp. 184-5, contains his hostile notice of *Der Nachsommer*, and pp. 189-93 a further attack.)

[2] 'He and Amalia together could polish off a goose and a large ham in a day . . .' (W. Muschg, *Tragische Literaturgeschichte*, Bern 1948, p. 372, based on A. R. Hein, *op. cit.*[1], Prague 1904, p. 443).

Friedrich Hebbel,[1] wounded him deeply; and his need for the reassurance of praise was never appeased. He had some contact with polite provincial society, and was given to dominating the conversation at aristocratic tea-parties by an astonishing display of erudition. He insisted (as he often does in his books) on giving a full genealogy and list of circumstances appertaining to the topic under discussion—his old friend Prince Peppi Colloredo called him 'ein Definitionsmagazin'; politics and contemporary events were excluded from his conversation. But neither the social life of Linz nor one or two close friends, among them his early biographer Johannes Aprent, did much to lighten the burden of his isolation.

Various family connections were taken up but ended in squabbles. On three different occasions young girls, distantly related, were brought in to share the life of the ageing couple; all three died young. The writer had shown[2] what retribution attended the passionate desire of the childless—the man could not reconcile himself to the deprivation; and consequently suffered one of the harshest blows he ever knew. One of the girls, an orphaned niece of Amalia's called Juliane, lived with them for a number of years as their foster-child. As she grew to womanhood, the girl's impetuous temperament and her 'tendency to untidiness and frivolity' irritated him a good deal; what he called 'a violent disturbance in her sex-life'[3] may well have been merely the symptoms of puberty. Late one night in March 1859 Juliane, then aged eighteen, secretly left the house; she was found drowned in the Danube a few days later. Her portrait is contained in one of the

---

[1] Hebbel's hostility to Stifter's outlook and work has its exact parallel in the notorious *Boon*-controversy chronicled in *Henry James and H. G. Wells, A record . . .*, London 1958. As Wells says (8.vii.1905), the difference 'is profound and incurable', and also typical. For James, as for Stifter, 'It is art that *makes* life, makes interest, makes importance . . .' (James, 10.vii.1915), and in this 'making' a high degree of formal artifice is involved; for Hebbel, on the other hand, the relevant criterion is not 'art' but 'life', the naturalism (as Wells puts it) of a 'raw, bleeding piece of life'. But unlike James, Stifter hasn't the *critical* intelligence to challenge Hebbel's point of view. Ultimately, the 'difference' is between a deliberated classicism and '*littérature engagée*'.

[2] *Der Waldgänger*, of 1847.   [3] To Heckenast, 24.viii.1859.

children's stories in *Bunte Steine*, written when she was seventeen. *Katzensilber* is the tale of an orphan, 'the nut-brown girl', whom some children and their grandmother find deserted in a forest. They take her back to the farm on which they live with their parents, but although they all love and cherish her, she is never happy among them. And at the end of the story, after a passionate outburst of sorrow, she suddenly leaves them:

> *The father and mother decided not to follow the girl, so that she might calm herself in solitude. They thought all would be well.*
> *But all was not well. They saw the girl go up the sandy ridge, and after that they never saw her again.*

The girl's last words had been, '*Sture Mure ist todt, und der hohe Felsen ist todt*'. ('My mother is dead, and the high rock is dead.') The note which Juliane left behind read, 'I go to my mother into the great service'. Why did 'the nut-brown girl' never feel happy among the people who had given her a home? Why did she so suddenly leave them? Why did Juliane disappear and die? We are never told. But in the work of art the withholding of motive turns the unexplained into a mystery, and thus something of the effect of tragedy is achieved; whereas the absence of a final reason in life left Stifter bewildered, and with a yet heavier burden of guilt.

The banishment, as he increasingly felt it, of his life in Linz was interrupted by occasional tours of inspection and journeys, usually with Amalia. Together they went to Vienna, to various Austrian and Bohemian towns and resorts, and in 1857, on concluding *Der Nachsommer*, to Trieste. There he beheld the sea for the first time in his life, and followed it along the coast westward, turning inland at Duino. The impression he received was overwhelming. Ten years before he had anticipated this moment and wondered whether, when it came, 'it would not be too late, and whether anything could enter my hardened soul any more'.[1] And now he writes:

> *My very dear friend! This little foretaste made me feel that I could burst into tears at having grown so old without seeing this. I know for certain now that I shall live*

[1] To Heckenast, 16.xi.1846.

for a month in Venice, that I shall see Florence, Rome and Naples, indeed that I shall perhaps remain for years in Rome. Goethe only became a great poet through Italy. If I had come to Italy for the first time twenty or twenty-five years ago and frequently afterwards, I too should have achieved something. A man's heart might break in contemplating certain impossibilities.[1]

And he adds, with a literary awareness which is unusual in him,

Der Nachsommer is a German book; even so, after such a journey I would have written it quite differently . . .

How different would it have been? Perhaps the seascape mentioned in a single sentence in the last chapter would have been more fully described. But the drift of his imagination—the imagination of a poet who dwells on forests and mountains— would not have been altered.

The mountains and the sea: in man's dealings with these two regions of nature the whole difference between the solitary and the social experience lies enshrined. Both are regions in which a man may prove himself; and the experience of the sea *can* be a solitary thing: we need only think of the agony of little Pip, abandoned by the crew of the whaling boat: 'Out from the centre of the sea, poor Pip turned his crisp, curling, black head to the sun . . . the awful lonesomeness is intolerable. The intense concentration of self in the middle of such heartless immensity, my God! who can tell it?'[2] But above all it is a social symbol: it is the company of men at sea, concertedly working towards a common end, under a common moral dispensation, that yields images of authentic life. And when an exile like Joseph Conrad chooses the sea, first as a profession and then as a theme, he chooses it because it allows him access to the authentic life of men engaged in one common pursuit as no other situation would have done.[3] To this social situation the poet of the mountains remains a stranger.

[1] To Heckenast, 20.vii.1857; Trieste and Venezia Giulia were then still an Austrian province.

[2] *Moby Dick*, Chapter XCII.

[3] See Graham Hough, *Image and Experience*, London 1960, Chapter VIII.

Alas, the journey to Italy never came off. Stifter's financial situation remained chaotic, even though he earned a good deal of money, for Heckenast, who in the earlier years of their connection had exploited Stifter's financial crises to his advantage, proved a generous and successful publisher. Money never plays an important part in Stifter's stories and is never a motive of action. When it is mentioned, it is always the reward of careful husbandry and a symbol of probity and human worth. As a matter of biographical fact Stifter lost a good deal of it speculating in railway-shares, and for several years lived in the firm conviction that all his financial worries would be cured by a win in the state lottery; the castles in Spain he was forever building with his certain win belong to the best tradition of contemporary Austrian comedy.[1]

In his last years Stifter frequently visited the villages on the southern slopes of the Bohemian Forest, where many scenes of his last novel, *Witiko* (1867), are set. While Amalia found the seclusion intolerable, to him it was a place of refuge.

From about 1855 onwards Stifter suffered from various abdominal ailments and colics, for which he was prescribed rigorous and to him intolerable diets, exercise, and the waters at Carlsbad. Whether or not the various complaints of the late 'thirties onwards were hypochondriac in origin, the illness which in 1863 was diagnosed as incurable cirrhosis is likely to have been of long standing; and it is certain that his ailments were at all times intimately related to his psychic states, in which violent depressions alternated with periods of deep, silent melancholia. He aged very rapidly—it is significant that in his stories he mostly describes either youths or old men, and only rarely dwells on the

---

[1] I mean the tradition of Raimund and Nestroy. Needless to say, Stifter was wholly hostile to the contemporary theatre. Raimund's plays (he writes) he used to think of as 'the aberrations of a considerable mind', but in comparison with the subsequent 'immeasurably low' standards of the 'Volksstück'—he probably has Nestroy in mind but never mentions him—Raimund's works 'now [1867] appear noble, true and natural'. (See *ed. cit.*, Vol. XVI, ed. Horcicka and Wilhelm, Prague 1927, pp. 386, 495).

period of manhood. In 1865 he was at last granted retirement on a full pension (together with the title of '*Hofrat*'), but he had little time left to enjoy it.

The end is confusion and darkness. We read of a flight from Linz into the mountains in fear of a cholera epidemic (October 1866); of his return, with feelings of guilt at having deserted Amalia; of a snowstorm which brought him to the limit of mental endurance (November 1867). Grave attacks of the *grippe* (October 1867), from which he never fully recovered, were added to the progressive cirrhosis. In the despair of pain he cut his throat in the night of 25 January 1868. His wounds were stanched and he died, having received extreme unction, in the morning of the 28th, aged sixty-two.

Of Stifter's religiousness, except as it enters his writings, it is difficult to speak. In his letters, especially in later years, he confines himself to words of conventional piety. The impression one receives is that, as with so many of his contemporaries, his Christianity was not a joyful faith: 'I cannot give over my suffering [he writes[1]], for otherwise I would have to give over the Divine also.' His faith was to him neither a solace nor an escape. He remained a Catholic all his life, and was bound to Amalia by a Christian conception of marital duty. In his prayers, which sprang from need rather than from plenty, from sorrow and repentance rather than from hope and joy, he resembles Dr Johnson; and so he does too in that heaviness of heart and temperament for which in German there is the apposite word '*Schwerblütigkeit*'. True, he seems to have lacked Dr Johnson's conversational gifts—but then, he also lacked any audience that would provide the conditions in which those gifts could flourish. (And one wonders, in the course of such a comparison, what effect the early death of Johnson's wife had on his literary and public career.)

Let me single out a few episodic moments from this life, none of them intimate or palpably tragic: the young, mud-bespattered

---

[1] To Heckenast, 13.v.1854.

tutor in the courtyard, the ageing provincial school-inspector yearning for a journey to Italy, the cactus-collector pottering among his plants, the elderly recluse writing letters of loving homage to his ignorant, shrewish wife. What deprivation, what narrowness of worldly experience, what need for solace and enrichment through Nature and mind are manifest in that life, contemporary French and English writers would have been hard put to imagine. Yet its tenor is not at all exceptional; in its narrowness and resignation, in its absence of dramatic turning-points, that life is entirely representative of the lives of most nineteenth-century German poets. Paris, London, the Empire overseas . . . the words have an exotic, adventurous sound to German ears, they speak of vice and splendour, of life, worldliness, of an established social order as well as of a freedom beyond German experience. A country-house party in Meredith—lords and ladies of dubious descent and rich genteel bankers, stripped of their finery by the shrewd pen of a tailor's son—is a party held on another planet; so is Stephen Blackpool's bitter conversation with Mr Gradgrind; so is the funeral of Poor Jo.

At some distance from the mainstream of English realistic fiction runs the current of mid-nineteenth-century American prose, whose affinities with German literature have hardly been noticed. Entirely lacking the social sophistication of the Old World, a writer like Hawthorne is conveying a range of spiritual experience which has much in common with Stifter's work. Take that central scene in *The Scarlet Letter*, by the solemn brook in the lonely forest, where Hester Prynne, after 'seven years of outlaw and ignominy', meets again her lover, the Reverend Arthur Dimmesdale. The child that is with her—'half-elf, half-demon', the burning stigma on her breast, the haunted, guilt-ridden man who 'kept his conscience alive by the fretting of an unhealed wound', the forest with its intimations first of wrath and then of forgiveness and a new life, the close allegorical correspondence of objects, moods, words, and gestures, even the slow, unwieldy language with its deliberate complex clauses, its archaic stiffness and its awkward pedantic arrangement of verbal tenses—all these belong as much to Stifter's stories as they do to Hawthorne's. The scarlet letter itself too, so much more a sign than a thing, is the product of an imagination whose need for significance is unappeased by the signs we find in our common world. And Arthur Dimmesdale, whose life is spent in the shadow of slow retribution, in a prison of guilt from which he cannot imagine an escape, weak in everything except his obsession, is the kind of character that springs from the innermost core of Stifter's experience. Finally, there is the single sinful act—Hester Prynne's adultery, buried in a past which Hawthorne's narration, like Stifter's, shuns exploring. The function of the act is to motivate the events of the story. But when we enquire to what extent it really does this—what freedom if any there is beyond the consequences, social and spiritual, of the act—the difference between the two writers looms up large. In Hawthorne's heroine that meeting in the forest releases an energy, an almost Lawrentian sense of life, which frees her from that bondage of guilt which her lover was never strong enough to break. In Stifter's *Novellen* such characters never emerge from the dire consequences of their transgression, they have none of Hester Prynne's energy and can never gain her kind of freedom. Hester is free from the moment she refuses to identify social obloquy with divine judgement; the moment she first realises that there is *a world* outside the New England settlement (though that world is never described). Stifter cannot conceive of such a world of freedom for his characters. Instead, he presents the consequences of the single act of impiety more nearly as determined by superhuman fate, so that the consequences are less capable of being defied than is the ignominy of the Puritan pillory. The imbalance between the act and its consequences is a part of Stifter's design—not always of his conscious intention perhaps, but of the achieved effect. With him the single act either unleashes a chain of disastrous events incommensurably larger than itself, or else its consequences are transformed into the grand image of 'What-might-have-been', of all that life failed to provide.

I have suggested that the tenor of Stifter's life runs counter to his work, but this is not to say that his living experience is omitted from it. On the contrary, the work never moves far away from the cares which his life inflicted on him, his creative imagination is fettered to them. The facts of his spiritual experience are not omitted but carefully veiled in his stories, and in examining the fabric of his work it is relevant to know that its purpose to him was that of a beautiful veil. His most recent—and most honest— biographer sees his writings as attempts at answering the central question, 'How is a life that is worthy of man possible in this world?'[1] And certainly, the dignity of man under a divine ordinance occupies Stifter in a great many of his stories. Yet even this question, it seems to me, is still a part of the beautiful veil. What lies behind it, veiled by the elaborate devices of Stifter's prose, only rarely emerging from them and then only in an exclamation of anguish, a sentence as brief as it is sudden, is the still simpler question, 'How is existence itself, the "ultimate unreason of Being",[2] to be borne?'

Apart from some minor poetry and a number of articles on political, moral and pedagogic topics, Stifter's work is confined to narrative prose. Of his two great novels one, *Der Nachsommer* (1857) has become a classic in the language, while the other *Witiko* (1865–7), the first and only part of a projected trilogy about medieval Bohemia, confronts even his most devoted readers with difficulties of style and presentation which critics have by-passed rather than solved. Even though the hundred years which Stifter said would be needed for its full appreciation have now passed, the book is acclaimed a great masterpiece more often than it appears to be actually read. It is on *Der Nachsommer* and on some thirty stories and *Novellen*—of which about a quarter appeared in two versions—that his reputation rests; some of them he published in the collections *Bunte Steine* (1853) and *Studien* (1844–7–50); a third novel, *Die Mappe meines Urgrossvaters*, was begun as a single story in 1841–2, incorporated in an expanded

---

[1] K. G. Fischer, *op. cit.*, p. 93.   [2] See below, p. 274.

form in *Studien* in 1847, and left unfinished at Stifter's death in 1868.

3

In structure and style, *The Ancient Seal*[1] is representative of Stifter's finest work. Like so many of his stories, it revolves round the idea of pathetic irony. Its characters—like those of Henry James's later novels—are endowed with an all but flawless moral perfection, where morality *is* perfection of mind and heart. This perfection is impaired by the merest single flaw, and it is through this flaw that hostile fate enters into the lives of the two principal characters. And, again as with James, the stylistic devices are concentrated in their intensity first on an infinitely gradual and circumspect evoking of the perfection; however, the sudden, flashlike stroke of fate that destroys all peace of mind and happiness, irrevocably and beyond the possibility of human repair, has no parallel in James.

The story opens two decades or so before the Napoleonic Wars. A boy, Hugo, is being brought up in a country mansion by his widowed father, an old soldier, and on reaching manhood is sent out to the distant city, to learn whatever honourable profession he shall choose. Hiding his feelings from the youth, the father sends him off with a self-denying severity which seems to rest on nothing more complicated than his sense of duty. With its expression of direct feelings and clear-cut moral problems the heartbreaking scene is not merely naïve—it moves us with the power of a Homeric farewell. Only when we come to the end of the story and cast our mind back on that scene do we perceive that the severity which Hugo inherited from his father was not merely self-denying but self-destructive.

The old man's secret hope is that his son will become a soldier, and that he will one day lead his men into battle against the foreign oppressor. Hugo's preparation for that day is described at some length (the atmosphere is something like that of young John Inglesant's life at the court of Charles II), the harshness of

---

[1] *Das alte Siegel*, published in 1843; all my quotations are taken from the final version in the second volume of *Studien*.

the trade he is learning is carefully hidden by the detailed pattern of his daily routine. Of the emotion that moves the patriotic young man and his contemporaries Stifter says,

Der Hass war sachte und allseitig herangeblüht . . .	*Hatred had blossomed forth gently and from every side . . .*

It is a strange sentence. It seems to intimate (as does Rilke's beautiful sonnet on the doves[1]) that hatred too is 'in the right', that it is a positive, life-giving thing. But at the same time it robs hatred of its violent, dramatic quality, veiling it, with a word or two, by a language of flowers. Just so in another story, *Abdias*, Stifter calls that ineluctable working of causality which wreaks utterly unintelligible destruction upon men, 'that serene garland of flowers—that chain of causes and effects—suspended across all cosmic infinity . . .'; or again, in *Der Hagestolz*, we read, 'I tell you that self-sacrifice for others, even unto death, . . . is really nothing but the most violent bursting open of the flower of one's life.' With such sentences as these thrust at us quite suddenly, out of the blue, we are outside the range of the Jamesian experience, outside the range of overt motivation. We seem rather, with these strange poetic ambiguities, to have come close to the world of Kafka—to his description of a wound festering in a boy's thigh, lethal yet suddenly taking on the shape of a pale mauve rose.[2]

The Ancient Seal is to be a love story. Brave, pure, infinitely industrious, enthusiastic apprentice of the art of war—how is such a hero ever to meet the heroine? How is the step out of innocence to be accomplished? The subterfuges Stifter is put to devising for a meeting are a part—the least successful—of his anxious narrative concern for gradualness, of his anti-dramatic mode. Nor does the story gather momentum when, on his way to church, Hugo meets the woman of his destiny and they at last exchange a few words. With religious solemnity their every glance is described, the stateliness of gestures verges on the liturgical, perhaps on the portentous. Elsewhere[3] it becomes intolerable. But here the slowness of the style is deliberate without being contrived. The mood

---

[1] *Sonette an Orpheus*, II/xi. [2] In the story *Ein Landarzt*.
[3] E.g. in *Der Kuss von Sentze*.

evoked here is that of 'The association of man and woman / In daunsinge signifying matrimonie—/ A dignified and commodious sacrament'.[1] And when this mood is disrupted by the untoward event, the effect is shattering.

The love that grows up between them is complete and passionate, except that she insists on keeping her past from him. Three times the bare little house is described in which she receives him and in which their love is consummated, each time the description is given and the scene enacted in almost the same words:

In dem Stübchen unter dem Thorwege sah er denselben Thürsteher aus dem oberen Theile der Glasthüre heraus sehen. Er war ein schon sehr betagter Mann. Hugo ging die Treppe hinan, klingelte an der äussern Thür der Wohnung, und dasselbe Mädchen, welches sonst immer da war, öffnete ihm auch heute, und geleitete ihn zu der Gebieterin hinein. Diese war ihm bis in das äusserste Zimmer entgegen gekommen, und führte ihn dann, wie das erste Mal, in ihr Arbeitsgemach zurück. Sie war heute wieder nicht in ihr Schwarz, in dem er sie kennen gelernt hatte, gekleidet, sondern, wie das erste Mal mit grauer Seide, war sie heute mit dunkelgrüner angethan. Jedes der Kleider war sehr einfach, aber sehr edel gehalten. Im Stoffe reich, spannten sie um die Hüften und flossen dann in ruhigen Falten hinab. So wie das vorige Mal hatte sie auch heute gar keinen Schmuck an sich, nicht einmal einen Ring an einem Finger—das Kleid schloss an dem Halse, dann war das Haupt mit den gescheitelten braunen Haaren, und den glanzvollen grossen Augen, mit	*In the little room under the archway he saw the same gate-keeper looking out through the upper half of the glass door. He was quite an old man. Hugo went up the stairs, rang the bell at the outer door of the apartment, and the same girl who had always been there opened the door and led him in to her mistress, who had come to the outermost room to meet him and then took him back to her workroom as on the first occasion. Today she was again not dressed in black, as he had first met her, but in a dark green silk dress like the grey silk one she had worn on his first visit. Each of her dresses was very simply but very gracefully designed. The material was cut full and draped round the hips and flowed down in easy folds. Just as on the previous occasion she was again wearing no jewellery, not even a single ring— her dress came close up to her throat, and then [there] was her head with its brown hair carefully parted and her great shining eyes looking at him as he came in. Now Hugo was in the room—today he had been better able to look at the other rooms as he*

[1] T. S. Eliot, *Four Quartets*, 'East Coker', I.

denen sie ihn ansah, als er herein-
getreten war. Hugo war *nun in dem*
Zimmer—heute hatte er schon mehr
Macht gehabt, die andern Zimmer,
durch die er gekommen war, zu be-
trachten. Sie waren ohne Prunk, fast
möchte man sagen, zu dünne, aber
sehr vornehm eingerichtet.[1]

passed through them. They were
furnished without luxury, one might
have said almost too sparsely, but
with great distinction.

'The inner freedom from the practical desire, / The release from action and suffering, release from the inner / And the outer compulsion, yet surrounded / By a grace of sense, a white light still and moving, / *Erhebung* without motion, concentration / Without elimination...'[2]—can prose ever communicate *this* mode of being? For that indeed is what this strange use of the bare ontological verb, this insistence on a high simplicity is attempting: '*Erhebung* without motion'; 'beauty unadulterated by anything beautiful'; an image of man 'so little articulated that it produces its effect through its simple being rather than through an excitation.'[3] This attempt to convey 'simple being' is reflected in Stifter's surprisingly synthetic working habits,[4] and hence in his style, in which causality and extended narrative are by-passed and the initial impetus of which are discrete scenes and 'stills' rather than intuitive glimpses of faces or situations. Here are characters almost (as Schopenhauer would say) beyond individuation, often without characteristic traits of face, figures in a solemn ritual. It isn't that this stylistic insistence and the repetitions are untranslatable. In German too they weigh down the narration

---

[1] Chapter 3, my emphasis.
[2] T. S. Eliot, *Four Quartets*, 'Burnt Norton', II.
[3] '... *wenn sich anders etwas so wenig Gegliedertes darstellen lässt, das eher durch sein einfaches Dasein, als durch seine Erregung wirkt.*' (*Der Waldgänger.*)
[4] 'My working method is this: First the main theme thought out in my mind, 2. working out of details in my mind, 3. outline of individual details, sentences, expressions, scenes, in pencil, all on separate pieces of paper (for this I use only the best hours of my day), 4. writing out of the text, in ink, on [whole sheets of] paper, 5. revision of this text, after some time, with many crossings-out, insertions, etc., 6. revision of the revision after a long period of time. Assimilation into the whole. Fair copy.' (Letter of 21.xii.1861, quoted from K. G. Fischer, *op. cit.*, p. 93.)

and splay it apart; its solemnity takes the description to the very margins of narrative prose.

Accordingly, the act of love itself is intimated in a sentence heavy with sensuous suggestion and verbal involution, yet the persons are almost without individuality, almost anonymous:

> Es war ihm wie ein Räthsel, dass sich die Pracht dieser Glieder aus der unheimlichen Kleiderwolke gelöset habe, und dass sie vielleicht sein werden könne.

> It was like an enigma to him, that the splendour of these limbs had loosed itself from the eerie cloud of raiment and that perhaps she might be his.

Three times the bare house is described. The rhythm of the fourth description is again the same—shades of boredom lengthen over the page: is Stifter asking us to go through these details yet once more?—but now the house is wide open and empty. The contrast—but to speak of contrast suggests deliberation where the text proceeds without mediating links—has been brought about by seemingly simple means, yet the end achieved is very far from simple: the end is a feeling of helplessness and exposure:

> Auf der Treppe hatte er Kehricht und Staub gefunden, durch die Zimmer, in welchen er jetzt stand, wehte die Luft des Himmels; denn die Fenster waren offen, und die Wände, an denen sonst die Geräthe, der Marmortisch, der Spiegel und Anderes gewesen waren, standen nackt.

> On the stairs he had found dust and refuse, the air of heaven[1] blew in through the rooms in which he now stood; for the windows were open, and the walls near which at other times had been various implements, the marble table, the mirror and other things, now stood naked.

No enumeration of absent objects (all the way to 'other things') can redeem the calamity.

The reason for this sudden ending of their perfect love is buried in the woman's past, in an earlier marriage. After a separation of eleven years they meet again and she, now free from past obligations, offers herself to him once more, with the same passion that had united them. But he responds with the same harshness with which his father had sent him out into the world: his

---

[1] Again, as in the description of 'hatred' (see above, p. 263), and of Abdias's calamity (see below, p. 276), we are overwhelmed by the unmediated placing of 'dust and refuse' side by side with 'the air of heaven'.

passionate moral sense of the wrong they had committed will not allow him to take her for his own. The self-destructive severity in him, that, certainly, is not veiled. In her anguish, she cries out to him, 'My sin is more human than your virtue.' The humanity to which she appeals and which she embodies is no less than earthly love itself, with all its beauty and anguish: 'Indeed, I was a sinner,' she says, 'but I did not sin lightly. You only saw the sweet fruit of my sin, the struggle I bore all alone.' Whereas the morality which made him reject her brings him no peace in a long life of solitude, no assurance even of having acted rightly. And that is all there is to it, to the reason-giving.

Stifter's narrative mode is anti-dramatic in the same sense as Kafka's: in the sense that both are unwilling—or unable—to prepare for the catharsis: which is thus not a catharsis so much as all-but-unmotivated calamity. The design of the story, its ideas and ideals, were to have been of the simplest and most direct, it was to be a 'naïve' tale of love and duty. But Stifter's original didactic intention of pointing a moral by presenting the love-story of two ideal human beings, their characters each impaired by the merest single flaw (his severity—her silence)—all this recedes behind a far from naïve design of sensuous intimations, enumerations, painstaking description and shattering disclosures.

But what of the elaborateness and expatiations with which Stifter's stories abound? Are not they designed to prepare and motivate? Nature in all its beauty, and all the precious 'things' that man has made, are for Stifter no 'setting', they remain disconnected from the calamity itself—there is only the garland of flowers by which the sufferer is said[1] to be tied to the world. Perhaps that is how Divinity sees him. But here on earth the garland lies round his mortal wound like an emblem of divine mockery. Sometimes—as in *The Ancient Seal*—the attempt is made, retrospectively, to give reasons and explanations. But even then our final impression is the lack of a just measure—the incom-

---

[1] Introduction to *Abdias*.

mensurateness of crime and punishment; the excess of suffering
over offence, and its irreparable finality. And the garland, the
natural setting, is a world apart:

Nur die Berge stehen noch in alter
Pracht   und   Herrlichkeit — ihre
Häupter werden glänzen, wenn wir
und andere Geschlechter dahin sind,
so wie sie geglänzt haben, als der
Römer durch ihre Thale ging und
dann der Alemanne, dann der Hunne,
und dann Andere und wieder
Andere——Wie viele werden noch
nach uns kommen, denen sie Freude
und sanfte Trauer in das betrachtende
Herz senken, bis auch sie dahin sind
und vielleicht auch die schöne,
freundliche Erde, die uns doch jetzt
fest gegründet und für Ewigkeiten ge-
baut scheint.[1]

Only the mountains still stand in
their old splendour and beauty—their
summits will gleam when we and
future generations have passed, as
they gleamed when the Roman went
through their valleys and then the
Aleman, and then the Hun, and then
others and still others——How many
will yet come after us, into whose
meditating hearts they will drop joy
and gentle sorrow, until they too are
gone, and perhaps our beautiful,
friendly earth also, which now stands
so firmly and as though built for
eternity.

4

Combining a wide sweep with precise detail, and an emphasis on
the architectonic, almost geometrical qualities of landscape,
Stifter's nature-descriptions outweigh, almost in every story,
human action and dialogue. Their firm, stylised designs, which are
those of a landscape painter, not a naturalist, place them among the
finest natural descriptions in any literature:

Endlich gelangten sie wieder zu
Gegenständen.
    Es waren riesenhaft grosse, sehr
durch einander liegende Trümmer, die
mit Schnee bedeckt waren, der überall
in die Klüfte hineinrieselte, und an
die sie sich ebenfalls fast anstiessen,
ehe sie sie sahen. Sie gingen ganz
hinzu, die Dinge anzublicken.

At last they came to some objects
again.
    They were gigantic ruins lying as
though overthrown, covered with
snow which was sifting everywhere
into the crevices and which they
almost fell over before they saw
them. They went up close to look at
these things.

[1] End of Das alte Siegel.

Es war Eis—lauter Eis.

Es lagen Platten da, die mit Schnee bedeckt waren, an deren beiden Seitenwänden aber das glatte grünliche Eis sichtbar war, es lagen Hügel da, die wie zusammengeschobener Schaum aussahen, an deren Seiten es aber matt nach einwärts flimmerte und glänzte, als wären Balken und Stangen von Edelsteinen durch einander geworfen worden, es lagen ferner gerundete Kugeln da, die ganz mit Schnee umhüllt waren, es standen Platten und andere Körper auch schief oder gerade aufwärts, so hoch wie der Kirchturm in Gschaid oder wie Häuser. In einigen waren Höhlen eingefressen, durch die man mit einem Arme durchfahren konnte, mit einem Kopfe, mit einem Körper, mit einem ganzen grossen Wagen voll Heu. Alle diese Stücke waren zusammen oder empor gedrängt, und starrten, so dass sie oft Dächer bildeten oder Ueberhänge, über deren Ränder sich der Schnee herüber legte, und herab griff wie lange weisse Tatzen. Selbst ein grosser schreckhaft schwarzer Stein, wie ein Haus, lag unter dem Eise, und war empor gestellt, dass er auf der Spitze stand, dass kein Schnee an seinen Seiten liegen bleiben konnte. Und nicht dieser Stein allein—noch mehrere und grössere staken in dem Eise, die man erst später sah, und die wie eine Trümmermauer an ihm hingingen.[1]

It was ice—nothing but ice.

Blocks were lying there, covered with snow, but with the smooth greenish ice showing on their two vertical planes, hills lay there that looked like huddled foam, but with an inner flickering of brilliance on their sides as though great beams and shafts of precious stones had been thrown together in a heap; then too there were rounded spheres completely enclosed in snow, and some blocks and other shapes were standing either obliquely or upright, as high as the steeple of the village of Gschaid, or as houses. Some of them were worn away in hollows big enough to drive an arm through or a head or a body, or a whole cart loaded high with hay. All these pieces were pushed together, or pressed upwards, and rigid, so that they often formed a roof or overhang, with the snow projecting over the edges and reaching down like big white paws. One huge frighteningly black rock as big as a house lay under the ice, and was held erect in such a way that it was standing on its pointed end and no snow could cling to its sides. And not this rock alone— many others, and bigger ones, were stuck in the ice, as they saw only later, and formed a kind of ruined wall in it.

These are not landscapes we know, nor the landscapes of Stifter's own experience. They are the products of an exact creative imagination, and as such they take the place of the world that Stifter knew and failed to conquer; they are to him society,

---

[1] From *Bergkristall*, the fourth story in *Bunte Steine*.

politics, requited love and the company of friends, solace and regions of a peace which goes beyond the human. They are indeed his 'compensations': except that the word implies a derivativeness where the texts speak in passionate intensity; for in these scenes above all lies Stifter's narrative strength.

Though he elaborately disclaims any 'literary' merit for his writings, he does insist on being counted among the last heirs of Goethe's estate;[1] yet the truth about his work is not to be found in the ambience of Weimar. What remains of the Goethean ideas on man and nature is radically altered in Stifter's work. Differences of personal temperament have a good deal to do with it; but, above all, the historical and social circumstances in which Goethe's ideas had arisen, the image of man itself in which Goethe had sought to embody them, all this has changed—and changed, in Stifter's view, for the worse. The truth is that the isolated greatness of Stifter's nature-descriptions, but also their excess over the human, their strenuousness, derive from his attempt to follow a precept that is no longer valid. The subtle Goethean balance between man and nature—the equi-valence of the two—has given way to a vast exaggeration, in which man is dwarfed into insignificance. And he is dwarfed especially where Goethe had shown him at his most human, in the throes of passion. There is now no dramatic conflict between the human and the natural, the die is loaded against man since in his passion he is always in the wrong; and there is something awesome in the relentlessness with which Stifter shows him to be in the wrong. We are charmed and beguiled by these forests and mountain solitudes, and we are appalled by the way their innocence and superiority are taken for granted. Nature is charged with an absolute spiritual value it never had for Goethe.

Here, I believe, lies the religious dilemma of Stifter's writings.[2] Is the Natural the measure of the Human, as it was once for Goethe, or is the Natural itself a divinity which imposes upon man its arbitrary ordeals? Does Stifter himself know? His Christian faith tells him that the natural cannot be more than a

---

[1] E.g. to Heckenast, 13.v.1854.
[2] As I have suggested (p. 258) this may well not be his personal dilemma.

mute image and parable of the human and divine—for (as St Augustine[1] tells us) the stones and the lambs and the green grass have no voice wherewith to speak, and it is only man who lends them his voice so that they may sing the paean of God's glory. But the images upon which Stifter's prose is lavished tell a different story. On seraphic fields of Alpine flora and in the sylvan vastness there is something of that *Naturphilosophie* which Heine had singled out as 'the German religion': more, certainly, than there is of the Christian idea of Nature as the great analogue of a benevolent God. Is Stifter himself aware of a dilemma? It seems hard to believe; the uncontentious, non-dialectic way he puts the two views side by side, almost in a single breath, muffles rather than solves the contradiction:

Man stand einen Augenblick stumm, die Herzen der Menschen schienen die Feier und Ruhe mitzufühlen; denn es liegt ein Anstand, ich möchte sagen ein Ausdruck von Tugend in dem von Menschenhänden noch nicht berührten Antlitze der Natur, dem sich die Seele beugen muss, als etwas Keuschem und Göttlichem,——und doch ist es zuletzt wieder die Seele allein, die all ihre innere Grösse hinaus in das Gleichniss der Natur legt.[2]	*They stood in silence for a moment— their hearts seemed to share in the feeling of solemnity and calm. For there lies a propriety, I might almost say an expression of virtue, in the countenance of Nature before it has ever been touched by the hand of man, to which the soul must bow as to something virginal, pure and divine, ——and yet it is after all man's soul alone which carries all its own inward greatness into the image of Nature.*

The two thoughts, separated by a mere dash, trace out a dilemma, not a conflict creatively worked out. The pathetic fallacy here is not the source of dramatic tension (as it is in *King Lear* or *Moby Dick*[3]). The characters in Stifter's stories don't rise up in hubris

---

[1] *Expositions of the Book of Psalms*, ad cxliv, cxlv (trsl. Oxford 1857, Vol. VI, pp. 327 ff.).

[2] *Der Hochwald*, 1842. This was the first story to make Stifter's work widely popular. The only non-German literary influence on Stifter, J. F. Cooper's *The Deerslayer*, is discernible in some of the events of this story: Cooper's American virgin forests clearly remind him of the Bohemian woods and mountains.

[3] Melville allows this tension to break at the highest point of crisis in the story, at Ahab's death (Chapter CXXXIV), when Starbuck calls out to him in

against the natural order of things, to be punished and shown
their human limits. Hubris and consequent punishment imply a
sense of order and a law. Whereas the 'gentle law of Nature'
which Stifter extols in the famous Preface to Bunte Steine is the
last place in which to find a rationale for the fate that befalls men
like Hugo, Abdias, or the heroes of so many of his stories for
grown-ups. In their calamity no order is vindicated, nothing
changes, Fate or Nature barely deigns to destroy them, the
pathetic fallacy is carried to a point from which the human figure
is barely discernible. An artist's truth lies where the life he creates
beats strongest; for Stifter, as for Claude Lorrain, it lies in the
golden and green distance of natural landscape.

The awesome imbalance between man and Nature does not,
however, pervade his entire work. When the reading public to
the end of the First World War[1] saw in Stifter above all the
author of idyllic and high-minded children's stories, their estimate
was partial but not wholly wrong. What they didn't understand
was that here was a creative mind capable of very much more—
whereas what recent existential criticism is in danger of ignoring
is that the beauty of the children's stories assembled in Bunte
Steine (and of many others besides) is a thing in its own right. It
is biographically true that his children's stories too were written
on the retreat from adult life. Yet it is equally true that in them
the achievement wholly silences the intention; so that there is
little or no suggestion here of a complexity deliberately by-
passed, of an involvement avoided. Nor is there that feeling of
human insignificance: the childish figures in the landscape (even
in a landscape of icy wastes) share its life, are protected not
dwarfed by it. Passion, the tragic (or absurd) flaw and the consequent disaster are neither avoided nor left unmotivated, they
quite naturally do not occur. And the moral lesson, which is here
a lesson taught by innocence and absolute trust, emerges in its

supreme anguish, '... See! Moby Dick seeks thee not. It is thou, thou, that
madly seekest him!'
[1] Der Nachsommer was not generally available before Max Stefl's reprint of
1919, nor was there much serious criticism of his work before Ernst Bertram's
essay of that year; see below, note 3 on p. 358.

purest and simplest form. It emerges not, as it does in Dickens, by the complex device of seeing the world through the child's eyes and thus throwing social life and institutions into a grotesque perspective; nor even, as in Henry James, by a child's conquest of the sordid adult world through its own knowledge, that marvellous mixture of precocity and innocence. Here the child is victorious because it is preserved from all adult knowledge and acts from an innocence of corruption, as by a miracle. These stories don't belong to that sophisticated cult of childish innocence which has Bettina von Brentano and her admirer Rilke among its votaries; the view that the complexities of adulthood are all unnecessary, all sad defections from some serene natural grace, is implied in them uncontentiously and clearly enough.

5

From the view I have presented so far it appears that everywhere except in the children's stories the tragic is either avoided or contaminated with the absurd. The opening two pages of the story *Abdias* (1842) contain an important clue,[1] not indeed to Stifter's way of writing, but to his profound awareness of the threat of absurdity. It is a tale of Ahasuerus, the eternal Wandering Jew. His wife dies in childbirth, he loses his worldly possessions during a raid by an Arab tribe, leaves his fantastic desert hide-out and flees to Europe, bringing with him his only daughter Ditha. Upon her he lavishes his every care and thought, for her comfort he amasses once more a fortune, for her protection he builds a very citadel of a house. But all Ditha's beauty and gentleness are a bitter mockery—she is born blind. ('She was a lie', we read, without a word of preparation.) And all his efforts and cares are in vain. There comes a flash of lightning which brings her sight, and then a second flash which kills her; that is all.

---

[1] The clue is, I believe, rather more important than the passage in his Preface to *Bunte Steine*, about the 'gentle law in all creation', which the critics never tire of quoting, and which says little more than does Walt Whitman's 'A leaf of grass is no less than the journey-work of the stars'; Stifter's collection itself contains at least two stories, *Turmalin* and *Katzensilber*, to which that 'law' is absurdly irrelevant.

Reading the story of the Jew Abdias, we look for reasons; and
Stifter's own introductory reflection justifies us in our expectation
of them:

Dieses war den Alten Fatum, furcht-
bar letzter starrer Grund des Ge-
schehenden, über den man nicht
hinaus sieht, und jenseits dessen auch
nichts mehr ist, so dass ihm selber die
Götter unterworfen sind: uns ist es
Schicksal, also ein von einer höhern
Macht Gesendetes, das wir emp-
fangen sollen.... Aber eigentlich
mag es weder ein Fatum geben, als
letzte Unvernunft des Seins, noch
auch wird das Einzelne auf uns
gesendet; sondern eine heitre Blumen-
kette¹ hängt durch die Unendlichkeit
des Alls und sendet ihren Schimmer
in die Herzen—die Kette der
Ursachen und Wirkungen—und in
das Haupt des Menschen ward die
schönste dieser Blumen geworfen, die
Vernunft, das Auge der Seele, die
Kette daran anzuknüpfen, und an
ihr Blume um Blume, Glied um
Glied hinan zu zählen bis zuletzt zu
jener Hand, in der das Ende ruht.
Und haben wir dereinstens recht ge-
zählt, und können wir die Zählung
überschauen: dann wird für uns kein
Zufall mehr erscheinen, sondern
Folgen, kein Unglück mehr, sondern
nur Verschulden; denn die Lücken,
die jetzt sind, erzeugen das Unerwar-
tete, und der Missbrauch das Un-
glückselige.

This was, for the ancients, Fate, the
terrible ultimate stark background of
events, past which one cannot see, and
beyond which there is in fact nothing,
so that even the Gods are subject to
it; for us it is destiny, that is some-
thing sent by a higher power which
we must accept... But no doubt
there is really no Fate, as the last
unreason of existence, nor yet is the
individual happening visited upon us;
but a bright chain¹ of flowers hangs
across the eternity of the cosmos and
sends its radiance into men's hearts—
the chain of causes and effects—and
into men's heads the most splendid
of these flowers was cast, called
Reason, the eye of the soul, that they
may fix the chain on it and count
along it flower after flower, link
after link until at last it comes to that
hand in which the end of the chain
is held. And if we have counted right
at last, and if we can muster the
whole account, then we shall see no
accidents but effects, no misfortune
any more but only guilt; for the gaps
that there are now produce the un-
expected, and abuse is the reason for
misfortune.

¹ The reference here is to the *catena aurea Homeri.* K. Hohoff (*A.S.*, Düsseldorf 1949, pp. 42-3) suggests that this flower-image is something like a contemporary cliché. This may well be so. What is more important is that Stifter's
emphatic use of it in a number of different and often unexpected contexts (e.g.
in *Der Hagestolz*, see pp. 263 f. above) is wholly original.

We could hardly hope for a clearer indication of the traditional story-teller's task: to convert chance into consequences, misfortune into guilt, to fill out the gaps with meaning . . . And so we put all indications of Abdias's guilt in the balance: his avarice and mistrust of all living beings (he fears his most devoted servant and causes him almost to die of exposure on the journey through the desert), his blind cruelty (he horribly wounds his dog and lets him bleed to death), his tortured, choleric temperament; his dark skin and pockmarked face (they are Stifter's own) are an outward sign of the desolate soul within.[1] But when we have put all the acts of Abdias's guilt together, when we have added his caution, cunning, hardness and vengefulness—how can we ignore that they all, together with his whole life, have their meaning and end in *her* life? Are we meant to feel that it is Abdias's idolatrous love for his helpless daughter which invites the retribution of fate? Retribution, guilt itself is only where there is choice, the proving of Job's faith has only a meaning in his final recognition, 'He doeth as He wills, He is of one mind.' Whereas Abdias has no choice, and attains to no ultimate *knowledge* however devastating, since Ditha's death robs him of his reason. He is an unlovable character, bereft of grace; the elaborate defences against the malice of men and fate with which he surrounds Ditha may be put down to his possessiveness; yet for all that, his love for her is protective and tender above all. To suggest that it is a sinful thing and thus deserving of punishment is to suggest the absurd, is indeed to acknowledge 'the ultimate unreason of Being'. It would be a suggestion more absurd than any Job or Abraham are asked to contemplate, because the power that robs Abdias of his all is an anonymous, silent power. But then, Stifter does not quite make the suggestion.[2]

---

[1] Depressingly, it isn't redundant to insist at this point that Stifter's image of the Jew as one shut out from Grace has nothing whatever in common with contemporary anti-Semitism. It is an image both of eternal alienation and of the infinite capacity for survival, and as such it also suggests something of the mentality of those early nineteenth-century Jews who had left the ghetto and wandered homeless among the Gentiles. Cf. E. Sterling, *op. cit.*, esp. pp. 63 ff.

[2] Nor, incidentally, does the story yield clues to a hidden Freudian motivation, but on that pitch no critic can win: failing to find is as 'significant' as finding.

One after another the images of desolation pass before our view.
Like the fairy-tale in *Woyzeck*, they have but one motto: 'And
all, all, all was lost.' There are many old men like the Jew Abdias
in Stifter's stories, hermit crabs barely moving through life, their
claws broken and their armour cracked, stunned by the blows of
fate, yet somehow living on, senselessly, beyond the reach of
comfort. Stifter does not expatiate on their desolation. On the
contrary—he puts it and its 'causes' as briefly, as suddenly as he
knows how. The second of the two flashes of lightning which
gave meaning to Abdias's life and then took it away is 'explained'
in a single sentence:

Das neue Wunder und Strafgericht, wie sie es nannten, flog sogleich durch das Land.	*The news of the recent miracle and terrible judgement,*[1] *as people called it, travelled quickly through the country.*

Which is it—miracle *or* terrible judgement? Is the event untoward *or* motivated? And if it is all one to the powers that
'barely deign to destroy us', how can it be all one to us?[2] Does
reason follow the thought of that sentence ('miracle *and* terrible
punishment') any more easily than it follows this one:

Einmal dem Fehlläuten der Nacht-glocke gefolgt—es ist niemals gut-zumachen.	*Once you have answered the false alarm of the nightbell—and all is lost.*

But the author who here adds the final touch of absurdity to the
story of a country doctor is not Stifter but his fellow-countryman
Franz Kafka.

This imbalance between causes and effects has for us a very
special appeal: lack of faith and *angst* combine to destroy our

[1] That '*Strafgericht*' has this meaning is confirmed from a context in *Der Nachsommer*, chapter 'Der Rückblick', in the young von Risach's exchange with Mathilde.
[2] Thus Hohoff (*op. cit.*, p. 44) is prepared to throw morality overboard in favour of a transcendent ontology: 'The true purport of Stifter's art [he writes] lies not in the moral answer, which is arbitrary and *ad hoc* [*beliebig*]. . . . The truth of Abdias's world is the extent to which that world participates in Being.' But elsewhere (see below, p. 360) Hohoff explicitly—and, I think, rightly—disclaims any Christian character for this Being.

sense of the distinction between the tragic and the merely absurd. A peculiar snobbishness of suffering makes critics speak of the 'impossibility of Christian tragedy', as though the Crucifixion were something less than tragic because St Paul asks us to 'bear reasonable witness' to it, in other words to understand it. Yet the distinction between the tragic and the absurd, which lies in the reason-giving, is surely fundamental to us as human beings, and *a fortiori* as readers. Of course it happens often enough that the reasons given in a literary work are 'apparently insufficient'. But the effect of such an apparent imbalance should be to refine and enrich our sense of what are adequate causes, of what is a just measure: I did not hitherto think (we should be able to say) that such a small act could lead to so great an iniquity, or that such another attitude has such dire consequences. (Something like this is the effect of *Der Waldgänger*.) Is the situation in *Abdias* of this kind? However willing we are to abandon our preconceptions of what is a just measure, we are not given an unambiguous alternative. Are we to see Abdias's lack of grace—of gratitude for the restoration of Ditha's sight, for instance—as the cause of his final calamity? His attempt to propitiate fate ('He deliberately inflicted pain upon himself [we read], or sacrificed something he loved, lest fate should demand a greater thing') suggests a mind as fearful and suspicious of divinity as it is of all men; yet then again we are told that when Ditha's sight was restored 'people said' that he had grown less avaricious and harsh, and we are shown that Ditha's loving presence was altering his character. . . . The question, 'miracle *or* terrible judgement?', is never unambiguously answered; twice the narrator asks it and each time he withholds his judgement behind the phrase, 'people said'—the flowers of the chain are never counted all the way to the hand in which the chain rests. Are we to conclude (as the first page of the story suggested) that *at our time in human history* a complete reason-giving is not yet possible? *Or*, that in our time an act of faith is no longer possible? The effect of the final ambiguity is not one of tragedy (of a calamity motivated) but of a combination ot the tragic (the punishment of a man bereft of Grace) *and* of the absurd (the stroke of untoward, arbitrary fate).

Our contemporary 'literature of the absurd', like its antecedents

RE-INTERPRETATIONS

in the lower reaches of nineteenth-century Romanticism, has challenged the distinction between the tragic and the absurd, but it has not, it seems to me, created works which have rendered that distinction invalid. On the contrary, the situation in which that literature has arisen makes the distinction more important than it has ever been before. The brief scenes of desolation in Stifter, like the extended scenes of desolation in Kafka, go some way towards giving a valid meaning to calamity; but its full validation is withheld.

Stifter's nature-scenes are offered as a substitute for the giving of reasons, yet their function is rather to delay the blow of fate, or to create a world that diminishes the reality of that blow when it comes. There is here no full mediation through the mind that understands. Instead, the mind creates images: such as that of the casemented windows of the citadel, their bars ending in locks shaped like roses.[1] The flowers of his poetry grow out of Stifter's fear of disaster, out of his fear of death, but in the garland he makes of them they are no longer connected with the common world of men.

And the story of the Jew Abdias, on the verge of the absurd, is not an exception to the view I put forward, that in the landscape of hostile fate as in the landscape of harmonious nature the human figure is dwarfed into insignificance. To face fate, the irreparable calamity, *and* to wring a meaning from it, is not wholly within Stifter's creative capacity. The citadel he will build is never to be assailed at all.

6

Stifter's stories are marked by a certain similarity of structure, their narratives are carried forward by a movement which is characteristically his own. To describe this movement it may be helpful to recall my suggestion that simple and unsophisticated means take him to complex ends. (This happens, I think, largely

[1] These images occur both in *Der Hagestolz* and in *Der Nachsommer*.

unawares; he appears to have no interest in making his technique explicit either to himself or to others.) Many of the narrative devices he employs can be found in German prose a hundred years before his time—he is 'old-fashioned', though, rather than archaic. Thus he is in a sense too naïve a writer to attempt characterisation by manner of speech or through the consistent use of a point of view. The relations between the people of his stories are hieratic and confined to a very small group (marriage, a family, a small village). The characters of those involved tend to be of the simplest, they are accounted for by 'humours' or centred on a single, invariably destructive passion. Men's characters at their best are shown in relations determined by their natural age (father–son, old man–adopted youth) and God-given position (master–servant); it is in the world of Nature and (as we shall see) of things that nuances and subtleties of configuration are achieved. The prose that is fashioned from these elements acquires increasingly a liturgical, sacramental quality, reaching its apogee in the monumental last novel *Witiko*; the same development is shown in the changes from the earlier versions of several stories to their worked-over last versions, which lead away from the idiosyncratic and personal and dramatic towards the even, undifferentiated tone of a solemn rite.

The characteristic narrative movement begins with the elaborate piling up of these elements. Extensive, enumerative, sometimes repetitious, circumstantial (at times clumsily so), the structure rises up, to the point where (so we feel) the very weight and quantity of the descriptions will surely keep all calamity away. And when all and more than all[1] has been done towards that *one* end—what then?

Up to this point the structure is similar in most stories, here it divides: into the tragic or absurd conclusion on one side, utopia on the other. The flash of lightning strikes, the arrow falls from

---

[1] Again the parallel with Kafka is striking, e.g. the Bürgel-episode in Chapter 18 of *Das Schloss*, ending with, '. . . one must show *everything*, in all its detail, without in the least sparing oneself. . . . But when that too has been done, Mr Surveyor, then indeed everything that was necessary has been accomplished, one must be content with that, and wait.'

the blue sky, the irrevocable word is said, passion irredeemably destroys:

Also ist es wahr, die Heimath, das gute Vaterhaus ist preisgegeben und verloren, all ihr früher Leben ist abgeschnitten, sie selbst wie Mitspieler in ein buntes Märchen gezogen, alles neu, alles seltsam und dräuend—in dem drohenden Wirrsal kein Halt.[1] . . .	*So then it is true, their homeland and ancestral house is forfeited, is lost, the whole of their earlier life cut off, they themselves drawn as actors into a pretty fairy-tale, everything is new, strange and threatening—no foothold anywhere in the menacing chaos. . . .*

Or there is the other conclusion, utopia: 'All, all will be well'[2]— *not*, however, because the citadel has withstood the onslaught but because it has never been attacked at all. So that here too, after the 'turning-point' where nothing turns, as after the one where everything is lost, the median of experience is avoided: I mean that most human of possibilities—the sacring of passion and the conquest, even if it be in the soul alone, of adversity through faith.

7

Der Waldgänger is Stifter's finest *Novelle* because it achieves a perfect balance between the two traits characteristic of his narrative art, the idyllic and the tragic: because here for once he leads us to the edge of the absurd and then, without taking refuge in distant utopia, away from it, to a meaningful conclusion.

The two people at the centre of the story, Georg and Corona, are happily married and lead a noble, fruitful life; we are told of Georg's successes as a young and gifted architect, of their beautiful house. The character of the man, impulsive, generous yet lacking in firm purpose, is exquisitely matched with the proud and

---

[1] *Der Hochwald*, 1841, Chapter 2, 'Waldwanderung'; here again, offered as wholly self-evident, is one of Stifter's devastating and unmediated antitheses, '*buntes Märchen . . . drohende Wirrsal*'.

[2] This is one of the leitmotifs of the old von Risach in *Der Nachsommer*; and when, in the last chapter, Heinrich Drendorf (the young hero) uses it for the first time, it is meant to signify his coming of age—yet the German words, '*Alles wird gut werden*', have something of the naïve fervour of a child's prayer.

passionate nature of the woman. Everything that two human beings can *do* towards achieving the good life is here done. One by one the details of their shared life are put in: tender care for each other inspires them, no impediments are admitted to this marriage of true minds—yet it is all of no avail. They have no children. They seem to be reconciled to that, until one day, at a party, they see a child playing the piano. They drive home, to their 'dark, very beautifully furnished rooms', in silence. On the next day, passionately and abruptly, Corona addresses Georg:

I have come into your room today to offer you the divorce of our marriage.

Corona's offer comes out of the blue—the edge of the absurd is skirted—yet for all its apparent suddenness her decision *is* motivated. Not by psychological explanations—it would not be Stifter's way to show anything so drab as their growing dissatisfaction with one another—but by the images of life revealed in the narrative (which is somewhat more complex than I have so far suggested). The scenes which precede and follow upon the moment of decision are intended to explain how Corona has acted on her understanding of her husband's character. The act is an act not of fate but of wrong-doing: their sin is rooted in the man and woman they are: for its expiation two long lives are required.

The circumstantial details of their happy marriage are not the only wall that is built round the act of wrong-doing. The first half of the *Novelle* is devoted to Georg's life as an old man, to the time long after the divorce, the years which he spends wandering through the forests. He takes to his heart a little boy, the son of a poor woodman, and with great love and patience teaches him the elements of knowledge. The description of virgin nature in which his and the boy's days are lived is unsurpassed in Stifter's writings. Its connection with the central event of the story appears at first inconsiderable. In fact, as an illumination of Georg's being, this grand image of a natural life with its undertone of what might have been is magnificently relevant. Here the knowledge on which Corona had acted is worked out—her knowledge that in the paternal relation, which their marriage could not provide, would have lain Georg's fulfilment. But this

life in the forest comes too late, the shadow of the past lies too
heavily on it. In his paternal love, the old man rears the boy to
an understanding of the natural beauty around them, only to part
with him when the boy's time comes 'to go out into the world'.
Their parting points to the incomplete and melancholy resignation Georg has attained no less than it evokes the elemental sad-
ness of all such partings. Of Georg's incomplete life the narrator
makes a thing at once perfect in itself and connected with the
rest of the story. The image of the little boy and the old man—
the one who 'has nothing to do yet' and the other who 'has
nothing to do any more'—as they walk together through the
forests of Southern Bohemia is as moving as any that literature
can yield.

The highest achievements in narrative literature, I suggested in
earlier chapters, lie where human conflict is fully evoked. And
this is true of this story also, for Georg has paid the full price of
adult passion and suffering. His expiation is incomplete, but it is
meaningful because it issues from a full understanding of his guilt.

He had allowed Corona's decision to prevail. A divorce took
place, he married again and was blessed with two sons, his work
as an architect prospered. And one day he takes his family into a
region which resembles the one in which Corona and he had
once lived:

Am zweiten Abende seines Auf-
enthaltes ging er mit seinen zwei
Knaben allein spazieren. Er schlug
einen Pfad durch das Thal ein,
welcher mit Obstbäumen gesäumt war,
und einen Zaun neben sich hatte,
der mit frischem Wassergebüsche um-
wachsen war, und richtig auch zu
seinen Füssen das klare, schiessende,
über Kiesel rollende Wasser hatte—
gerade so wie ein Pfad gewesen war,
an dem er sehr gerne mit Corona ge-
gangen war, da sie noch mit einander
das Haus am Waldhange bewohnt
hatten. Als er um eine Gruppe hoher,
kleinblättriger Birnbäume bog, wo
ein hölzernes Gitter war, und der

On the second evening of his stay he
went for a walk alone with his two
boys. He took a path through the
valley which was lined with fruit
trees and ran beside a fence that was
overgrown with young water-plants
and indeed had at its feet the clear
rushing water flowing over gravel—
just like a path there had been where
he had been fond of walking with
Corona when they still lived together in the house on the wooded
hill. As he turned the corner round a
group of tall small-leaved pear trees,

Pfad in zwei Theile auseinander ging, wandelte eine dunkel gekleidete Frau ihm entgegen—er erkannte sie—es war Corona. In dunkle Kleider gekleidet, wie sie wohl auch früher geliebt hatte, ein Häubchen, wie früher, nur viel bescheidener, auf dem Haupte, und eine Tasche, wie früher, nur etwas grösser, an ihrem Arme tragend. Das Antlitz war so schön wie sonst—aber es war alt geworden. In den geliebten Zügen, die einst so seine Freude gewesen waren, waren sehr viele kleine, klare und deutlich geprägte Fältchen, auch war sie blasser als gewöhnlich, wie es ja das heranrückende Alter mit sich bringt. Sie blieben Beide stehen, und blickten einander an.

'Corona,' sagte er.

'Georg,' antwortete sie.

Sie reichte ihm die Hand—er fasste sie, und meinte, er könne gar nicht mehr loslassen.

'Geht es Dir wohl, Georg?

'Wohl, Corona—Dir auch?'

'Ja, Georg.—Das ist eine schöne Gegend, nicht war?'

'Ja, sie ist schön——sehr schön ——bist Du lange hier, oder reisest Du bloss durch?'

'Ich lebe schon mehrere Jahre in dem kleinen Städtchen dort—Du reisest wohl eben hier durch?'

'Ich bin in dem einzelnen Gasthause über Nacht.'

'Reisest Du dann wieder weiter?'

'Ja.'

'Georg——sage—ich möchte fragen: sind diese Deine Kinder?'

'Ja, Corona.'

'Wie alt sind sie denn?'

'Der Eine ist neun, der Andere zehn Jahre alt.'

where there was a wooden paling and the path divided, a woman dressed in dark clothes came towards him—he recognised her—it was Corona. She was dressed in dark clothes, as she had always preferred, with a little cap, as in the old days, only much simpler, on her head, and a bag, as always, but rather larger, on her arm. Her face was as beautiful as ever, but it had grown old. In her beloved features, which had once been his joy, there were many tiny, clear and distinctly marked lines, and she was paler than before, as people usually are when age advances. They both stood still and looked at each other.

'Corona,' he said.

'Georg,' she answered.

She gave him her hand—he took it, and thought he would never be able to let go.

'Are you well, Georg?'

'Well, Corona.—And you?'

'Yes Georg. This is a lovely place, isn't it?'

'Yes, it is beautiful—very beautiful——have you been here long, or are you only travelling through?'

'I have lived for several years now in the little town there—I suppose you are just travelling through?'

'I am at the lonely inn for the night.'

'Are you travelling on again tomorrow?'

'Yes.'

'Georg——tell me—I would like to know: are these your children?'

'Yes, Corona.'

'How old are they?'

'This one is nine and that one is ten.'

'*Es sind freundliche Kinder.—*
Weil Du nur Kinder erhalten hast.'
'*Bist Du auch vermählt, Corona?*'
'*Es haben sich Anträge gefunden.*'
'*Also bist Du vermählt?*'
Sie wurde sehr roth und sagte: '*Ich
habe es nicht vermocht.*'
*Er antwortete kein Wort—nicht
ein einziges Wort sagte er auf diese
Rede.——
Nach einem Weilchen reichte er
ihr die Hand hin und sagte:* '*Gute
Nacht, Elisabeth.*'
'*Warte noch ein wenig,*' *antwortete
sie, dann suchte sie in ihrem
Täschchen, das sie am Arme trug,
herum, brachte zwei Aepfel heraus,
und gab jedem der Knaben einen.
Dann gab er die Hand hin, sie
reichte ihm die Rechte, an der sie, wie
es auch früher gewöhnlich der Fall
war, keinen Handschuh hatte, er
drückte die Hand, in welcher die
seinige so oft geruht hatte, Beide
wandten sich ab und gingen ohne
ein Wort die verschiedenen Wege
fort. Die Knaben bissen in die
rothen Aepfel und assen sie auf dem
Heimwege.*

'*They are nice children. Oh, to
think that you should have had
children.*'
'*Are you married too, Corona?*'
'*I have had suitors.*'
'*Did you re-marry?*'
She became very red and replied:
'*I could not.*'
*He did not reply—not one single
word did he say in reply to this
speech.——
After a while he gave her his hand
and said:* '*Good night, Elisabeth.*'
'*Wait a little,*' *she said, searched
in the bag on her arm, brought out
two apples, and gave one to each of
the boys. Then he gave her his hand,
and she gave him her right hand, on
which, as had formerly been her
habit, she wore no glove. He pressed
the hand in which his own had so
often rested, both turned away and
went their different ways. The boys
bit into the red apples and ate them
on the way home.*

In no other story of Stifter's is dialogue used at once so sparsely
and so meaningfully. The simplicity and stateliness of their
exchange have many parallels in his work, but nowhere else do
the words that two beings exchange relate so closely to, and
convey so fully and deeply, what has happened to them. The
dialogue begins with their greeting—the act of recognition and
name-giving, almost religious in its intensity. (At the end of their
meeting Georg calls his wife by her second name, which in their
married life he had used only on solemn occasions.[1]) Then,

---

[1] Perhaps Stifter had in mind Zacharias's wife Elizabeth, who had remained
childless until her old age, when God rewarded her for her faith with a son,
John the Baptist.

slowly they move close to each other, once again and for a last time, and again their only means are a few bare words. And, coming closer still, step by step, they complete in their brief accounts all the years that have passed, and their present condition: until they are there, in the core of their living intimacy, which is also their cruel wound. He had always been impulsive and generous, she passionate and determined, and so it is again. In a single muffled cry she gives her blessing to his life ('*Weil Du nur Kinder erhalten hast*'), and then it is her turn to answer for her life. It is difficult for her to bare again her past: almost shyly she intimates her suffering, which is also her glory; saying, not 'I have kept faith', but more humbly, 'I could not remarry'.

This is all there is to the story. The guilt and remorse, Georg's long life of expiation which follows upon this meeting, are related to this moment of recognition. Yet he remains something of a stranger to that faith, that law of love, which she never broke. And it is meaningful, as meaning is known among men, that nothing he will ever do should expunge the wrong decision from his consciousness. For when we look back on the story, on the completed experience it conveys, we become aware of an effect which is as strange and untoward as it is powerful. The true centre of the tale is not Georg, the restless, solitary wanderer in the forests, but Corona, his beloved, passionate wife. We have seen much less of her, and yet her decision and knowledge—her sin and expiation—overshadow all that he is. Stifter neither avoids the tragic flaw that he sees in human lives nor is he overwhelmed by it and incapacitated for his creative effort. Here tragedy belongs to the very core and texture of his work, and around it nature, judge and solace, finds its rightful place.

8

Like the complex and many-hued lines of grain in the highly polished wood of a Baroque altar chest, so the experiences of Stifter's years are ingrained in the prose of his greatest novel: or rather, not the experiences but their opposite, the inversions of reality, the images of what might have been. *Der Nachsommer* (*Indian Summer*) is a meeting-place of several genres: the strongest element in its composition is that of the *Bildungsroman*, the novel of education and growth through spiritual refinement. In its centre lies a *Novelle* of passion, buried deep in the past, its calamity touched on as briefly as in Stifter's other stories; its function is that of a cautionary tale. The narrative element is heavily over-laid with pedagogic intention conveyed by minutiae from the spheres of nature and art. The setting is idyllic and still owes something to Jean Paul, though it lacks both his fancy and his lightness of touch. Finally, the village-tale of almanac and family magazine, too, with its hints of the propriety of possession and of the distribution of the stations in life in which it has pleased God to place men, belongs among the sources of the novel. The world, in short, of Maria Edgeworth?

The most astonishing literary fact about the work is the com-plex and in a sense sophisticated use to which these simple and unambitious elements are put. For they are all intensified and exaggerated to the point where they join in support of a narrative of unique originality and import. Its central theme is the planning and gradualness and total protection of experience.

Consider the opening of the story. Heinrich Drendorf, a young man at the end of his formal education, is the only son of a wealthy merchant in an unnamed city (presumably Vienna). The father is conscious of the honourable but humble nature of his calling, his rôle in the story is therefore confined to providing his son with the freedom to develop his gifts and sensibilities to the full; Heinrich's mother and sister remain indistinct, they are there merely because they belong to the idea—the symmetry—of a complete family. In the course of one of his travels through the Alpine foothills Heinrich arrives at the gates of a country man-sion and, believing that a storm is imminent, asks the owner of the house for shelter. Although the storm doesn't come, he is granted hospitality and stays for three days. In the course of that time his host—an old man whose name he learns only many months later—opens before him a world of unique order and beauty. The appointment of the house, its furniture and rare panellings and patterned marble floors; its library, pictures, scientific instruments and *objets d'art*; the roses which cover its main wall; the park with its elaborate lay-out, its orchards, birds, beasts and insects; the estate itself with outlying farms, workshops, fields and woods—all this is revealed to the young man for the sole purpose of educating his mind, refining his perception and forming his character.

Inherent in this opening are several opportunities for—I will not say dramatic action but at least narrative contrasts. Thus we might expect in Heinrich some vitality or even crudeness which would make him impatient in the presence of so much harmony and perfection; in fact he is merely receptive and thoughtful. Then again, something of a contrast inevitably arises between the atmosphere of his home, which is relatively humble, and the world into which he is being initiated; between Heinrich's father and his host: nothing is made of these either, the world of the *Asperhof* is exalted while the city recedes into indistinctness. The minute episode of the storm that doesn't come—intended to illustrate the young man's inexperience and the old man's wisdom —points to the strangely tautologous mood of the whole, to the beautiful boredom that encompasses the main story.

Heinrich Drendorf's visits to the *Asperhof* are repeated. Between them he lives for a few winter months with his family—to be estranged not indeed by them but by the social bustle of the city, of which we see very little. Once more he sets out on long excursions, to study the geology and climatic conditions of the region. He crosses a snow-covered mountain-pass; visits lonely villages where he acquires neglected antiques, which are then restored in his host's workshops. At the House of Roses (as he has renamed the *Asperhof*) a few simple relationships develop. Heinrich makes friends with his host's foster-son, Gustav; and at last learns that his host's name is Freiherr von Risach, and that he once held an important post in the civil service,[1] from which he retired at the height of his career. Two more people are added to their company, Gustav's widowed mother Mathilde, the owner of a neighbouring manor, who turns out to have been secretly engaged to Risach many years before, and her daughter Natalie, with whom Heinrich eventually falls in love. *Their* engagement, Heinrich's

---

[1] W. Rehm (*Nachsommer: zur Deutung von Stifters Dichtung*, Bern 1951, pp. 75 ff.) suggests that the figure of Risach was partly modelled on the Prussian *savant* and statesman Wilhelm von Humboldt, whose writings Stifter knew.

subsequent journey to many foreign lands (lasting two years and disposed of in half a page), and their wedding, which is attended by both families and a ceremonial of infinite solemnity, complete the main story.

Heinrich's education towards this happy end is guided by von Risach in such a way that the things of nature and of art should speak to him, one after another, and intimate to him a message of spiritual perfection. It is in fact planned for him with infinite forethought, somewhat as Wilhelm Meister's journey through experience turned out to be secretly guided by the *Society of the Tower*, or as the hero of Wieland's *Agathon* (1766) has been guided in his progress towards wisdom by the philosopher Archytas. But Heinrich's progress is what Meister's or Agathon's had escaped being—it is wholly undramatic. Not a breath of tension, not a stirring of passion is admitted, all occasions for conflict are passed by. There is (for instance) among the labourers and artisans employed at the House of Roses a young carpenter called Roland, whose eyes rest on Natalie 'for a long time and significantly'. The profane reader longs for an involvement, a rivalry, but the idea is unthinkable: Natalie merely happens to remind Roland of a girl in his native village to whom he is engaged. The idyll, set out with an overwhelming strength of narrative purpose, with an immovable determination to avoid all calamity, is complete. Here, in this vast exaggeration of the patches of tranquillity which we know experience can yield, lies the unique creative act.

Hidden behind the battlement of things and moods and characters all in perfect harmony, hidden deeply in the main story's past, lies the *Novelle* of passion, the episode from Risach's and Mathilde's youth, when they had been in love—he a poor and humble young tutor, she the daughter of a noble family. (Something of Stifter's relation with Fanni is here re-enacted, though on a level of sublime tact and high nobility.) After a fervent avowal of mutual love, but without consulting Mathilde, the young Risach had disclosed his feelings to her mother, who had withheld her consent to a union. Shortly after this the young tutor left, Mathilde married a nobleman—Gustav's and Natalie's father— Risach rose in the world, was himself ennobled, and we find him at the opening of the novel retired from the world, in the Indian Summer of his life. With Mathilde, now widowed, living close by, they are recapturing something of the love they once bore each other, though their love is now freed from all passions: '... what a summer it could have been if there had been one' is the listless tautology in which Stifter himself[1] sums up von Risach's life. This—the remembrance of passion, of its untoward avowal and of the act of disobedience to which it led—is the experience which is to enable von Risach to guide Heinrich and show him the path of moderation and virtue: this is the precept for Heinrich's education. And when, in the penultimate chapter, von Risach tells him his own story, Heinrich's education is virtually completed and he is ready to marry Natalie.

But even if we don't demur to the loss of living tension entailed by this jump from youth to the wisdom of restraint and serene contentment, even if we accept as plausible that the lesson of old age can ever be conveyed to youth, there still remains a certain unclarity[2] in the centre of the book. For what *was* the sin that it took Risach a lifetime of successful but uncongenial work to expiate, and what, consequently, the lesson for Heinrich to learn? What was the fault repaired only in the Indian Summer of von Risach's and Mathilde's days? Disobedience and breach of trust towards her parents? This is the burden of their accusation, this is what Risach feels guilty of. But Mathilde, when he told her of her parent's decision and of his readiness to give her up, had charged him with the opposite fault—with a lack of passion, and with timidity. It is with her that he broke faith (she tells him), it is their love he betrayed. And when, with the passage of intervening years, she grew contemptuous of him, it was not because he had shown too much passion but too little. Was he wrong in his weakness or she in her strength? If the former were the true view,

---

[1] To Gustav Heckenast, 2.i.1855.

[2] It is this unclarity I had in mind when (p. 249) I spoke of the direct relevance of Stifter's life to his work.

then the story would be irrelevant to the lesson it is intended to teach. And if the latter? Then Mathilde's impassioned and beautifully perceptive accusation would be false. But Mathilde *is* right: her understanding of his weakness is the truest and most vital passage in the book:

'Ich muss gehorchen,' rief sie, indem sie von der Bank aufsprang, 'und ich werde auch gehorchen; aber du musst nicht gehorchen, deine Eltern sind sie nicht. Du musstest nicht hieher kommen und den Auftrag übernehmen, mit mir das Band der Liebe, das wir geschlossen hatten, aufzulösen. Du musstest sagen: Frau,[1] Eure Tochter wird Euch gehorsam sein, sagt Ihr nur Euren Willen; aber ich bin nicht verbunden, Eure Vorschriften zu befolgen, ich werde Euer Kind lieben, solange ein Blutstropfen in mir ist, ich werde mit aller Kraft streben, einst in ihren Besitz zu gelangen.'

'I must obey,' she called out, jumping up from the bench, 'and I shall obey; but you need not obey, they are not your parents. You were not obliged to come here and accept the task of dissolving the bond of love which we had concluded. You should have said: Your daughter will be obedient to you, tell her what is your will; but I am not bound to obey your instruction, I shall love your child as long as there is a drop of blood in me, and I shall strive with all my might to make her my own one day.'[2]

The main line of Stifter's intention is hardly in doubt. The situation which Grillparzer had followed out to the end Stifter wants to draw out to its opposite conclusion: where Jacob's weakness had been turned into a solely spiritual redemption, von Risach's weakness (for that is what it is, even though Stifter only

---

[1] I find the German untranslatable: 'Frau' here conveys a forthrightness and a directness of address quite unlike anything the young Risach can muster—Stifter's insight into Mathilde's disappointment is perfect.

[2] K. Hohoff(*A.S.*, Düsseldorf 1949, p. 134), the only one of the critics I know who enters on this central argument of the book, sees the predicament differently: in giving up Mathilde (Hohoff writes) 'Risach places the alien law of [his] obedience towards [her] parents above' his own love for her. Hence (Hohoff implies) Risach is entitled, having learned from his *error*, to teach Heinrich the *right* kind of obedience (to his own 'law', i.e. to his love for her.) But surely here it is not a question of choosing one 'law' rather than another; as Mathilde points out, his act, in the context of their love, was not an error but a *weakness*, a defection from love. And the only possible lesson for Heinrich would be, 'Avoid my weakness, be passionate!', the very opposite of the message of *Der Nachsommer*.

calls it so in the *Novelle*) is to yield a triumph in this life. Risach is to be proved right—his defective love is somehow to be validated and shown as his strength—and he is to teach not only Heinrich but also Mathilde the true value of harmonious living freed from all passion. Yet his triumph is a *non sequitur*, it is based on the taming of a passion he never felt. Of *her* 'error' nothing is made. It is smothered by all the *things* with which she and they all are surrounded; like an anguished cry drowned in the tolling of a bell, her passion is muffled by the sound of his 'All, all will be well.' Perhaps one had expected a Jamesian solution, something like that firm velvet ribbon on which the remarkable Mr Verver leads Charlotte to *his* collection of exquisite objects. But nothing remotely like it is hinted at. We are to conclude that from the experience of their abandoned love von Risach drew the strength and wisdom of which we see him possessed in his old age, but our doubt as to the logic of these emotions remains unanswered.

I think we can do no more than state the dilemma between the achieved splendour of the part (the *Novelle* of passion) and its less than complete relevance to the whole novel. We can only try as best we may to keep the value of the single experience from being impaired by its disconnectedness. The next step, which would be to show the hiatus as symbolically relevant, can no more be justified by what Stifter has written than such a reading would be justified in respect of the incompletely motivated earlier stories; no more than would be the attempt to identify his natural piety with the Christian.

What we are once more left with is Stifter's strange and relentless *will* to harmony and perfection, a will that shrinks from self-knowledge and replaces the true consequences of an experience by a made-up world. This conclusion, it must be admitted, is flatly contradicted by Stifter's own view of his mature work; thus he writes to Heckenast (*à propos* of *Witiko*) in January 1861:

> *The form which I impart to the material is quite independent of me . . . I must discover, not invent it.*

And again:

> *When I wrote* Der Hochwald [1841], *I was young and frivolous enough to do violence to my story and then stuff it into the drawers of my fancy. Now I am almost*

ashamed of such a childish proceeding. For now that which has happened [das Geschehene] *stands almost like an awesome rock before my eyes, and the question* [*I ask*] *is not 'What shall I do with* [*my hero*]?' *but 'What is he?'*

In order to portray 'that which has happened', Stifter would have to accept the real world as a place not wholly empty of God; but for him the world as it is *is* empty, and hence unacceptable. This is the reason (so it seems to me) why his creative attention is directed not towards what is but towards what ought to be.

In such a dispute[1] the critic can only go on by his own best understanding, and leave the reader to decide. To me the conclusion seems inevitable that *ultimately* Stifter is no more prepared to entrust his art to 'that which has happened'—the logic, in this case, of the human heart—than he is ready to entrust it to the actuality of the social and political world. Ultimately: that is, when it comes to connecting the perfectly achieved story of the single experience of passion with the novel as a whole; when it comes to drawing out its fullest meaning. That, for him, does not lie in the human scene.

9

In the reflection from which I quoted at the beginning of this chapter Nietzsche asks how 'the poetry of the future', which he sees foreshadowed in some contemporary writings, will be related to the 'national and social conditions of our modern world and reality'. It must seek out the places (he continues) where, in the midst of that world, 'the great and beautiful soul is still possible'; and it should convey the beauty of that soul 'without any artificial resistance' against the modern world, without betraying any feeling of 'deprivation', or abstracting from that world.[2] Without any artificial resistance? One wonders whether Nietzsche can have

---

[1] For most critics, including for instance Emil Staiger, there is no dispute: for them Stifter's intention and realisation are one. Yet even Staiger concludes (à propos of *Witiko*) that Stifter's conception of the Middle Ages corresponds to 'nothing that ever existed'. (*Adalbert Stifter als Dichter der Ehrfurcht*, Zürich 1952, p. 63); the contradiction is left unresolved.

[2] '*Der Künstler als Wegweiser für die Zukunft wird . . . jene Fälle auswittern, wo mitten in unserer modernen Welt und Wirklichkeit, wo ohne jede künstliche Abwehr und Entziehung von derselben, die schöne grosse Seele noch möglich ist . . .*'

had Stifter in mind after all, whether he of all readers could have failed to notice the signs of the magnificent contrivance. These signs are to be found in almost any part of *Der Nachsommer*, but they cannot be conveyed briefly. My quotation comes from the seventh chapter, 'The Meeting' of Heinrich and Natalie; von Risach is describing the appointments made in his workshops for the rebuilding of Mathilde's manor house:

'Als wir einmal den Plan gefasst hatten, die Zimmer Mathildens nach und nach mit neuen Geräten zu bestellen,' erwiderte er, 'so wurde die ganze Reihe dieser Zimmer im Grund- und Aufrisse aufgenommen, die Farben bestimmt, welche die Wände der einzelnen Zimmer haben sollten, und diese Farben gleich in die Zeichnungen getragen. Hierauf wurde zur Bestimmung der Grösse, der Gestalt und der Farbe, mithin der Hölzer der einzelnen Geräte geschritten. Die Farbezeichnungen derselben wurden verfertigt und mit den Zeichnungen der Zimmer verglichen. Die Gestalten der Geräte sind nach der Art entworfen worden, die wir vom Altertume lernten, wie ich euch einmal sagte, aber so, dass wir nicht das Altertum geradezu nachahmten, sondern selbstständige Gegenstände für die jetzige Zeit verfertigten mit Spuren des Lernens an vergangenen Zeiten. Wir sind nach und nach zu dieser Ansicht gekommen, da wir sahen, dass die neuen Geräte nicht schön sind und dass die alten in neuen Räumen zu wohnlicher Zusammenstimmung nicht passten. Wir haben uns selber gewundert, als die Sachen nach vielerlei Versuchen, Zeichnungen und Entwürfen fertig waren, wie schön sie seien. In der Kunst, wenn man bei so kleinen Dingen von Kunst reden kann, ist eben so wenig

Once we had decided on the plan to re-furnish Mathilde's rooms gradually . . . ground plans and elevations of this set of rooms were made, the colours of the walls of the different rooms were chosen and these colours painted into the drawings. Then we proceeded to decide on the size, shape and colour of the individual pieces of furniture, as well as the woods they were to be made from. Coloured drawings of them were prepared and compared with the plans of the rooms. The shapes of the furnishings were designed in the manner we have learnt from ancient times, as I once told you, but in such a way that we were not directly imitating the antique, but designing independently articles for modern times with traces of what we have learned from the past. We arrived gradually at this point of view after observing that modern furniture is not beautiful and that old pieces do not adapt themselves harmoniously to new rooms. When the things were finally ready, after many attempts and many new drawings and sketches, we ourselves were surprised to see how beautiful they were. In art, if one can speak of art in such small things, it is just as

294

*ein Sprung möglich als in der
Natur. . . . Nur dass in der Schöpfung die Allmählichkeit immer rein
und weise ist; in der Kunst aber, die
der Freiheit des Menschen anheim
gegeben ist, oft Zerrissenheit, oft
Stillstand, oft Rückschritt erscheint.
Was die Hölzer anbelangt, so sind
da fast alle und die schönsten Blätter
verwendet worden, die wir aus den
Knollen der Erlen geschnitten haben,
die in unserer Sumpfwiese gewachsen
sind. Ihr könnt sie dann betrachten.
Wir haben uns aber auch bemüht,
Hölzer aus unserer ganzen Gegend
zu sammeln, die uns schön schienen,
und haben nach und nach mehr zu-
sammengebracht, als wir anfänglich
glaubten. Da ist der schneeige, glatte
Bergahorn, der Ringelahorn, die
Blätter der Knollen von dunkelm
Ahorn—alles aus den Alizgrün-
den—, dann die Birke von den
Wänden und Klippen der Aliz, der
Wachholder von der dürren, schiefen
Haidefläche, die Esche, die Eberesche,
die Eibe, die Ulme, selbst Knorren
von der Tanne, der Haselstrauch,
der Kreuzdorn, die Schlehe und viele
andere Gesträuche, die an Festigkeit
und Zartheit wetteifern, dann aus
unseren Gärten der Wallnussbaum,
die Pflaume, der Pfirsich, der Birn-
baum, die Rose.'*

*impossible to proceed by leaps as it is
in Nature. . . . With the reservation
that in creation the gradualness is
always pure and wise; but in art,
which is subject to man's free will,
there often appears to be discontinuity,
lack of progress, or even regression.
As for the woods, we made use of all
the most beautiful planks that we had
cut from the roots of the elders that
grew in our marshy meadow. You
can see them afterwards. We also
took great pains to collect from the
whole of our region woods that we
considered beautiful, and gradually
assembled more than we thought at
first. There is the smooth snowy
mountain-maple, planks from the
trunk of the dark maple—all from
the ravines of the Aliz—then the
birch from the slopes and cliffs of the
Aliz, elder from the dry, bare, slanting
heath, ash, rowan, yew, elm and
even the roots of fir, hazel; black
elder, blackthorn and many other
bushes vying with each other in
delicacy and strength; then, from our
own gardens, wood of the walnut,
plum and peach, pearwood and rose-
wood.*

The 'art' that is here so humbly exalted ('if one can speak of
art . . .') is something like the art that Stifter himself practises.
Its condition is a kind of total planning ('Once we had decided
. . .') and premeditation, and in this sense it too[1] aspires to a
'scientific' exactitude. This art is defiant of all sudden moves as it
is lacking in spontaneity. It is connected with the natural world
through its materials and with the human through its ultimate

---

[1] See above, p. 251.

purpose, but stands away from both as a thing of beauty, self-contained and with an import of its own. It proceeds *via* exhaustive enumeration ('size, shape and colour'), its being and becoming are carefully, anxiously accounted for. The explicit praise of its archaic character ('. . . but old pieces [*Geräthe*] . . .') is heavily underscored by a deliberate, involuted arrangement of past tenses. The contrasts (nature—art: freedom—arbitrariness) are played down, the ideal of gradualness, of a *complete* account, is driven home with relentless circumstantiality. And the passage ends (after a brief pathetic appeal to man's best endeavour in all this, '*Wir haben uns aber auch bemüht* . . .') with a litany of trees . . . All this has a certain heavy charm, a charm as surprising, after all ('we ourselves were surprised . . .'), as is the effect of a completed piece of work each part of which had involved much toil of trial and error.

Yet the beauty and the charm are limited. Not that these descriptive passages are lacking in tension, even in a certain strange narrative energy. But the source of that tension is the anxiety lest anything should be forgotten,[1] the fear lest even all these 'things' should not be enough to ward off the blow. But these obsessive feelings are never clearly seen for what they are. To understand such fears for what they are would be to contrast them with a strength from another source, for all conveyed insight, in literature, is strength. But since here they are denied, merely stifled by the enumeration, since in fact nothing is made of these fears, no living conflict issues and no human illumination comes from them.

Here, in this *mystique* of things religiously assembled[2] and shored up against the ruins of time and fate, lies the core and import of

---

[1] Von Risach concludes the above discourse by referring Heinrich to an artisan who 'can show you the drawings one day in the *Asperhof,* and tell you of all the many kinds that I have not named here. . . .'

[2] In a less reverent mood one is reminded of H. G. Wells's searing comments on James's work: 'It is like a church, lit but without a congregation to distract

this strange novel; these are the emblems of Stifter's *pietas*, the essence of his re-interpretation of the world of men. No longer connected with Goethe's supreme openness and generous love of man and of Nature, Stifter's art points to Rilke's recreation of '*die Dinge*' within the 'heart-space' of poetic inwardness: the novel becomes the most memorable of the many documents[1] in which the religion and ethos of 'things' is laid down.

Are they not just like the objects that surround us in the real world? Indeed, it is from their close resemblance that they derive their plausibility and effectiveness. But the cult for which they are assembled is not the cult of a living faith. There is nothing esoteric about the premise from which Stifter sets out. After all, both Stifter's poetic vision of '*Geräthe*' as vessels of human worth and Marx's definition of commodities as tokens of 'congealed labour' spring from a similar protest against the ethos of contemporary society, against what Marx calls the 'alienation of things-for-use' from their true purpose; and both issue into utopia. But whereas Marx's protest is vigorously critical—what he attacks is the hypostatization of commodities into 'fetishes' of capitalist commerce[2]—and his utopia is forward-looking, Stifter's 'protest' is nostalgic and vague, and his utopia deliberately archaic and pastoral. He is of course wholly unconcerned with economic data and their detailed criticism—what he expresses is a 'feeling', not a 'judgement.'[3] Things are to be given back their true value—their value-for-man—by a return to individual craftsmanship and a reunion of craft with the arts, by their recon-

---

you, with every light and line focused on the high altar. And on the altar, very reverently placed, is a dead kitten, an egg-shell, a bit of string...' (*op. cit.*, p. 248).

[1] The beautiful objects of Mörike's and C. F. Meyer's poetry belong to the same ethos, but they aren't as important a part of their work.

[2] See the end of the last chapter of *Das Kapital*, ed. K. Kautsky, Stuttgart 1914, pp. 35–46.

[3] In Stifter's own scheme of values 'feeling' is a defective form of 'judgement'; thus Heinrich Drendorf speaks of his own education: '*Bei mir war es damals nur Gefühl gewesen, bei Risach war jetzt es Urteil*' (Chapter XVII). The odd word-order in the final clause is one of the countless examples in which the strange relentlessness of the vision is bodied forth.

secration to the purposes of man and thus of man to the purposes of God. Yet 'die Dinge' end up by always engaging Stifter's care and creative attention more fully than the men whom they are to serve. And so they become, not symbols of human values and dignity, but fetishes of Stifter's own fears.

The conclusions that emerge from Stifter's argument have their reflection in the social reality of his and the subsequent era. The *mystique* of things is translated into the characteristic ethos of the Wilhelminian Empire. The satisfaction, the emotional reassurance which springs from material comforts is elevated into a cult—a culture—of solid building, solid furnishing and solid cooking;[1] it is by a highminded and as it were 'spiritual' materialism that the *Bürgertum* attempts to grapple itself to the real world. Uninterested in social questions and uncreative in the political life of Germany, the *Bürgertum* becomes merely an efficient provider of means towards ends which are not its own. It creates an 'abstract *élite*' of legal, technological and financial experts, but leaves the political direction of the civil and foreign services and of the army in the hands of an isolated aristocratic 'natural *élite*' unleavened by new arrivals from the other classes.

All this does not take us as far away from the world of Stifter's *Der Nachsommer* as it may seem. His work is a sign and symptom, not an influence. The fact that he makes von Risach into a distinguished civil servant suggests that he was not oblivious of the need to connect the spiritual with public affairs; and Risach's humble peasant origin suggests the untapped source from which the Austrian administration might draw new life. But when all is said and done, the meaning of Risach's successful public past is as disconnected from the wisdom he teaches Heinrich as is the meaning of his melancholy personal past. Unlike that episode of a defective love, von Risach's career is presented sketchily and with little conviction, as a mere stepping-stone to higher things;

[1] A description of this cult is to be found in the section on '*Gemütlichkeit*' in Harold Nicolson's *Good Behaviour*, London 1955, pp. 209–24.

it is a mere stage of experience through which Heinrich doesn't
have to go; nothing that Risach has achieved in his life as a statesman is handed on to Heinrich—in short, in the world of the
Asperhof Risach's public and political past is without value. 'He
was a great statesman', Stifter writes of him, '*but* his powers were
by nature [*ursprünglich*] *creative*, he had to suppress them, and it
is only *after* his career as a statesman is over, in his leisure, that these
powers become effective. . . .'[1] This, surely, is indication enough
of how unspiritual Stifter too considered the social and political
sphere, and how unworthy of his own creative powers.

Realism (to return to an earlier argument) I have taken to mean
no more than the fulfilment of an expectation which we carry
from the social world into the work of art. It is distinct from
blatant naturalism by the nature of the expectation it elicits in
us; our expectation is not statically fixed by the facts of the social
world but constantly modified, enriched and refined, by the
work of art: by the art at work upon our sensibility. That is,
instead of being merely told what we know anyhow, we are
shown what, but for the realism of the work, we would know
less clearly, less meaningfully. Where a work of art raises no
expectations derived from our knowledge and experience of the
social world, and therefore disappoints none, it is irrelevant to
criticise it for being unrealistic; accordingly, most of *Der Nachsommer* is immune from this kind of criticism. And were the work
absolutely to attain to that hermetic condition of being sealed off
from the social world—were it to be the sort of self-contained
artifact that Stifter intends in *Der Nachsommer*—such criticism
would be irrelevant. But that absolute isolation is not attained.
The world of the city is there, and its image is sketchy—the
contrast between it and the House of Roses is by-passed, and no
tension is allowed to develop. A set of social relations is there—
between master and servants; between artisans and consumers;

---

[1] Letter to Heckenast, 2.i.1855, my italics; the end of the sentence is quoted
above, p. 289.

between employers and labourers; between merchant and
rentier; between *Kleinkapital* and a feudal manorial community—
but the relations are not explored. The terminology itself, in
which I have presented these relations, sounds inappropriate: any
reader of the novel is certain to find it so. But though the words
are crude, the relations are *there*—not omitted but left un-
developed.

10

In Rilke's *First Elegy* the '*mystique* of things' is completed and
made explicit:

. . . But who, alas, is there
that we can use? Not angels, not men, and the knowing animals are aware
that we are not very reliably at home
in the interpreted world. There remains, perhaps, some tree on a slope, that we
   might each day
see it again.[1]

In a world where 'everything is new, threatening—no foothold
in the menacing chaos',[2] the trees of Stifter's litany are offered up
as the ultimate propitiations and last refuge. Is it not strange that
Nietzsche, reading *Der Nachsommer*, should have had no eye for
the cult that is being celebrated there? That he, who praised
authenticity as the last surviving value (and defined it as the
identity of living and thinking), appears to have been unaware
of the deep anxiety that speaks from every description in this
novel, of the relentless will of the artist who would *make* the world
into that which the man knows it not to be?

Is this, one wonders, to be the literature of the age of the
Superman? To the Christian values which Stifter professed, at all

---

[1]   '. . . *Ach, wen vermögen*
wir denn zu brauchen? Engel nicht, Menschen nicht,
und die findigen Tiere merken es schon,
dass wir nicht sehr verlässlich zu Haus sind
in der gedeuteten Welt. Es bleibt uns veilleicht
irgendein Baum an dem Abhang, dass wir ihn täglich
wiedersähen; . . . .'
[2] See above, p. 240.

events, it is no longer related. The faith that takes no thought for
the morrow is not to be found in the House of Roses; the foolish
Christian Knight who goes out among men armed only with his
faith in a good end is not among its inhabitants; at *that* remove
from his personal experience not even Stifter's creative imagination could work. We have hardly had occasion to measure *Der
Nachsommer* with realistic standards, because the realistic expectation is never raised. If we are left with a last impression of disappointment it is because the expectation of a Christian solution,
commonly held to be the least realistic of all, is raised and not
fulfilled.

VII REALISM AND
TOLERANCE:
THEODOR FONTANE

I

'THE CHARACTERISTIC accomplishment' of the French realistic
novelists, Lionel Trilling writes,[1] 'was the full, explicit realisation
of the idea of society as a definite external circumstance, the main
condition of individual life.' Viewed from this vantage point, the
German novels and *Novellen* of the nineteenth century fall
readily into place on a scale whose least realistic—that is, most
characteristically German—point is the work of Stifter; the work
of Theodor Fontane marks the other end of that scale. Fontane's
last great novels—and it is with these that I shall be concerned—
are the fruits of a creative compromise between the 're-interpreta-
tive' and the realistic traditions. Their particular charm and value,
as well as their limitations, derive from a felicitous and fruitful
adjustment of two cultures; of which adjustment, incidentally,
Fontane himself—the son of a Gascon Huguenot father and a
Cevennoise mother, born and bred on the North Sea coast of
Prussia—was the uncontentious and fairly happy product.

However, in pointing to the cosmopolitan character of Fontane's personal and literary background I don't at all wish to
give the impression that his work is in any way alien to the literature of his native country. On the contrary: he is *the* Prussian and
German novelist of the Second Reich 'as it really was', and his
long sojourns abroad as well as his lively contacts with contemporary French, English and Scandinavian literature all serve
to bring out and secure the German nature of his literary undertaking. Furthermore, the realism to which he commits his work

---

[1] *The Opposing Self*, London 1955, p. 176.

has of course its antecedents in German literature. And if, in the
course of this book, I have taken no account of the works of
Jeremias Gotthelf, Karl Immermann, Theodor Storm, Gustav
Freytag, Otto Ludwig or Wilhelm Raabe (not to mention a host
of *clearly* minor authors), it is merely because their various
compromises between the realistic vein and their several literary
aims and preoccupations don't seem to me to have produced
writings of comparable distinction at either end of the scale. To
say this is to leave unexamined their local worth and interest. In
terms of European realism at all events they cannot be said to
transcend the limitations imposed upon them by their provincialism; and in terms of the 'interpretative' tradition, too, they don't
seem substantially to modify the situation I have endeavoured to
describe. A brief examination of the work of the Swiss writer
Gottfried Keller, on the other hand, whose place on the scale is
nearest to Fontane's, requires no apology. Keller's work is
typical and representative of German provincial realism because
it 'combines in an extraordinary degree, exceptionally, the
various qualities which are usually present only partially'[1] in
diverse, less distinguished authors.

2

Keller's *Der grüne Heinrich*,[2] though not his greatest work, is
perhaps the last major original work in the German language to
stand under the direct impact of the Goethean tradition; at the
same time it represents a compromise between the Goethean
notion of 'becoming', of the human potentialities for positive
development, and the trammels and responsibilities of social life.

---

[1] See Roy Pascal, in a discussion of Gotthelf's work, in *The German Novel*,
Manchester 1957, p. 127; see also Lukács's argument (see below, note 1,
page 328).

[2] In its first version (published in 1854) the novel was such a flop that Keller's
sister used the unsold copies as winter fuel; the second version (1879) differs
from the first in presenting the events of Heinrich's life consecutively in the
first person, and it ends on a positive note; furthermore, 'the final version asserts
the vitality of social life and makes the individual, even in his eccentric course,
a representative man' (Pascal, *op. cit.*, p. 35); quite how strong this vitality is
remains to be seen.

The novel describes the boyhood, adolescence and early man-hood of Heinrich Lee, known from his manner of dressing (and also from a certain callowness) as 'Green Henry'. Through pride, affectation and fortuitous circumstances the boy comes to think of his minor talent for drawing and painting as a great gift; leaves his native Swiss town to study art in Munich, fails to make his way, and finally returns, via some unconvincing romantic detours, to a modest post in the civil administration of his home town. His mother and rustic relations, schoolfriends, several art-teachers, two girl-friends, the companions of his Bohemian life at Munich, and the aristocratic protector who turns out to have had a watchful eye on the young man—these are the main back-ground figures against which Heinrich's 'development' is traced out.

The remarkable and refreshing honesty of the book lies in Keller's clear-minded and accurate impartiality: in his consistent refusal to sentimentalise his hero's self-imposed predicament or extenuate his failings. The accuracy of Keller's psychological in-sights (especially in the early chapters) has often been remarked on. At least as striking, I think, are his forthright moral indict-ments, the scenes in which the circumstances of Heinrich Lee's life are pared away, one by one, until this or that effect of his self-indulgence emerges with startling clarity. At these points the road on which the hero has been travelling becomes so narrow that he cannot avert his eyes from the indictment.

The moral structure of Keller's narrative scheme emerges in such episodes as Heinrich's encounter with Römer, one of his teachers. Römer, a genuine artist, has come to the town (Zürich) after many failures; sinister rumours about his past life accompany him. Heinrich lends him some of his mother's money and, at a critical point in Römer's haunted life, in a pique of vanity and self-righteousness, extracts it from him again by means of a letter that borders on blackmail. Römer instantly returns the money and leaves. The venomous letter he writes to his 'dear young friend' from Paris makes it clear that Heinrich's act was the *coup de grâce* which has brought Römer to the point of abject poverty and moral disintegration. Sometime later Heinrich confesses his perfidy to Judith, the more mature of the two girls to whom he is attached. To his show of contrition and his claim that 'the story

will be a warning to me', she replies indignantly that the reproaches he has felt are a diet which should last him a lifetime:

> '... *this bread is good for you and I'll certainly not spread the butter of forgiveness
> on it!'*
> *Then she stood still, looked at me and said: 'Do you really know, Heinrich, that
> you already have a human life on your green conscience?'*[1]

In such forthright statements of the irretrievable nature of past
experience, of the finality of wrong-doing, Keller's novel presents
an advance on Goethe's *Wilhelm Meisters Lehrjahre*, where the
genre itself, with its underlying view of experience as a series of
experiments, had run counter to the making of irreversible
moral judgements. But then again we can see the philosophy of the
Entwicklungsroman reasserting itself when, a little later, Heinrich
all too readily assimilates the experience 'because it belongs to
my person, to my story, to my nature, otherwise it wouldn't
have happened!'

Here, then, is an advance on, not a denial of, Goethe's view of
character-development. Wholly free from any kind of abstract
moralising, Keller's narrative manner in such passages stands in
something like the same relation to Goethe's as does George
Eliot's to Jane Austen's: each of the later writers brings nearer to
the light of day the moral implications finely hidden in the novels
of their predecessors.

Keller's engaging honesty consists quite simply in his refusal
to make Heinrich Lee into a great artist; that is, he is ready to
show that what Heinrich is abandoning when he decides to give
up his artistic ambitions is merely a mediocre dilettantism, that
here all is gain, nothing sacrifice. The detailed way[2] in which

---

[1] Vol. III, Chapter 5: '*Weisst du wohl, Heinrich, dass du allbereits ein Menschen-
leben auf deiner grünen Seele hast?*'
[2] Keller's exposures go through three stages: first (Vol. I, Chapter 20) comes
Heinrich's failure in straightforward representational terms, when he tries to
get a beech tree on to his drawing paper; secondly (Vol. II, Chapter 6) Heinrich
tries to eke out his inadequate draughtsmanship by concentrating on grotesque
natural shapes and exaggerating them romantically into lurid caricature;
finally (Vol. III, Chapter 15, in Munich) Heinrich abandons all ideas of representation and lapses into surrealist doodles.

Keller exposes Heinrich's failure reveals the process at work in all unauthentic displays of talent. Unsparingly he presents to us the turgid dilemma and frustrations known to every man who has applied himself to a creative task for which he is inadequately suited by nature, and which he has chosen on false grounds and for the wrong reasons. All this is anti-romantic and honest, but ultimately it is also somewhat undramatic. The equation of personal irresponsibility with bad art may come as something of a relief to a reader saturated with the literature of 'the Demonism of Art'. But on the other hand he may wish for a clearer indication than he ever receives that Keller is equally aware of the danger of the opposite attitude, that of a philistinism which equates responsibility with good art. A possible conflict between the social and the aesthetic is not explored (on the contrary, it is never made clear how the lesson of his drastic failure is to be relevant to Heinrich's life as a respectable pen-pusher). True, there is a good reason why this source of narrative tension is not used—the artist-versus-society theme has been done too often before, by 1870 it has lost whatever broad human relevance and freshness it had once possessed. But when no other conflict takes its place, the book begins to flag, and well before the end all but collapses; similarly, the naturalism of the *petit-bourgeois* metaphors, of the 'bread-and-butter' style, drops from sobriety to flatness. The paean in praise of adult social responsibility on which the novel closes is as unexciting, not to say insipid, as perhaps only life in one of the German cantons of the Helvetic Confederation can be.

Der grüne Heinrich is a 'novel of development': that is, it shows the spiritual progression of a single individual from the comparative isolation of childhood and adolescence to an attitude in which the claims of society are acknowledged. And Keller shows all this—or most of it—in a straightforward and accurate realistic manner. It is in a comparison with *Le rouge et le noir*, another variation on the theme of *Entwicklung*, that the weaknesses of his novel become manifest. And what the comparison reveals seems to me characteristic not only of Keller's work, but also of the tradition within which he writes.

The most obvious thing to insist on is the tremendous vitality of almost every one of Stendhal's characters. The forces in conflict with each other in his novel are incomparably greater, incomparably more violent, the resistance which the world offers to Julien Sorel's ambition is magnificently powerful; the measure of these forces is not so much that they lead to a violent end but that each gives as good as it gets. The moment Julien leaves his father's sawmill we enter a world depicted with such assurance, such singlemindedness of reference, as is displayed in no German novel of the nineteenth century. And to compare the political cabbala in which Julien gets involved in Paris with the lengthy discussions on road planning and civic duties which teach Heinrich Lee how to become a responsible member of a community, is to recall the narrowness of the German (or, for that matter, the Swiss) literary scene, and Keller's acquiescence in it. The irony with which Stendhal reports on Julien's progress has an almost Flaubertian wryness about it. It also implies a supreme narrative confidence, a perfect and unambiguous *rapport* between author and public. The idea that world and society are anything but the firm *données* of the hero's situation simply doesn't arise. The idea that society in some mysterious way will yield before the hero's *weaknesses* (as it does in the last quarter of Keller's novel) is quite alien to Stendhal's scheme—and, it may not be irrelevant to add, to life as we know it. Whatever Sorel wants he must fight for, and the passion displayed in the course of that fight gives Stendhal's novel a dimension wholly lacking in Keller's. Hence the scheme of moral values, intimated through Julien's transgressions, is consistently more important. Heinrich's 'conflict', on the other hand, is a protracted tussle with his art. It is, also, a conflict with selfishness, heartlessness, irresponsibility . . . yet all these are *his* qualities after all. And though the problems of his artistic career intimate much more than a mere 'aesthetic' concern (since his art is also shown as the manifestation of a defective moral sensibility), yet in this too the circle of the self is merely widened, never breached—all *comes* at him, scarcely anything *is*, 'in and by itself'.

Nowhere is this more manifest than when we compare the women of the two novels. The two women in Heinrich's life—spirit and flesh—are literary clichés, they have been done countless times throughout the nineteenth and early twentieth century. Anna has certain affinities with the Mignon of *Wilhelm Meister*, without the poetic overtones which are an integral part of Goethe's conception; Judith, too obviously Anna's opposite, makes her entries and exits to suit narrative convenience. Unlike Mme de Rênal or Mathilde de La Môle, they don't exist outside Heinrich's emotional and moral need of them, and even on that premise they don't come to life.

Underlying Stendhal's novel is the suggestion that, given a different historical setting, Julien's qualities might have led to different, positive ends. A less hypocritical and self-seeking world would be less likely to excite his contempt—were not M. Valenod among the judges at his trial, he might not so readily put his head under the guillotine. Yet that suggestion is conveyed by means of that most delicate balance between self and world which belongs to the finest accomplishments of realism: the self responding to the world but not its victim, the world real and powerful yet not wholly overwhelming. A freedom of choice is there, yet it is a choice of actual possibilities: *that* Julien chooses is his business, *what* he chooses is the world's. And Stendhal's business is to show as ultimately inseparable the two elements—world and self—which determine the course of events and the shape of the novel. Early sociologists—among them Marx, but also Max Weber—and Marxist literary critics have insisted that the self in any living sense is, even as a self, already involved in a social whole. In doing so they did little more than provide the theoretical framework for a situation which, to a man like Stendhal, contains an obvious fundamental truth about life.[1]

On this intuitive recognition Stendhal bases a character at once unscrupulous and attractive, intelligent and vain, calculating and reckless, and passionate in all things: it is these qualities which make both for life and for an intimation of values in the novel. Moral values, even when they are shown forth negatively, by being trespassed against, are a concentration of human experience

---

[1] Besides, in literary criticism too it is a commonplace; which is why I suggested (above, p. 3) that a good deal of the Marxist barrage is aimed at straw men.

at a certain degree of intensity. The passions engaged in human strife—embodiments of moral values—yield images that go to the roots of the human condition. This is Stendhal's major theme, but it is not quite Keller's in *Der grüne Heinrich*. The taint of the provisional—as though somehow it were possible *not* to enter the river of experience: as though a man could ever *choose* whether he will enter the social world or not—is indelibly imprinted on the novel.

3

Keller's difficulties in hitting on a satisfactory form for his story have often been described. Yet not all of them were solved when he decided to adopt the manner of a first-person narrator. His main difficulty, it seems to me, lies in his 'going through to the end' with his story; which in turn derives from his tendency to allow many a chapter of the book to turn into a self-contained whole, into an episode, a *Novelle*. Nietzsche's remarks on the *'petits genres'* is very much to the point here. Attacking Wagner's conception of the 'total work of art', Nietzsche writes: 'Nowadays it is only the small thing that can be truly well made. Only in that is integrity still possible.'[1] And when he praises the excellence of Keller's prose,[2] it is not the novelist he has in mind but the author of a group of *Novellen* whose very form turns to good account the compositional weaknesses of *Der grüne Heinrich*.

Not only that. In the course of exploring that smaller *genre*, Keller in *Die Leute von Seldwyla* achieves the cohesion of theme that had at times eluded him in the more ambitious novel. The ten stories which he saved up in the bottom drawer of his desk against a rainy day seem at first sight to be only loosely connected.[3] They are all set in 'Seldwyla', an imaginary little Swiss town which, in its slothful and foolish ways, owes something to the

---

[1] *Der Fall Wagner* (1888), *ed. cit.*, no. 77, p. 42; in his rejection of Wagner's *Gesamtkunstwerk* he agrees with Keller (see Georg Lukács, *G.K.*, Berlin 1947, p. 88).

[2] *Menschliches, Allzumenschliches II* (1886), *ed. cit.*, no. 72 (ii), p. 227.

[3] The first volume of the collection, containing five stories, appeared in 1856, the complete work in 1874.

'Abdera' of Aristophanes and Wieland. Yet for all their variety of mood, narrative manner and sophistication, these *Novellen* form a unity which is reflected in something more than their common setting. Each of them is built round a single mania, a single *idée fixe*.

The first tells of a drastic cure for sulking. The second, tragic in tone, is on the Romeo-and-Juliet theme. The third is the story of a wastrel's ruin made good by a prudent wife and son. The fourth uses harsh satire to drive home the absurdity of maniacal thrift. Even in the fifth, a humorous fairy-tale, a Faustian cat cheats a Mephistophelean magician by appealing to his greed for money. The next, which resembles the first story in style, ridicules the inhabitants of a neighbouring town for being taken in by fine clothes and an elegant coach and horses. The seventh satirizes the love of titles and noble ancestry, while the eighth mocks the *précieuses* affectations of a housewife who has fallen in love with literature. The ninth is a historical tale less directly related to the rest (though its atmosphere of violence is reminiscent of the fourth, the heroine's possessiveness, which she eventually abandons, is again typical of the main theme). And the tenth, which returns to the more or less contemporary setting, takes for its subject the destruction of family life by religious bigotry.

The narrative manner of each story is determined by the kind of *idée fixe* of which it treats. Thus the cautionary tale of sulkiness is told in the tone of a child's story—not of a fairytale but of a curious anecdote about the real world as it might be told to a child. Sometimes the characters move jerkily, like marionettes; the charm of such stories lies in their lifelike artifice. From wit, lighthearted irony, farce, burlesque and caricature, through oblique and direct social criticism, all the way to the tragic manner, harsh satire and the grotesque—Keller's stylistic range is remarkably wide. Among these, caricature is the most frequent device, because it is the most direct expression of that 'terrible constriction of life in one-sidedness',[1] of those *idées fixes* which are Keller's main theme.

---

[1] The phrase, '*die schreckliche Gebundenheit des Lebens in der Einseitigkeit*' is from Hebbel's Preface to *Maria Magdalene* (1844).

And all this is crowded into Seldwyla, an imaginary yet largely realistic nineteenth-century small-town setting and its environs. And now, because Keller takes issue with the petit-bourgeois constriction—because he no longer acquiesces in it—the taint of provincialism is gone. Nowhere is this more patent than in *Romeo and Julia auf dem Dorfe*, in the way that he alters the grand Shakespearean theme to fit a totally different social situation. When we witness the deterioration of the two fathers from proud, patriarchal figures to litigious maniacs; when we watch their quarrel over a stony piece of land intensifying, and see the two families abandon their farmsteads and move into the squalid quarters of the Seldwyler *Lumpenproletariat*; when we see how, for all their innocent tenderness, all the love they bear each other, the two children-lovers are held and ultimately crushed by the world of their parents which is the only world they know, then indeed we understand that the Seldwyla setting is no fortuitous or fanciful framework but the precise and fitting condition of their lives: what is enacted in the Swiss backwater is a European theme.

In his illuminating study of the grotesque in painting and literature, the late Wolfgang Kayser[1] drew a good deal on the greatest of these stories, *Die drei gerechten Kammacher*. This is the tale of the monstrous passion of thrift, mean industry and singleminded devotion to an absurd end. The three journeymen comb-makers lying motionless in their single bed like sardines, the meanness of their surroundings, and especially the last scene of all, the race in which they compete for the business in which they have been working and for the woman whom everybody except them knows to be a shrew—these are among the finest of Keller's unsophisticated triumphs. They are also instances of the grotesque— of a Breughel-like intermingling of the idyllic and the obscene, of the jolly and the scurrilous, the effect of which is to leave the reader in a curious kind of imbalance, with a vertiginous feeling in which illumination and insight derive from a new, bizarre,

---

[1] *Das Groteske in Malerei und Dichtung*, [Rowohlt ed.] Hamburg, 1960.

indeed 'grotesque' disposition of familiar facts. Here are the two journeymen racing through the town (the third has deserted them and is disporting himself with the shrew in a nearby copse). The scene opens as on a gay festival—

Schon waren sie dem Thore nah, dessen Thürme von Neugierigen besetzt waren, die ihre Mützen schwenkten;	*They had almost reached the town gate, its towers crowded with inquisitive spectators waving their caps;*

and yet, when we look closer, the laughter dies on our lips:

die zwei rannten wie scheu gewordene Pferde, das Herz voll Qual und Angst;	*the two of them ran like a couple of bolting horses, their hearts full of fear and torment;*

Everything these two misers stand for, everything they have worked and hoped for these many years, is now at stake, and the competition is for them the supreme test. Within the terms of his non-religious point of view Keller invokes all the pangs of their terror. A street-urchin trails one, Jobst, hanging on to his carpet-bag 'like an evil troll', while the crowd express their delighted approval. The fierce tone rises—'*er flehte ihn an*' [he implored the urchin to let go]—but is juxtaposed with the merry '*der Junge duckte sich und grinste ihn an*' [the boy ducked and grinned at him] —on and on, until the fiercest point of the grotesque, of the man-made horror, is reached—

Sie weinten, schluchzten und heulten wie Kinder und schrieen in unsäglicher Beklemmung: 'O Gott! lass los! Du lieber Heiland, lass los Jobst! lass los Fridolin! lass los du Satan!'	*The two journeymen wept, sobbed and screamed like children, and cried in indescribable anguish: 'Oh my God! let go! Lord Jesus Christ, let go Jobst! let go Fridolin! let go, you devil!'*

—yet the horrible climax is enveloped in an almost serene description, from afar their movements resemble a ballet:

Sie hielten sich gegenseitig fest und drehten sich langsam zum Thore hinein, nur zuweilen einen Sprung versuchend . . .	*Holding each other fast and slowly revolving they entered the town gate, only occasionally attempting a leap . . .*

and again,

dazwischen schlugen sie sich fleissig auf die Hände,	*in between they were busily hitting one another on the hands,*

until, at the end of the passage, the full medieval horror of the mob-scene is invoked, this time by the juxtaposing of the rabble with the refined Seldwyla *haut monde*:

Voran und hinter ihnen her wälzte sich der tobende Haufen; alle Fenster waren von der Damenwelt besetzt, welche ihr silbernes Gelächter in die unten tosende Brandung warf, und seit langer Zeit war man nicht mehr so fröhlich gestimmt gewesen in dieser Stadt.	*In front of them and behind, the frenzied crowd was surging along, every window was occupied by Society ladies who dropped their silvery laughter into the surf raging below; it was a long time since they had been so merry in that town.*

And this use of the grotesque in the portrayal of people Keller also applies to his description of things. Several times in these stories, as well as in *Der grüne Heinrich*, we find ourselves caught up in a paragraph of strange doodles, or collections of books, or weird paraphernalia of this kind:

> *In the course of many long nights and holidays the young man* [one of the shrew's previous wooers] *had built an elaborate and precious monument of his admiration. It was a huge Chinese temple, made of cardboard, with countless receptacles and secret drawers, which could be taken apart into many pieces. It was covered with the finest coloured and embossed papers and decorated everywhere with golden borders. Walls with mirrors on them alternated with pillars, and on removing a piece or opening a room you could see more mirrors and hidden pictures, vases with flowers and loving couples, and from the extended gables of the roofs everywhere hung little bells. A casing for a lady's watch was attached to the pillars by means of pretty little hooks on which the golden chain could be suspended so that the watch swung from the building. Endless effort and art were wasted on this ingenious temple, its geometrical design being no less elaborate than the neat way in which it was executed.* [The young man's] *work rested on top of* [her] *ancient wardrobe, protected from dust and the prying eyes of the unworthy by a piece of seagreen gauze. So sacred was it to her that she never used it. . . .*

What exactly is the purport of these Dali-esque—or Dickensian—objects in Keller's stories? It is hard to tell how conscious the Clerk to the worthy Councillors of Zürich was of the feelings he was committing to paper through these contraptions. If, in his epistolary injunctions to friends and reviewers, Keller was anxious to recommend the *bürgerlich* virtues of thrift and hard work, and a responsible use of the franchise, these images tell a different story. In trying to understand the full meaning of such images we receive some help from Dickens, who indulged in very similar 'things'. We think of Miss Haversham's wedding cake (in Chapter XI of *Great Expectations*), of the weird reflections in the Veneerings' looking-glass (in Chapter II of *Our Mutual Friend*), of Miss Tox's little bags (in Chapter I of *Dombey and Son*), of Mr Dombey's own fungoid parlour (Chapter XXX), of the figure of 'the Law' and the 'entanglement of real estate in meshes of sheepskin, in the average ratio of about a dozen of sheep to an acre of land' (Chapter XXXII of *Bleak House*) or the 'soiled knives and tablecloths [that] break out spontaneously into eruptions of grease and blotches of beer' (*ibid.*, Chapter XX). Keller is a less conscious writer—and a less purposeful satirist—than Dickens. Yet his 'things' too have a symbolical value. They are true emblems ('... monuments...') of pointlessness, crystalloid growths of frustration, grotesques of *bourgeois* application. They are the satirical counterparts to Stifter's sacred 'implements', to his '*Geräthe*', encrusted not with metaphysical values but with drab *accidie* and turgid failure.

Yet though Keller is less conscious than Dickens of the in-herent social symbolism, on a personal level he is explicit enough. In describing the moods of his *alter ego*, of the penniless Heinrich Lee in his Munich hovel—

In order to be doing something and perhaps to stimulate my mind I began to ink in with a reed pen one of the trees I had sketched in charcoal, wondering what would come of it. But before half an hour had passed, when I had covered a few branches with pine-needles, I fell into a deep mood of distraction and began, without thinking, to draw unrelated lines, as one does when trying out a pen. These scribbles soon grew into an infinite network of penstrokes, which in the course of many days of aimless brooding I spun into an enormous grey spider's web, covering with it the greater part of the board. Yet if you looked closer at the chaos, you could see in it signs of coherence and admirable industry, for the continuity of strokes and twists of the pen (which added up to thousands of yards in length) formed a maze that could be traced from its beginning all the way to its end. Every now and then there appeared a new style, as it were a new compositional period; new patterns and motifs emerged, often subtle and attractive; and if I had used the sum total of care, purposefulness and application which went into this senseless mosaic to a real purpose, I would certainly have produced something worth looking at. Only now and then could you see stoppages and knotty places in the labyrinths of my distracted gloomy soul, and the

*careful way in which the pen had tried to get out of the difficulty showed how my
dreaming consciousness was caught in the net.*[1]

—here at all events he knows exactly what the 'thing' is and what
it stands for.

Keller's use of the grotesque, then, is a source of insight—into
what? The morality of *Die Leute von Seldwyla* is an implied and
satirically inverted scheme of values. The only story where it is
positively asserted (*Frau Regel Amrain und ihr Jüngster*) is unconvincing, its values thin and conventional. The satire, on the
other hand, is at its most effective where the double optics of the
grotesque focuses on the juxtaposition of jollity and infamy, of
Gemütlichkeit and *Niederträchtigkeit*. Keller's view here is perhaps
best summed up by a poem of Goethe's, which begins:

> *Ueber's Niederträchtige*
> *Niemand sich beklage;*
> *Denn es ist das Mächtige,*
> *Was man dir auch sage.*

His social realism is not at its best but at its most boring where
he preaches the social and political responsibility for which Georg
Lukács has praised him.[2] And in his inability to give a convincing
picture of the positive social values behind his satirical scheme,
Keller shares the predicament of his fellow-realists throughout
Europe. In Dickens too the 'socially responsible' characters are
mostly pallid and stereotype, and true goodness of heart is only
to be found on the margins of the social world.

Keller is at his best where he shows that trivial baseness is not

---

[1] *Der grüne Heinrich*, Vol. III, Chapter 15. The Freudian and surrealist aspect
of this remarkable passage lies in its emphasis on free association ('they soon
grew into . . .'), in the way the 'Id' takes over from the 'distracted gloomy'
'Ego'.

[2] But Lukács also shows that Keller 'formulates the *process* of development,
not the concrete problems, and the conflicts of the developed type with reality'
(*op. cit.,* p. 95, his italics)—*i.e.* that 'utopian ideas' of Swiss democracy (which
Lukács sees intimated in Keller's works) are neither worked out nor tested.

really trivial, that the mood of *Gemütlichkeit* may on occasion stand in a terrifying alliance with depravity and cruelty; where he understands how close and powerful the alliance is, and how it is bound up with the stifling setting of the *petite bourgeoisie*; in fine, where he fully explores the social facts of his world. What gives his work a European quality and relevance is the fact that this provincial milieu and its inbred morality are a European phenomenon. In the stories of Gogol, Dostoyevsky and Jan Neruda[1] the satirical vein of Keller's *Seldwyla* is continued and intensified, the *petit-bourgeois* mentality dissected, the *idée fixe* which informs it shown up in all its harshness and, ultimately, its dæmonic obsessiveness.

4

Theodor Fontane's major novels and *Novellen* are founded fairly and squarely in the social setting of his time and country, the Prussia and Berlin of the Second Reich. He depicts the whole scale of *milieux* from the lower to the upper middle classes and their servants, to the Prussian Junkers, including the civil service and military aristocracies; the working-classes are on the whole outside his range. So fascinated is he by this complex setting that on occasion[2] he contents himself with presenting it as the main substance of a 'story', as a five-finger exercise on an instrument which he plays with unparalleled virtuosity and assurance. So complete is his grasp of the social *données* that of more than one of his characters may be said what an academic joker said of the President of an American College, that 'he was so well adjusted to his environment that sometimes you could not tell which was the environment and which was the President'.

The given condition of life as Fontane sees and portrays it is society as an ordered, tradition-directed and custom-bound community of human beings with certain common needs and certain common habits to gratify those needs; a community of men and women whose reactions are at least partly and often wholly

---

[1] See his *Malostranské povídky*, 1878, translated as *Tales from the Little Quarter* [of Prague], London 1957.
[2] For instance in *Die Poggenpuhls*, 1896.

determined by that which their fellow-men hold dear or pro-
scribe. Also, society is for him a static body determined by con-
ventionally and uncritically held beliefs which at times thwart
individual aspirations. And all this he portrays not uncritically.
But his criticism is directed against particular failings and
deficiences of that society, and in a very particular manner,
not against the existence of nineteenth-century urban society
as such.

'The woman's predicament', a critic wrote à propos of *Anna
Karenina*,[1] 'is the test of the moral and human worth of any given
state of society.' For Fontane too, in a large number of his stories
and novels, 'the woman's predicament', especially in adultery,
enables him to probe the qualities of the contemporary social
world; and this he does most finely in *Effi Briest* (1895). Since the
adulterous situation has, for the nineteenth-century realists,
assumed the function of a typical theme, Fontane's particular
contribution to it may best be made clear by a set of comparisons.
On this theme, Flaubert and Tolstoy too write from indisputably
given points of view; and in all three instances the characters of
their heroines are fashioned, in the course of the three novels I
propose to compare, partly by their socially determined qualities
and partly by their inwardly generated impetus away from the
normal conventions and proprieties of their enveloping world.

All three heroines seek happiness, which for them takes the form
of erotic fulfilment. Yet each seeks it differently, partly because
each is determined in her search by a social environment whose
pressure and sanctions are different, and partly because the character of each responds differently, that is more or less vigorously,
to that pressure.

In *Effi Briest* the social determination is the most severe. Effi's
whole life, even the form of her violation of the social proprieties,

---

[1] Ernest Rhys, in his Introduction to the *Everyman* translation (London
1935); the quotations in the latter part of this chapter are drawn from this
translation by R. S. Townsend.

is determined by the severe code of the Prussian civil service aristocracy in which she was born, into which she marries, and in which she spends almost all her days. She begins life on the carefree margins of the code, in her parental home in the Prussian provinces, in a scene of delicious and unforgettable exuberance. When her mother calls her away from the swing on which she has been playing, to tell her that a suitor has arrived to ask for her hand in marriage, she calls back to her companions, 'Go on playing—I'll be back very soon . . .'; and in a sense her brief life in the world is encompassed by that phrase, 'I'll be back very soon.' In the course of that life she undergoes certain changes—from her childlike attitude to childishness, and thence, at the end, she returns to her childlike innocence. Yet throughout, her outlook is wholly limited by the aspirations and taboos of her own class. Her marriage to Gert von Instetten, upright, honourable, her senior by twenty years, is suggested to her, not forced upon her, by her parents; it is forced upon her by the social setting of which she is an absolute product in the sense that she is incapable of conceiving any independent aspiration of her own. She has a sort of vague longing for that greater thing which neither her husband nor anyone else around her can appease, the longing for love. But this longing is neither strong nor intelligent, it remains childish or at best childlike, merely tucked away in a parenthetic aside. Her lover, 'der arme Crampas', a slightly roué Army major, can be no better than he is nor more significant as a lover, since he represents a fairly exact gratification of her childish longing and no more. Twice in the course of the novel the theme of love is explicitly broached by Effi, both times in conversation with her mother. Early on, just after the opening scene, she describes what she hopes for from her marriage to von Instetten:

Und wenn es Zärtlichkeit und Liebe nicht sein können, weil Liebe, wie Papa sagt, doch nur ein Paperlapapp ist (was ich aber nicht glaube), nun, dann bin ich für Reichtum und ein vornehmes Haus, ein ganz vornehmes, wo Prinz Friedrich zur Jagd kommt, auf Elchwild oder Auerhahn, oder wo der alte Kaiser	*And if it isn't to be tenderness and love because, as Papa says, love is just fiddle-faddle (though I don't really believe him)—well, then I'm all for being rich and having a fine house, a really fine house, where Prince Frederick might come for the deerstalking or the grouse-shooting or the old Emperor might drive up*

vorfährt und für jede Dame, auch	*and address a gracious word to all*
für die jungen, ein gnädiges Wort hat	*the ladies, even the young ones.*
(Chapter 4).[1]	

Throughout the story Effi's experience of love remains immature, it never emerges from those brackets into which she put it in her early mood of childish sophistication. And at the end, when 'being rich and having a fine house' have ceased to matter, she thinks once more about that love which she had neither dismissed nor taken seriously. At the point of death, she has matured at least so far that she understands von Instetten, and in her description of him she describes her own predicament:

Er hat ganz recht gehabt. . . . Lass es	*He was right. . . . Let him know that*
ihn wissen, dass ich in dieser Ueber-	*I felt sure of that before I died. For he*
zeugung gestorben bin. Denn er	*had a great deal of good in his nature*
hatte viel Gutes in seiner Natur und	*and was as noble as anyone can be*
war so edel, wie jemand sein kann,	*who is without real love.*
der ohne rechte Liebe ist (Chapter	
36).	

And her characterisation is both similar and complementary to von Instetten's understanding of Effi, the main tone of which is set with the words 'Liebenswürdigkeit' and 'heiterer Charme'. Of course, the causes of the fundamental deficiency at which she hints are different: in von Instetten the cause is very likely natural, in Effi it is social; in other words, he and his like determine her outlook while she remains passive. Yet they both live the normal life of a society which has no place for love, no central place at any rate, a society whose laws and morality are built on a foundation of formal honour, of appearances.

Hand in hand with this determination of the central character

---

[1] The phrase 'ich bin für . . .' for instance, or, in other passages, the omission of definite articles to suggest ease of reference and the speaker's *dégagé* attitude, are among the many signs of Fontane's sureness of touch, of his virtuosity in conveying the social dimensions in conversational turns; so is his use of foreign words, mainly French but also English, which for most *German* novelists (as for Tolstoy, but not for Austrians) become clichés connoting alienness and insincerity or affectation; in Fontane's conversations they are signs of social ease and of perfect accommodation.

as well as the major subsidiary personages goes Fontane's narrative manner, which is predominantly social. The houses in Effi's native Hohen-Cremmen and in Kessin, where von Instetten is posted, the two flats in Berlin, are a direct measure of the character's social standing. Guests and parties and recitals and office discussions, the honeymoon journey and visits to spas, servants, neighbours, and state-visits—these are the daily round of the Instettens' life, it is these that are most fully and carefully described. Thus every discussion of Effi's parents turns on the relation, as they see it, between their child's fortunes and what is done in their station in life. It is, again, characteristic of the manner in which Fontane presents his story that, while the parents are only vaguely and uneasily conscious of their responsibility for their child's personal happiness, they are very precisely conscious of their obligation towards the society to which they belong. The perfection and sustainedness with which Fontane evokes this entire social world have no equal in earlier nineteenth-century German prose, and only in Thomas Mann a worthy successor. The only blemish in the novel—the imagery of a mysterious Chinaman which Effi discovers on a set of chairs in Kessin, symbolical of her longing for freedoms far away—is a very minor one, a piece of bric-à-brac left over by 'poetic realism'.[1] For the rest—and it is virtually the whole work—theme, agents, and narrative manner achieve a rare degree of integration.

Emma Bovary's outlook and marriage (the novel was published in 1857) are no less directly determined by the society of Yonville and Rouen; she too suffers from a feeling of deprivation whose first sign is boredom. Since hers is a character with a potentiality for passion, she is in a sense more successful in replacing the life which her society forces upon her by another kind of life. Here again husband and enclosing society are identified. Charles—with

---

[1] Similarly Keller feels the need to introduce a bit of 'poetic' symbolism into *Romeo und Julia auf dem Dorfe* in the form of a sinister fiddler who is said to be the rightful owner of the disputed strip of land.

all his dullness and oafishness and mediocrity and perpetual
financial worries—is as much the representative of French provincial society as the severe, schoolmasterish and righteous Gert von
Instetten is of the Prussian code. However, unlike Effi, Emma has
vast imaginative resources at her disposal. It is irrelevant to our
comparison that in describing Emma's fanciful dream-life
Flaubert's aim was to denigrate the Romantic outlook; it is the
fancies and dreams themselves that matter, not their literary
pedigree. Both her lovers are only rarely presented to us as independent of Emma's fanciful view of them. They are what she
desires them to be—an escape, for her, from the world in which
she is constrained to live. The determination of the social scene
here is if anything more powerful than in Fontane. For while in
Effi Briest we meet characters—like the apothecary Gieshübler and
Effi's maid Roswitha—who, by virtue of their own strength of
mind and integrity, stand outside the code, there are no such
characters in *Madame Bovary*. Flaubert, it has been often remarked,
does not portray a single wholly lovable character. Every one of
them, even Emma's father, is tainted by some silliness or vanity
or lack of dignity, each belongs inescapably to a world of pettiness, greed, rancour or malice. Even Charles, in that last foolish
remark of his after Emma's funeral, is deprived of the dignity of
true suffering—

> Il ajouta même un grand mot, le seul qu'il ait jamais dit: 'C'est la faute de la
> fatalité' (Book 3, Chapter 11).

—which is a foolish remark because it is in no sense fate that has
been her undoing but the life of inauthenticity to which she was
reared and which she chose, knowing no other; and thus Charles
too remains ignorant of Emma's true character. Only Flaubert
knows her, and he portrays her singlemindedly, with a telling,
at times a deadly precision. Her emotional strength intimates to
us that she (unlike Effi) might not be incapable of love, and this
awareness we have is almost the only source of sympathy for her
that Flaubert allows us to feel. Yet her lovers fail her, because they
are the creatures of her wayward imagination and of her trivial
longings. Even Rodolphe and Léon she does not love, but what
she loves is herself loving them:

Elle se répétait: 'J'ai un amant! un amant!' se délectant à cette idée comme à celle d'une autre puberté qui lui serait survenue. (Book 1, Chapter 9).

With all this sultry, sentimental temperament of hers she never steps outside the society of Yonville and Rouen. She desires what her neighbours desire, she spurns what they spurn, she measures with their yardstick, she would use them as they use her, both her heedless desire to get to Paris and its utter frustration are what every other provincial lady has experienced, though less vividly; they are all potential adulteresses, while Emma is both a potential and an actual one, being more determined than they are to gratify her desires. Measured by any adult standards—that is, by the standards implied in Flaubert's harsh irony—her own sensibility is fundamentally defective, it is spent on voluptuousness and trivialities. Though superior to Effi in the purposefulness of her desires, she too never envisages human love in its fullest, wholly untrivial form, she too is incapacitated for such a love by being imprisoned in her world. This condition of hers is reflected in the very structure of the novel, which opens and closes not with her but with Charles. Yet the manner in which this impact on her is portrayed by Flaubert is not social (as with Fontane) but psychological. L'Heureux, Homais, Binet, the beggar and the priest—all these live in some small measure lives of their own. But to an overwhelming extent they are a part of Emma's character— they are a part of that exquisitely woven and intricate web of motives and reactions which is Emma's mind. Thus, without hesitation and without scruples, Flaubert 'unmasks' (as his admirer Nietzsche would have said) her religiosity as the most intensified form of her self-love, of her self-indulgence and complex senti- mentality.[1] And to this psychological 'unmasking' belong also Flaubert's detailed descriptions of Emma's sexual life—fairly

---

[1] In Book 1, Chapter 5, the girl's religiose temper (*'Les comparaisons de fiancé, d'époux, d'amant céleste et de mariage éternel qui reviennent dans les sermons lui soulevaient au fond de l'âme des douceurs inattendues'*) is fundamentally the same as the dying woman's mood in Book 3, Chapter 8 (*'Elle tourna sa figure lentement, et parut saisie de joie à voir tout à coup l'étole violette, sans doute retrouvant au milieu d'un apaisement extraordinaire la volupté perdue de ses premiers élancements mystiques . . .'*).

daring for their time and fairly reticent for ours. These can have no parallel in Fontane, because the social dimension in which he presents Effi's life doesn't allow for such explicitness. Although Fontane is very far from acquiescing in the code, he offers no effective alternative to it—it is part of his realism that in the Prussian set-up liberal-mindedness *is* ineffective—nor does he allow himself anything like Flaubert's radical rejection; he is as little sarcastic as Flaubert is tolerant.

How catching was the Flaubertian manner of psychological unmasking may be seen in a Portuguese novel on the same theme, Eça de Quieroz's *Cousin Basilio* (1878),[1] set in contemporary Lisbon. Once again we have the exposure of an oppressive, sultry *milieu*, done unsparingly, with deadly accuracy and a cold eye for every sham detail; once again an unsuspecting husband, a worthless lover, a heroine, Luiza, who has little beyond her 'romantic' imagination to fall back on. Like Rouen, Lisbon is to the heroine an all-too-distant suburb of Paris. At the same time Eça introduces two interesting variations. The social pressure is sanctioned, more directly than in Flaubert, by an obscurantist religious ethos in the person of an old family servant, who effectively blackmails the adulteress and whose death Luiza takes as a sign of divine wrath. Luiza is thus weaker than Emma (as Jorge, her husband, is less oafish than Charles), Luiza's superstitions have a greater hold on her mind. (The religious pressure thus resembles somewhat the social pressure to which Effi is subjected, but Effi's maid, Roswitha, is on the side of charity and forgiveness.) Not that Eça's sympathies are with the religious point of view. On the contrary, by introducing a third man, Sebastian, a bachelor-friend of the married couple, who is humane, warm-hearted and free from all bigotry, Eça is pointing the way towards that tolerance and understanding which are the greatest virtues in Fontane's moral scheme of things, though as with Fontane tolerance and compassion make no difference to the course of events. Sebastian fulfils a rôle somewhat similar to that of the apothecary Gieshübler, Effi's liberal-minded friend at Kessin, but is more closely involved when the adultery is dis-

[1] It was recently translated by Roy Campbell, London 1953.

covered. The more melancholy is Sebastian's ineffectiveness. In the moment of crisis he is entirely powerless to prevent its worst consequences, the forces not of passion but of bigotry triumph, and Luiza's death confirms their victory.

The novels I have been considering so far have in common the social determination of their heroines in their acts of adultery. The intensity of that pressure differs, the quality of the heroines' response differs; and so does the manner in which the ensuing situations are analysed: in Fontane this manner is social, in Flaubert it is psychological.[1] Turning now to Tolstoy's *Anna Karenina* (1875-7), we are above all struck by the heroine's abundant strength to fashion her life. She too, of course, has her own 'circle', which follows her, inescapably, from St Petersburg wherever she goes, even to Italy; yet her relation to it is not anywhere nearly as passive as it is in Flaubert and Fontane. The society to which she belongs is less rigid, less righteous and less petty; it is not beyond a bit of nepotism here, a minor bribery there; things can be hushed up in St Petersburg in a way they cannot be hushed up in Yonville or Berlin. Because of this, and because the laws of this society are entirely embodied in the people around Anna (while Fontane's society is conscious of a Hegelian '*etwas*' over and above the individual members that compose the Berlin 'set'), the Russian aristocracy and even Anna herself can decide, on this or that specific occasion, what is and what is not 'done' according to the convention. This is seen most clearly in her relationship with Count Vronsky. It is significant that, quite unlike Emma and Effi, Anna does not have to go through a degrading phase of lies and subterfuges. She tells her husband of her adultery, she forces him—and he too, like the other two husbands,

---

[1] Fontane does not mention Flaubert's name, either in his published works (see E. E. F. von Helms, *German Criticism of Gustave Flaubert*, New York 1939, p. 3), or in his posthumously published letters (see *Briefwechsel von T. F. und Paul Heyse*, ed. E. Petzet, Berlin [1928], and *T.F.: Briefe an Georg Friedländer*, ed. K. Schreinert, Heidelberg 1945).

is representative of the world into which she was born—she
forces him and therefore all society to recognise and even to
accept what she has done. She thus creates a situation which is
quite unthinkable in *Effi Briest*, for Instetten and his 'set' would
never accept it. And such a situation is difficult to imagine with
Emma, if only because the secrecy of her love-affair is an integral
part of that turgid sensuality on which she lives, and thus a part
of the structure of the novel itself. For Anna alone secretiveness is
psychologically redundant: she is forced to face the issue of her
adultery directly, with a minimum of distraction from social
pressure—a minimum determined by the realistic convention
within which Tolstoy is writing.

Of the three women, Anna is the only wholly adult character.
Her beauty and her generosity, her warmth of heart and her
compassion, above all her capacity—not merely her potentiality
but her true capacity—for a feeling which is neither immature
nor precocious, neither weak nor wayward, but unabatingly
passionate—it is all these qualities which give her character a
dimension of depth that in the other books is lacking. Tolstoy, it has been said, has an 'almost sexual love for his heroine',[1]
and it is this love for her (as opposed to Fontane's tolerant compassion, and Flaubert's detached psychological knowledge) which
informs almost every phase of Tolstoy's presentation of Anna.
Turgenyev, Matthew Arnold and a host of less distinguished
critics have all given the novel that highest praise which is
traditionally associated with the names of Homer and Shakespeare: it is Life, not Art, they exclaimed. And they meant by this,
I think, that the experience encompassed in the novel, and the
novelist's criterion of selection and presentation, are uniquely
generous, uniquely wide. Yet the compass is meaningfully (not
haphazardly) limited, and the criterion of selection is still strict.
Take the Levin story. It is very far from being a Utopian self-
indulgence on Tolstoy's part, as some critics have condescendingly
called it. On the contrary, it dovetails with and complements the
story of Anna's own life, for through his marriage and his work
with his peasant community Levin has at least a glimpse of that

[1] See Lionel Trilling, *op. cit.*, p. 69.

good life which Anna cannot attain.[1] And the fact that Tolstoy
views Levin's 'moment of truth' with irony and shows it to be
brief and unsustained—that he sees Levin realistically—should not
deceive us about the importance of Levin's insight for the balance
of the novel as a whole: it is a moment in a moral development
which goes in the opposite direction to Anna's. When he shows
Anna flirting with Levin (during one of his rare visits to town),
Tolstoy leaves us in no doubt as to the precariousness of Levin's
hard-won virtue; more than that, he points to the potential
danger that lurks at the intersection of the two opposing lines of
moral development.

And with this term, moral development, we are at the centre of
Tolstoy's preoccupation in *Anna Karenina*. It is neither social nor
psychological, though both these narrative modes play important
rôles in the unfolding of the story. If the novel is 'like Life', it
is not the 'life' of Naturalism, it is an image of life shot through
with morality. The development which Anna experiences—and
there is virtually no development in the other two novels[2]—takes
a moral form. The development consists in Anna's gradual
realisation that the life she leads with Vronsky is unjustifiable on
moral grounds, that almost all that presses in upon her embodies
the morality from which she has defected. Take Alexei Karenin
himself. He has of course nothing of Charles Bovary's oafishness.
His manner reminds us a little of von Instetten's pedantry and
self-righteousness, he too is a bit of a schoolmaster, and has a
great deal of the inhuman bureaucrat. Beyond this, he fails his
wife in her emotional and erotic demands, he is unable to respond
to her yearning for love. At Anna's sick bed 'something like life
begins to stir in his deeply buried human core, but . . . this stirring
is much too weak to establish new human relations between
them.'[3] And since she not only yearns for love but is capable of

---

[1] Thomas Mann, who calls Levin 'the real hero of the novel', points to the
many occasions when Tolstoy voices through Levin his own beliefs and doubts;
see Mann's essay on the novel in *Adel des Geistes*, Stockholm 1945, pp. 323, 329 f.

[2] Effi's return to her childlike innocence has already been noted. Emma too
does not develop—she merely runs the whole gamut of her fancies.

[3] Georg Lukács, *Studies in European Realism*, London 1950, p. 188.

it, her deprivation is indeed more vital than either Effi's or Emma's. Yet when all is said and done, Karenin unlike Charles Bovary retains his human dignity; and unlike Instetten he remains free from great moral guilt. In the face of the authentic demands which he cannot meet he does what men in such situations are prone to do—he shelters behind a façade of righteousness. He becomes a hypocrite, anxious to keep up appearances, he turns religiose and 'holier than thou'—and yet, for all that, imperfectly and intermittently he does represent the morality of family life against which Anna has offended. It is because she knows this that Anna speaks to their son of Karenin only charitably and without reproach; and her words move us because they have the ring of passionate sincerity. Tolstoy (unlike Flaubert) is unable to portray a single character as wholly unlovable. And this implies, not a lack of moral discrimination, but on the contrary Tolstoy's innermost moral belief that all manner of people, simple and sophisticated, innocent and foolish (like Dolly) and corrupt (like Anna's brother Stiva) are, in spite of all their feelings, capable of *some* degree of moral goodness; that the moral commandment remains valid even when it is enforced through such a dessicated character as Karenin; and that the divergent insights all go to prove that life is what it is: a highly moral affair. This absolute anti-gnosticism of Tolstoy's has caused some misunderstanding and censure among his critics, beginning with Peter Kropotkin[1] and ending with the Soviet critics of our own times. They make the same accusation against him, roughly speaking, as that which Hebbel[2] had made against the author of *Die Wahlverwandschaften*: that he conforms to the social taboos of his day. Yet all that Tolstoy (and, incidentally, Goethe) does here is to express a subtlety and a wisdom of which a writer like Lawrence was not capable. The wisdom lies in the belief that society—the society of his day—and institutions—the institutions of marriage —are not wholly incapable of showing forth the moral law, the highest governance that men have set up above themselves; that it is not—or not only—the universal historical process or some

---

[1] *Russian Literature: Ideals and Realities* (London 1916), p. 134.
[2] In his Preface to *Maria Magdalene*.

other large abstraction which embodies this law, but certain facets of our own conscious lives within the concrete limitations of a given society.

Of course, to single out the moral strand of the novel is to do violence to Tolstoy's design, which shows the moral embedded in the social. Yet it is hard to see how without such a distinction we can ever come close to the fullness of his achievement. It is just this fullness that Marxist criticism, even at its finest, fails to convey when it insists that there is no distinction, that the moral is a product of the social—when it does violence to that balance of self and world which is among the realists' finest human insights. Georg Lukács shows convincingly enough how Anna (not to speak of Karenin and Vronsky) is the product of her environment:

> *Anna Karenina lives—with a husband whom she does not love and whom she has married for conventional reasons, and with a lover whom she loves passionately—a life just like the life of other women of her own sphere.* The only difference *is that she follows this road consistently to the end, ruthlessly drawing every conclusion and not permitting insoluble contradictions to blunt their edges in the banality of everyday life.*[1]

And elsewhere he suggests, a little less relevantly, how Tolstoy's genius avoids the naturalistic *impasse*, because he never presents merely 'the average man', in whom 'the social contradictions blunt each other' and thus lead to 'immobility [and] monotony in ... artistic presentation'.[2] This is somewhat less relevant, because it describes a mode of writing it would never have occurred to Tolstoy to adopt. But in all this argument the important question to ask is not: Why does Tolstoy portray Anna rather than some other, 'average' woman?, but: Why is Anna precisely *not* like the women around her? To which the only answer the Marxist scheme has to offer is the depressingly 'literary' answer: Because Tolstoy needed an outstanding character, etc. Whereas the true answer lies in Anna's passion. And that passion, which precisely distinguishes her, is, by virtue of that very distinction,

---

[1] *Op. cit.*, p. 172, my emphasis.   [2] *Op. cit.*, p. 170.

not a product of social circumstances but of her own freedom,[1] and her freedom is her point of contact with morality.

Anna's changing and deteriorating relationship with all the people around her shows that Tolstoy too was intent upon showing the social implications of her adultery. And again, his detailed and precise tracing out of her gradual loss of Vronsky's love (in Book 5) is presented in psychological terms more restrained than, yet every whit as precise as, Flaubert's. Not only that—the deterioration, in Vronsky certainly, is caused by the lack of social purpose and the uprooting which his affair with Anna entails for him. All this leaves its imprint on Anna as nothing comparable ever would on the other two heroines. Her very beauty—severe and passionate and grave from the very beginning, at the ball where she meets Vronsky for the second time—becomes graver, distraught and haunted as the story comes to its climax; it comes to reflect her distraught mind—her beauty records her own maturing awareness of her moral situation. Tolstoy's analysis of Anna's mind (for instance in the *monologues intérieurs* during her last carriage rides) shows him a master of that psychological motivation for which Flaubert has often been praised. Yet the psychological illumination of her state of mind is no more Tolstoy's end than is an attack on capitalist society. Her dilemma—that she cannot live with Vronsky and that she cannot live without him— presents itself to her in concrete terms: she sees him growing cold towards her, she sees that her jealousies drive him away from her: we know, and she comes to know, that her jealousies reflect her inability to live apart from her family. Yet hers is fundamentally neither a psychological nor a social dilemma, but a moral one.

---

[1] Lukács asserts (but does no more than assert) the opposite: 'What is outside the average in Anna Karenina's figure and fate is not some individually pathological exaggeration of a personal passion, but the clear manifestation of the social contradictions inherent in *bourgeois* love and marriage' (*op. cit.*, p. 176)— as though the only kind of experience that lies outside the 'social contradictions' were pathological. He then goes on to say that 'When Anna Karenina breaks through the limits of the commonplace, she *merely* brings to the surface in tragically clear intensification the contradictions latently present (although their edges may be blunted) in every *bourgeois* love and marriage.'; the '*merely*' which I have italicised amounts to no less than the distinction of Anna's character.

REALISM AND TOLERANCE: THEODOR FONTANE 329

Unlike Effi, she is not afraid of being found out. Unlike Emma, she does not find that her lover falls absurdly short of the creations of her sultry imagination, for though he has 'spots of commonness', Vronsky is a man for all that, and the Epilogue shows him to be a man if not of honour and sensitivity, yet aware, at least, of his own share of guilt.[1] Ultimately her problem is as simple as its resolution is tragic: Anna is desperately afraid of losing him because she knows, in her heart of hearts, that she has no moral right to keep him.

Now, the moral theme enters into the other two novels also, but it is never embodied in the heroines. In Flaubert's novel it is embodied in nobody, it is merely asserted by the author. The implicit judgement he passes on the actions of his heroine is fastidious rather than moral, it is in his precise and sharp vision of her ineptitudes (at the end of the novel the vision is shared, at least in some degree, by Emma herself). Yet the fullest treatment of the life of inauthenticity is not 'aesthetic' nor fastidious but moral. And when (inevitably, I believe) Flaubert's moral concern does emerge, most unexpectedly, when he suddenly blurts out a judgement as if he could restrain it no longer, the judgement is unsustained by the rest of the story; it is strangely naïve, a mere indignation. Such an unmotivated outburst occurs for instance when Emma, now at the end of her tether, goes to see her old lover Rodolphe, to borrow from him the money she owes L'Heureux:

> Elle partit donc vers la Huchette, sans s'apercevoir qu'elle courait s'offrir à ce qui l'avait tantôt si fort exaspérée, ni se douter le moins du monde de cette prostitution (Book 3, Chapter 7).

At other times (as in the death scene) the grounds for a moral judgement are more carefully laid—but even then some triviality, some irremediable absurdity of the situation catches the novelist's eye and deflects his pen into irritation or nausea. In Flaubert, then,

---

[1] Thus the function of the last part of Tolstoy's novel is different from that of Flaubert's concluding chapters. While the latter are designed to complete the presentation of Emma's mind, the former presents a validation—at least a partial one—of Anna's love.

the moral theme, although not wholly absent, is presented poorly and intermittently, it remains unrelated to the main theme of the novel, unsustained by the substance of the story itself.

In Fontane the matter is more complex. The nearest we ever come to a statement of the moral theme is in Chapter 27, in that magnificent scene between von Instetten and Wüllersdorf, his friend and colleague, at the Berlin ministry, which Wandrey in his excellent book on Fontane has called 'the greatest conversation scene in the German novel'.[1] Yet the scene is not a converging of two opposite points of view[2] but the elucidation of a single complex one. Wüllersdorf is Instetten's *alter ego*: by disclosing to him the details of Effi's infidelity with Crampas, von Instetten forces himself to do what is his duty according to the code by which he lives. His brief reluctance to challenge Effi's lover to a duel betrays neither cowardice nor moral scruples but his lack of passion, his lack of a passionate conviction of anything, even of 'the Code'. By calling it 'our service to an idol', Wüllersdorf intimates (and von Instetten agrees) that the code is different from true morality, that society does not embody morality. By calling it 'an auxiliary construction' (an expression, incidentally, which Fontane was fond of using in his letters), Wüllersdorf argues that we must for ever make do with provisional measures, which we must beware of taking too absolutely. The other meaning of '*Notkonstruktion*', implied but not expressed in the novel, relates to the origin of the Prussian code in the legendary rigours of life under Frederick the Great. The emergency atmosphere of those days is now 'really' outdated—yet the code is designed to perpetuate it; there is nothing else to hold society together. Wüllersdorf suggests a different set of values. His motto is, 'Forget and forgive'. And he shows up the code at its most absurd when he asks Instetten exactly how many years (over and above the six and a half years since Effi's adultery) would have to pass for Instetten to let bygones be bygones. (Effi's parents too 'count the years' before they agree to take her back to Hohen-

Cremmen.) But Wüllersdorf knows that tolerance is something that men like Instetten and the society to which they both belong cannot afford. They both know that a duel will only bring misery or worse to everyone concerned; why then fight, asks Wüllersdorf.

'*Because it must be so* [Instetten replies]. *I've thought about it a great deal. One isn't merely a single person, one belongs to a whole—and we must constantly consider that whole, we're entirely dependent on it* . . . *One doesn't have to be happy, one has no claim at all to happiness* . . . *But there's a* something *that evolves*[1] *when people live together. Well, that* something *exists, and it has certain rules and regulations, and according to these rules we're used to judging everything, other people and ourselves. You just can't offend against them. Society will treat you with contempt, and you end up by putting a bullet through your head*. . .*!' Wüllersdorf had jumped up. 'I think it's terrible that you should be right, but you* are *right.* . . . *The world is what it is, things don't happen the way we want them to happen but the way others do. All that about "Divine Judgement", as some people highfalutinly call it, is of course a lot of nonsense—it's nothing of the sort—on the contrary, our cult of honour is service to an idol. But as long as the idol is accepted we must submit.'*

The dissociation of the moral from the social that is expressed here lands Fontane in a dilemma which he cannot solve on the social plane. The very fact that he makes Instetten the advocate of the social code is significant: for Instetten of course is treated with detachment and irony throughout.[2] Since Instetten is treated ironically, the view he stands for is *a fortiori* of problematic value in moral terms. Yet what else is there? The code is all-powerful and iniquitous, yet Effi certainly doesn't show it up as such, because she is too weak, because (it comes to the same thing) she is too much involved in it. And the morality that exists *outside* the ordinance of the code is an untested thing.

Effi, then, is not the code's antagonist. She too, after all, is merely a victim, an example of that 'morality of inertia' which

---

[1] '*Aber im Zusammenleben mit den Menschen hat sich ein Etwas herausgebildet.* . . .' My translation is not very satisfactory. An English reader may wish to be assured that Fontane is, here too, using nothing but the *conversational* tone of German.

[2] It is the sort of irony that is heightened and also a little hardened in Thomas Mann's portrayal of Thomas Buddenbrook; other parallels, with similar changes, are Effi—Tony, Gieshübler—Gosch.

consists in '*not* making moral decisions'. It may well be true that
such an attitude 'constitutes a large part of the normal life of
mankind',[1] but by confining himself to it the novelist misses the
finest and most powerful effects his art can yield, those moments
of which we can say, 'What a fall was there!' Consistently enough,
Fontane has portrayed characters who are lacking in passion and
who may consequently be shown within a range of experience
for which a direct invocation of the moral theme is not required.
Effi has no doubt offended against morality as well as against the
social taboos. But by the time the code becomes operative she is
no longer considered guilty. All we know is that her guilt was
not beyond the possibility of expiation, whereas von Instetten's
duel with Crampas is, since it makes him into something much
like a cold-blooded murderer. At the very end of the book,
when Effi returns to her parents' house in Hohen-Cremmen, a
higher kind of justice is hinted at: 'The plane-trees with which
the book opens and closes are its only metaphysical symbols,' a
student once wrote. Metaphysical or not, the plane-trees do
symbolise that higher justice whose law Effi has fulfilled. Yet
what is significant here, what a comparison with Tolstoy makes
abundantly clear, is that the fulfilment of that justice has been
achieved wholly outside the complexities of adult society, outside
Fontane's social theme, apart from what Mr Forster once called
'the world of anger and telegrams'.

'Vengeance is mine: I will repay', is the motto that Tolstoy takes
for his book from St Paul's letter to the Romans. Yet the critics, in
their eagerness to point to the 'life' of Tolstoy's novel, have been
curiously reticent about the moral theme. 'It is difficult to believe',
writes one of them, 'that Tolstoy considered Anna's unhappy end
to be the righteous dispensation of an avenging deity.'[2] In fact,
Tolstoy leaves the question of a supernatural sanction for the
moral law unasked. Another critic confines himself to saying

[1] See Lionel Trilling in his essay on Edith Wharton, *op. cit.*, pp. 37 ff.
[2] D. Leon, *Tolstoy, his Life and Work*, London 1954, p. 174.

that 'Anna defied the laws of nature—nature quietly extracted retribution'.[1] Again, it was her *nature* which remained unsatisfied in her marriage with Karenin, it was natural inclination and longing which found their fulfilment in her life with Vronsky. Not nature but her innermost awareness of the moral law—wholly concrete, never (in her) explicit or abstract, always sustained by actual, living situations—it is her growing inward preoccupation with her moral guilt which first imperils her love and finally disables her for life itself. Her 'unhappy end' is intimated again and again throughout the story by *leitmotif*, symbol and anticipation, the moral law is terribly vindicated in that anguish which is born with her love for Vronsky, which becomes inseparable from it and which grows as that love becomes impossible. Percy Lubbock[2] has criticised the book by saying that Anna's crisis—that is, her falling in love with Vronsky—comes too early in the story, before we know her well enough. Yet surely such criticism presupposes a complexity of character and outlook which we do not look for in Anna at all. When she married Karenin, she was presumably an 'average' society lady. After that, all we need to know of her is in fact all we are told: that she is now a full-grown, normal, passionate woman, capable of a human relationship fundamentally different from that of her marriage. The rest— and it is virtually the whole story—follows on directly from that original and utterly normal situation.

The *form* of Anna's death, suicide, is determined by her psychological and social situation. So is Emma's suicide, and so (with very little less convincingness) is Effi's early death. But only of Anna's death can we say that it is the vindication of a *moral* law, since it is only she who has drained the cup of human passion. Effi's is a thirst for excitement; Emma's for refinement; Anna's is a thirst for love. And 'the greatest of these is love', for it alone, of these three, reaches to the wholly untrivial ground of morality. Anna's suicide is an instrument of punishment, the only form of expiation open to her.

But how can Anna's suicide be a *morally* motivated act? To see

---

[1] Ernest Simmons, *Leo Tolstoy*, London 1949, p. 347.
[2] *The Craft of Fiction*, London 1926, pp. 243-4.

it as a form of punishment is not to say that it is the form decreed
for her by God. (Anyway, the 'I' of the Pauline motto is for
Tolstoy not God but the moral universe, whose relation to God
Tolstoy here leaves unexplored.) Nor is this form decreed for her
by morality. The matter is less abstruse: This is how (Tolstoy is
saying) the voice of conscience speaks in *that* human soul, this is
what, in her particular circumstances, *she* chooses, how *she* understands her moral situation. (And the fact that she intends her deed
also to bring punishment on others, especially Vronsky, is further
proof of its particularity.) In decreeing her punishment, Tolstoy
never goes beyond the *human* view of the moral-spiritual law.
Morality is his narrative mode. He 'judges' her only in the sense
of showing the consequences of her conduct according to the
logic of the novel's morality—as a painter 'judges' the distances
in his picture according to the logic of his composition. It is an
ironical thought that Tolstoy alone among these three writers
was not much concerned with the final form of his work, that
by the time he had finished it, in 1877, he was already off on his
'religious crisis', and left the final pruning to his friend, the
philosopher Strakhov.[1] The style is discursive, apparently loose
and undisciplined, apparently without any other distinction than
that it traces out, unemphatically and without any conceits, one
event of the story after another. Yet this very accumulation of
words is organised and shot through with a moral purpose, the
descriptive words and symbols being kept in their proper relation
to the theme unobtrusively, the precision and sharpness of outline heightening into brief moral judgements at the points where
the story's narrative structure is most firmly established.

The 'law' is to Tolstoy palpable and palpitating reality—a fact,
out there in life and in the 'life' of his novel. In one sense Tolstoy's
attitude towards it[2] is not wholly unlike Fontane's attitude towards 'the Code': he may well wish the law to be different, yet
he cannot change it. But the final impression with which he leaves
us is incomparably more powerful than anything in Fontane.

---

[1] See Simmons, *op. cit.*, p. 346.
[2] Is it relevant to add that in 1877 Tolstoy's own family affairs were in a
disastrous muddle?

The law that is at work here is shown to have an objective, *anti-existentialist validity*: Tolstoy's intimation is not that 'they' (Karenin and his entourage) are right but that she is wrong—yet, in her pride and passion, beautifully wrong.

Given Tolstoy's deep involvement in Anna's life *and* in the working out of the moral law, it is not surprising that his attitude towards Anna changes in the course of the novel. Many of the things she does—she rides in a man's habit, smokes, plays tennis, practices birth control, takes morphine against insomnia, keeps a disreputable English nurse, discusses Zola and Daudet[1]—he strongly disapproves of. And his judgments on all these iniquities are reflected in her moral disintegration. While she, at first imperfectly aware of the moral implications of her adultery, comes gradually to recognise the law and ultimately (with these implications ever more clearly before her) to detest herself, Tolstoy's attitude too changes and returns to compassion: so that at last his love meets her self-hate, his concern with the moral theme finds its echo in her matured conscience, and she comes as it were to understand his mind. The measure of Tolstoy's achievement is simple enough: he cannot save her, but he never abandons her. His love *and* his judgement make for the same tension as that which informed the Paolo and Francesca story.

Let me now narrow down the comparison I have attempted. Flaubert's preoccupation in *Madame Bovary* is predominantly psychological, and the consistent judgement he passes on his heroine is fastidious or 'aesthetic'. Fontane's preoccupation in *Effi Briest* is social: in that sphere he passes no direct judgements: but he implies an outlook of tolerant humaneness which is embodied in one or two characters on the margins of society, but which is alien to that society and to the code by which it lives. The line of Tolstoy's narrative in *Anna Karenina* is moral, and he shows the moral law at work in a passionate character, that is, in the kind of character that can most fully and most consistently

---

[1] I owe these points to a letter of René Wellek's.

exhibit morality in a novel. I would like to illustrate these three
modes once more by pointing to the three women's relations
with their children. All three children—Emma's Berthe, Effi's
Annchen and Anna's Seryoja—are the offsprings of their unhappy
marriages.

For Emma, her child is as much of a wish-fulfilment as are her
lovers, and as disappointing. At the child's birth she faints from
sheer frustration, because she so intensely wanted a boy. Towards
Berthe she is as fitful and moody as she is towards every single
thing in the world—the child is no more to her than a part of
that romantic miasma which envelops her whole outlook. When
it is burdensome to her she gives it to a woman to look after—
the scene in which she goes to visit Berthe is reminiscent of
Dostoyevsky's child scenes in its squalor and heartlessness.
Flaubert's treatment here has all the sarcasm of his outraged
sensibility, it has all the fastidiousness which in his novel takes the
place of a direct moral judgement:

> ... elle recoucha la petite qui venait de vomir sur sa collerette. La nourrice aussitôt
> vint l'essuyer, protestant qu'il n'y paraitrait pas. 'Elle m'en fait bien d'autres',
> disait-elle. . . . (Book 2, Chapter 3)

and Emma quickly puts the baby down. The child means nothing
to her, it has no life outside her extravagant imagination.[1]

Of this kind of heartlessness Effi Briest is of course quite incapable. Like Anna, she has been forcibly separated from her
child, but a meeting has been arranged—and it turns out as un-
satisfactory as could be. The child has been trained, parrot-wise,
to reject her mother; but what of Effi's attitude towards her?
She is affectionate and loving, she has been longing to see her
little girl, she would give almost anything in the world to see her,
she is prepared to humble herself . . . yet there is a limit to her
affection for the child beyond which she cannot go. Question
after question is rebuffed:

---

[1] See also Book 2, end of Chapter 10, where Emma suddenly—'comme au
retour d'un voyage'—remembers the child, 'qui restait fort ébahie devant cet excès de
tendresse.'

'Will you come to see me often?'
'O yes, if I am allowed . . .'
'Then we can go for a walk in the Prince Albert Gardens.'
'O yes, if I am allowed . . .'
'Or we'll go to Schillings and have ices, pineapple or vanilla.'
'O yes, if I am allowed. . . .'

And at this point Effi's patience is at an end. She says good-bye to the child as gracefully as her frustration, her resentment and her incipient hysteria will allow her. It is her pride that revolts. Of course she will miss the girl. But when all is said and done she can live without her, the presence or absence of the child is for her not a determining factor in her life; in other words, wherever the embodiment of the novel's moral scheme may lie, it is not where we might expect it, in the child-mother relationship.

Finally, there is Anna's meeting with her son Seryoja on the morning of his ninth or tenth birthday. It may well be one of the greatest narrative passages ever written, simply because its greatness, its 'life-likeness', springs from Tolstoy's ability to infuse the meeting with all the passionate tenderness, all the joy and all the anguish of which Anna, of which a complete human being, is capable. This in itself radically distinguishes it from the other two scenes. And this love, this absolute passion which Anna bears for her little boy, is a moral love, a love shot through with knowledge of good and evil. The anguish of her desperate dilemma—that she must leave the boy and that for the life of her she cannot leave him—is perfectly shown forth in her every gesture:

Smiling sleepily, with his eyes still shut, he threw his little arms about her shoulders, and pressing close to her began rubbing his face against her neck and shoulders, exhaling that sweet odour of warmth and sleep that only children have. 'I knew it! I knew you would come on my birthday! I'll get up at once!' And saying this, he began to doze off again. Anna devoured him with her eyes: she could see how much he had changed during her absence. His long bare legs that stretched under the bed-clothes, his thin neck, his short closely cropped curls on the back of his neck, appeared to her now familiar, now strange. She passed her hand all over him, but could not utter a word: the tears choked her. 'Why are you crying, mamma?' he asked, completely awake by this time (Book 5, Chapter 29).

It is in such a detailed and circumstantial way, in this alternation of 'now familiar, now strange'[1] for instance, and in hundreds of little touches lavished mainly upon physical details, that Tolstoy achieves his perfection. Yet we have not done with the scene. With the wisdom of hindsight (which is so often the critic's only insight) we say that the only thing which is needed to complete this scene is the boy's response to his mother's love. In the other two novels it would not occur to us to look for the children's independent response: only here the child too is brought to bear upon the novel's major theme. Hence the scene becomes perfect and complete only when the mother's love-and-anguish is answered by the boy's love-and-anguish. Marvellously, wholly within the compass of the knowledge that is available to him, he responds:

> Now she was unable to say anything. Seryoja understood her. He understood that she was unhappy and that she loved him ... The only thing that puzzled him was that her face should express fear and shame.[2]

Of course he does not and cannot understand the complexity of his mother's moral and social situation: he does not understand the causes of that fear and shame on her face; but he does understand that she loves him with an anguish that nothing can assuage.

Anna's violation of the social code is a trivial matter in comparison with the moral problem which she cannot solve. For a recent Soviet critic to claim that 'Anna's fight with Karenin for her son grows into a fight with fashionable society'[3] is false since she does not fight, since she knows she cannot fight. Her deepest reason for refusing to fight is that she is aware of having violated that which Tolstoy presents to us as the greatest and widest and most absolute law of all, the moral-spiritual law. It is this law which Levin is trying to realise in his marriage and in his farming

---

[1] 'Ona uznala i nyeuznala yevo ...'

[2] 'No Seryozha ponial' vsyo ... No odnovo on nye mog ponyat': pochemu na yeye litsye pokazalis' ispug i styd?' An earlier draft of Anna's meeting with Seryoja (Polnoye sobranie sochinjenii, xx [Moscow 1939], pp. 447–8) does not contain nearly as convincing a working-out of Anna's moral dilemma or of the boy's instinctive grasp of it.

[3] Quoted from H. Gifford's review, 'The Continuity in Russian Criticism', Essays in Criticism, Oxford 1955, pp. 258–9.

activities; it is the reason why Anna's second child—begotten by Vronsky—can never displace Seryoja from her heart; it is this law which is at the root of all those lengthy discussions of the peasant question; even Alexei Karenin has a glimpse of it once or twice; even Vronsky, though not prepared to act on this law, not, at any rate, during Anna's lifetime, even Vronsky is not ignorant of it. To Anna all the world appears as one monstrous accusation, one great cry for punishment. Morality is for her neither gently implied (as it is in the ironical tolerance of Fontane), nor is it deflected beyond her range of awareness (as Flaubert deflects it beyond Emma's range). It is here fully expressed and fully sustained. Tolstoy invokes it as inexorably as Dante had invoked Christian morality in the punishment of Paolo and Francesca; but again, as in Dante, the full meaning of the punishment is inseparable from the beauty of the trespass, from the splendour of Anna's pride. In the bodying-forth of this conflict lies the true aesthetic of the great work of art: Tolstoy's novel is a precise working-out, this side of transcendence, of its motto.

5

The theme of tolerance, which goes through Fontane's entire work, reflects the character of the man, often resigned and occasionally serene, and his self-knowledge: 'We don't belong to the race of Christian martyrs,' he writes to his wife from Brussels in April 1852, at the age of thirty-three, 'and we shall hardly reach the stage where we can rejoice in our suffering—so let us at least take comfort in the knowledge that what we have to bear is precisely what we have been destined for from the beginning.' It is the Schopenhauerian comfort[1] without the Schopenhauerian escape into aestheticism.

Fontane's lack of moral and political fanaticism has its counterpart in his attitude towards his art. Never was there a writer who took the grades to Parnassus more clearsightedly and with finer deliberation. In 1849, aged thirty, Fontane gave up a reasonably good job as a pharmaceutical dispenser and, stimulated by the

---

[1] See his essay, 'On the apparent intent [*anscheinende Absichtlichkeit*] in the destiny of the individual', *ed. cit.*, Vol. VI, pp. 230 ff.

Berlin Revolution, launched out on the uncertain seas of political journalism. In 1870, having made a reputation for himself in the Austrian Campaign of 1866, and as a foreign correspondent, he resigned his post on the Berlin *Kreuz-Zeitung* to start a career as a free-lance journalist. He covered the Franco–Prussian War, and spent a short time as prisoner-of-war on the Ile d'Oléron. Then, in 1876, he accepted a secretaryship in the Prussian Royal Academy of Arts. The post had promised to be a sinecure, turned out to be a humiliating imposition, and again he resigned from it, this time after a few months. Each decision had been taken against the strongest pressure from his wife and family—and what was there to show for it all? Two war books, four volumes of travels in Mark Brandenburg, a slim volume of ballads (sired by Walter Scott), another of impressions of London (the outcome of three long visits). . . . At all events, it seemed late in the day to start complaining: 'When all is said and done,' he writes, 'I've now achieved just about all there is to achieve: love, marriage, two decorations, and an entry in Brockhaus. Only two things are lacking: Privy Councillor and death. The latter I'm sure of, the other I'll manage to do without.'[1]

And now, at the age of fifty-six—the lateness is unparalleled among great writers—he took the last step towards his art. A whole life, varied and not unadventurous, fell into place. Commercial experience, service in the Army, the Civil Service, landed *Junkers* and ironical generals, small shopkeepers, the Jewish and Gentile *nouveaux riches*, Protestant parsons and Catholic *dévots*, Conservative *Von und Zu's* and progressive schoolmasters, a few dogs and elegant Englishmen and picturesque Austrians in the margin, marriages and divorces, bankruptcies and get-rich-quick schemes, duels and illnesses and the gentle sloping down of life towards death—he 'knew it all inside out', it was all merely waiting for him to set it down. And the glory of it was that he had enough time left to do just that. When he died, twenty-two years later, on 20 September 1898, he had accomplished 'what he had been destined for from the beginning'; and when a friend

---

[1] Quoted from Wandrey, *op. cit.*, p. 37. The reference is to a sort of *Who's Who* and encyclopaedia combined.

wrote 'that perhaps more would have become of me if I hadn't been kept back by perpetual "hard struggling",' Fontane replied, 'All that business about "struggling" is superficially true. But even if I had had to struggle less [*wenn ich weniger gestruggelt hätte*], I wouldn't have achieved more. The little that was in me came out that way too. I've no complaint against my fate.'[1] And that, his characteristic understatement apart, is true enough. Seventeen novels and *Novellen*, perhaps half of them major achievements, were indeed a harvest worth waiting for. Though the order in which he lived his life and wrote his books is the opposite to Mr Forster's, the work of both is informed by the same ironically veiled hatred of injustice, by the same acute intelligence and tolerant humaneness. Every one of the characters of 'the least indefatigable of our novelists' could come from Fontane's pen; 'two cheers for aristocracy' could easily be *his* motto.

Yet he had few if any of Mr Forster's literary advantages. The social realism with which he enriched German literature is, as I have suggested, not without its precedents; in Fontane's hands it attains to a subtlety and assurance which it never had before. There is no question here of a problematic attitude towards society, no utopia, and little otherworldliness. All the same, in one important aspect Fontane's work does belong to the tradition I have described: the suggestion is never absent from his novels that private life and morality are one thing and social and political life another, and that the relation of the one to the other is a *passive* one. The particular narrative energy that would show both the social world *and also* the way its ethos is *actively determined* by personal decisions and acts, is not to be found either in that tradition or in his novels. It is as though the creative act of his work—its realism—had exhausted his narrative energy; so that he is left with characters who exhibit the social forces always only by being their victims.

What he gives us, therefore, is not the whole picture: '*il constate seulement*' is no answer to this criticism. The courage which a few of his characters show is the courage of nonconformity

---

[1] Wandrey, *op. cit.*, p. 47.

outside society, not the courage of direct opposition to society. All radical attitudes he sees as liable to deteriorate into fanaticism, personal inadequacy or comic failure. Yet his tolerance implies no lukewarmness, it does not reconcile him to the lot of the victim. Presenting the unwisdom of moral absolutes, he occasionally allows himself a moral condemnation which is no less powerful for being made implicitly and uncensoriously. If he is tolerant of both sides in a social dilemma,[1] this is not because he is unsure of the rights and wrongs of the case, but because he has so much sympathy with those who are neither very sure in their knowledge nor very strong in acting upon it. It is they who engage his imagination—but not in the Flaubertian manner, not as a mere spectacle. True, his political sympathies are 'after all' aesthetically tinged, as when he writes, 'Every day I become more democratic, and the most I can take is the real aristocracy. All that lies between— *Spiessbürger, bourgeois*, officials, the "cultured" class generally —gives me little joy.'[2] But his avoidance of all moral and political absolutism, of all ideology, is not 'compensated for' by an 'absolute aestheticism': he is as unstrained in his attitude towards the art which he had nurtured in a lifetime of preparation as in everything else. Hence he is incapable of that radical irony and distance which Thomas Mann occasionally puts between himself and *his* characters. Yet Fontane's ironical sympathy and affection are not the least part of Mann's heritage—as is made abundantly clear in the two essays[3] in which Mann's pays homage to the mentor of his early work: this is why his summing-up of Fontane's attitude—'responsible disengagement'[4] remains the last word on the subject. Fontane's 'disengagement' is obvious enough; but its qualifying condition is 'responsibility' towards his own work: that is, not towards the absolutism of *fin de siècle* aesthetics—in *that* controversy he was on the side of Ibsen and Hauptmann—

---

[1] E.g. towards both Botho and Lene in *Irrungen, Wirrungen*, 1888, or again towards Holk and his wife in *Unwiederbringlich*, 1891.

[2] 29.i.1894, in *Familienbriefe*, Vol. II, Berlin 1909, p. 302.

[3] 'Der alte Fontane', 1910, and 'Anzeige eines Fontane-Buches', i.e. Wandrey's, 1920; both in *Rede und Antwort*, Berlin 1922.

[4] *Op. cit.*, p. 93: '*verantwortliche Ungebundenheit*'.

but towards his own work as an integral part of the social world which it portrays and criticises.

The humour and wisdom of Fontane, the charm of his style and story-telling—all these are a matter of delicate balance. He 'is for' preservation rather than destruction, yet he knows well enough that 'so long as one takes all things around one for granted, everything is fine; but the moment criticism begins, it all collapses. Society is a horror.'[1] He has no illusions about this world or himself, yet he takes no great pride in his disillusionment; instead, his sympathy enables him to sum up in a humorous aside a good many literary and personal aspirations of his century (and, incidentally, a good many arguments of this book):

Wer was hat, nun ja, der kann das Leben so nehmen, wie's wirklich ist, der kann das sein, was sie jetzt einen Realisten nennen; wer aber nichts hat, wer immer in einer Wüste Sahara lebt, der kann ohne Fata Morgana mit Palmen und Odelisken und all dergleichen gar nicht existieren.[2]	*If a man has something—well, of course, he can take life as it really is, he can be what nowadays they call a realist. But a man who has nothing, and who has always to live in a Sahara desert—why, he simply can't exist without a fata morgana with palms and odelisques and all that sort of thing.*

He lives for his literary work, and confesses that his 'occupation with politics [is] after all only literary', yet in the same breath turns against 'our habit of overestimating *art* at the expense of life'.[3] Of course, it is not the 'literary' attitude as such but his particular kind of literary insight and sympathy that prevent him from penetrating to the personal sources of power in his society. But although these *personal* sources remain hidden, the force of *tradition*—of that superannuated yet powerful Frederician ethos

---

[1] 22.viii.1895, in *Briefe an seine Frau*, Vol. II, Berlin 1905, p. 316.
[2] *Die Poggenpuhls*, Chapter IV.
[3] In a letter from London, 25.iv.1856 (see *Gesammelte Werke*, II, Vol. X, Berlin 1909, p. 145). It was this attitude which produced the 'literary' precepts of politics (see above, p. 342).

which makes the dry-as-dust Instetten fight a duel—emerges
clearly enough. This force, he shows again and again, is now
waning. The rise of the *entrepreneurs*, industrialists and financiers
is accompanied by the decline and decay of the old-fashioned
Prussian Junkers with their large and economically unviable lati-
fundia—the double movement of 'historical necessity' is not
wholly unlike the double movement that Thomas Mann retraces
in *Buddenbrooks*. And it is this process, this spectacle of life sloping
down towards death, that engages Fontane's imagination at its
finest and most perceptive.

6

At the close range at which Fontane observes the social world,
the generalisations about the 'Prussian Code' begin to look
problematic; especially if we look at them through the eyes of
Major Dubslav von Stechlin, rtd, the hero of Fontane's last
novel. A brief and uneventful service in the Prussian Army, a
happy married life cut short by the early death of his wife, and
long years spent in the not very successful management of his
estate in the Grafschaft Ruppin, north-east of Berlin—the tale of
Stechlin's life is soon told. The old country-house with its courtyard and its oddly assorted architectural curiosities, the village
with school, church, and—harbinger of the modern world—its
not very efficient glass-factory: all these localities are as typical of
German provincial life as are their inhabitants: the Protestant
parson Lorenzen, the schoolmaster Krippenstapel, Stechlin's old
servant Engelke, Oberförster Katzler and his wife Ermyntrude,
née Prinzessin von Ippe-Büchsenstein, Baruch Hirschfeld and son
(with an eye on the Stechlin estate), von Gundermann and wife,
'*auf Siebenmühlen*', owner of a chain of sawmills . . . Typical?
Fontane has not a little of Tolstoy's capacity to let the 'type'
recede behind the particular and unique and yet to preserve its
representative character. What is certainly unique in this Prussian
backwater is Stechlin itself—the mere from which village, house
and family take their name. There are a good many little lakes
in that part of Mecklenburg, but Stechlin (as the old Baron is
fond of pointing out) is something special. On the 'evidence of
science' ('which', Stechlin says, 'is nowadays the highest authority'),

the lake has subterranean connections with other parts of the world, including Sicily and Java—it is volcanic in origin; and, according to the law of connected vessels, it has been known to invert itself into a deep vortex and then into a mighty fountain—with even a flaming-red cockerel rising from its depths—whenever Mount Etna or its Javanese fellow-volcano erupted. Which is as much as to say that its very uniqueness is once again typical and representative, and that the quiet backwater is, after all, part of a far-from-quiet world.

Der Stechlin (1899)—and I now mean neither the old Baron nor his son Woldemar nor the mere, but the novel—throws some doubt on most generalisations, including the one made earlier in this book:[1] for here, certainly, the absence of anything like a strongly marked plot does not imply a lack of concern with the social world. On the contrary, the social reality which fills three quarters of the novel is conveyed with enormous subtlety and richness. Take the social ladder itself: the Stechlins are minor aristocracy, and they go back far enough to regard the Hohenzollerns as upstarts. But when Woldemar becomes engaged to the younger daughter of the cosmopolitan Graf Barby, the old Junker looks forward 'with mixed feelings' to the visit of his prospective daughter-in-law and her sister:

'*The rich and the great*' [he writes to his son Woldemar] '*are always something special. Of course they get on with us, but they'd much rather get on with those who are higher than they, you know, because that's much more important to them. The saying always is "The humble are the salt of the earth," but when you look at it more closely you will find that* [in our position] *it's always a case of being pushed rather than pushing ... Same old story, as with Moneybags and the proletarians. All the proletarians were ever good for—at least when they were genuine, nowadays it's probably different—was to pull other people's chestnuts out of the fire; and when things went wrong, it was Brother Havenot who went to gaol and Brother Moneybags who lay down in his own bed. It's almost the same with the high nobility and us Junkers.*'[2]

And the visit, which turns out a great success in spite of Dubslav's misgivings, is in a sense the centre of this almost plotless,

<hr/>

[1] See above, p. 139.

[2] Chapter XXVI, '*... Bruder Habenichts wanderte nach Spandau und Bruder Protz legte sich zu Bett ...*'.

apparently shapeless book. It is here that its main strands unite: the Berlin world of Melusine, the Barbys' elder daughter; the far from optimistic progressive attitude of Pastor Lorenzen; the frosty conservatism and backwoodsmanship of Domina Adelheid, Dubslav's elder sister, who is prioress in a neighbouring lay 'convent'; the antiquarian and patriotic discourses of Krippenstapel—all under the affectionate and bemused eye of the old Stechlin.

Yet for all its indulgence in anecdotes, reminiscences and 'typecasting', this great *causerie* is not really shapeless. And the form which Fontane has imparted to this last work of his old age is, simply enough, the form of decline—old Stechlin's decline—towards death. There are many signs, strewn throughout the story, of its approach. Dubslav's unsuccessful candidature for the *Reichstag*, his financial difficulties, his sceptical appraisal of the future of his class, are among the signs of that decline on the social level; and—in personal terms—a strange, almost sinister, feeling of personal dissolution hangs over the story when, shortly before his end, Dubslav rejects the advice of his doctor and turns to a local soothsayer who prescribes her own magical medicines. Shades of Thomas Buddenbrook's dissolution? Fontane doesn't press the point—Dubslav's dealings with the 'witch' turn out to be his way of coming to terms with his own past, and of settling his present account before the greater reckoning.

Dubslav withdraws from the world into the privacy of death without loss of dignity, of humour even. Like Fontane, he hasn't been able to solve the problem of personal power, of 'who is the régime', who runs history: 'Is it the machine itself, whose old-fashioned works just keep on clattering away, or is it the fellow in charge of the machine?' However that may be, there *is* a 'law' that remains valid. It isn't the Prussian Code, after all, by which Dubslav lived and by which he is now preparing for the end; or rather, it is the basis, the personal and intimately moral sense of that code, the homely sense in which the old Prussian Junker had understood the teaching of his fellow-countryman, Immanuel Kant:

> *Engelke left, and Dubslav was alone again. He felt that the end was near. 'The Self is nothing—that knowledge one must keep hold of. An eternal law fulfils itself,*

and we mustn't be afraid of that fulfilment, even though its name is "death". To accept the law in peace and resignation, that is what makes a man moral and raises him up.'

He thought about that for a while, and was glad to have conquered his fear. But then the pangs of anguish returned, and he sighed: 'Life is short, but the hour is long.'

But this, the solitude of death, is not the end of the novel—Fontane's sense of the world knows better than that. Dubslav's son and his young wife return from their honeymoon—a new life is about to begin, a new page in the history of Stechlin. Fontane was, after all, too deeply involved in his world to take his own fears for its future very seriously: too involved to be a 'good' prophet of the bad.

EPILOGUE

AT THE BEGINNING of the new century, which Fontane didn't live
to see, stands *Buddenbrooks*; looking back on that early masterpiece almost fifty years later, Thomas Mann wondered whether
it would not 'in the end' turn out to have been his greatest.
Thomas Mann's work begins where Fontane's ends. His first
novel is built on Fontane's achievement, and surpasses it because
it places the conflict with which I have here been concerned—that
between the claims of the social world and of the individual
spiritual interpretation—firmly in the centre of the stage. In
comparison with Thomas Mann's, Fontane's world is unsophisticated, his losers are mere victims and no more. *Buddenbrooks*
concludes on a note at once more radical and ambiguous. The
social world, life itself, is defeated by a spirituality which in its
turn emerges as a thing corrupted by its isolation from life. This
double defeat, which is informed with a literary self-consciousness
unparallelled in Fontane, belongs to a different age. But the battle
is fought out in a wholly realistic—that is, in Fontane's—manner;
and it is from this contrast between a by now 'old-fashioned'
elaborate realism and a new, 'modern' search for meaning, that
Thomas Mann derives his finest effects.

At the beginning of this book I suggested that after the First
World War the dissociation of literature from the political and
social realities had ceased to be a phenomenon peculiar to Germany; this is the reason why the works of Mann, Rilke and Kafka
found a ready European audience. For these new writers—and
for Stefan George, Georg Trakl, and Hofmannsthal—the situation I have described is something like a premise they take for
granted. From the retrospect of the first of his *Duino Elegies* Rilke
proceeds to a novel interpretation of the lot of modern man. Yet
the work of his maturity remains informed by that acute
historical consciousness which had been bequeathed to him by

Nietzsche, and it is his consciousness of the immediate past rather than that of more distant cultures which speaks to us from his greatest poetry. When Rilke translates the theme of solitude to an existential plane and offers a validation of modern man in terms of pure inwardness, his poetic images are no less original for being connected with that past. When Thomas Mann, in his last great work, *Doktor Faustus*, attempts to symbolise the course of German history in the first thirty years of this century, the explanation he offers for his country's frenzied outbreak into violence follows something of the old pattern that Heine had traced out: what Mann describes is a desolate otherworldliness that is trying, with the help of the Devil himself, to 'bruise or break its way' into the real world. And even Brecht's achievement may be seen against this background; for it is from his satirical attack on all 'idealist' values and sentiments that much of his dramatic energy derives. Whatever Brecht's ambiguously 'positive' conclusions, he begins where Büchner began, and his theory of the 'epic' theatre is foreshadowed not in Shakespeare but in the discontinuities of Büchner's plays.

Yet for all that, German literature in the twentieth century is unmistakably different. New styles and complexly self-conscious attitudes towards language emerge; and the new visions of man too are more radically alienated than any I have considered here, except Büchner's—and he is a twentieth-century discovery. 1912, the year of Rilke's first elegy, marks the beginning of a new literary era.

THREE NOTES

1. *On Goethe's* Campagne in Frankreich 1792 (see p. 34)

The Jacobin wave of terror which followed upon the false truce of July 1790 was watched with growing apprehension from across the Rhine. To forestall a hostile move, the French National Assembly declared war on Austria in April 1792, which brought Prussia, and thus also the Duchy of Weimar, into the conflict. The Duke commanded a brigade in the vanguard of the Prussian troops, which Goethe joined at Longwy on 23 August 1792, a few days before his forty-third birthday. The journal of the campaign was written up, from notes and memories, in the years 1820–1. It contains a number of splendid passages which invite comparison with *War and Peace*. The movement of large bodies of men is powerfully conveyed: so are landscapes, the chaos that broods over them, rumours, requisitionings, retreat. Rain and fog, mud, dysentery, dying horses and hunger—here is realism in plenty. The feeling for the obscurity of purpose behind the military actions—a feeling akin to that which, in *Die natürliche Tochter*, had led to a dramatic *impasse*—is here conveyed to great effect; the diarist-narrator is so involved in the story that his is almost the only point of view presented. But beyond the living details and powerful scenes of daily life in the field, the book contains two or three passages in which Goethe attempts to place the whole episode historically: that is, to say something in explanation of why Karl August's men, under Prussian leadership, occupied Verdun, Longwy, prepared to enter Paris, and on 30 September 1792 were repulsed by the cannonade at Valmy. These attempts at writing history are the weakest parts of the book (or rather of its first half; the second is disfigured by major flaws); but it is on them that Goethe's reputation as a critic of his

age is often founded. In particular, Goethe's remark when returning to camp from the front line on the evening of the cannonade
(19.ix.1792), 'Here and today begins a new epoch in world
history', has been made much of, though actually it sounds less
authentically Goethean than the lightly ironical afterthought,
'and you may say that you were present'. The remark has caused
Oswald Spengler (*Der Untergang des Abendlandes*, Vol. I, Munich
1920, p. 35) to speak of Goethe's 'divine vision' and to add, 'No
army commander, no diplomat, let alone any philosopher, has
ever shown such an intuitive feeling for history in the making.
It is the most profound judgement ever pronounced in respect of
a great historical act in the moment of its happening.' Of course
it doesn't matter when the remark was really made, and by whose
esprit d'escalier (cf. *J.A.*, Vol. XXVIII, p. 279). More important is
the fact that there is little anywhere else in the book to disclose
an understanding of or even interest in the wider political situation that could be seen to lead up to and substantiate the remark;
there is, in other words, little to show it is anything but an *obiter
dictum*. And as such it does not really mean very much. If it were
true, the meaning associated with it would have to be put there
by our own understanding of subsequent events; but it isn't true,
because the event itself was without consequences. The campaign
of intervention was halted by bad weather, epidemics and dis-
affection rather than by enemy action, and eventually ended in a
complete fiasco; the Sansculottes occupied all the fortifications
previously held by the allied armies; and the Revolution proceeded to new terrors: the September massacres, and the assassina-
tion of Louis XVI on 21 January 1793. The 'new epoch in world
history' had begun three years before Valmy.

2. *Stifter's Childhood Impressions* (see p. 245)

On three different occasions Stifter tried to recapture his earliest
childhood impressions, each time the undertaking was abandoned.
The following fragment is the longest and finest of these attempts;
parts of it were quoted in the first chapter of Urban Roedl's
biography, the full version has only recently become available.
It is reprinted here from the *Insel Almanach auf das Jahr 1963*,

Frankfurt/M. 1962, pp. 28–33; the manuscript is in the archives of the Czechoslovak Academy of Sciences in Prague.

Es ist das kleinste Sandkörnchen ein Wunder, das wir nicht ergründen können. Dass es ist, dass seine Teile zusammen hängen, dass sie getrennt werden können, dass sie wieder Körner sind, dass die Teilung fortgesetzt werden kann, und wie weit, wird uns hienieden immer ein Geheimnis bleiben. Nur Weniges, was unserem Sinne von ihm kund wird, und Weniges, was in seiner Wechselwirkung mit anderen Dingen zu unserer Wahrnehmung gelangt, ist unser Eigentum, das Andere ruht in Gott. Die grossen Körper, davon es getrennt worden ist, und die den Aussenbau unserer Erde bilden, sind uns in ihrer Eigenheit unbekannt wie das Sandkörnchen. Sie sind, und wir sagen Manches von ihnen aus, das auf dem Pfade unserer Wahrnehmungskräfte zu uns hereinkömmt. Und dann sind die Planeten, die wie unsere Erde als andere Erden in dem ungeheuern Raume schweben, der uns zunächst an uns durch sie geoffenbaret wird. Dann sind weiter ausser ihnen die Fixsterne, die in dem noch viel grösseren Raume, den sie darstellen, bestehen, und deren Grösse so wie die Grösse des Raumes wir durch Zahlen ausdrücken, aber in unserem Vorstellungsvermögen nicht fassen können. Dann geht, wie unsere Fernröhre zeigen, der körpererfüllte Raum fort und fort. Wir nennen das Alles die Welt, und heissen sie das grösste Wunder. Aber auf den

The smallest grain of sand is a miracle we cannot fathom. That it exists, that its parts hold together, that they can be divided into further grains, that the division can be continued and how far, will always remain a mystery to us here on earth. Only the little that our senses apprehend of it is our own, and the little of its interaction with other things that reaches our consciousness; the rest remains with God. The great bodies from which it has separated and which form the outer fabric of our earth are in themselves as unknown to us as is the grain of sand. They exist, and we relate many things of them that come to us by way of our perceptions. And then there are the planets, other earths, that float, like ours, in the vast space which is revealed to us in the first place through them. Then, beyond the planets, are the fixed stars. They exist in a much larger space still, of which they are the representation— their size and the size of that space we express in figures but cannot grasp with our imagination. And still, as our telescopes show, space full of celestial bodies goes on and on. We call all that the World, and say it is the greatest wonder. But upon these things of the World lies a greater wonder still: Life. We gaze into the abyss of this enigma in helpless amazement. Life touches us so nearly and dearly that everything in which we can discern it we feel to be akin to us, and everything which

Dingen der Welt ist ein noch grösseres Wunder, das Leben. Wir stehen vor dem Abgrunde dieses Rätsels in Staunen und Ohnmacht. Das Leben berührt uns so innig und hold, dass uns Alles, darin wir es zu entdecken vermögen, verwandt, und Alles, darin wir es nicht sehen können, fremd ist, dass wir seine Zeichen in Moosen, Kräutern, Bäumen, Tieren liebreich verfolgen, dass wir sie in der Geschichte des menschlichen Geschlechtes und in den Darstellungen einzelner Menschen begierig in uns aufnehmen, dass wir Leben in unseren Künsten dichten, und dass wir uns selber ohne Leben gar nicht zu denken vermögen. Ich bin oft vor den Erscheinungen meines Lebens, das einfach war, wie ein Halm wächst, in Verwunderung geraten.

Dies ist der Grund und die Ent-schuldigung, dass ich die folgenden Worte aufschreibe. Sie sind zunächst für mich allein. Finden sie eine weitere Verbreitung, so mögen Gat-tin, Geschwister, Freunde, Bekannte einen zarten Gruss darin erkennen, und Fremde nicht etwas Unwürdiges aus ihnen entnehmen.

Weit zurück in dem leeren Nichts ist etwas wie Wonne und Entzücken, das gewaltig fassend, fast vernichtend in mein Wesen drang, und dem nichts mehr in meinem künftigen Leben glich. Die Merkmale, die fest ge-halten wurden, sind: es war Glanz, es war Gewühl, es war unten. Dies muss sehr früh gewesen sein; denn mir ist, als liege eine sehr weite Finsternis des Nichts um das Ding herum.

Dann war etwas Anderes, das **sanft** *und lindernd durch mein*

lacks it, alien; that we lovingly pursue its traces in mosses, plants, trees and animals; and avidly seek it in the history of the human race and the representations of individual men; that we invent life in our arts, and cannot think ourselves without life at all. The events of my own life, which was simple as the growth of a blade of grass, have often moved me to wonder.

This is the reason and the excuse for my writing down the words that are to follow. They are intended in the first place for myself alone. If they reach further, then let my wife, my brothers and sisters, friends and acquaintances recognise them as a gentle greeting, and strangers see in them something not unworthy.

Far back in the empty nothingness is something resembling rapture and delight, which grasped my being with a powerful, almost annihilating force, and with which nothing in my later life could compare. The characteristics I remember are these: it was brightness, it was turmoil, it was below. This must have been very early on, for it seems to me as if there were a large dark space of nothingness about the thing.

Then there was some other thing, that went gently and soothingly

Inneres ging. Das Merkmal ist: es waren Klänge.

Dann schwamm ich in etwas Fächelndem, ich schwamm hin und wider, es wurde immer weicher und weicher in mir, dann wurde ich wie trunken, dann war nichts mehr.

Diese drei Inseln liegen wie feen- und sagenhaft in dem Schleiermeere der Vergangenheit, wie Urerinnerungen eines Volkes.

Die folgenden Spitzen werden immer bestimmter. Klingen von Glocken, ein breiter Schein, eine rote Dämmerung.

Ganz klar war etwas, das sich immer wiederholte. Eine Stimme, die zu mir sprach, Augen die mich anschauten, und Arme, die Alles milderten. Ich schrie nach diesen Dingen.

Dann war Jammervolles, Unleidliches, dann Süsses, Stillendes. Ich erinnere mich an Strebungen, die nichts erreichten, und an das Aufhören von Entsetzlichem und Zugrunderichtendem. Ich erinnere mich an Glanz und Farben, die in meinen Augen, an Töne die in meinen Ohren und an Holdseligkeiten, die in meinem Wesen waren.

Immer mehr fühlte ich die Augen, die mich anschauten, die Stimme, die zu mir sprach, und die Arme, die Alles milderten. Ich erinnere mich, dass ich das 'Mam' nannte.

Diese Arme fühlte ich mich einmal tragen. Es waren dunkle Flecke in mir. Die Erinnerung sagte mir später, dass es Wälder gewesen sind die ausserhalb mir waren. Dann war eine Empfindung, wie die erste meines Lebens, Glanz und Gewühl, dann war nichts mehr.

Nach dieser Empfindung ist wieder eine grosse Lücke. Zustände, die

through my inner being. Its characteristic is that it was sounds.

Then I was floating in something gently rippling, I floated to and fro, there was an ever greater softness inside me, then I became as if intoxicated, and then nothing more.

These three islands lie fairylike and legendary in the veiled sea of the past, like primordial memories of a race.

The following three peaks become more definite: the ringing of bells, a great brightness, a red dusk.

Something quite clear always repeated itself: a voice that spoke to me, eyes that looked at me, and arms that had the power of soothing. I cried for these things. There was also wretchedness and vexation, then sweetness and gentle calming. I remember strivings which never achieved anything, and I remember the cessation of the terrible and annihilating. I remember brilliance and colours in my eyes, sounds in my ears, and blessed delights within my being.

More and more I felt the eyes that looked at me, the voice that spoke to me, and the arms that soothed everything. I remember that I called this 'Mam'.

I remember these arms carrying me once. Dark patches were inside me. Memory told me later that these were woods outside myself. Then came a sensation like that first one of my life, of brightness and turmoil, and then there was nothing.

This sensation is again followed by a large gap. Circumstances that

*gewesen sind, mussten vergessen
worden sein.*

*Hierauf erhob sich die Aussenwelt
vor mir, da bisher nur Empfindungen
wahrgenommen worden waren. Selbst
Mam, Augen Stimme Arme, waren
nur als Empfindung in mir gewesen,
sogar auch Wälder, wie ich eben gesagt habe. Merkwürdig ist es, dass
in der allerersten Empfindung meines
Lebens etwas Äusserliches war, und
zwar etwas, das meist schwierig und
erst spät in das Vorstellungsvermögen gelangt, etwas Räumliches,
ein Unten. Das ist ein Zeichen, wie
gewaltig die Einwirkung gewesen
sein muss, die jene Empfindung her-
vorgebracht hat. Mam, was ich jetzt
Mutter nannte, stand nun als
Gestalt vor mir auf, und ich unter-
schied ihre Bewegungen, dann der
Vater, der Grossvater, die Grossmutter, die Tante. Ich hiess sie mit
diesen Namen, empfand Holdes von
ihnen, erinnere mich aber keines
Unterschiedes ihrer Gestalten. Selbst
andere Dinge musste ich schon haben
nennen können, ohne dass ich mich
später einer Gestalt oder eines Unterschiedes erinnern konnte. Dies be-
weist eine Begebenheit, die in jene
Zeit gefallen sein musste. Ich fand
mich einmal wieder in dem Entsetzlichen, Zugrunderichtenden, von
dem ich oben gesagt habe. Dann war
Klingen, Verwirrung, Schmerz in
meinen Händen und Blut daran, die
Mutter verband mich, und dann war
ein Bild, das so klar vor mir jetzt
dasteht, als wäre es in reinlichen
Farben auf Porzellan gemalt. Ich
stand in dem Garten, der von damals
zuerst in meiner Einbildungskraft ist,
die Mutter war da, dann die andere
Grossmutter, deren Gestalt in jenem*

intervened must have been forgotten.

After this the external world rose
up before me, for until then experience had all been sensations. Even
Mam, eyes voice arms, had only been
sensation within me, even woods, as
I have just said. It is remarkable that
that very first sensation of my life had
some external quality about it which
usually comes to the imagination
with difficulty and not until much
later, a spatial quality, a sense of
being below. This is an indication
of how strong the influence must have
been which caused that sensation.
Mam, which I now called Mother,
now stood as a shape before me and I
distinguished her movements, and
then my father, grandfather, grandmother, aunt, I called them by these
names, experienced bliss from them,
but I remember no differences in their
shapes. I must have been able to
name other things too, without later
remembering their shapes or any
differences between them. This is
borne out by an event which must
have happened at that time. I found
myself once again in that terror and
annihilation which I mentioned
above. Then there was a shrill noise,
confusion, pain in my hands and
blood on them, my mother bandaged
them, and then came a picture which
still stands before me as clearly as if
it had been painted in pure colours on
porcelain. I was standing in the
garden, which exists in my imagination from that time on, my mother
was there and the other grandmother,

Augenblicke auch zum ersten Male
in mein Gedächtnis kam, in mir war
die Erleichterung, die alle Male
auf das Weichen des Entsetzlichen
und Zugrundrichtenden folgte, und
ich sagte: 'Mutter, da wächst ein
Kornhalm.'
Die Grossmutter antwortete darauf: 'Mit einem Knaben, der die
Fenster zerschlagen hat, redet man
nicht.'
Ich verstand zwar den Zusammenhang nicht; aber das Ausserordent-
liche, das eben von mir gewichen war,
kam sogleich wieder, die Mutter
sprach wirklich kein Wort, und ich
erinnere mich, dass ein ganz Un-
geheures auf meiner Seele lag. Das
mag der Grund sein, dass jener
Vorgang noch jetzt in meinem
Innern lebt. Ich sehe den hohen
schlanken Kornhalm so deutlich, als
ob er neben meinem Schreibtische
stände, ich sehe die Gestalten der
Mutter und Grossmutter, wie sie in
dem Garten herum arbeiteten, die
Gewächse des Gartens sehe ich nur
als unbestimmten grünen Schmelz
vor mir; aber der Sonnenschein, der
uns umgab, ist ganz klar da.
Nach dieser Begebenheit ist aber-
mals Dunkel.
Dann aber zeichnet sich [deut]lich
und bleibend die Stube ab, in der ich
mich befand. Ganz vorzüglich sind
es die grossen dunkelbraunen Trage-
balken der Diele, die vor meinen
Augen sind, und an denen allerlei
Dinge hingen. Dann war der grosse
grüne Ofen, der hervorspringt, und
um den eine Bank ist. Dann sagte die
Mutter, der Zimmersepp wird uns
einen Tisch machen, auf dem das
Osterlämmlein ist. Der Tisch wurde
fertig, und bildete meine grosse

a shape who also entered my
consciousness for the first time at that
moment, inside me there was the
relief which always followed the
cessation of the terrible and annihilating, and I said, 'Mother, there's a
stalk of corn growing.' My grandmother answered, 'People don't talk
to a boy who has broken the windows.'
I did not understand the connection,
but the extreme condition which had
just left me returned immediately, my
mother really would not speak a
word, and I remember that something quite monstrous weighed on my
soul. This may be the reason why
that occurrence is still alive within me
today. I can see the tall, slim stalk of
corn as clearly as if it were standing
beside my desk. I see the figures of my
mother and my grandmother working
at this and that in the garden, the
plants in the garden are only a vague
green mist before my eyes, but the
sunlight about us is there quite
clearly.
After this incident there is darkness once more.
But after that it is the parlour
which assumes clear and lasting outlines, and I am in it. Most particularly it is the great dark-brown
beams in the ceiling which are before
my eyes and from which a number of
things were suspended. The large,
green-tiled stove projected into the
room, with a seat built round it.
Then my mother said, Sepp the
carpenter will make us a table with
the Easter Lamb on it. The table was
completed and was my great joy.

Freude. Dessen, der früher gewesen war, erinnere ich mich nicht mehr. Der Tisch war genau viereckig, weiss und gross, und hatte in der Mitte das rötliche Osterlämmlein mit einem Fähnchen, was meine ausserordentlichste Bewunderung erregte. An der Dickseite des Tisches waren die Fugen der Bohlen, aus denen er gefügt war, damit sie nicht klaffend werden konnten, mit Doppelkeilen gehalten, deren Spitzen gegeneinander gingen. Jeder Doppelkeil war aus einem Stück Holz, und das Holz war rötlich wie das Osterlamm. Mir gefielen diese roten Gestalten in der lichten Decke des Tisches gar sehr. Als dazumal sehr oft das Wort 'Conscription' ausgesprochen wurde, dachte ich, diese roten Gestalten seien die Conscription. Noch ein anderes Ding der Stube war mir äusserst anmutig und schwebt lieblich und fast leuchtend in meiner Erinnerung. Es war das erste Fenster an der Eingangstür. Die Fenster der Stube hatten sehr breite Fensterbretter, und auf dem Brette dieses Fensters sass ich sehr oft, und fühlte den Sonnenschein, und daher mag das Leuchtende der Erinnerung rühren. Auf diesem Fensterbrette war es auch allein, wenn ich zu lesen anhob. Ich nahm ein Buch, machte es auf, hielt es vor mich, und las: 'Burgen, Nagelein, böhmisch Haidel.' Diese Worte las ich jedes Mal, ich weiss es, ob zuweilen noch andere dabei waren, dessen erinnere ich mich nicht mehr. Auf diesem Fensterbrett sah ich auch, was draussen vorging,

The one which had been there before I do not remember. The table was exactly square, white and large, and in its centre was the reddish Easter Lamb with a pennant, which excited my extreme admiration. In the thickness of the table, the planks of which it was made were held together by pairs of wedges so that they would not come apart, and the points of the wedges were towards each other. Each wedge was made of a single piece of wood tinted red like the Easter Lamb. I loved these red shapes in the light table top. Since at that time the word 'conscription' was spoken frequently, I thought that these red shapes were the conscription. There was yet another thing in the room which was extremely agreeable to me and which remains lovely and almost glowing in my memory. It was the window nearest the door. The windows of the room had very wide windowsills and I often sat on the sill of this window and felt the sunshine on me, and that may be the source of the glowing quality of the memory. It can only have been on this windowsill that I began my reading. I took a book, opened it, held it before me and read: Castles, Cloves, Villages.[1] These words I read every time, I know it well; whether there were others too I cannot remember. From this windowsill I also saw all that was happening outside, and I often said: 'There's a man going to Schwarzbach, there's a man driving to Schwarzbach, there's a woman going

---

[1] 'Nagelein' [= carnations or cloves] is followed by the name of a village, probably Okfolderhaid, in the vicinity of Stifter's native Oberplan.

*und ich sagte sehr oft: 'Da geht ein
Mann nach Schwarzbach, da fährt
ein Mann nach Schwarzbach, da
geht ein Weib nach Schwarzbach, da
geht ein Hund nach Schwarzbach,
da geht eine Gans nach Schwarzbach.' Auf diesem Fensterbrette legte
ich auch Kienspäne ihrer Länge nach
aneinander hin, verband sie wohl
auch durch Querspäne, und sagte:
'Ich mache Schwarzbach.' In meiner
Erinnerung ist lauter Sommer, den
ich durch das Fenster sah, von
einem Winter ist von damals gar
nichts in meiner Einbildungskraft.*

to Schwarzbach, there's a dog going
to Schwarzbach, there's a goose going
to Schwarzbach.' And on this
windowsill I laid out pieces of
kindling-wood lengthwise, and perhaps laid others across them, and
said, 'I am making Schwarzbach.' In
my memory it is always summer
when I looked through the window,
there is no winter in my memory of
that time.

3. On Some Criticisms of Stifter's Work (see p. 272)

For the first half-century after Stifter's death his reputation was that of a minor Austrian prose writer in the tradition of the village story. Around the time of the First World War his work was re-discovered by a number of influential critics, including Hermann Bahr in Vienna, Max Stefl in Munich, August Sauer and Josef Nadler in Prague, and Ernst Bertram, a member of the George Circle, in Cologne. This early criticism is predominantly bio-graphical and ideological, its emphasis still lies on the 'naïve' and idealising poet, the heir to Goethe's *Naturphilosophie*, though even here we notice that the rustic values (which Stifter and his work are said to represent) blend with nationalistic strains. The opening and conclusion of Bertram's essay (1919) explicitly invoke Stifter's 'German' spirituality and anti-political wisdom as a comfort and precept to Germany in her hour of defeat. As against this, Hofmannsthal (1924) and Josef Hofmiller (1924 ff.) stress the humanity and European nature of Stifter's vision; it is now that the timeless ideal of culture enshrined in *Der Nachsommer* comes into its own. At the same time Hofmiller points to Stifter's occasional pedantry and stylistic mannerisms; his view of *Witiko* comes very close to that of Hermann Hesse, who described it as 'a novel in which three people sit down on three chairs'. In the middle 'thirties, especially in the biography of Urban Roedl (1936), a different note is struck. Now for the first time attention is drawn to the disparities between Stifter's life and his writings, though the latter are still seen as creatively integrated answers to his personal doubts. What in Roedl's biography had been discreet hints becomes the focus of the existential study of the Dane Erik Lunding (1946). Written during the Second World War and wholly under the impact of Heidegger's *Sein und Zeit*, Lunding's book turns the tables on the older conception. No longer is Stifter the naïve and idyllic writer of rural virtues and nature-studies; Lunding concentrates on the ideas of *Angst* and personal solitude, seeing these reflected in almost every line that Stifter wrote. With its note of apocalyptic doom[1] this is existential biography with a vengeance, and as such it leaves little room for an appreciation of Stifter's actual literary achievement; all the same, many of the corrections that Lunding's book implicitly provides to the high-minded simplicities of earlier writers remain permanently valid. Meanwhile, in Germany, the national-socialist critics take up Stifter's work. In Julius Kühn's book (*Die Kunst Adalbert Stifters*[2], Berlin 1943) the nationalistic strains of a Sauer, Nadler and Bertram become predominant; Stifter is now seen as the prophet of *Grossdeutschland*, of pristine peasant wisdom, racial purity, and of the *Führer*-principle (pp. 275-6). All sugges-tions of a discrepancy between life and work, of religious and personal doubts, are rejected as destructive; indeed all 'criticism' of Stifter's work is branded, with the help of quotations from *Der Völkische Beobachter*, as 'Jewish machinations' (pp. 293-4, 331). The writings of most post-war critics come under the heading of 'After Strange Gods'. Emil Staiger (1952, see above, p. 292). writes an almost unqualified panegyric of Stifter as the poet whose aim it was to recall us to the lost feeling of awe and veneration before the world as a creation of God; for him Stifter 'resembles the priest who, with his back to the community, performs the divine office.' That such an attitude amounts to a denial of the actual world: that no *poet*, not even Hölderlin, had ever seen his office in such a light—these considerations Staiger ignores.

---

[1] Thus on its last page the book contains the remarkable statement: '*Im Mittelalter wurde noch ordnungsgemäss nach Kategorien gestorben*', which may well be as hard to verify as it is to translate.

Similarly, Walter Rehm (1954) takes up one strand of *Der Nach-sommer*—the wisdom and serenity of old age—and, without entering on any of the actual details of events and story, at length retraces the character of Risach; here homage takes the form of a fine paraphrase decked out with classical allusions. H. Augustin, after first devoting a monograph (1944) to a comparison of Stifter, Dante and Goethe, in 1959 writes an explicitly and un-reservedly Christian panegyric on Stifter; both Augustin and K. Steffen, 1955 (and, incidentally E. A. Blackall, 1948) return again to that language of sublime praise, spiritual uplift and quietism which, in so many of the earlier studies, had taken the place of critical enquiry. However, this style can sometimes be deceptive. Thus Kurt Hohoff's book (1949) conceals a number of very search-ing arguments (see above, p. 276). He alone among these critics points out that the values which inform Stifter's work are no longer Christian (pp. 110–15, 176–79): 'Christianity has many mansions, but it has not one for enlightened man as the high classicism [of Weimar] saw him' (p. 179). His conclusion that 'the religious is so holy for [Stifter] that it remains hidden: in this hidden form it stands behind the classical image of man,' is rendered problematic by Hohoff's own argument. Furthermore, Stifter's one overtly religious tale (*Kalkstein*, 1848, fashioned on the pattern of Grillparzer's *Novelle*) shows that he did not regard the religious theme as ineffable, for it is there set out plainly enough; whereas the 'classical image of man' of which Hohoff speaks implies a serenity, and a balance between the human and the natural, which (this was the burden of my argument) are no longer available to Stifter. Turning now from the high-church style to the low, we shall hardly be surprised to find that con-temporary Marxist criticism almost entirely ignores the subject. Georg Lukács (*Der historische Roman*, Berlin 1955, p. 268) quotes Hebbel's notorious dismissal (that as a result of his preoccupation with trivial minutiae 'Stifter loses sight of man entirely . . .'), but Lukács doesn't think Stifter important enough for a full study. His disciple Hans Mayer (*Von Lessing bis Thomas Mann*, Pfullingen 1959, pp. 303–4, 314) includes *Der Nachsommer* among German novels which describe and recommend a socially responsible attitude, but—surprisingly enough—he too makes nothing of the

fact that the life which von Risach plans for Heinrich Drendorf
amounts to a denial of the value of his own career as a statesman.
Finally, there are F. G. Fischer's 'contributions towards a [defini-
tive] biography', 1961; based upon a critical evaluation of the
entire literature, this is the first wholly unprejudiced and truthful
account of some of the major phases and aspects of Stifter's life.

It is not in order to quarrel with this or that writer that I have
mentioned these few works from the vast list of Stifter studies,
but to illustrate the peculiar paradox typical of much of German
criticism. By and large, Stifter is regarded as the non-political
writer *par excellence*, while at the same time many of the criticisms
of his work follow more or less closely the course of German
political history; it is not too much to say that the critical opinions
are determined by political events in something like the same way
as they are in Soviet criticism. True, the parallel is not always as
close as in Soviet literature, yet it is much closer—that is, the
studies are less independent of political considerations—than in
any comparable critical trends in England or America. Why?
The obvious answer is that, up to the present at all events, national
and political life in England and America has been sufficiently
self-assured not to need to go to literature for support and validation; and that, for the same reason, it has been less open to
intellectual and literary influences. But to say this is to suggest
why the need hasn't arisen in the West, not how it was supplied
in Germany. Given that need, what intellectual jump makes it
possible to claim that a work is non-political, and in the same
breath to derive from it support for the current political ideology?
The spurious link in this argument is provided by the twin claims
to absolute validity: both the work and the ideology are somehow
(against disconcerting evidence to the contrary) recommended as
total accounts of the human situation, as absolute precepts.
'Criticism', whether literary or political, is identified with fault-
finding, and becomes a dirty word; and, in its 'total' support of
the ruling ideology, the work of art is endowed with a preceptive
function which it doesn't have in a democratic context. Yet of
course the act of recommending the work of a given author as a
precept is, in itself, a critical act (whatever its intellectual level),
just as the recommending of its political attitude is itself a political

act (whether or not it is recognised as such). And just as the
national-socialist politicians could successfully appeal to the
German electorate on a 'non-party' ticket, and proclaim that
their government would resolve for them 'absolutely' the dreary
compromises and choices of democratic politics, so writers like
Kühn or Gregor Heinrich (1937) could claim that they held no
'critical opinions' about Stifter; that his work contains an absolute
and timeless answer to all problems; that he was at once a true
'*Volksdichter*' and intelligible only to an 'élite'; that all 'criticism'
is lacking in proper respect; that critics who hold different views
('*hier scheiden sich die Geister*' is the hideous phrase) are somehow, for instance congenitally, or racially, incapable of understanding Stifter, and so forth. I have called this sad confusion
typical, for I doubt whether there is a major German author whose
work was not treated in a similar way.

INDEX

INDEX

2

*Figures in bold type denote main references,
raised numerals refer to footnotes*